T0323018

HUMANITARIAN ECONOMICS

GILLES CARBONNIER

Humanitarian Economics

War, Disaster and the Global Aid Market

HURST & COMPANY, LONDON

First published in the United Kingdom in 2015 by
C. Hurst & Co. (Publishers) Ltd.,
41 Great Russell Street, London, WC1B 3PL
© Gilles Carbonnier, 2015
All rights reserved.

The right of Gilles Carbonnier to be identified as the author
of this publication is asserted by him in accordance with the
Copyright, Designs and Patents Act, 1988.

A Cataloguing-in-Publication data record for this book is
available from the British Library.

978-1-84904-552-0 *hardback*

www.hurstpublishers.com

Printed by Bell and Bain Ltd, Glasgow

In memory of Laurent Du Pasquier

CONTENTS

List of Acronyms and Abbreviations   ix
Preface and Acknowledgments   xiii

Introduction   1
1. Reason, Emotion and Compassion   11
2. The Humanitarian Market   37
3. War Economics   67
4. Terrorism Economics   99
5. Disaster Economics   127
6. Survival Economics   149
7. The Transformative Power of Humanitarian Crises   177
Conclusion   195
Appendix: PEA: the Example of Food Aid in Angola   205

Notes   213
References   261
Index   281

LIST OF ACRONYMS AND ABBREVIATIONS

AADMER	ASEAN Agreement on Disaster Management and Emergency Response
ASEAN	Association of Southeast Asian Nations
AU	African Union
BBB	Building Back Better
BHP	Business-Humanitarian Partnership
CAR	Central African Republic
CCRIF	Caribbean Catastrophe Risk Insurance Facility
CDD	Community-Driven Development
CERP	US Commander's Emergency Response Program
CFT	Countering the Financing of Terrorism
COIN	Counterinsurgency
CPA	Comprehensive Peace Agreement (Sudan/South Sudan)
CRED	Centre for Research on the Epidemiology of Disasters
CSO	Civil Society Organization
DAC	Development Assistance Committee of the OECD
DALY	Disability-Adjusted Life Years
DFID	UK Department for International Development (UK Aid)
DRC	Democratic Republic of the Congo
DRM	Disaster Risk Management
DRR	Disaster Risk Reduction
EM-DAT	Emergency Events Database
EMMA	Emergency Market Mapping and Assessment
ETA	Euskadi Ta Askatasuna (Basque Country and Freedom)
EU	European Union
FARC	Fuerzas Armadas Revolucionarias de Colombia

LIST OF ACRONYMS AND ABBREVIATIONS

FATF	Financial Action Task Force
FDI	Foreign Direct Investment
FMLN	Frente Farabundo Martí de Liberación Nacional
FTS	Financial Tracking Service (UN OCHA)
GAM	Gerakan Aceh Merdeka/Free Aceh Movement
GCC	Gulf Cooperation Council
GCTF	Global Counterterrorism Forum
GDP	Gross Domestic Product
GHA	Global Humanitarian Assistance
GNI	Gross National Income
GTD	Global Terrorism Database (University of Maryland)
GWOT	Global War on Terror
HDI	Human Development Index
HEA	Household Economy Approach
HFA	Hyogo Framework for Action
HiCN	Households in Conflict Network
IASC	Inter-Agency Standing Committee
ICRC	International Committee of the Red Cross
ICT	Information and Communications Technology
IDMC	Internal Displacement Monitoring Centre (Geneva)
IDP	Internally Displaced Person
IFPRI	International Food Policy Research Institute
IFRC	International Federation of Red Cross and Red Crescent Societies
IHL	International Humanitarian Law
IMTS	Informal Money Transfer Systems
INGO	International Non-Governmental Organization
IRC	International Rescue Committee
ISIS	Islamic State of Iraq and Syria
ITERATE	International Terrorism: Attributes of Terrorism Events (Cornell University)
J-PAL	Abdul Latif Jameel Poverty Action Lab
K&R	Kidnap and Ransom
LIC	Low-Income Country
LMIC	Lower Middle-Income Country
LRA	Lord's Resistance Army
LSMS	Living Standards Measurement Study
LTTE	Liberation Tigers of Tamil Eelam

MAG	Market Analysis Guidance
MIC	Middle-Income Country
MIFIRA	Market Information and Food Insecurity Response Analysis
MLC	Mouvement pour la libération du Congo
MSF	Médecins Sans Frontières
NATO	North Atlantic Treaty Organization
NFIP	US National Flood Insurance Program
NGO	Non-Governmental Organization
NRC	Norwegian Refugee Council
NSP	National Solidarity Programme (Afghanistan)
OCG	Organized Criminal Group
OCHA	Office for the Coordination of Humanitarian Affairs
ODA	Official Development Assistance
ODI	Overseas Development Institute
OECD	Organization for Economic Co-operation and Development
OHA	Official Humanitarian Assistance
PEA	Political Economy Analysis
PMT	Proxy Means Testing
PPP	Public-Private Partnership
PRIMS	Philippines Risk and Insurance Scheme for Municipalities
RAM	Rapid Assessment of Markets
RCD	Rassemblement congolais pour la démocratie
RCD-G	RCD-Goma
RCD-K	RCD-Kisangani
RLS	Risk-Linked Securities
SCF	Save the Children Fund
SOMIGL	Société minière des Grands Lacs
SPLM/A	Sudanese People's Liberation Movement/Army
SWIFT	Society for Worldwide Interbank Financial Telecommunication
TCIP	Turkish Catastrophe Insurance Pool
TCO	Transnational Criminal Organization
UCDP	Uppsala Conflict Data Program
UMIC	Upper Middle-Income Country
UN	United Nations
UNDP	United Nations Development Programme
UNHCR	United Nations Office of the High Commissioner for Refugees
UNICEF	United Nations Children's Fund
UNISDR	United Nations International Strategy for Disaster Reduction

LIST OF ACRONYMS AND ABBREVIATIONS

UNITA	Uniao Nacional para a Independência Total de Angola
UNOCHA	United Nations Office for the Coordination of Humanitarian Affairs
UNODC	United Nations Office on Drugs and Crime
UNRWA	United Nations Relief and Works Agency
URNG	Unidad Revolucionaria Nacional Guatemalteca
VASyR	Vulnerability Assessment of Syrian Refugees
VSL	Value of a Statistical Life
WFP	World Food Programme
WHO	World Health Organization

PREFACE AND ACKNOWLEDGEMENTS

This book is about humanitarian economics as an emerging field of study and practice. It is about the economic aspects and political economy dynamics of humanitarian crises and responses to them. Linking theory with practice, *Humanitarian Economics* is intended not only for interested scholars and researchers, but also for policymakers and practitioners. To the greatest extent possible, I have avoided specialized (economic and humanitarian) jargon in order to make this book accessible to a broad audience beyond trained economists and humanitarian practitioners.

This book lies somewhere between a primer and an essay. It is a primer to the extent that it is a first attempt to define and cover the field of humanitarian economics. It is an essay to the extent that, throughout the book, I bring personal arguments to the fore and select topics that I believe deserve particular scrutiny, while leaving others aside. For instance, I examine terrorism and counterterrorism economics from a humanitarian viewpoint in some detail but I do not delve into the privatization of violence and the rise of the private security and military service industry, nor do I dwell on monetary policy in war and post-war contexts.

Drawing on twenty-five years of study and practice, this book is influenced by the fortuities of my personal trajectory in the field of humanitarian economics. At the end of the 1980s I joined the International Committee of the Red Cross (ICRC) as a fresh graduate in economics to serve as a humanitarian worker in the field at a time when the Cold War was still tearing apart many conflict-ridden countries in the developing world. The fall of the Berlin Wall precipitated the end of the civil war in El Salvador, where I was working at the time. But it took several years to replace the analytical mould of the East-West rivalry and ideological confrontation with a new analytical framework to understand so-called 'new wars', notably by paying greater attention to civil war economies and the political economy of armed conflict.

In 1990, I witnessed extreme violence between Hindu and Muslim Tamils in Eastern Sri Lanka. I interpreted the massacres as largely driven by a competition over the agricultural rent: the violence prevented farmers from bringing their rice harvest onto the market, pushing prices down to record lows in production enclaves. The traders who were able to buy rice at rock-bottom prices and transport it across frontlines made extraordinary profits. A few years later, having now left the humanitarian sector, I attended a lecture shortly after the 1994 Rwandan genocide by an economic adviser who had served in Rwanda until the genocide started. He was aware of the fact that he and other economists working in international financial institutions pushed for economic reforms that contributed to heightened political tensions. He lamented that economic advisers to Rwanda were not expected nor allowed to address political issues. Their role was to advocate for macroeconomic orthodoxy irrespective of the explosive political situation, which was compounded by a fragile peace process and falling coffee prices. This motivated me to start doctoral research on the politico-economic interactions in relation to aid conditionality in war-torn countries.

A decade after the fall of the Berlin Wall, the ICRC opened a new position of economic adviser, so I went back to the organization from 2000 to 2006. Many of the practical examples that I use in this book to illustrate conceptual and theoretical issues are drawn from fieldwork experiences and exchanges with colleagues who specialized in domains such as nutrition, agronomy, water engineering and health. Other examples are drawn from the time I spent with Médecins Sans Frontières (MSF, 'Doctors Without Borders' in English) as a board member of the Swiss section and in the finance committee where many issues related to the humanitarian marketplace were debated.

I would like to express my gratitude to all those who have contributed to my reflections on humanitarian economics over the past two-and-a-half decades. This book owes much to the people in crisis-affected communities who, despite their plight, have displayed great generosity in welcoming me as a humanitarian worker or as a researcher, spending hours addressing my questions or, more simply, sharing time that allowed me to better understand specific dynamics related to household livelihood, coping strategies and survival in the midst of disaster and war. I am grateful to my former colleagues, both nationals and expatriates, who shared their experiences and expertise in diverse contexts and sectors.

PREFACE AND ACKNOWLEDGEMENTS

I greatly benefited from regular exchanges with my colleagues at the Graduate Institute of International and Development Studies in Geneva, as well as with my students who enthusiastically debated and worked on several of the key questions raised in this book. I have had the opportunity to teach and conduct research in the field of humanitarian economics first at Sciences Po in Paris and, since 2007, at the Graduate Institute. I am particularly grateful to my doctoral students as well as to the masters students who have participated in my seminar on the economics on conflicts and disasters and in the annual 'applied research seminar', where students work on research projects commissioned by humanitarian organizations. I am also grateful to the humanitarian professionals who shared their thoughts and experiences while following executive training programmes at the Centre for Education and Research in Humanitarian Action in Geneva. As the list of references makes clear, this book owes much to numerous scholars and researchers who have pioneered work on the economics of war, terrorism and disaster, as well as on the political economy of armed conflict.

While writing this book, I spent two months at the Lee Kuan Yew School of Public Policy of the National University of Singapore to work on the Disaster Economics chapter, looking at disaster risk management and the political economy of disaster response in South-East Asia. I am particularly grateful to Caroline Brassard who greatly contributed to making my stay highly productive and enjoyable. I wish to thank also Kishore Mabhubani, Kanti Prasad Bajpai and Paul Kenneth Tan for welcoming me at the Lee Kuan Yew School, as well as Rick Perdian and his colleagues for their many insights into the disaster risk insurance industry. My thanks go also to Mehmet Kerem Coban, Andrew Maskrey and Anne Florini for stimulating exchanges while in Singapore, as well as to the Swiss National Science Foundation for financial support.

I spent another month at the American University of Beirut with the Issam Fares Institute for Public Policy and International Affairs. This allowed me to look in particular at the impact of the ongoing Syrian crisis in Lebanon, while working on the chapter entitled Survival Economics. I wish to thank Rami Khouri, Tarek Mitri, Karim Makdisi, Nasser Yassin and Sarine Karajerjian for welcoming me at the Issam Fares Institute. My appreciation goes also to Ivan Vuarambon, Ugo Panizza and Riccardo Bocco for facilitating contacts in Lebanon, where I benefited from rich exchanges in particular with Thomas Batardy, Jean-Nicolas Beuze, Antoine Bieler, Fabrizio Carboni, Myriam Catusse, Philippe Chite, Frédéric Dumont, Carmen Geha, Hala Ghattas, Filippo Grandi, Heba Hague-Felder, Carla Lacerda, Nisreen Salti and Rabih

Shibli. I am grateful to the Swiss Embassy in Beirut for financial support and in particular to François Barras, Boris Richard and Chasper Sarott.

A few chapters in this book partly draw on previously published articles, with relevant sections revised and updated for consistency with the whole volume. I thank the respective publishers for permission to reproduce parts of the original articles in adapted form, as detailed:

- Chapter 1: 'Reason, Emotion, Compassion: Can Altruism Survive Professionalisation in the Humanitarian Sector?', *Disasters* 39, 2 (2015), pp. 189–207.
- Chapters 4 and 7: 'Humanitarian and Development Aid in the Context of Stabilization: Blurring the Lines and Broadening the Gap', in Muggah, Robert (ed.), *Stabilization Operations, Security and Development—States of Fragility*, New York: Routledge, 2014, pp. 35–55.
- Chapter 5: 'The Rise of Disaster Risk Insurance and Derivatives', in Brassard, Caroline, David Giles & Arnold Howitt (eds), *Natural Disaster Management in the Asia-Pacific*, Tokyo: Springer, 2015, pp. 175–188.
- Chapter 7: With Liliana Andonova, 'Business-Humanitarian Partnerships: Processes of Normative Legitimation', *Globalizations* 11, 3 (2014), pp. 349–367; with Piedra Lightfoot, 'Business in Humanitarian Crises—For Better or for Worse?' in Dijkzeul, Dennis & Zeynep Sezgin (eds), *The New Humanitarians in International Practice: Emerging Actors and Contested Principles*, London: Routledge (forthcoming).

Several experts kindly agreed to comment on draft versions of individual chapters and I extend my sincere appreciation to Charles Anderton, Ravinder Bhavnani, Thomas Bierstecker, Philippe Le Billon, Riccardo Bocco, Caroline Brassard, Francis Cheneval, Agnès Dhur, Paul Dunne, Jacques Forster, Oliver Jütersonke, Urs Luterbacher, Olivier Mahul, Alessandro Monsutti, Hugo Slim, Achim Wennmann and two anonymous reviewers for their insightful remarks and suggestions. I further benefited from regular, substantive exchanges with both scholars and leading humanitarians including Bruno Bochum, Yves Daccord, Dennis Dijkzeul, Oliver Jutersonke, Robert Muggah, Kevin Savage and Fiona Terry. All errors remain my own.

I thank Annie Hylton for the meticulous copyediting of the entire book and lively exchanges on individual chapters, as well as Marie Thorndahl and Jacqui Tong for editorial suggestions, Yann Pablo Corminboeuf for graphic design support, as well as Matthias Nowak and the Small Arms Survey for providing specific data on armed violence. From the outset, this book proposal received a warm welcome from Hurst and I express my appreciation to Michael Dwyer and his colleagues.

Last but not least, I thank Sophie, Baptiste, Arthur and Clémence for being supportive of my long stays abroad and bearing with me once back home and writing this book.

I dedicate this book to my cousin Laurent Du Pasquier who, like hundreds of other humanitarian workers in 2014, was the victim of a grave security incident while on field assignment. He was thirty-eight when he was killed on 2 October in Donetsk, Ukraine, while working with the ICRC.

Geneva, April 2015

INTRODUCTION

Then every soldier kills his prisoners.

William Shakespeare, 1599[1]

Protecting prisoners and civilians in war has long been a major humanitarian concern. The contemporary kidnap-and-ransom boom in conflict zones is particularly worrying from a humanitarian perspective. On 2 December 2014, as I was working in Beirut on this book, I was struck by the news of a 'high-value catch': the Lebanese army arrested a woman and an eight-year-old boy, allegedly the wife and son of Abu Bakr al-Baghdadi, the leader of the Islamic State of Iraq and Syria (ISIS).[2] Around the same time, Lebanese authorities separately detained the wife and brother-in-law of the al-Nusra Front's military commander Anas Sharkas.

Lebanese officials hoped that the arrest of close relatives of jihadi leaders would improve their bargaining position to obtain the release of over twenty security officers held captive since August 2014. The Lebanese soldiers and policemen were taken prisoner following clashes in Arsal, a town in the northeast of the Bekaa Valley, considered to be a strategic smuggling centre for the trafficking of arms, money and people in support of jihadists in neighbouring Syria. As of December 2014, they were still in the hands of Syrian jihadi groups, including ISIS and al-Nusra. What the Lebanese hoped to use as leverage, however, did not improve their bargaining power. On 5 December 2014, al-Nusra executed a Lebanese policeman, stating: 'executing prisoners of war in our custody is our response to the filthy Lebanese Army detaining our wives and kids. If our sisters are not released we will execute another soldier in our custody in the very near future.'[3] A few days later, the Lebanese government released the so-called 'high-value detainees' from custody.[4] Although the epi-

1

sode received both Western and Middle Eastern media attention, hardly anyone publicly questioned the legality of regular security forces detaining civilians, including an eight-year-old child, for leverage in a prisoner swap. Sadly, this exemplifies that trading civilians and combatants has become regular business in a booming kidnap-and-ransom market.

Ransoming prisoners is nothing new, however. The near universal adoption decades ago of international conventions on the treatment of civilians and prisoners in war has not prevented the perpetuation of egregious abuses. History actually reveals considerable variations in the fate of civilians and prisoners of war across space and time. Academics from different disciplinary backgrounds have provided a wide range of explanations to account for such diversity in belligerent behaviour. Scholarly work has primarily involved international law experts and, to a lesser degree, political scientists, historians and ethicists. Since the end of the Cold War, economists have started to take a closer look at many issues central to contemporary humanitarian crises and responses, such as the rationale and incentives for kidnap and ransom and how best to address them (see Chapter 4).

Values, Norms and Cost-Benefit Calculus

Economists tend to emphasize cost-benefit calculus to explain variations in the treatment of war prisoners. An economic inquiry into the treatment of war prisoners during medieval times provides insights relevant to the contemporary kidnap and ransom crisis, including the case of Lebanon. The age of chivalry in medieval Europe has been hailed as a time when the lot of the vanquished improved. Many social scientists have highlighted the role of knightly values that glorified acts of mercy in war, with an emphasis on warriors' concern for reputation and inner emotions of pride, guilt and shame. Economists have emphasized the changing costs and benefits of keeping prisoners alive: granting captors property rights over their prisoners raised the incentive to keep them alive, at least those prisoners expected to be ransomed for a good price.

In economics, combatants are assumed to behave as opportunistically as any other rational, maximizing agents, including when it comes to killing or sparing the vanquished. In an article on property rights over prisoners of war in the Middle Ages, Frey and Buhofer remarked that a ruler with limited resources to pay for the war had an interest in granting each soldier the rights to their own spoils of war. Battles pitting man against man made it possible to clearly identify who was made prisoner by whom and to assign property rights accordingly. Under these circumstances,

> [A soldier] acts rationally when he decides either to kill or to spare a defeated enemy. If he kills him he eliminates any risk of the defeated soldier striking back. The advantage of sparing a defeated enemy, on the other hand, is the monetary benefit of selling him at a price determined by the prisoner himself, his family, or whoever else is interested in his release. A greater benefit, of course, can be expected from a rich prisoner than from a poor one, from a healthy prisoner than from a wounded or sick one … The (net) value of a defeated enemy thus depends on a number of empirically observable factors influencing benefits and costs, given the particular form of property rights.[5]

During the Hundred Years' War, Henry V departed from the prevailing normative system of chivalry that favoured sparing the vanquished. The English king, victorious over the French at Agincourt in 1415, ordered the execution of all the prisoners including 'the flower of French nobility and chivalry',[6] with the exception of a few of the highest ranking prisoners whose ransom belonged to the king.[7] The massacre was later explained, if not justified, on grounds of necessity: the sheer number of French prisoners made it risky and costly to keep them alive in the event of another French assault. Guarding the prisoners to prevent them from taking up arms would have diverted English forces away from combat.[8]

The rise of nation states, forced conscription and new military technology altered incentives to take part in war. The adoption of the first Geneva Convention for the Amelioration of the Condition of the Wounded in Armies in the Field in 1864 coincided with the final transfer of property rights over prisoners from individual combatants to states. Aware of the budgetary constraints to pay for modern warfare, Henry Dunant, the founding father of the Red Cross and promoter of the Convention, drew attention to the benefits of effective sanitary services for the wounded: 'by reducing the number of cripples, a saving would be effected in the expenses of a Government which has to provide pensions for disabled soldiers'.[9] Signatory states formally relinquished some of their rights over prisoners by adopting subsequent international covenants, in particular the 1949 Third Geneva Convention relative to the Treatment of Prisoners of War, which requires the release of prisoners of war at the end of hostilities without compensation.

Despite considerable advances in establishing a stronger legal framework and some remarkable successes in effectively promoting and enforcing the laws of war—international humanitarian law (IHL)—millions of individuals have suffered from massive, repeated violations of basic rules and principles of

IHL. As Frey and Buhofer concluded in their article on prisoners and property rights, it is far from easy to 'substitute moral (humanitarian) principles and rules for material incentives.'[10] The examples of Agincourt centuries ago and Lebanon today illustrate the relevance of looking at the multifaceted variables that influence individual and collective behaviour in war beyond values, norms and international law. Consideration of costs and benefits, distributional issues and economic incentives can assist in understanding the behaviour of key actors in humanitarian crises. More broadly, humanitarian economics can greatly contribute to humanitarian studies as well as humanitarian policy and practice.

Humanitarian Economics

Humanitarian Economics is a field of study and practice that deals with the economic and political economy dimensions of humanitarian crises and responses. It focuses on the (re)distribution of power, wealth, income and destitution in specific historical and institutional crisis settings. Humanitarian economics is thus concerned with the economics and political economy dynamics of humanitarian crises accruing from war and natural hazard. Departing from previous work where disaster, war and foreign aid tend to remain separate fields of study, I consider humanitarian response not as an exogenous reaction to adverse shocks, but as part and parcel of humanitarian crises, as deeply embedded in today's disaster and war economies.

The humanitarian aid market is booming: funding for international humanitarian assistance steadily increased over the last three decades. From 2012 to 2013 alone, government funding increased by a quarter and private funding by a third, reaching a total of $22bn by the end of 2013.[11] Total international humanitarian funding rose again in 2014 to reach $24.5bn. Hundreds of thousands of professionals work in the humanitarian sector, which has become a pillar of today's global governance. Yet, humanitarianism is in crisis. Renewed criticism from within and outside the sector hint at the failings of the humanitarian system. Acute needs for assistance and protection simply remain unaddressed, in particular in the heart of the deadliest armed conflicts. Our understanding of humanitarian crises remains largely insufficient. Against this background, humanitarian economics offers a largely untapped field that has much to contribute, as developed throughout this book.

The humanitarian sector is stretched to the limit as it attempts to address the plight of crisis-affected communities in Afghanistan, the Central African

Republic, the Democratic Republic of the Congo, Haiti, Iraq, Liberia, Myanmar, the Palestinian Territories, Sierra Leone, Somalia, Sri Lanka, Syria and Ukraine, to name a few recent crises. A study by Médecins Sans Frontières (MSF) covering three of these contexts, aptly entitled 'Where is Everyone?', finds aid effectiveness to be largely unsatisfactory despite increased funding and enhanced expertise in the field. The reasons for poor outcomes include bureaucratic hurdles, conflicts of interest, insufficient priority to emergency response, risk aversion and, worryingly, a lack of resolve and ability to assist the vulnerable in difficult-to-reach locations.[12]

In spite of highly dedicated people and relentless efforts, the humanitarian sector too often fails to provide proper assistance and protection to millions of civilians in distress. In an article entitled 'Humanitarianism Besieged,' the former head of the UN Office for the Coordination of Humanitarian Affairs in Damascus lamented that the standard toolkits brought by the international humanitarian system simply did not work in Syria. To respond more effectively to the crisis, he called for more creativity, pragmatism and 'some cold, calculating realism' from humanitarians. He further bemoaned that 'any divisions between aid agencies were exploited by government and security agencies.'[13] That said, humanitarian action alone would obviously not provide any solution to the Syrian crisis, which requires a political settlement. The primary purpose of humanitarian action is to save lives, alleviate suffering and protect human dignity in crisis situations. In the best cases, it achieves some of these objectives. In the worst, it fails and is instrumentalized by domestic and foreign political actors to pursue other objectives. Too often, it serves as a foreign policy option by default, a smokescreen for diplomatic and military failure that makes the unacceptable more tolerable.

In this context, factoring humanitarian economics into the analysis offers critical insights to better understand and address humanitarian crises, as well as the crisis facing the humanitarian sector itself. Humanitarian economics can greatly contribute to research and education related to humanitarian action. Over the past two decades, an increasing number of economists have turned to the study of civil war, terrorism and disasters, albeit generally leaving humanitarianism aside. Humanitarian economics draws on conflict economics, terrorism economics and disaster economics with a specific focus on humanitarian concerns. It further overlaps with development and household economics. As a discipline, economics has expanded and today applies to the whole spectrum of issues ranging from the micro-determinants of rebellion and suicide bombing to the role of commodities in armed conflict or the vulnerability and coping mechanisms of affected households. By examining protection rackets, informal taxation, aid diversion, the impact of economic sanctions and the payment of ransoms, economic analysis helps to uncover how humanitarian assistance risks becoming—inadvertently or not—a resource fuelling conflict, and how to better deal with that risk.

This book bears witness to the fact that over the past two decades hundreds of scholars, researchers and practitioners have expanded on the work of a few pioneers, greatly broadening our knowledge base on the economics and political economy of humanitarian crises and responses. Much of this literature does not look at war or disaster from a humanitarian perspective or out of an explicit humanitarian concern. Conducting research for the sole purpose of enhancing our understanding of war and disaster is of course welcome; a lack of sensitivity for humanitarian problems can however raise serious ethical issues when it comes to carrying out research involving people who are affected by war, terrorism and counterterrorism.

Humanitarian economics is situated in the broader interdisciplinary field of humanitarian studies, which covers the origin and evolution of humanitarian crises, their impact on affected individuals, institutions and societies, as well as the responses that they trigger at local, national and international levels. As I argue throughout the book, it is essential to enhance our capacity to analyze and understand humanitarian crises and responses from an interdisciplinary perspective. Wherever possible, I present and discuss theoretical and empirical economic inputs in conjunction with relevant insights from other disciplines such as political science, anthropology, sociology, the life sciences, law and psychology.

About this Book

This book draws on twenty-five years of research and practice in the field of humanitarian economics. While preparing seminars and training sessions on the economic and political economy dynamics of humanitarian crises and responses, I realized that there was no book or relatively comprehensive reference document on humanitarian economics.[14] As I thought about filling this gap, my starting point was to write a book about what economics tells us about war, disaster and humanitarianism, and how this can contribute to enriching humanitarian studies and practice. I soon came to consider the reverse question as well: to what extent the study of humanitarian crises and responses contributes to enriching, but also challenges, economics as a discipline.

Indeed, economics evolves in a universe of opportunistic individuals whose 'rational' behaviour and decisions result from cost-benefit and maximization calculus. War, in turn, is associated with emotions such as fear, hatred and resentment. Humanitarian action arguably thrives on selfless, altruistic engagement. Chapter 1, entitled 'Reason, Emotion and Compassion', introduces some of the major theoretical foundations that underpin the field of humanitarian economics. In doing this, I address the epistemological tensions embedded in the nexus between economics and humanitarianism, for instance when factoring the role of emotions and altruism into a rational choice framework, when explaining suicide terrorism as a result of opportunistic, maximizing behaviour or when evaluating the impact of foreign aid geared to 'win hearts and minds' in counterinsurgency campaigns.

The book invites the readers to take a journey from fundamental epistemological issues to the specific contributions of conflict, terrorism and disaster economics to humanitarian studies. It is organized around three clusters: first, the economics of humanitarianism and the humanitarian marketplace; second, war, terrorism and disaster economics and how people survive in the midst of crises; and third, the transformative power of humanitarian crises and responses. The book bridges macro approaches with micro-level analysis that captures the impact of humanitarian crises on individuals, households and institutions. The focus is on the costs and benefits of war and disaster as much as on how the vulnerable strive to survive and make a living in such crises. This book also examines the evolution of supply and demand in the humanitarian marketplace. I use many concrete examples in an attempt to bridge theory with practice, to bring humanitarian economics to life, and to illustrate its relevance for context analysis, strategic planning and operational management.

Several issues permeate through all chapters, such as: questioning the explicit and implicit assumptions behind theoretical models and empirical research; delving into the interactions between global humanitarian, development and statebuilding agendas and the transformative power of crises; research ethics and the role and use of evidence in informing humanitarian policy and practice. Getting solid data in the midst of humanitarian crises is often highly challenging. It can be a serious obstacle to rigorous needs assessment and impact evaluation. Drawing on advances in development microeconomics and applied microeconometrics,[15] evidence-based decision-making and field experiments have started to be more frequent in emergencies, not least with a view to improving impact evaluation related to the effectiveness and efficiency of humanitarian action and other interventions in conflict and disaster situations.

Chapter 2 examines the humanitarian marketplace. I question the extent to which the supply boom of the past two decades was triggered by a surge in the needs for humanitarian assistance and protection. Facts and figures highlight that the boom has rather been driven by a surge in donors' demand for humanitarian action in a context where humanitarian morality, discourse and practice have become a central tenet of global governance, next to concerns over global issues such migration, public health and security.

Chapters 3, 4 and 5 deal with conflict, terrorism and disaster economics respectively. Chapter 3, 'War Economics', focuses notably on the costs and benefits of war, conflict finance, war economies and the political economy of aid. Chapter 4, 'Terrorism Economics', delves into the rational-choice literature on terrorism and addresses the consequences and financing of terrorism. In this chapter, I also examine the policies and instruments devised to combat terrorism, including foreign aid and economic sanctions, with a focus on contexts of greatest interest to humanitarians: situations of armed conflict. Chapter 5, 'Disaster Economics', analyzes the costs and impact of disasters triggered by natural hazards. I focus in particular on the surge in disaster risk insurance and risk-linked securities on global financial markets, which transfer part of the disaster costs out of the affected country. These new instruments lead to increasing collaboration between the humanitarian sector and the financial services industry, but also raise moral hazard and other political economy issues and may eventually lead to increasing competition between the two sectors.

Chapter 6, 'Survival Economics', focuses on the impact of humanitarian crises at the micro level. I look at how individuals, households and communities attempt to cope in crisis and how humanitarian organizations react accordingly. The impact of the Syrian crisis in Lebanon serves as a case study to illustrate the complexity of assessing the needs for humanitarian assistance in a middle-income country where refugees are scattered across the whole country, living within host communities mainly in urban settings. The spread of multisector cash assistance allows beneficiaries to pay not only for food, but also to cover housing, education, transport, heating, water and other requirements. The spread of cash assistance is not a silver bullet, but is a game changer that challenges long-established sectoral boundaries and relief modalities.

Humanitarian crises and responses profoundly affect national and regional development trajectories. They can be seized as opportunities to challenge or cement the prevailing global order. Building on the preceding chapters, the seventh and final chapter is entitled 'The Transformative Power of Humanitarian Crises'. It critically assesses the tensions embedded in comprehensive approaches that combine political, security, development and humanitarian agendas. I focus in particular on the paradigms of resilience, stabilization and 'building back better' that underpin the expansion of the humanitarian marketplace, notably through a web of collaborative arrangements with a variety of actors outside the humanitarian sector. As an illustration, I examine the case of business-humanitarian partnerships and discuss the risks, opportunities and legitimacy issues involved in such cross-sector collaborations. In the post-2015 context of Sustainable Development Goals, it is critical to look for synergy between the humanitarian, development and environment sectors, as much as it is to reassert the purpose and legitimacy of humanitarian action in and of itself.

It is my hope that this book will contribute to developing humanitarian economics as a vibrant field of study on the economic aspects and political economy dynamics of war, disaster and humanitarian action. *Humanitarian Economics* is also a call for more interdisciplinary and cross-sector collaborations, which are critical to support the humanitarian enterprise in addressing many of today's thorniest humanitarian challenges. I am convinced that the field of humanitarian economics has a great, largely untapped potential in this respect.

1

REASON, EMOTION AND COMPASSION

[T]he age of chivalry is gone. That of sophisters, economists, and calculators, has succeeded; and the glory of Europe is extinguished forever.

Edmund Burke, 1790[1]

Since the expansion of the international development aid enterprise in the 1950s, civil wars have dramatically impacted the developing world. The Cold War was rather 'hot' in countries like Vietnam, El Salvador and Angola where an increasing number of humanitarian organizations became operational. Despite the prevalence of armed conflict in developing countries, it was not before the mid-1990s that development economists started to seriously address civil war as a topic worth studying. Why so late? Getting reliable quantitative data on war-torn economies can be highly challenging, which tends to discourage database-hungry and time-pressed researchers. Besides, civil war was regarded as a research topic better suited to political scientists, historians or anthropologists than economists.

More fundamentally, the encounter between *homo economicus, homo bellicus* and *homo humanitarius* raises basic questions concerning how to analyze individual and group behaviour in humanitarian crises. Rational choice theory serves as a framework for economists and many political scientists to analyze and model human behaviour. 'Rational' here does not mean sound or sane, but refers to an instrumental form of rationality whereby self-interested individuals look for the most cost-effective way to achieve their goals (for example, maximizing wellbeing, power, income, happiness). It is assumed that

11

individuals have consistent preferences over a range of options and opt for the alternatives that maximize net outcome. Notwithstanding the explanatory power of such an analytical framework, there is much to gain from interdisciplinary research which factors reason, emotion and compassion into the analysis to the extent that they all come into play in humanitarian crises.

Before examining the nexus between humanitarianism and economics, let us dig back a bit into the past and then look at the theoretical underpinnings of economic research on humanitarian crises and responses. In 1790, the Irish philosopher Edmund Burke (quoted above) lamented the imprisonment of Queen Marie-Antoinette. He equated the end of the eighteenth century marked by the French Revolution with the end of chivalry—a normative system largely based on custom and attaching value to honour and mercy—and the simultaneous advent of economists and calculators. Over the two centuries that followed, economics emerged as a scientific discipline of its own while chivalry and the glory of Europe have indeed suffered serious blows. At the same time, humanitarianism emerged as a modern version of chivalry. Today, the international humanitarian aid sector is a multi-billion dollar enterprise with more than 270,000 workers involved. It remains Western-dominated. Yet, humanitarian engagement from emerging economies and Gulf countries is fast increasing.

How fundamental is the antagonism between humanitarianism and economics, as implied by Edmund Burke? Economics evolves in a universe of rational, opportunistic agents who pursue their own individual interests, seeking to maximize wellbeing and minimize pain. War, in turn, is associated with resentment, fear, hatred, longing for revenge and other emotions that arguably compete with cost-benefit calculus and utility maximization in motivating individual behaviour.[2] As for humanitarianism, it is a movement that arguably thrives on the selfless, altruistic engagement of volunteers in favour of distant strangers in distress. Think, for example, of volunteers with Médecins Sans Frontières (MSF) in 2014 flying to Guinea-Conakry, Liberia and Sierra Leone in an attempt to contain the spread of the Ebola haemorrhagic fever. These volunteers put their own lives in danger and had to endure wearing warm protection 'spacesuits' under tropical conditions. In addition, angry community members attacked their treatment centres, accusing the foreign volunteers of having imported the disease. Instead of gratitude, they often received death threats.[3]

The perceived antagonism between altruism and rationality has emerged relatively recently. The world's major religions and philosophical traditions have long been concerned with human traits such as compassion. Over the past century, rational choice models assuming utility-maximizing behaviour became the hallmark of orthodoxy in neoclassical economics, political science and other social sciences, while human morality remained the preserve of theologians and philosophers.[4] Under neoclassical economics,[5] war appeared as a paradox or an anomaly: why would rational, self-interested, maximizing actors not simply prefer a peaceful negotiated settlement to costly hostilities? Why wouldn't they seek to avert the costs of armed conflict and seize the potential gains from peaceful trade relations?

To address such theoretical questions, it is useful to consider political economy dynamics related to the distribution of war costs and benefits, looking for instance at rebels, warlords and the Western military-industrial complex. As discussed below, the economic profession has rediscovered that combatants can make more than a decent living by looting or protecting what others have produced, or simply by preying on each other. In the aftermath of the Cold War, the East-West ideological rivalry as the dominant explanatory framework for armed conflict disappeared. Scholars and reflective humanitarian workers sought to develop a new analytical framework to understand civil war. The seminal book *Economies des Guerres Civiles* (Civil War Economies), edited in 1996 by Jean and Rufin, brought many empirical insights to the attention of scholars and humanitarian practitioners alike.[6] Novel insights from the economics of war and the political economy of armed conflict led humanitarians to reconsider how best to negotiate with warring parties and influence combatant behaviour.

The extension of rational choice approaches to civil war in the non-Western world resonates with a debate that raged within economic anthropology in the 1970s and 1980s between the proponents of formalist and substantivist economic models.[7] The formalist model applies standard economic theory to all cultures, including 'primitive societies' where self-subsistence and barter trade prevail over monetized exchanges. Against this idea of the universal validity of neoclassical economics, substantivism argues that decision making in non-Western, pre-industrial societies is based less on individual choice or market signals than on moral values and social relations based on reciprocity and redistribution, further shaped by clientelism and fear.[8] The formalist-substantivist debate raises a set of questions that remain relevant for humanitarians seeking to support the livelihood (or enhance the 'resilience') of vulnerable communities, especially in countries like South Sudan, the Central African Republic or Afghanistan.

In this chapter, I turn first to the theoretical foundations of conflict economics, and then factor altruism and emotions into the analysis to highlight epistemological tensions in the nexus between economics and humanitarianism.

Economics and War

As a discipline, economics can be defined with reference to its object and project: it deals with the production, distribution, exchange and consumption of goods and services, and pursues the optimal allocation of scarce resources. It is a social science interested in the study of human behaviour and decisions, notably in relation to interactions in markets. Neoclassical economics expects rational, self-interested individuals to generate Pareto-optimal equilibrium outcomes.[9] Importantly, exchanges are supposed to be voluntary and property rights clearly defined as well as enforced. These assumptions do not always hold true under normal and peaceful circumstances, let alone under civil war and anarchy. Hence, while neoclassical economics fully recognizes the power of self-interest in 'the ordinary business of life'—as Alfred Marshall puts it[10]— it ignores what Jack Hirshleifer referred to as the dark side of force: war and crime. It seems obvious that war, crime and politics influence human behaviour in the context of scarce resources and fierce competition.[11] Yet, as economics established itself as a discipline of its own, it evacuated politics altogether. Armed conflict came to be regarded as abnormal, disrupting the ordinary business of life, or as an exogenous event neither amenable to economic analysis nor worthy of scholarly interest (except a handful of remarkable instances in relation to World War I and II).[12] Conflict economics applies the principles, concepts and methods of economics to study war and terrorism. It factors armed violence into the analysis by considering not only production and exchange, but also appropriation through force or the threat thereof. Anderton and Carter define conflict economics as '(1) the study of violent or potentially violent conflict using the concepts, principles, and methods of economics and (2) the development of economic models of appropriation and its interaction with production and exchange activities.'[13]

Rational choice theory rests on the assumption that individuals behave opportunistically, making choices that maximize their benefits (or pleasure) and minimize their costs (or pain), accurately captured by Gordon Tullock's assertion that '[T]he average human being is about 95 percent selfish in the narrow sense of the term.'[14] However, as discussed below, many scholars and recent advances in neurobiology challenge that assumption. One may further question to what extent individuals behave as 'the average human being' in the midst of a humanitarian crisis. The study of humanitarian crises and responses begs the question of the role that emotions and altruism play in explaining the behaviour of warring parties, humanitarian workers or disaster victims. In this context, interdisciplinarity should by no means be seen as just a 'fashion of the day'; it is an epistemological necessity required to reconstruct the complex social reality prevailing in disaster and war.

From the classical economists of the eighteenth and early nineteenth centuries to the neoclassicists and neomarxists, interest in war has waxed and waned over time.[15] Two or three centuries before the emergence of neoclassical economics, Niccolo Machiavelli and the mercantilists largely regarded war as part of the ordinary business of life. The conquest of new markets and trade matters were intimately linked with war. The appropriation of gold and other assets by force rather than by mutual consent was instrumental in strengthening the monarchs' power and statebuilding. Economic activities included looting, extorting, sequestrating and the likes. This radically changed with the liberal revolution. Ricardo's theory of comparative advantages did away with a vision of trade as a zero-sum game. Mutually advantageous exchanges together with the primacy of individual interests enhanced the opportunity costs of opting for war and offered strong incentives for peaceful cooperation. It is, however, important to note that Ricardo intended his theory to apply to nineteenth-century England and Portugal, but certainly not to their African and Asian colonies where the logic of extraction and forced acquisition prevailed over peaceful, mutually advantageous exchanges. That said, the main theoretical issue is that, from a consequentialist perspective, negotiating a compromise came to be seen as more advantageous than waging a risky, costly war.

Neoclassical economists and other social scientists have provided several explanations for the paradox of war under a rational choice framework.[16] These can be categorized along four main, heterogeneous arguments:

- *Violence as inherent to capitalism and development*: armed conflict can be a vector of progressive change and development. War has played and still can play a critical role in spurring primitive capital accumulation leading to development.[17] Conversely, conflict is inherent to capitalism and is congenial to the profound social, political, cultural and economic transformations that characterize development processes. Civil war is thus not simply 'development in reverse'.[18] In addition, the national mobilization that is required as countries prepare for war has been singled out as an essential ingredient of statebuilding, as demonstrated by Charles Tilly in the case of state formation in Western Europe.[19] Even today, how rational would it be for the world's major powers not to wage war for an entire decade while seeking to maintain superior military capacity?[20] In the same vein, intervening in humanitarian crises has become a new strategic mission for the armed forces of major and emerging powers alike. So-called 'humanitarian interventions' provide a justification or pretext to request higher budgetary means from parliaments and an opportunity to upgrade operational military capacity through real-life field operations.

- *Political economy*: under the liberal paradigm, a major reason for ending war is to realize potential gains from trade. But even when such gains are high, the costs and benefits of peace and enhanced trade are not evenly distributed. Political economy models help identify how adjustment costs are distributed among different groups and how the likely losers may violently oppose both peace and trade liberalization. Thus, it may be helpful to design compensations or transitory measures for those who stand to lose wealth and power from peace. Political economy approaches challenge the liberal peace paradigm by relaxing the unitary actor assumptions that consider each warring party or trading nation as a single homogenous group. Instead, it concentrates on conflict over distributional issues both within and between groups.

- *Asymmetric or incomplete information*: the lack of accurate information leads to rational miscalculation about the actual strength and preferences of the adversary. This is compounded by a natural tendency to bluff: leaders tend to overstate their strength and resolve to wage war in the hope of negotiating a more favourable peace deal. Theoretically, such an argument may hold on a short-term, ad hoc basis. A few battles should suffice to improve information about the relative strength of warring parties and lead to a peaceful bargain. Since this is often not the case in reality, several explanations have been advanced for the apparent paradox of conflict as equilibrium behaviour. When one warring party feels cornered and hard pressed, it may adopt more risky behaviour, as individuals tend to be less risk averse under the prospect of loss than of gain. In other words, individuals tend to take more risks when facing the prospect of losses,[21] triggering fearful reactions that make conflict more likely in spite of the higher costs associated with such an outcome. In addition, individuals display a tendency to overweigh low-probability, high-consequence events.[22]

- *Commitment problem*: parties to a conflict are unable to credibly commit to disarming and maintaining peace over the long haul—or at least are unable to commit to refraining from allocating peace dividends to gain future military advantage and reneging on the peace accord (time consistency problem). There is a significant body of literature on incomplete contracting that seeks to explain when and why parties are unable to write down and enforce binding contractual arrangements. One problem is that many aspects of the peace deal may not be verifiable throughout the implementation phase. Besides, the parties may not have sufficient knowledge to envisage every likely scenario and set mutually agreeable conditions accordingly. Another issue is that, in the absence of institutions enforcing property rights and the rule of law, conflict may no longer be channelled towards peaceful outcomes. Lastly, the dispute may centre on something that cannot be divided and thus does not lend itself to any compromise on resource sharing or power sharing, such as holding power in a highly centralized state with a strong presidential regime.[23]

Several strands of conflict theory have developed on the basis of the very same rationalist, maximizing assumptions that made war irrational in the eyes of neoclassical economists.[24] Despite the prominent role of emotions in war, many contributions to conflict theory by economists and political scientists paradoxically rest on the same hypotheses.[25] Since the pioneering work on conflict theory by Trygve Haavelmo in the 1950s,[26] Jack Hirshleifer in the 1980s and a few others,[27] economists have started introducing armed conflict into economic modelling.

In conflict theory, the contest model basically considers the trade-off between two options regarding wealth accumulation: production associated with voluntary exchange—often mediated by the market—and appropriation or expropriation mediated by force (or the threat of force). The chances of successful appropriation depend on variables such as fighting capability and available technology. This, in turn, determines the extent to which a party may opt for appropriation. At a more micro-level, the individual resolve to take part in hostilities accrues from a cost-benefit analysis. Individuals make a calculus of how much there is to gain through appropriation ('greed') and how much they risk losing by joining an armed group ('opportunity cost').[28] While there may be more to gain in resource-rich countries, the opportunity costs of joining a rebellion are obviously higher in rich countries where people have more to lose than in poorer ones. This would partly explain why civil war tends to be more frequent in low-income than in high-income countries, or in countries where much of the youth is well educated but unemployed, or does not enjoy access to higher education or vocational training.[29] Violent conflict might be prompted when parties fail to negotiate a peaceful deal on the sharing of resources, for instance when such resources are indivisible or because of information asymmetries.[30] The contest model framework has become a theoretical fundament of economic research on civil war, transnational criminal organizations, and violent regime change (see Chapters 3 and 4).

Such rational choice models have contributed to explaining the frequency and intensity of deliberate massacres of civilians. The Worldwide Atrocities Dataset reports over 7,000 events of deliberate killing of non-combatants between 1995 and 2012.[31] Rather than being an instance of the unfortunate collateral damage of war, killing and maiming civilians can be a profitable option for perpetrators who wish to advance their objectives, which points to the disturbing rationality of war crimes, terrorist acts and counterterrorist attacks.[32] While civilians suffer the brunt of war, warring parties may find it more advantageous to keep waging war than winning it. Powerful outsiders can influence the cost-benefit equation of warring parties and their ensuing behaviour vis-à-vis the civilian population via (the threat of) sanctions and rewards. Against this background, a critical question is to what extent humanitarian assistance represents yet another resource or spoil in belligerents' cost-benefit calculus (see Chapter 3). At the same time, fighting a 'useful' enemy can provide the best chance of survival for a regime under threat.[33] Think of Bashar al-Assad and Islamist insurgents, where the Syrian regime eventually appears as a bulwark against the rise of the Islamic State in Iraq and Syria (ISIS).

In sum, conflict economics is the application of economics to the study of war, and considers appropriation in interaction with production and exchange activities.[34] It rests on the belief that the concepts, methods and principles of economics are valid and relevant to the study of armed conflict and terrorism. Of course, cost-benefit calculus is not all that matters. Armed conflicts are complex, multi-causal phenomena deeply engrained in specific historical and institutional contexts. Grievances play a key role as a mobilizing factor, in particular when combined with a sense of group identity along ethnic, religious, territorial or linguistic lines. Besides, leaders matter in conflict settings and often don't seem to act in a rational manner. Understanding the specific history of a leader's clan and individual trajectory can provide essential insights into understanding seemingly irrational behaviour. Yet, this is not our traditional remit as economists, nor are we trained to factor emotions such as fear, hate, resentment and revenge into our analyses.[35]

Economic Imperialism Versus Interdisciplinarity

Several studies over the past twenty years show that economics stands out with respect to its lack of cross-disciplinary engagement and its dominant position within the social sciences, in particular in the US.[36] With a humour that typically infuses economic imperialism, Hirshleifer predicted a bright future for economists as they finally turned to conflict analysis in the early 1990s:

> As we come to explore this continent, economists will encounter a number of native tribes—historians, sociologists, philosophers, etc.—who, in their various intellectually primitive ways, have preceded us in reconnoitring the dark side of human activity. Once we economists get involved, quite properly we'll of course be brushing aside these a-theoretical aborigines.[37]

Engaging such 'aborigines' is essential for economists seriously interested in improving our understanding of war, disaster and humanitarianism. Economics has a lot to contribute to humanitarian studies as part of a deep, structural interdisciplinary endeavour that confronts and integrates the concepts, models and paradigms from relevant disciplines. Conversely however, disciplinary insularity combined with an obsession to fit social reality into theoretical models can be a recipe for adding catastrophe to disaster in the context of humanitarian crises.

The study of humanitarian crises would gain from deeper confrontation and collaboration between different approaches to social inquiry, combining positivist, interpretative, historical and critical social research. Approaching humanitarian crises through inductive research methods grounded in the observation of field reality can greatly enrich hypothetico-deductive approaches typically favoured by economists interested in testing the validity of theory-based models. The 'Econ' tribe has much to gain from interdisciplinary exchanges with 'Native tribes', starting precisely with those whom Jack Hirshleifer coined 'a-theoretical aborigines'. Cross-tribal collaborations can be enriching all the way from collecting and questioning the validity of primary data to challenging research findings, for instance by confronting the outcome of qualitative field research that relies heavily on perception surveys and discourse analysis with the results from quantitative studies that consider 'hard facts' (see Chapter 4).

Interdisciplinary dialogue would further help address the implicit political inclination behind 'scientific' inquiry. From a humanitarian perspective, much of the economic literature on civil war presents a problematic bias against rebels. Empirical studies tend to focus on non-state armed groups and their leaders, assumed to be greedy, rather than to question repressive states. This bias contributes to the common conception of rebels as economic criminals rather than warring parties with rights and obligations under international humanitarian law (IHL). This reinforces the natural tendency of states to label armed opposition and their sympathisers as thugs, and more often as terrorists. State repression has received much less attention despite the fact that, in many cases, it accounts for most of the violence.[38] For example, the Guatemalan Historical Clarification Commission found the state responsible for more than 90 per cent of the 200,000 civil war casualties and forced disappearances between 1960 and 1996, while the guerrillas, the Guatemalan National Revolutionary Unity (Unidad Revolucionaria Nacional Guatemalteca, URNG), was found guilty of a mere 3 per cent of all human rights abuses.[39] More recently, researchers have resorted to state-centred approaches to examine state-building and peacebuilding processes in relation to a shift from violent extraction to taxation. This echoes what Mancur Olson described as a move from roving bandits solely interested in looting to stationary bandits. The latter typically start nurturing a tax base in order to have more to tax from in the long run and may thus take on state-like functions of protecting people against roving bandits.[40] A high dependence on valuable natural resources such as oil or gemstones may render repression more likely since it provides the state with an alternative source of revenue while increasing the opportunity cost of losing power.[41]

A Rationalist Approach to Humanitarian Negotiations

Rational choice models and insights from conflict economics eventually made it into humanitarian policy and practice. At the turn of the millennium, securing safe access to conflict zones arguably became more difficult. Humanitarian organizations increasingly expressed concern about the shrinking of the humanitarian space.[42] They elaborated negotiation manuals to help their staff and operational managers to successfully engage warring parties and other key stakeholders. This was part of a broader drive to professionalize such engagements, involving a shift from reliance on personal virtue towards developing training curricula and transferring professional skills. In this context, conflict theory and the growing economic literature on civil war influenced the humanitarian sector in many ways. To start with, humanitarian negotiation manuals adopted the assumption that individuals are selfish and utility maximizing, despite considerable evidence that challenges this assumption in the normal business of life in general, and in war situations in particular.

In 2004, the Centre for Humanitarian Dialogue (known as 'HD) released a 'Handbook for Securing Access, Assistance and Protection for Civilians in Armed Conflict' in collaboration with staff of the International Committee of the Red Cross (ICRC) and of the UN Office of the High Commissioner for Refugees (UNHCR).[43] Two years later, the UN Office for the Coordination of Humanitarian Affairs (OCHA) released a humanitarian negotiation *Manual for Practitioners* in response to an earlier request by the UN Secretary General.[44] Both manuals posit that combatants are rational, self-interested actors. They insist on the need to identify and understand the interests of each party to a conflict as a basis for successful negotiations, whereby 'interests are the most important things to identify',[45] and can comprise 'desire for recognition, economic gain, personal advancement or military victory, and more basic needs ... including physiological needs and personal security needs.'[46]

This emphasis on interests requires looking behind the veil of rhetoric, political discourse and negotiating positions. The assumption is that warring parties may be more or less amenable to granting access to humanitarian organizations or to changing their behaviour towards greater respect of IHL when this does not equate with a military or economic disadvantage (see Chapter 3). The key question is to ascertain what warring parties have to lose or to gain by granting access to humanitarian organizations and abiding by IHL. To what extent can an armed group or an individual fighter be conferred any economic, military or political advantage? The training manuals for humanitarian negotiators rest on the assumption that armed groups routinely resort to cost-benefit calculus when deciding whether to abide by the laws of war or to grant access to relief organizations. This includes questions such as the extent to which greater respect of IHL or improved relations with humanitarian agencies would result in enhanced international legitimacy and domestic popular support. Interestingly, the OCHA Manual envisages the possibility of moving the reservation price of an armed group by leveraging the political clout of the UN, including the use of force. The 'HD manual does not; it rests on a Dunantist vision of humanitarian action that strictly adheres to the principles of humanity, impartiality, neutrality and independence.

In an edited volume entitled *Humanitarian Negotiations Revealed*, MSF released an account of some of the organization's murkiest humanitarian negotiations conducted in the world's most troubled spots.[47] The case studies highlight the centrality of warring parties' interests and the political transactions involved in deciding whether aid activities can go on or not. The book editors contend that the 'lofty rhetoric of humanitarian principles' or the 'illusory ideals of humanitarian principles and humanitarian space' too often obscure the reality: what allows an organization like MSF to provide medical assistance in war is its ability to address the vested interests of warring parties in the context of grubby negotiations.[48] Would then greater professionalization and aid effectiveness afford humanitarians a greater capacity to identify and address the interests of belligerents, using cold, calculating realism at the expense of 'illusory ideals'?

Compassion and Emotion in Humanitarian Crises

In her book *A Paradise Built in Hell*,[49] Rebecca Solnit looked at a number of catastrophes and concluded that, in situations of emergency, human beings respond with naturally altruistic tendencies, even if chaos, looting, and panic can also be part of the picture. The author claimed: 'The great majority of people are calm, resourceful, altruistic or even beyond altruistic, as they risk themselves for others.'[50] Are standard assumptions behind rational choice models suited to the study of humanitarian crises? Would altruism be more relevant than egoism in explaining the behaviour of social actors in emergency situations, and that of humanitarian actors in particular? Does the ongoing professionalization of the humanitarian sector bear the risk of stifling altruism over the altar of efficiency and result-based management? I attempt to address these questions in the following sections.

Humanitarian gestures may be as old as humanity itself.[51] Historians have identified heroic initiatives to save lives and alleviate human suffering going back to antiquity. However, humanitarianism as we understand it nowadays emerged in the mid-nineteenth century.[52] The founding of the ICRC in 1863 and the adoption of the first Geneva Convention a year later represent foundational milestones in the emergence of modern humanitarianism, today embedded in the four fundamental principles of humanity, impartiality, neutrality and independence.[53] Jean Pictet provided an authoritative exegesis of these humanitarian principles in his famous 1979 *Commentary*, in which he drew a distinction between essential principles and derived principles: humanity and impartiality reflect the very essence or substance of humanitarian action; they are essential or substantive principles. Neutrality and independence are more operational or instrumental in that they are a means to an end and derive from the essential principles.

Notwithstanding the variety of humanitarian traditions and approaches, these four principles are now widely endorsed by the majority of actors in the humanitarian sector and feature as constitutive elements in the definition of contemporary humanitarian action. For Jean Pictet, 'humanitarianism works toward the establishment of a social order which should be as advantageous as possible for the largest possible number of people.'[54] This is a surprisingly utilitarian take on humanitarianism. In practice, the humanitarian movement seeks to minimize suffering and pain rather than to instil a social order that would be as advantageous as possible for the largest number of us. As an ideology, humanitarianism coincides with precepts embedded in several religious and moral philosophies. It rests on a form of utilitarianism where the good is dissociated from the right and, in a Rawlsian perspective,[55] would equate what is right with the maximum good or, rather, the minimum bad.

In his *Commentary*, Jean Pictet equates humanity with the very objective of humanitarian action, which is to prevent and alleviate human suffering, and to protect the lives, health and dignity of all human beings. He further postulates that the Red Cross 'has no interests of its own, or at least that its interests coincide with those of the persons it protects or assists.'[56] Humanity thus closely relates to the notions of selflessness and altruism. Impartiality implies that humanitarian action must respond to the needs of victims of armed conflict or disaster depending on the intensity and urgency of such needs, without any distinction as to nationality, religion, sex, gender, ethnicity, political leaning, etc. Neutrality implies abstaining from taking sides for or against parties to an armed conflict, in the hope of maintaining their confidence and preventing the politicization of humanitarian aid wherever possible. As for the independence principle, it requires effective autonomy of humanitarian actors in relation to state and non-state actors. It arguably adds credibility to the claim of relief agencies to be driven strictly by humanitarian motives.

Voluntary service is another fundamental 'Red Cross principle' that has also been adopted by many other humanitarian organizations. That principle implies that humanitarian workers should not be prompted in any manner by desire for material gain.[57] Volunteerism refers to the unconstrained willingness of aid workers to dedicate time and effort to promoting the core humanitarian values of their organizations outside the intent of personal monetary gain. Volunteering in the Anglo-Saxon tradition stresses the lack of remuneration. In French, we further distinguish between *bénévolat* and *volontariat*: both imply unconstrained service for the community.[58] The *bénévole* gets no remuneration for services performed outside of family, school and any professional or legal relations and obligations, while the *volontaire* usually has a legal employment-like contract and gets paid, albeit modestly. Volunteering is also booming outside the Western world. A recent study hints at the robust growth of international volunteering by Asians,[59] which is largely state-sponsored and geared first and foremost to development assistance in Asia, even if about half of the organizations surveyed also send volunteers to Sub-Saharan Africa. The study also underlines a clear trend towards greater professionalism, especially in disaster relief, and an increasing concern with containing 'voluntourism'.

Humanitarianism thus appears to be intimately associated with altruism. We may actually envisage the postulate of altruistic, selfless humanitarian engagement as the flipside of the postulate of rational, self-interested, opportunistic agents under neoclassical economics. The word 'altruism' was first coined a decade before the creation of the Red Cross, in 1852, by the French sociologist Auguste Comte in the *Catéchisme Positiviste* ('Catechism of Positive Religion'). Comte defined altruism as the opposite of egoism: it meant giving priority to the interests of others over one's own.[60] In common parlance, altruism refers to the selfless motives for an act. Such a psychological conception of altruism follows deontological ethics whereby an act is deemed altruistic if it is the product of a motivation directed towards the interests and wellbeing of another person.[61] Altruism typically represents a measure of good moral behaviour in the world's main philosophical and religious traditions.[62]

Biologists tend to define altruism not in normative terms but in an evolutionary perspective, stripped of intentionality. Altruism that favours non-kins results in a lower ability of the altruist to pass on genes to future generations, which results in a diminution of reproductive fitness.[63] For living organisms in a small group consisting mainly of closely-related individuals, behaving in an altruistic manner contributes to passing on the altruist's own genes to future generations since most neighbours are likely to be of the same family. Altruism amongst related individuals (kin altruism) can make perfect sense from a biological perspective. In fact, altruism towards siblings who share half of the genetic material of a parent is widely regarded as rational. However, humans and other species like bonobos often behave altruistically towards strangers. The puzzle for evolutionary biologists is to explain such 'non-kin altruism'. This puzzle is also well known in the social sciences. Based on game theory, many test experiments have shown how reciprocity can explain part of the puzzle.[64] Repeated interactions between non-kins can make cooperation more profitable and punishing non-cooperators more likely.[65] In addition, non-kin altruism can be associated with the search for alliances beyond family for both biological and strategic purposes associated with the incest taboo and greater bonds. Thus, *homo economicus* would arguably be more aptly described as *homo reciprocans*. But this does not explain why cooperation among humans and other species outside close relatives and with little probability of repeated interaction is frequently observed. The two main competing explanations for non-kin altruism are based on cultural and biological transmittance respectively. There is a vivid 'nature versus nurture' debate to determine if, and to what extent, non-kin altruism is the product of genes or culture. As we shall see, recent advances in neuroscience and evolutionary biology bring novel insights to this debate.

Agreeing on a working definition of altruism relevant across disciplines is not an easy task since the term does not necessarily carry a universal meaning. In his 'Introduction to the Economics of Altruism, Giving, and Reciprocity', Kolm proposes a definition of altruism that focuses on motives rather than outcomes:

> [A]n altruistic view of a person is a view that values positively and for itself what is good for another person or what it deems to be so. And [altruistic] giving is an unconditional action of a person, purposefully favorable in some way to another and costly in some way for the actor.[66]

This definition can be contrasted with a consequentialist perspective according to which it is not the intention behind an act that determines if it is altruistic or not, but rather the eventual outcome of that act. In this framework, religiously-motivated 'altruism' can be seen as self-interested since it is usually associated with the promise of a reward that can sum up to eternal life in paradise... not a negligible profit in the faithful's cost-benefit calculus.

Altruists and Bureaucrats

Organizational theory posits that bureaucrats, like other economic agents, seek to maximize utility, which can be more or less aligned with their narrow personal interests or with the humanitarian mission of their organization.[67] A number of surveys show that the vast majority of aid workers[68] today do not contest the need to professionalize the humanitarian sector. Yet some of them fear that professionalization may lead to bureaucratic meritocracies, sacrificing humanitarian values for the sake of efficiency.[69] For the International Federation of Red Cross and Red Crescent Societies (IFRC), voluntary service is of the essence for the whole International Movement of the Red Cross and Red Crescent: 'If the Movement fails to recognize the value of voluntary service it is in danger of becoming bureaucratic, losing touch with a vital source of motivation, inspiration and initiative, and of cutting off the roots which maintain its contact with human needs and enable it to meet them.'[70] Another major concern is that increasingly professional and efficient humanitarian workers focus on technical fixes only to address symptoms, neglecting the political engagement that is required to address the causes of chronic humanitarian crises.

Looking at such concerns, it is as if the advent of modernity portrayed by Max Weber over a century ago finally affected the humanitarian sector. Weber equated the rise of modern nation states with the expansion of bureaucratic organization and impersonal institutional relations associated with the primacy of the rule of law. The 'disenchantment of the world' was not only associated with the retreat of religion, but also with the generalization of instrumental rationality involving cost-benefit calculus at the expense of value-based forms of rationality. Weber further highlighted a shift of the legitimation of domination from traditionalism and charisma of leadership to legality and bureaucracy. This echoes transformations within the humanitarian sector over the past four decades. Just as Max Weber saw the increasing dominance of bureaucrats devoid of any sense of political responsibility as a threat to modern states,[71] humanitarian bureaucrats can be seen as a threat to the vibrancy of humanitarianism. Yet, there is no determinism. The generic issue is: how can altruism thrive in bureaucracies within professions that may require a degree of selfless engagement or personal sacrifice (such as fire-fighting and the health professions)? More specifically, can the altruistic impulse that fuels humanitarianism survive professionalization?

To address this question, let's return to the nature versus nurture controversy. If altruism is an innate trait, as we shall suggest when exploring advances in the cognitive sciences, there is not much to fear since it would be deeply ingrained in human nature anyhow. But if altruism is rather the product of individual experiences, organizational cultures and societal expectations, there is much cause for concern if it is not adequately nurtured. The development of functional magnetic resonance imaging in the early 1990s represents a big leap for the study of potential biological roots of morality. Recent advances in neuroscience and experimental evidence suggest that altruism is a powerful human trait, yet with great heterogeneity between individuals.[72] Altruistic impulses find different expressions depending on the institutional, cultural and ideological environment as well as on prevailing material conditions. More generally, our emotional and cognitive faculties are the product of genetic evolution with propensities for both violence and cooperation. The behaviour adopted by different individuals partly depends on the normative context that influences decisions involving moral dilemmas.[73]

Altruism as an Innate Human Trait

One hypothesis that assumes non-kin altruism to be a hereditary trait sees it as a form of evolutionary misfiring or 'maladaptation'.[74] The hypothesis posits that non-kin altruism developed over a very long period of time when humans lived in small groups with interactions primarily among kin. In sum, people interacting with each other were either relatives or, at least, likely to enter into repeated interactions. In today's highly urbanized and globalized world, daily encounters with non-kin are more likely to be one-off. Hence, our innate altruistic preference 'misfires' as a leftover of the times when people lived in small tribes. The environment in which we *homo sapiens* currently live changed too fast to allow for a parallel evolutionary adaptation.[75]

Centuries before the emergence of brain imaging techniques, the father of modern economics had the right intuition—as he often did—when he famously wrote:

> How selfish soever man may be supposed, there are evidently some principles in his nature, which interest him in the fortune of others, and render their happiness necessary to him, though he derives nothing from it except the pleasure of seeing it. Of this kind is pity or compassion, the emotion, which we feel for the misery of others, when we either see it, or are made to conceive it in a very lively manner. That we often derive sorrow from the sorrow of others, is a matter of fact too obvious to require any instances to prove it; for this sentiment, like all the other original passions of human nature, is by no means confined to the virtuous and humane, though they perhaps may feel it with the most exquisite sensibility. The greatest ruffian, the most hardened violator of the laws of society, is not altogether without it.[76]

For Adam Smith, sympathy was part of human nature rather than the product of virtue. His understanding of 'man' went far beyond that of a self-interested, economic fiction, which does not mean that sympathy cannot be reconciled with utility maximizing behaviour. Reducing the suffering of fellow human beings contributes to the altruist's wellbeing as well. In addition, Smith not only implied an individual utility function that includes the wellbeing of others but also underlined the role of what we, today, would refer to as empathy:

> [W]e conceive ourselves enduring all the same torments, we enter as it were into his body, and become in some measure the same person with him ... His agonies, when they are thus brought home to ourselves ... begin at last to affect us, and we then tremble and shudder at the thought of what he feels.[77]

Smith outlines the idea of an impartial spectator in each human being, an idea which could arguably be seen as an early conceptualizing of a 'theory of mind' that has developed since the 1970s with regard to the capacity to put oneself into someone else's mind. The theory posits an innate ability to attribute mental states not only to oneself, but also to others, while understanding that the latter may not share one's own intentions, beliefs and desires. This theory of mind has also been used to explain altruism in other animal species, consistent with reciprocal altruism and kin selection.[78] This innate ability must however be nurtured through social interactions and experiences over many years, especially during early childhood.

Smith's notion of compassion is also echoed in the recent discovery of mirror neurons in primates' brains. These neurons are involved in the capacity to feel what others may be experiencing. Mirror neurons are activated in a similar way when someone directly performs an action or observes someone else carrying out that same action.[79] Neuro-imaging techniques have been used to study specific brain areas activated in conjunction with utilitarian and non-utilitarian moral judgments that can lead to altruistic or egoistic behaviour.[80] Since the famous case of Phineas Gage in the mid-nineteenth century, the study of people's changing behavioural patterns after specific brain damage reinforced the argument in favour of a natural tendency for non-utilitarian judgment. People with damage to their ventromedial prefrontal cortex tend to lose their capacity to elicit emotional responses in front of others' pain and come to judge moral dilemmas in a more utilitarian fashion than healthy control groups. Besides, the capacity to identify and empathise with others also seems to play a key role in preventing cruelty.[81] But if altruism clearly appears as embedded in human nature, it is also the outcome of social norms and institutions.

Altruism as a Product of Socialization

'We in China do not think like that!' This is how a Chinese student expressed her doubt about the idea that altruism is hardwired in human nature in a class on the economics of humanitarian action. This led to a lively discussion on the manifestation of humanitarianism under different traditions and, more fundamentally, on altruism as culturally constructed. Since the course dealt with economics in an interdisciplinary masters programme, we discussed the extent to which training in economics can influence student behaviour. How far does exposure to the self-interest model, commonly used in economics, reinforce the tendency to behave in a self-interested manner? In an early study carried out in the US, graduate students in economics were significantly more likely to free ride on financial contributions to public goods.[82] Does this mean that, in a self-fulfilling prophecy, we begin to resemble our *homo economicus* construct as we plunge into the study of economics? Or is it rather that those of us who resemble *homo economicus* in the first place choose to study economics? Research on charitable giving in the US concluded that exposure to self-interest models wields an influence. Based on a questionnaire sent to 1,245 college professors across twenty-three disciplines, the results showed that economists were among the least generous in terms of median gifts. Despite higher incomes on average, a higher share of economists did not give anything compared to those in other disciplines.[83] The researchers concluded that education has an impact on altruistic giving and invited economists to stress a broader view of human motivation in their teaching, 'with an eye to both the social good and the well-being of their own students.'[84] A recent experiment involving over a hundred traders and investment bankers suggests that banking culture encourages dishonest behaviour among employees, showing a greater tendency to cheat in order to secure financial gains.[85]

In stark opposition to the evolutionary misfiring hypothesis, it has been argued that altruism results rather from a cultural adaptation that developed with *homo sapiens* living in increasingly larger groups. Larger and more complex societies made the development of norms and institutions necessary to function and prosper. This resonates with Kant's concept of the categorical imperative, under which cooperation becomes rational when it is widely recognized as a shared norm or moral rule.[86] Herbert Simon, the 1978 Nobel Memorial Prize in Economic Sciences laureate, argues that bounded rationality explains why human and other species do not actually behave optimally for their fitness and adopt frequent non-kin altruistic behaviour. Contrary to the *homo economicus* model, individuals do not enjoy access to full and perfect information in the real world. They are unable to identify all the options at their disposal and cannot ascertain the environmental factors that will influence the outcome of different decisions. Even if they could, they would not be able to process all of the information nor to compute the different outcomes in order to make the optimal decision. Consequently, humans tend to take decisions based on the information, suggestions and recommendations given by others. In highly complex economies, social networks provide better information on what is good and bad in terms of reproductive fitness than what an individual can learn independently and gather from experience. This, in addition to reciprocity over long-term iterative encounters, makes cooperation more profitable.[87] As the psychologist (and 2002 Nobel Laureate in Economics) Daniel Kahneman highlighted, people tend to assess alternatives very quickly and tend to take decisions based on what first comes to mind, which largely hangs on culturally dominant mental models.[88]

Incentives and institutions play a critical role in rewarding cooperative behaviour and, more importantly perhaps, in sanctioning social norm violations. Empirical tests in the context of evolutionary game theory show that voluntary cooperation is widespread across the globe, but rapidly diminishes when free riding is widespread. Punishing free riders is key to maintaining a sense of fairness for sustained voluntary cooperation. There is no determinism in the expansion of cooperation; the sudden onset of civil war in Syria in 2011 illustrates how quickly social fabrics can be radically torn apart. On the other hand, sociality implies that cooperation may also be achieved even when cooperative individuals represent only a minority of a given population that, under specific conditions, can swing an entire group towards large-scale cooperation.

To the extent that altruism is at least partly hardwired or innate, the evolutionary biologist Richard Dawkins perhaps pushes the envelope too far when stating: 'Let us try to teach generosity and altruism, because we are all born selfish'. Indeed, Dawkins has since retracted this statement.[89] But he had a point in that cooperative and altruistic behaviours are also the products of social norms, institutions and experience.

Emotions

War elicits deep emotions, which in turn play a crucial role in the evolution of conflict and in generating a humanitarian response. Factoring emotions into economic analysis is no easy task. Several strands of research attempt to integrate psychological research on the regulation of emotions with the study of complex political processes.[90] Psychologists have distinguished between primary emotions, which are immediate, instinctive feelings in response to a situation (e.g. fear, happiness), and secondary emotions, which emerge later in response to primary emotions (e.g. jealousy, anxiety, hostility, self-esteem or the lack thereof).

Internal rewards and sanctions in the form of secondary emotions, such as pride or remorse and guilt, play an important role in conditioning human behaviour, next to external ones such as bonuses, enhanced social status, economic sanctions or imprisonment. How such emotions develop partly depends on the economic conditions of each individual and the extent to which basic needs are met: Maslow famously posited a pyramidal hierarchy of needs where physiological and safety requirements must be met before individuals strongly pursue higher-level objectives such as self-esteem and pride, which indeed seem to play a role in altruistic behaviour.[91] Disinterested behaviour may thus also be regarded as a form of social elitism practiced by those materially and/or spiritually wealthy enough to afford and enjoy it.

The World Bank's 2015 World Development Report, entitled *Mind, Society and Behavior*, appeared in the wake of renewed interest in the power of social norms, intuitions and mental models in explaining human behaviour, beyond the influence of (bounded) rationality.[92] For example, recent empirical work in economics questions the role of monetary incentives and social norms in motivating civil servants such as health workers to perform, or in reducing corruption and enhancing tax compliance. A recent study concludes that fire fighter volunteering seems to be positively correlated with both altruism and a concern for social reputation, whereas monetary incentives can crowd out one's concern with reputation.[93] Already in the early 1970s, sociologists comparing different blood donation systems concluded that giving for free produces superior societal outcomes than giving against the promise of financial rewards in industrialized countries.[94]

The case of kidney transplantation provides a counter-example from a developing country. According to a study published by the Cato Institute in 2008,[95] Iran is the only country that enjoys a sufficient supply of kidneys for transplants. When no family member is able or willing to donate a kidney to a relative suffering from kidney failure, that person may then legally purchase a living one from a stranger. Rewards may include one year of health insurance coverage for free and remuneration that typically varies between $2,300 and $4,500. From a utilitarian perspective, the cost of giving a kidney for free may be too high compared to the pleasure of saving the life of a stranger. This provides an interesting example since there is a sample bias in many experiments where test subjects are selected out of Western industrial nations. Recent research, however, provides increasing evidence that some basic principles would apply to all cultures,[96] even where it is considered that the utility-maximizing *homo economicus* does not adequately provide the sole anthropological reference to predict or explain human behaviour. Indeed, empirical tests seem to conclude that both emotions and rationality are elements of moral behaviour across cultures.

So far, the social science literature does a poor job of integrating emotional and rational choice explanations of conflict, in particular when it comes to economics and political science. Rather than putting reason and emotions at opposite ends of an explanatory continuum, 'a common ground can be found if one follows the intuition that emotions are associated with rare and unusual

31

events such as serious threats to existence or the prospect of severe losses of wealth, property, territory or physical integrity.'[97] What can we conclude with regard to humanitarianism? Even if the precise contribution of emotions remains unclear, when individuals are confronted with the plight of disaster victims, primary emotions seem to play an important role in providing the initial impetus for the so-called humanitarian imperative to react. The ensuing rationalization process typically seeks to channel those emotions into effective action and to formulate a rational justification for that action. The humanitarian principles of humanity, impartiality, neutrality and independence serve as guiding principles in this process of channelling emotions into action under teleological rationality.

Factoring Humanitarian Principles into the Equation

The principle of *humanity* is closely related to the notion of selflessness, a feeling or sentiment of active goodwill toward mankind as a whole. As we have seen, our conception of humanity can be related to the theory of mind and our ability to attribute mental states to other human beings and react accordingly. This capacity for empathy is critical in spurring the sentiment of compassion associated with the initial emotion or affective reaction to the suffering of others, which spurs a humanitarian response. In his *Commentary* on humanitarian principles, Jean Pictet implies that the spirit in which a charitable act is performed does not much matter, and adopts a consequentialist view in that effective humanitarian outcomes count more than the purity of motives.[98]

The principle of *impartiality* implies non-kin altruism. Impartiality requires repressing one's initial impulse and engaging with a degree of rational restraint to assess the urgency and intensity of needs objectively. The principle can be divided into three sub-principles: non-discrimination, proportionality and the individual impartiality of humanitarian workers. Non-discrimination means assisting and protecting victims of disasters or armed conflict—even enemies—without discrimination of any sort. Proportionality dictates that as a matter of priority humanitarian aid programs address the most urgent and dire needs. The third sub-principle, impartiality at the individual level, is 'a personal quality of an individual called upon to make a judgment or choice ... to distribute relief or give care ... without taking sides, either for reasons of interest or sympathy.'[99] Whereas non-discrimination discards objective distinctions between individuals and communities, or between kin and non-kin, impartiality requires one to discount subjective distinctions or to leave one's *ego* aside in order not to favour the interests of ethnic affiliates, friends or political allies over those of distant strangers or even enemies. This echoes Adam Smith's concept of having an 'impartial spectator in one's breast' and the theory of mind in relation to the human ability for empathy.

Neutrality includes abstaining from taking sides for or against any party to a conflict in order to maintain trust and prevent the politicization of humanitarian aid wherever possible. In the face of atrocities, neutrality may require abstaining from an immediate outcry of indignation in order to preserve minimal trust for dialogue, including with war criminals and designated 'terrorists'. Like impartiality, neutrality requires restraining one's own feelings and natural impulses in the face of acute suffering. Neutrality does not mean suppressing emotions in the face of suffering, but imposes a rationalization process with regard to expressions of such emotions.

Independence from political, religious and economic influence enables humanitarian organizations to abide by the other principles. It adds credibility to relief agencies' claim to be driven only by humanitarian motives. Claiming to be independent implies humanitarian organizations seek a large degree of autonomy in relation to states and non-state actors. This is obviously far-fetched for UN agencies whose agenda is largely driven by member states and that may operate hand-in-hand with UN peacekeeping forces that often *de facto* take a side in armed conflict. Besides, these agencies may be operating in countries whose leaders are targeted by UN sanctions and do not consider the organization as neutral and independent. In terms of funding, independence may require turning down a large donation with strings attached. It means sometimes rejecting offers for badly needed logistical support or armed escort that would provide the means and security required for the provision of immediate relief in the hope that adhering to humanitarian principles will pay off in the long run in terms of field access and humanitarian outcomes.

In sum, the essential principles of humanity and impartiality require a degree of altruism, refraining from acting only out of self-interest. But together with the derived principles of neutrality and independence, they further require channelling, or constraining, the altruistic impulse in order to pursue greater effectiveness by factoring the potential negative side-effects of emotionally-driven responses into the decision-making process. The point is not to rigidly stick to humanitarian principles as sacrosanct commandments nor to dismiss them as illusory ideals and throw the baby out with the bathwater. In the rationalization process that channels the initial humanitarian impulse into plans and action, humanitarian principles offer useful beacons in the rough seas of war.

Concluding Remarks

We have approached the apparent tension between reason, emotion and compassion in the context of humanitarian crises. Gordon Tullock's assertion that 'the average human being is about 95 percent selfish in the narrow sense of the term' is not supported by evidence, with instances where altruism may be as valid a postulate as that of selfish utility-maximization. At the same time, Henry Dunant in his *Memory of Solferino* implicitly refers to cost-benefit calculus in support of his vision, while Jean Pictet in his *Commentary* takes a consequentialist view when interpreting the essential principles of humanitarianism. On that basis, can humanitarianism survive and strive in the age of economists and calculators? Should we be concerned with the current professionalization drive in the humanitarian sector?

The humanitarian impulse that fuels humanitarianism rests on altruism both as an innate human trait and the product of culture and experience. More broadly, some moral principles seem hardwired into human brains, yet with substantial cultural variations, paralleling Chomsky's idea of a universal grammar for different languages.[100] As international humanitarian actors from diverse cultural and geographical backgrounds take a more prominent position in the marketplace, further research on the emergence and persistence of humanitarian ventures in different historical and institutional settings would help us to better grasp how altruism is nurtured and to find diverse expressions in different humanitarian traditions.

Professionalization does not necessarily come at the expense of altruistic commitment. Sociological studies on pro-social behaviour confirm that socialization and identity development can play an important role in nurturing altruism as a professional virtue.[101] Bureaucracies can learn from on-going research in behavioural and development economics, for example on the role of extra-financial incentives and reward systems—including internal rewards mobilizing emotional triggers—in encouraging supererogatory acts. Further research can shed light on how in-house and external humanitarian training programmes coupled with appropriate incentive systems can nurture altruistic impulses and avoid the risk of organizational anomie. A key prerequisite is that training curricula and institutional reward systems do not discharge aid workers from critical, reflective thinking.

Humanitarian policymakers and practitioners routinely take decisions in the face of acute moral dilemmas involved in the rationalization process that channels primary emotions into operational plans and action. The relationship between emotions and cognitive structures deserves deeper scrutiny, which is beyond this book's purview. The forthcoming chapters illuminate how humanitarian economics can contribute to assisting humanitarian actors in taking informed decisions, be it in the design of assistance and protection programmes or in the management of staff security in high-risk environments.[102] In a rational choice framework, humanitarian negotiation manuals insist on leverage points related to the underlying interests of warring parties and other powerful political and economic actors. While reason is of the essence in humanitarian negotiations, empathy is critical to bring both rational calculus and emotional intelligence to bear when seeking to influence the behaviour and decisions of the key actors in war. Even in the digital age, this requires field presence and direct contact not only with affected communities, but also with the perpetrators of violence.

2

THE HUMANITARIAN MARKET

What matters is not only the good the ICRC brings, but even more the bad it prevents.

Nelson Mandela[1]

The humanitarian market has been booming for over two decades. Between 2012 and 2014, total funding for international humanitarian assistance is estimated to have increased by more than a third, reaching $24.5bn in 2014. On the supply side, the number and variety of actors providing emergency relief has exploded. The humanitarian labour market not only expanded in size—involving an estimated 274,000 workers in 2010—but also in diversity of professions and career trajectories. This has been accompanied by a multiplication of suppliers and sub-contractors along increasingly complex supply chains. Regional hubs have emerged in places like Nairobi and Dubai next to the traditional global hubs in Geneva and New York.

What accounts for this supply boom? Is it need-driven or rather donor-driven? In other words, does the supply boom respond to a surge in the need for humanitarian assistance and protection in armed conflicts and disasters? Or is it rather that donors' demand for humanitarian action has increased in an environment where humanitarian morality, discourse and practice have become central to the global political order, and where humanitarian response has become a default foreign policy instrument of choice? To address these questions, I start by defining key concepts and examining how the humanitarian marketplace has evolved over the past twenty-five years, looking at the supply and demand sides. I then turn to the labour market and supply chains, with a focus on the growing diversity of actors in the marketplace.

What Are We Talking About?

There is no universal definition of 'humanitarian' or of 'humanitarianism'. Their meanings vary across space and time, which, in itself, is a critical topic for research. The definitions that enjoy greater consensus nowadays are self-referential and self-serving: they have been advanced by those actors who define themselves as humanitarian, or by the major donors that shape the market. Critics question the universality of such definitions, which are anchored in Western moral philosophy and Christian tradition.

The word 'humanitarian' relates to the principle of humanity, which implies a concern and a wish to act for the wellbeing and happiness of mankind as a whole. As discussed in the previous chapter, the essential principles of humanity and impartiality refer to the very purpose of humanitarian action, which is to prevent and alleviate human suffering, and to protect the life, health and dignity of all human beings without any discrimination. As a noun, 'humanitarian' designates an actor whose actions and behaviour display solely humanitarian characteristics. As an adjective, 'humanitarian' generally serves to qualify an action, an objective, a crisis, an actor or a principle. 'Humanitarianism', in turn, refers to an ethics, to a corpus of doctrines and to a global movement embedded in an ideology born out of the philosophy of the enlightenment and the evangelical revival of the eighteenth century. As Albert Schweizer put it, 'humanitarianism consists in never sacrificing a human being to a purpose.'[2] Nowadays, humanitarianism refers also to a growing international humanitarian industry whose turnover has kept increasing at a fast pace over the past two decades.

As a buzzword, 'humanitarian' has gained so much traction that it has been increasingly used and abused for highly questionable purposes. For example, in 1999 the then Czech President Vaclav Havel expressed support for the North Atlantic Treaty Organization (NATO) air strikes in Kosovo. In an article in Le Monde, he wrote that 'the air attacks, the bombs, are not caused by a material interest. Their character is exclusively humanitarian,'[3] which led to ironic comments on the notion of 'humanitarian bombing'. Likewise, under a strategy known as 'information operations', coalition forces in Afghanistan provided relief dubbed 'humanitarian assistance' to local communities in Faryab and Badghis Provinces in return for intelligence to 'track down anti-government forces.'[4] Labelling a counterinsurgency instrument 'humanitarian' and other such gross language abuses dangerously erodes whatever moral authority may be conferred to 'genuine' humanitarian action and actors. The bottom line is that aid, which is not imparted in an impartial manner, does not qualify as humanitarian, as confirmed in a Decision of the International Court of Justice regarding US support to the Contras in Nicaragua.[5] In other words, aid that uses criteria other than the urgency and intensity of recipients' needs is, in essence, discriminatory and does not qualify as humanitarian aid.

This is not to deny that the military may have humanitarian concerns, for instance in disaster response or when commanders take all reasonable steps to avoid collateral damage as they plan an air strike, consistent with international humanitarian law (IHL). Yet this of course does not transform the military into a humanitarian actor. The same applies to business executives who may display genuine humanitarian concerns when they volunteer time and resources to assist hurricane or earthquake victims, which does not make them or their companies humanitarian actors. Indeed, I consider it essential that an actor displays at least two fundamental characteristics to qualify as humanitarian. First, its core business must be strictly humanitarian in that its prime objective is to save lives, alleviate suffering and protect human dignity. Second, it must act consistently with the principle of impartiality and thus address needs based on their urgency and intensity without any discrimination based on religion, ethnicity, political inclination, gender or otherwise.

An agreed definition of 'humanitarian aid' was adopted in 2007 by the group of so-called 'traditional' donors under the Development Assistance Committee (DAC) of the Organization for Economic Co-operation and Development (OECD) in Paris. The DAC is the main forum where rich country donors meet and discuss foreign aid policies and practices. The DAC also manages aid statistics. In 1969, the DAC adopted a definition of official development assistance (ODA), which covered both development aid and emergency relief but excluded military assistance.[6] Until the end of the 1980s, humanitarian aid fluctuated between 1 and 3 per cent of total ODA. As it was relatively marginal, DAC members did not establish a specific category for humanitarian aid. Instead, ODA comprised a food aid category that included both emergency and developmental food aid, and another category entitled 'emergency relief' whose definition referred to the occurrence of an abnormal event, such as a disaster or an armed conflict, which the affected state was unable to handle on its own. In the aftermath of the Cold War, humanitarian aid increased rapidly both in volume and as a share of ODA. This led DAC members to first distinguish between developmental food aid and emergency food aid in 1995. But it was not until April 2007 that a definition of 'humanitarian aid'[7] was adopted and defined as:

> Assistance designed to save lives, alleviate suffering and maintain and protect human dignity during and in the aftermath of emergencies. To be classified as humanitarian, aid should be consistent with the humanitarian principles of humanity, impartiality, neutrality and independence.
>
> Humanitarian aid includes: disaster prevention and preparedness; the provision of shelter, food, water and sanitation, health services and other items of assistance for the benefit of affected people and to facilitate the return to normal lives and livelihoods; measures to promote and protect the safety, welfare and dignity of civilians and those no longer taking part in hostilities and rehabilitation, reconstruction and transition assistance while the emergency situation persists.[8]

In this book, I adopt the DAC definition of humanitarian aid and use it interchangeably with humanitarian action and humanitarian response. Under the DAC definition, humanitarian aid indeed equates with humanitarian action: it encompasses not only medical and material assistance, but also protection activities in favour of civilians as well as combatants who are no longer taking part in hostilities. The definition covers emergency response, disaster prevention and preparedness as well as post-war and post-disaster recovery. Following a developmental logic, (early) recovery captures efforts to restore the ability of domestic institutions and communities to recover from disaster or conflict and to avoid relapses.[9] The DAC definition of humanitarian aid thus entails an overlap between the typical remits of the humanitarian and development enterprises.

For statistical purposes under the DAC, aid should be consistent with the principles of humanity, impartiality, neutrality and independence to be registered as humanitarian aid. A major bone of contention is what this concretely means for donor states and humanitarian organizations and how such consistency should translate into operational reality. In sum, definitions remain fraught with tensions and ambiguities. The tensions accrue from the instrumental, self-serving definitions of what qualifies as 'humanitarian'. The ambiguities relate to the varying ways of interpreting and operationalizing the fundamental principles that frame what qualifies as humanitarian and what does not.

The Humanitarian Marketplace

On the supply side of the humanitarian market, we find a broad range of actors and institutional arrangements. Suppliers involve multilateral, governmental and non-governmental organizations as well as non-profit and commercial actors. On the demand side, the sector's turnover depends on government and, increasingly, private donor generosity.

As a statistical aggregate, humanitarian aid refers to international aid flows to countries affected by war and disaster, and thus excludes domestically-funded responses. The DAC collects data on funding from its member states, which it releases annually together with information provided by a few non-DAC countries (e.g. Kuwait and Turkey, but not China) on a voluntary basis, without necessarily abiding by the DAC guidelines on what exactly qualifies as humanitarian aid. The UN Office for the Coordination of Humanitarian Affairs (OCHA) operates the Financial Tracking Service (FTS), which is another major information source on international humanitarian aid. FTS data is aggregated by funding appeals and provided on a voluntary basis by governments, humanitarian organizations and a few private donors.[10]

Drawing mainly on these two datasets, market analysis and reporting have markedly improved over the past decade, not least thanks to annual and special reports by the Global Humanitarian Assistance (GHA) Programme.[11] Importantly, the drive towards transparency goes hand-in-hand with a concern for quality and reliability, since much of the data is biased or incomplete. For example, the valuation of in-kind donation is problematic and the reported value of food aid often bloated: it is reported at the purchasing price in the donor country rather than based on international commodity prices or the actual value in the recipient country. High shipping costs are added to the bill. Another issue is that we do not have much information on domestically-funded humanitarian assistance despite anecdotal evidence of its increasing prominence, in particular in middle-income countries. For example, between 2009 and 2012 India reportedly allocated $7bn to domestic disaster relief and risk reduction while it received a mere $137m from foreign donors.[12] Humanitarian response by home governments and local communities goes largely unrecorded at the global level and is too often neglected by researchers and policymakers alike.

With these caveats in mind, Figure 1 illustrates the evolution of total humanitarian aid from 1970 to 2012 as reported by the DAC[13] in billions of US dollars (constant prices, 2012).[14]

The volume of official humanitarian aid funding followed an upward trend driven by the repeated occurrence of one or two major crises, bringing aid volumes to new heights. Looking at Figure 1, we see repeated increases in humanitarian aid starting with a surge at the end of the 1970s related to the Cambodian refugee crisis, followed by the Ethiopian famine in the mid-

1. Official humanitarian assistance, all donors, 1970–2013 (US $ billion, constant 2012 prices)

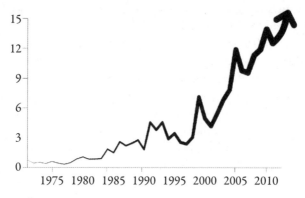

Source: Data from OECD/DAC.

1980s, humanitarian crises of the 1990s in Iraq, Bosnia-Herzegovina, the Great Lakes region and Kosovo. The Asian tsunami and the Haiti earthquake respectively largely drove the 2005 and 2010 funding peaks. With the crises in Syria, South Sudan and the Central African Republic in 2013, international humanitarian funding has reached new heights. According to the GHA 2014 Report, international humanitarian assistance reached $22bn, 30 per cent of which came from private donors. The following year, it reached $24.5bn.

Until the 2000s, DAC donors provided the overwhelming share of overall international humanitarian aid. Since then, private funding has soared. Its value was a quarter of the size of government contributions between 2008–2013.[15] Private funding consists mainly of contributions from individuals, but also from private foundations, trusts and companies. The exact volume of private humanitarian funding is difficult to ascertain since the data is not systematically reported, and must be extracted notably from the annual reports and audited accounts of humanitarian organizations.[16] Private funding tends to be particularly substantial in response to sudden and large disasters with high media coverage. It presents a few advantages for humanitarian organizations to the extent that private funding is often more flexible than government contributions, which often involve the strict allocation of funds to specific programmes or regions (earmarking). Besides, private funds can often be spent over a longer time horizon. On the flipside, fundraising costs can be high since reaching out to a large number of small individual donors requires more resources than maintaining a relationship with a few large public donors.

In the humanitarian sector, Médecins Sans Frontières (MSF) stands out with regard to private funding: it is estimated that the organization raised more than a quarter of total private humanitarian assistance in 2012.[17] MSF's consolidated accounts show that it raised 1,008 million euros in 2013 (or $1,335m), about 90 per cent of which came from private sources that reportedly included about five million active individual donors.[18] By way of comparison, the International Committee of the Red Cross (ICRC) received less than 7.5 per cent of its funding from private sources to cover its 2013 expenditure, totalling $1,264m.[19]

The bulk of private funds come from individuals. Contributions from trusts and foundations remain limited, the Bill and Melinda Gates Foundation ranking first. Private companies have contributed $1.1bn over five years (2008–2012). This corresponds to a mere 4.6 per cent of total private humanitarian funding.[20] Beyond cash donations, amounting to slightly less than 1 per cent of total humanitarian funding between 2008 and 2012, the business sector has favoured broader partnerships with humanitarian organizations that encompass the provision of goods and services together with skills, know-how and technology whose value goes largely unrecorded (see Chapter 7). Faith-based giving or funding from religious groups and networks, channelled notably through faith-based organizations, represents a significant part of private humanitarian funding whose magnitude and potential remains to be ascertained. This is for instance the case of Zakat, which is one of the fundamental pillars of Islam and a religious obligation whereby one donates a percentage of one's annual income in support of the poor and needy.

Humanitarian funding from non-DAC countries has also increased over the past few years. While it was relatively negligible at the turn of the millennium—except a few instances when Gulf States made substantial donations—the contributions of non-DAC donors increased from 7 to 14 per cent of overall government funding between 2011 and 2013.[21] This increase has been largely driven by Turkish contributions in response to on-going crises in neighbouring Iraq and Syria and the ensuing influx of refugees to Turkey. In 2012 and 2013, Turkey was the fourth largest humanitarian donor after the US, the EU and the United Kingdom.

As recorded by the DAC, total official humanitarian aid (OHA) represents just a marginal share of overall resource transfers from richer to poorer countries when compared to ODA, foreign direct investment (FDI) and migrants' remittances, as illustrated in Figure 2.

2. FDI, ODA, OHA and remittance flows to developing countries, 1990–2013 (US $ billion, constant 2012)

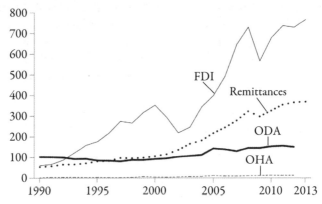

Source: ODA and OHA data from DAC (QWIDS). FDI and remittances data from UNCTAD (UNCTADstat).

Back in 1990, ODA still represented the largest source of North-South resource transfers, ahead of FDI and migrant remittances. Figure 2 shows that, by the mid-1990s, both FDI and remittances sent back home by migrant workers surpassed ODA. Globally, the share of ODA has become less significant, while remittances have continued growing at a robust pace. FDI has also been on the rise, but with large fluctuations along economic boom-and-bust cycles. The relative decline of foreign aid compared to remittances is even more significant considering that ODA data does not reflect the reality of what eventually gets transferred to people in developing countries. Virtually all of what is recorded as migrant remittances goes to people in the South, except transfer fees. By contrast, a large share of expenditures registered as ODA, including humanitarian aid, actually end up covering headquarters costs including administrative, communication, coordination and fundraising costs, not to mention staff salaries and contractors' remuneration.[22] It is not rare that less than half of the aid volume recorded as humanitarian assistance actually ends up in the hands of the beneficiaries. Even if a substantial portion of these costs may be justified or even essential to ensure effective humanitarian action, the evolution of headquarters/field and support/operations expenditure ratios deserves close scrutiny from the governing boards of humanitarian agencies.

Global remittance and FDI volumes are now much larger than foreign aid flows. This however does not mean that ODA and even humanitarian aid have become insignificant across the board. There are huge variations in aid dependency ratios from one developing country to another, as well as from one region to another within the same country. While in 2012 ODA accounted for less than 0.1 per cent of gross national income (GNI) in India, it represented more than a third of GNI for Afghanistan and Liberia, accounting for 80 and 132 per cent of central government expenditure respectively.[23] In such contexts, international humanitarian aid remains an essential resource inflow.

In constant US dollars (2012), ODA dropped from $102.5bn to $88.7bn during the 1990s. This can partly be explained by the end of the Cold War, which meant that Western donors lost interest in ODA as an instrument to contain the spread of communism. Additional factors include the partial reallocation of aid from developing to East European countries. In sharp contrast, humanitarian aid escaped such aid fatigue: it rose from $1.8bn to $7.1bn over the same decade. Consequently, the share of humanitarian aid in total ODA[24] increased from 1.8 percent in 1990 to 8.2 percent in 1999. Since then, this ratio remained relatively constant while both humanitarian and development aid volumes increased.

Over the same two decades, major aid donors sharply increased their contributions to peacekeeping operations. UN-sanctioned peacekeeping operations first experienced a peak in terms of budget and number of peacekeepers between 1993 and 1996. The focus was on basic peace enforcement together with traditional post-conflict interventions and was not accompanied by any surge in ODA. By contrast, the post-9/11 period saw a second, prolonged boom in peacekeeping expenditures that went hand-in-hand with an increase in ODA in volume and as a percentage of DAC members' GNI. The growing aid-security nexus has been particular pronounced in countries like Afghanistan and Iraq, which have ranked among the top aid recipients worldwide.[25]

The Demand Side Versus Humanitarian Needs

What makes up demand on the international humanitarian market? In policy circles, the demand for humanitarian aid commonly equates with 'needs', that is the need for assistance of people affected by war and disaster as assessed by relief agencies. In economics, however, market demand equates with solvent demand, that is the demand expressed by consumers who are willing and able to pay the price required to acquire goods and services. On the humanitarian market, such demand is expressed by donors' willingness to pay for the delivery of humanitarian goods and services to assist crisis-affected people. The humanitarian market displays various specificities, one of which is that donor governments not only provide funding to external suppliers such as humanitarian NGOs and multilateral organizations but also run humanitarian aid programmes themselves via their governmental aid agencies.

In this framework, demand on the humanitarian market does not generally equate with actual needs for assistance and protection. Those needs are impossible to measure with certainty (see Chapter 6). They accrue as a result of humanitarian crises that comprise situations of armed conflict, collective armed violence, and disasters triggered by natural hazards, epidemics and the likes. The problem is that such crisis situations tend to limit both the access and the time available to accurately assess the needs for humanitarian assistance and protection. As the 2014 GHA Report puts it: 'it is impossible to know exactly how many people are directly or indirectly affected by crises.'[26] To start, the relevant baseline data and precise population census may be missing. Population movements may go unrecorded, with individuals who would qualify as refugees or internally-displaced persons (IDPs) being unaccounted for.

Officially, donors seek to adapt their demand for humanitarian aid to the needs of people in distress. In the absence of accurate data, a variety of proxy indicators serve the purpose of estimating the evolution of needs for international humanitarian aid. The number and intensity of armed conflicts and disasters provides a first indication of how those needs fluctuate over time. In a self-serving mode, demand tends to be equated with humanitarian organizations' ex-ante appeals for funds—notably UN-coordinated appeals—and ex-post operational reports and financial statements. The multilateral humanitarian system has embraced the programme cycle logic whereby needs assessments lead to the design of aid programmes, which in turn determine resource mobilization. GHA 2014 reckons that UN-coordinated appeals for funds provide a partial measure of funding according to needs. But it is far-fetched to claim that just two thirds of the needs were met between 2004 and 2013 because one-third of the UN funding appeal requirements were unmet.[27] In its 2014 Overview of Global Humanitarian Response, the UN outlines that the 2014 global humanitarian appeal for funds targets fifty-two million people, compared to thirty to forty million a decade earlier. Yet, the report adds that this represents just 'a portion of true global needs, as many millions more will seek help from their families, communities and Governments directly.'[28]

Conceptually, the annual humanitarian funding appeals of the UN and of other agencies such as the ICRC do not only relate to forecasted needs. They also set out the operational ambitions and capacities of those agencies vis-à-vis potential donors. Annual appeals are prepared well in advance, typically over the summer and autumn of the preceding year. The needs for assistance are thus anticipated months ahead, which would seem odd to anyone who perceives humanitarian action as geared towards responding to unexpected emergencies. In practice, the majority of humanitarian aid goes to protracted crises.[29] Relief agencies have been operational for more than two decades in contexts like Afghanistan, Ethiopia, Somalia, Sudan (North and South), or the West Bank and Gaza Strip, which consistently ranked among the top twenty humanitarian aid recipients over the past years (this may continue to be the case for years to come).

Among the thirty countries that received humanitarian aid for at least eight years in a row by 2013, twenty-five of them qualify as 'fragile states'.[30] In addition, over half of them ranked among low-income countries (LICs), which are countries where the average per capita income is below $1,046 (see Figure 3). Conversely, nearly half of all LICs are long-term recipients of humanitarian aid, a majority of which are in Sub-Saharan Africa. In presenting its 2014 consolidated appeal for funds, the UN insists on the need to set clear boundaries on humanitarian action in situations of general deprivation and poverty-related needs.[31] This raises tough questions on the overlap and interaction between the humanitarian, development and peacebuilding enterprises (see Chapter 7).

20 per cent of the long-term recipients of humanitarian aid are lower middle-income countries (LMICs, per capita income between $1,046 and $4,125), while the remaining 27 per cent are upper-middle income countries (UMICs: per capita income between $4,126 xand $12,745), primarily located in the Middle East and North Africa.

3. Long-term aid recipients by income groups, 2013

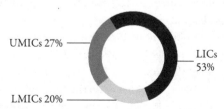

Source: Data from GHA (2014).

Armed Conflicts

The definition of armed conflict remains a sensitive and contested issue. The Mexican authorities strongly disagreed with the authors of the *War Report 2012* that classified Mexico as a country at war, ranking second in terms of war-related casualties in 2012 with an estimated 9,000 people killed, behind Syria (55,000) but ahead of Afghanistan (7,500).[32] The Mexican case raises the question of whether 'for-profit armed groups', such as drug cartels and urban gangs whose primary motive is economic gain, could or should be seen as warring parties and, by extension, be granted such status under international law. The Mexican example raises the question of how to classify 'infra-political' armed violence associated with wealth accumulation through illegal means and the partial privatization of violence.[33]

Social scientists use a plethora of additional adjectives to categorize conflicts: conventional, asymmetric, ethnic, environmental, communal, and so on.[34] IHL case law actually sets two main criteria to determine if a given situation amounts to a non-international armed conflict, as is arguably the case in Mexico: violence intensity and level of organization of the groups involved.[35] IHL further distinguishes between international and non-international armed conflicts, depending on the parties involved in the conflict, with specific rules and criteria applying in each case.[36]

Polemology centres[37] have adopted varying definitions of armed conflict for the purposes of recording their number and intensity. In conflict studies, the most frequently used dataset is the one operated by the Uppsala Conflict Data Program (UCDP). UCDP defines armed conflict as a 'contested incompatibility that concerns government and/or territory where the use of armed force between two parties, of which at least one is the government of a state, results in at least 25 battle-related deaths in one calendar year.'[38] As we shall discuss in Chapter 6, such definitions based on the number of battle-related deaths is of little help to humanitarians: it does not say much about the extent to which armed conflict affects the livelihoods of those who survive. Assessing the evolving needs for humanitarian aid requires micro-level studies that focus on individuals, households and communities.

In an attempt to establish an instrumental definition of conflict for conducting socioeconomic surveys in conflict-affected areas, researchers of the Households in Conflict Network (HiCN) developed a definition of conflict aimed at capturing the impact of violence on the daily lives of affected people. They suggest considering conflict as 'the systematic breakdown of the social contract resulting from and/or leading to changes in social norms, which involves violence instigated through collective action'.[39] This definition encompasses different conflict intensities from riots, coups and terrorism to civil war and genocide. Importantly, it highlights the transformative impact of conflict on institutions and focuses on the micro level: it considers how individuals, households and communities experience conflicts of different intensity. Yet, there is no worldwide dataset based on such an instrumental definition of armed conflict that would permit one to trace the evolution of the needs for humanitarian assistance related to armed conflict. Deprived of such information, I consider the UCDP dataset on armed conflict as a proxy to trace the evolution of humanitarian crises where assistance is required (together with an additional dataset on armed violence and another on disasters).

The UCDP dataset reports a sharp drop in the number of active armed conflicts in the aftermath of the Cold War (see Figure 4), in contrast with humanitarian aid, which increased sharply over the same time period. After a peak of fifty-two active armed conflicts in 1992, that number went down to twenty-nine in 2003. Since then, the number of active armed conflicts has fluctuated between 30 and 40, the overwhelming majority of which are non-international armed conflicts. A so-called 'dyad' is made up of two armed and opposing actors. There can be several dyads in the context of a single armed conflict, for instance in Syria where the state is opposed to several armed groups at the same time. The drop in the number of dyads has been less pronounced since a number of contemporary conflicts have several dyads involved in the fighting, suggesting greater fragmentation of rebel groups.

4. Number of armed conflicts (and dyads), 1946–2013

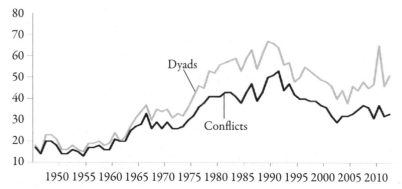

Source: Data from UCDP Dataset.

Other armed conflict datasets confirm this trend. According to Maryland University's Center for International Development and Conflict Management, the magnitude of global warfare dropped by more than 60 per cent from the mid-1980s to 2004. Conflict magnitude refers to the overall effect 'on the state or states directly affected by the warfare, including numbers of combatants and casualties, size of the affected area and dislocated populations, and extent of infrastructure damage.'[40]

What explains the paradox of a surge in humanitarian aid and the concurrent decline of armed conflict in the 1990s? This may be partly explained by the former Communist Bloc opening up and providing enhanced access to the Western humanitarian enterprise. More importantly, instant media coverage of humanitarian crises worldwide has contributed to increased political support and funding of humanitarian aid, with international TV channels and news agencies reporting instantly on humanitarian crises around the globe.[41] I tend to favour the band-aid argument, whereby humanitarian assistance has become a default foreign-policy instrument to make up for the lack of political will to stop war crimes and crimes against humanity in the face of mounting domestic public pressure in donor states. Supporting international relief operations has enabled those states to signal sympathy and a concern for ongoing humanitarian crises, while at the same time discharging them from taking more costly measures from an economic and political viewpoint, such as military intervention or taking on a large influx of refugees.

Examining the evolution of the number of refugees and IDPs tends to confirm this explanation. Displacement may result from a combination of insecurity, environmental degradation and natural hazards. For example, semi-pastoralists in the Horn of Africa may be driven out of their usual areas of pasture as a result of drought and civil war. Civilians in northern Nigeria have had to flee their homes under the combined effect of armed violence, deforestation, desertification and recurrent floods.[42] Even if establishing the precise causal links can be a complex endeavour, refugees and IDPs often leave their homes to escape insecurity and abuses associated with armed conflicts. The total number of uprooted people increased markedly over the past three years. The United Nations Office of the High Commissioner for Refugees (UNHCR) estimated that over 56.5 million people were either refugees or IDPs in 2014, with more than thirteen million of direct concern to the Organization, Syrians and Afghans ranking first and second. Over the past two decades, the total number of refugees oscillated between ten and fifteen million. An additional 4.8 million Palestinian refugees were registered with the United Nations Relief and Works Agency for Palestine Refugees in the Near East (UNRWA) in 2013. Overall, developing countries host up to 86 per cent of the total refugee population; industrialized countries bear a much smaller share of the global burden.

Figure 5 illustrates the evolution of the number of forcibly uprooted people between 1990 and 2013. Following the trend in the number of armed conflicts, the number of refugees peaked in 1993 and then followed a downward trend until 2005.[43]

While refugees were almost as numerous as IDPs in 1990, their number decreased while the number of IDPs increased markedly between 1997 and 2013. The number of IDPs is difficult to ascertain since they are not systematically registered and a majority of them do not live in camps. The data is often outdated, omitting, for example, information on IDPs who have found a durable solution and can be considered as relocated on a relatively permanent basis. According to estimates from the Geneva-based Internal Displacement Monitoring Centre (IDMC), there were over thirty-three million IDPs by the end of 2013, two thirds of them being located in only five conflict-ridden countries: Syria, Colombia, Nigeria, the Democratic Republic of the Congo and Sudan. In 2013, there were thus about twice as many IDPs than refugees. This evolution is partly due to the mounting reluctance of neighbouring countries and, even more, of distant and richer countries to accept any large influx of refugees. It also results from major donors calling on the UNHCR and other relief agencies to assist people in their home country before they cross the border.

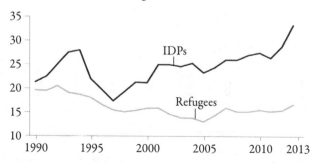

5. Number of refugees and IDPs, 1990–2013

Source: IDMC and NRC, 2014, p. 10.

The growth of the humanitarian market in the 1990s and 2000s cannot be explained by the evolution of the number and intensity of armed conflicts. Since 2010, however, there has been a renewed surge in the number of refugees and IDPs (in great part because of civil war in Syria and Iraq), which has certainly contributed to the recent market growth.

Armed Violence

Can the paradox of an expanding humanitarian market in the face of a reduced number of armed conflicts be explained by attempts to respond to situations of armed violence that do not amount to armed conflicts? Such situations, which lie below the threshold of IHL applicability, include different forms of collective violence,[44] such as criminal or inter-communal violence. The latter concerns groups fighting along ethnic lines, regional boundaries and social classes, which can be aggravated by the feeling of one's identity being threatened in the face of abrupt social transformation associated with the advance of globalization.

The Geneva Declaration on Armed Violence and Development—an international initiative to address the interactions between armed violence and development—highlighted that between 2004 and 2009, over 740,000 peo-

6. Direct conflict-related deaths vs. intentional homicides in non-conflict settings, 2004–2012 (in thousands)

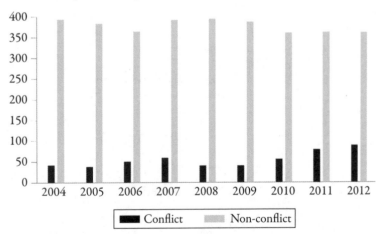

Source: Data from the Global Burden of Armed Violence (GBAV) 2014 Database. Geneva: Geneva Declaration Secretariat.

ple have died annually as a result of armed violence, two-thirds in countries that were not affected by armed conflict.[45] Figure 6 reports the number of direct conflict deaths and the number of intentional homicides in non-conflict settings. It clearly appears that the majority of violent deaths have taken place outside of armed conflicts.

Would the high prevalence of armed violence in non-conflict settings explain the surge in humanitarian aid over the past two decades? No. Figure 7 lists the twenty countries that recorded the highest yearly average for direct conflict death and homicide rates between 2010 and 2012, expressed in number of homicides per 100,000 residents.[46] None of the fourteen countries where no armed conflict is registered rank among the top twenty recipients of humanitarian aid. In fact, humanitarian organizations have not significantly

7. Top 20 most violent countries in and outside armed conflict, 2010–2012 (Homicides and direct conflict deaths, annual average 2012–12, per 100,000 inhabitants)

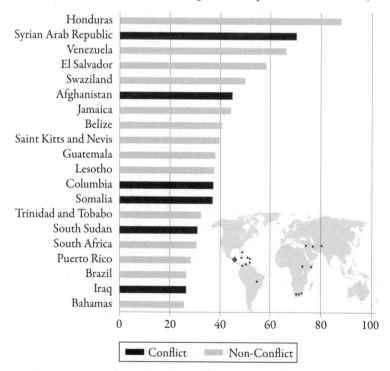

Source: Homicide data from the GBAV 2014 Database. Geneva: Geneva Declaration Secretariat. Armed conflict classification from the War Report 2013.

invested in the areas of armed violence found in Central America and Southern Africa, notwithstanding pilot projects aimed at providing medical and psychosocial assistance in violent suburbs, for example in a few Brazilian favelas.

Disasters

The label 'natural disaster' is misleading: disasters are not natural. The hazards that trigger disasters may be natural, but the ensuing disasters—or lack thereof—are the products of human commissions and omissions such as investment in disaster prevention and preparedness or incentives to settle down in highly exposed locations. Disasters refer to emergency situations that result primarily from natural hazards, but also from epidemics or technological and industrial accidents.[47]

There are over fifty disaster databases, but just a few of them systematically attempt to provide worldwide data on the human and economic costs of disasters:[48]

- The primary reference for empirical research on disasters is the Emergency Events Database (EM-DAT) of the Centre for Research on the Epidemiology of Disasters (CRED) at the Catholic University of Louvain (Belgium). Disasters, as defined in EM-DAT, result from an unforeseen and often sudden event that causes damage, destruction and human suffering. Disasters refer to situations or events that overwhelm local response capacity and spur a national or international request for assistance.[49] The CRED notably distinguishes between disasters induced by biological, geophysical and climate-related causes, the latter being further sub-divided between hydrological and meteorological hazards.[50]
- The world's two largest reinsurance companies, MunichRe and SwissRe, release annual reports on worldwide disasters with estimates on life and asset losses. The data is obviously more accurate when it comes to insured losses—typically found in industrialized countries—than with regard to the uninsured losses that prevail in poorer countries.[51] Lloyd's of England, a long-time leader in insuring risks typically encountered in humanitarian crises, also provides information on disasters with a focus on the transport, shipping and insurance industry.[52]

Comparisons across datasets are problematic since there are differences in the definitions of disaster, the minimal thresholds for recording disaster events, data collection methodology and information sources.[53] Figure 8 tracks the evolution of the number of disasters from 1975 to 2011 according to EM-DAT, showing a steep increase until the turn of the millennium, followed by a downward trend in particular after 2005.[54]

Interpreting the data requires caution. The increase in the number of disasters does not only reflect a greater occurrence of such events, but also improved reporting practices over time: developing countries have established or strengthened their national disaster agencies tasked with monitoring and reporting disaster events. There has also been an increase in the recording of small disasters,[55] even if a substantial share of small and medium-sized disasters that hit the developing world are not recorded at the international level despite their cumulative costs being considerable.

With this note of caution in mind, Figure 8 shows a steep increase in the number of disasters during the last decades of the twentieth century.[56] The number of disasters triggered by natural hazards actually increased six-fold from the 1960s to the early 2000s. This has essentially been the result of a surge in hydro-meteorological events such as storms and floods that, in recent years, account for more than 90 per cent of disaster events.[57] Available evidence suggests that the number of such extreme events will increase as climate change intensifies. Besides, rapid urbanization results in greater risk exposure. The number of people exposed to cyclones and earthquakes in large cities may

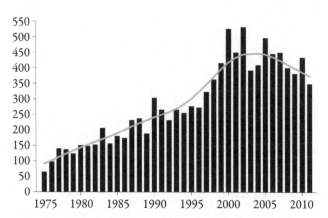

8. Number of natural disasters, 1975–2011

Source: EM-DAT: The OFDA/CRED International Disaster Database—www.emdat.be—Université Catholique de Louvain, Brussels—Belgium.

increase from 680 million people in 2000 to 1.5 billion in 2050, according to one forecast.[58]

Did the surge in disaster events in the 1990s result in increased need for assistance that would partly account for the rise in humanitarian funding over the same period? It seems unlikely. Figure 9 reveals that the surge in the number of disasters has not been met with a concurrent increase in the number of disaster-related deaths. Figure 9 considers the number of people killed, injured and made homeless. In order to detect trends, we smooth strong annual variations and show five-year moving averages. There is no clear trend outside the relatively large and sudden fluctuations related to the occurrence, location and scale of disasters from one year to another.

In contrast to the number of people affected, there is a clear upward trend in the reported economic losses from disasters. These losses include both the direct economic impact of disasters such as the destruction of infrastructure, housing and crops, and the indirect consequences such as losses in productivity, income and business opportunities.[59] The value of the lives lost is not included in economic losses (see chapter 4 for a discussion on the value of a statistical life, or VSL, in the case of war and terrorist attacks).

Figure 10 shows that a few disasters that hit Japan and the US drive the estimated costs of disasters up in certain years. Even if more than 30 per cent

9. Disaster-related deaths, injured and homeless, 1975–2013 (in thousands, 5-year moving averages)

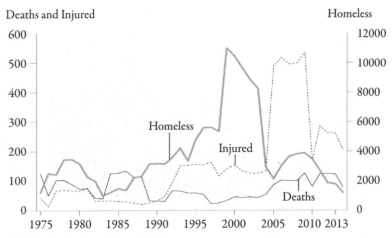

Source: The author, based on data from EM-DAT.

of the direct disaster losses in developing countries are not internationally recorded,[60] economic losses tend to be higher in rich countries. In relative terms, however, economic loss as a share of gross domestic product (GDP) tends to be higher in poorer countries. CRED experts have calculated that the total disaster-induced economic damages between 1961 and 2010 do not even amount to 0.5 per cent of GDP in high-income countries, while those damages reach an average of 3 per cent of GDP in low-income countries. The number of deaths and injured people tend to be much higher in poorer countries, with a mortality rate of 6.5 per 100,000 inhabitants in LICs between 1961 and 2010 compared to a negligible rate in high-income countries.[61]

The costliest disasters are not the deadliest. For example, the economic losses recorded for Hurricane Katrina (USA, 2005) are thirty-three times higher than those recorded for Cyclone Nargis (Myanmar, 2008), but the latter killed seventy-five times more people. In other words, there are huge differences in the ratio of casualties to economic losses. The number of casualties per billion US dollars of damages was ninety-four in the case of the Honshu or Tohoku Tsunami that hit Japan in 2011. This ratio was even lower when considering the Kobe earthquake of 1995 and Hurricane Katrina: thirty-six and thirteen deaths per billion US dollars of damages respectively. This compares—or rather stands in sharp contrast—with 26,816 casualties per billion US dollars in the case of

10. Estimated damage caused by natural disasters, 1970–2013 (US $ billion, current, with peaks explained mainly by one major disaster)

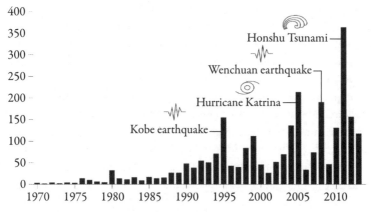

Source: EM-DAT: The OFDA/CRED International Database, Université Catholique de Louvain, Brussels, Belgium: www.emdat.be/

the Haiti earthquake of 2010 and 32,178 casualties per billion US dollars for Cyclone Nargis.[62] Investment in disaster prevention and preparedness is known to be highly cost-effective in reducing the harm inflicted by natural hazard but remains grossly under-funded (see Chapter 6).

It may be tempting to conclude this section on disaster by hailing the success of investments in ex-ante prevention and disaster preparedness, such as the building of cyclone shelters in Bangladesh. Indeed, the number of disaster victims has not increased in spite of the greater number of weather-related disasters. There is, however, insufficient evidence to provide a rigorous evaluation of the actual impact of specific measures in different environments.[63]

Suppliers and Contractors

There are various ways to categorize international humanitarian organizations, starting with traditional versus new actors. The traditional actors can be classified into four distinct groups: UN agencies[64] and other multilateral organizations, non-governmental organizations (NGOs)[65] including secular and faith-based organizations, the International Movement of the Red Cross and the Red Crescent,[66] and bilateral or governmental aid agencies. Some of them operate on a global scale while others have a more limited regional or national reach. Many of the new actors are not humanitarian actors strictly speaking, but intervene in the design and delivery of humanitarian aid: the military, private for-profit companies and contractors, regional organizations, diasporas, or virtual communities of volunteers who wish to actively support relief efforts. New actors include an increasing number of operational government agencies and humanitarian organizations in developing countries.[67]

Among humanitarian actors with a truly global reach, another distinction can be made between a few of them who deliver aid directly to the end beneficiaries in an independent manner and the majority that intervene at specific stages along complex supply chains that involve an expanding web of affiliates, contractors and sub-contractors. Humanitarian organizations have taken different make-or-buy decisions along a continuum between providing the goods and services directly to the ultimate beneficiary or outsourcing most of the operation to other organizations, often to private for-profit contractors when it comes to communications, transportation, construction, logistics and security services.[68]

This make-or-buy dilemma is well known in the business world in relation to transaction costs and the theory of the firm.[69] Many humanitarian organizations have embraced outsourcing and sub-contracting, moving away from the direct provision of humanitarian aid to focus more on coordination, fundraising and advocacy work while contracting out the effective implementation of the actual relief work to others. To the extent that brokers and intermediaries levy overhead costs and other margins that typically vary between 5 and 20 per cent, this can result in substantial gaps in value between the relatively generous initial donor funding and the resources that eventually reach the beneficiaries. Besides, outsourcing has serious implications in terms of governance, institutional strategy and accountability. In a study on aid governance, accountability and participatory approaches in the post-tsunami housing sector in Aceh, Indonesia, researchers conclude that 'the distance between the donors and beneficiaries caused by the wide-scale use of intermediate implementers, contractors, and sub-contractors undermined vertical accountability, upward to the donors and downwards to beneficiaries, with significant implications for the overall recovery efforts'.[70]

The donors' initial or first-level recipients of humanitarian funding comprise mainly traditional humanitarian organizations. Multilateral organizations represent the largest first-level recipient groups, receiving 58 per cent of international humanitarian aid funding between 2008 and 2012 (see Figure 11). The NGO sector comes second with 19 per cent, followed by the public sector or government agencies (11 per cent) and the International Red Cross and Red Crescent Movement (10 per cent).

11. First-level recipients of total humanitarian funding, 2008–2012

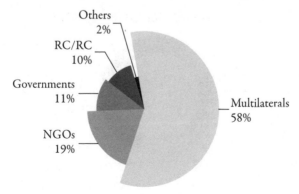

Source: Data from GHA (2014), p. 58.

The Labour Market

Even during episodes of economic crisis, the humanitarian labour market has continued to grow rapidly, reaching an estimated 274,238 workers in 2010. The average growth rate between 2007 and 2010 has been estimated at 5 per cent.[71] Over half of the labour force works in the NGO sector and nearly a third with the UN (see Figure 12).

The NGO galaxy is vibrant and diverse. In a report entitled 'The State of the Humanitarian System 2010', the authors reported 4,400 NGOs active in the humanitarian sector, 64 per cent of which are national NGOs and 18 percent of which are international NGOs (INGOs).[72] The sector is dominated by a handful of large INGOs. Five of them accounted for 38 per cent of total INGO humanitarian expenditures in 2009, MSF ranking first, followed by Catholic Relief Services (CRS), Oxfam International, the International Save the Children alliance, and World Vision International. The latter ranks first when including non-humanitarian expenditures such as development aid.[73] Promoting or following the drive towards greater globalization, many INGOs have established international networks, global alliances, federations or confederations involving both Northern and Southern national and local organizations, sometimes referred to as civil-society organizations (CSOs) or community-based organizations (CBOs).[74] An increasing number of Southern NGOs are themselves running operations abroad.[75]

The humanitarian labour market has long been highly segmented between expatriates ('expats') and national staff ('locals'). Expats typically get internationally competitive remuneration packages, while locals receive a much lower

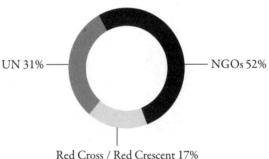

12. Breakdown of humanitarian personnel, 2010

UN 31% —— —— NGOs 52%

Red Cross / Red Crescent 17%

Source: Data from *The State of the Humanitarian Sector* (2010)

salary, deemed to be commensurate with local market conditions. Several arguments have been put forth to justify this dual salary system. First, they operate in different labour markets. Second, granting higher salaries to national staff would distort local labour markets and intensify the brain drain out of the domestic public and private sectors. The Inter-Agency Standing Committee (IASC) specifically recommends that humanitarian organizations refrain from offering exceptionally high wages in order to avoid weakening local institutions.[76]

On the other hand, lower salaries, more limited career opportunities and weaker job security can breed a sentiment of injustice and has been singled out as a stress factor that can lead to national staff demotivation and burnout.[77] This can create further tensions within relief organizations, especially as the overall level of education and expertise found on the domestic labour market has improved in middle-income countries and even in low-income countries.[78] There are regular accounts of national staff going on strike to push for higher wages. This was the case for example in 2006 when Ugandan medical staff working at a MSF therapeutic feeding centre demanded better wages. Their demand was turned down by the head of mission who wrote: 'I would wish that MSF is not seen as an employer but rather as a movement and a non-profit organization where we together as a team have a wish to assist others who are disadvantaged, living in distress, lacking a perspective.'[79] The head of mission subsequently fired the employees whose strike had put the lives of severely undernourished children in danger and who had further threatened other employees who wanted to work. For MSF, this revealed a lack of the commitment that is expected from people working for a humanitarian organization that thrives on volunteerism. The national employees who went on strike obviously saw things differently.

The growth of the humanitarian sector is met by increasing pressure from host states to tax humanitarian organizations (a trend also found among non-state armed groups as discussed in Chapter 3). The number of host countries that require expatriates to pay income tax is on the rise. Some organizations have no qualms about paying taxes that are meant to support national capacity building. Others seek tax exemption as a matter of principle, justified on the basis of the voluntary, not-for-profit nature of their work. Others still pursue tax optimization strategies akin to transnational corporations.[80] Emerging practice involves tax protection and tax equalization. Under the tax protection scheme, the employer continues to pay identical gross salaries to its employees and, in addition, pays the income tax directly to the host country.

In the tax equalization approach, the employer deducts a standardized estimated tax amount from the gross salary of all expatriate workers to pay the income taxes in host states where this is required. Submitting expatriates to income taxation like national staff can be seen as an equalizing factor, in particular when expatriates are not committed to paying income tax in their home countries.

As humanitarian organizations grow into large multinational organizations, they face issues that multinational corporations have long been dealing with: institutional decisions regarding internationalization, increased fiscal pressure leading to different options regarding tax optimization, strikes for improved wages, local content issues and rethinking labour force segmentation, make-or-buy decisions in the face of ever more complex supply chains, and so on. This can be seen as a symptom of the professionalization and success of the humanitarian sector, or of the disenchantment and bureaucratization of the sector.

Mandates, Principles, Competition: A Divided Aid Sector

In the 1990s, there was much talk of the humanitarian 'community', implying a shared identity and common interests between humanitarian actors, and even of the 'aid community', comprising the humanitarian and development aid sectors. Renewed polarization following the terrorist attacks of 11 September 2001 has shed stark light on the inherent tensions and contradictions within these sectors, further characterized by competition for funds and visibility. Even if many INGOs are driven by shared values, 'insecurity and competition, however, often pushes them to behave in rational and rent-seeking ways ... When placed in competitive, market-like settings, non-profit groups are likely to behave like their for-profit counterparts'.[81] A 2014 study on the impact of MSF's withdrawal from Somalia is telling in this regard. The medical organization had been operating in Somalia since the early 1990s, becoming one of the few major health care providers in the country. Because of deteriorating security conditions and a lack of effective support from community leaders, MSF decided to withdraw from Somalia altogether in August 2013. The study reveals that most of the other aid agencies did not seize the opportunity of MSF's withdrawal to collectively take stock of the deteriorating security conditions nor to influence Somali elders to take greater responsibility for the safety of aid workers in Somalia. Instead,

> There was just a 'pissing contest' (as one donor agency so eloquently put it) among agencies to see who was best suited to claim a share of MSF's spoils. The Emergency

Health Cluster meeting held on 26 August [2013] in Nairobi to discuss a take-over of MSF's facilities was attended by some 60 participants (a record!) and got straight down to the technical task of discussing which agencies were eligible.[82]

The variety of mandates, identities and histories of aid agencies results in a wide range of institutional positioning and operational modes.[83] Much depends on how strictly different organizations interpret and adhere to humanitarian principles. For example, many of the UN humanitarian agencies may wish to strictly abide by the principles of impartiality, neutrality and independence for operational purposes. Yet, they must deal with the fact that they are part of a larger political organization. The UN plays first fiddle in the peacebuilding, statebuilding and development agendas pushed forward in war-torn countries. Invariably, some warring parties do not perceive UN Security Council decisions nor missions established under Chapter VII of the UN Charter as neutral. Hence, it is difficult for UN humanitarian agencies to claim the same degree of neutrality and independence as strictly humanitarian NGOs. Indeed, the UN General Assembly (UNGA) Resolution of December 1991 on the Strengthening of the Coordination of Humanitarian Emergency Assistance states that 'Humanitarian assistance must be provided in accordance with the principles of humanity, neutrality and impartiality' (Art. 2): the principle of independence is not included in the Resolution, which is aimed at the UN humanitarian system.[84] Likewise, multi-mandated NGOs that pursue broader aims than saving lives and alleviating suffering, such as promoting peace, democracy and human rights, may not claim the same degree of neutrality.

In a schematic manner, Peter Walker and Daniel Maxwell distinguished between four humanitarian tribes.[85] Principle-centred or Dunantist organizations, named after the founding father of the Red Cross, Henry Dunant, claim to be strictly impartial, neutral and independent (e.g. MSF, ICRC, Pharmaciens sans frontières). The pragmatists or Wilsonians, named after the promoter of the League of Nations, US President Woodrow Wilson, receive a substantial funding share from their home governments and tend to act in line with their home countries' foreign policy objectives (e.g. CARE). Solidarist organizations do not only pursue humanitarian objectives: their action can be partisan depending on their agenda, which may include social justice, women's empowerment, environmental sustainability, democracy and so forth (e.g. Oxfam).[86] The fourth category consists of faith-based organizations (e.g. World Vision, Islamic Relief). A humanitarian agency can move from one to another category over time, and depending on the context, or can simultaneously run a solidarist advocacy branch and a Dunantist operational one. Dunantists typically tend to refuse protection from armed escorts, even at the cost of losing access to people in distress. Gaining access thanks to armed escort in the short-term could compromise the perception of independence and neutrality in the eyes of warring parties, which could cause a backlash at a later stage. By way of contrast, other agencies have actively sought out the protection and logistical support of international military coalitions or peacekeeping forces without relinquishing their claim to impartiality and neutrality.

Faith

The issue of faith-based organizations—the fourth category of relief organizations listed above—relates to a much broader debate on religion and humanitarianism. Disasters have long been perceived as acts of God(s). In major religious traditions, God's wrath found expression in war and catastrophes. Today, in many parts of the world, victims still attempt to make sense of the ensuing desolation by conceiving of disasters as implicating divine forces.[87] All major religions are interested in ways to 'avert misfortune, overcome crises, and provide salvation.'[88] Religious rituals often play a major role in post-crisis healing processes. Conversely, modern humanitarianism is rooted in the evangelical revival that considerably influenced the emergence of a culture of compassion in Europe over two centuries ago. But it is also rooted in the philosophy of the Enlightenment, which went beyond charity and advanced human dignity and rights, reason and secularism. In *Empire of Humanity*, Michael Barnett underscores the progressive dissociation of humanitarianism from its Christian origins during the twentieth century.[89]

All humanitarian actors may arguably be seen as driven by spiritual ideals that push them to continuously strive for elusive global standards in spite of repeated setbacks.[90] Yet, the humanitarian sector widely regards secular humanitarianism as the norm and faith-based organizations as special cases. The Code of Conduct for the International Red Cross and Red Crescent Movement and NGOs in Disaster Relief, adopted at the end of 1994, explicitly states that 'aid will not be used to further a particular political or religious standpoint.'[91]

Conflict can occur between secular and religious actors who compete over the legitimacy and authority associated with the generous delivery of relief. Besides, some religious actors reject modern humanitarianism based on the perception that it is a threatening vector of secularization and desacralization. The search for truth and meaning—for instance with regard to disasters—comes to rely on scientific investigation instead of religious beliefs, myths and magic. This goes hand-in-hand with political modernization that implies a transfer of power from religious to secular state institutions and the emergence of a rational legal order under the authority of non-religious social institutions. As Max Weber claimed, the rationalization process associated with the Western development or modernization model leads to the 'disenchantment of the world'.[92]

But those who have predicted the death of religion have been proved dramatically wrong. Despite the rapid spread of the modernization or 'development' project in Asia, Latin America and Africa, major religions prove resilient. Globalization is expanding in parallel with religious revivals rather than the death of religion.[93] In his book *Humanitarian Reason*, Didier Fassin adds that Western humanitarianism is not only infused with a legacy from the Christian missionary venture but the humanitarian imperative to succour the suffering and save the lives of fellow humans, even if they are distant strangers, is also premised on Christian moral values. The advent of humanitarian reason brings this religious heritage firmly into the heart of today's liberal democratic order. Fassin sees this as the ultimate victory of religion, which does not lie 'in the renewal of religious expression throughout the world, but in its lasting presence at the heart of our democratic secular values.'[94]

Concluding Remarks

This chapter is premised on a paradox: over the past two decades the supply of humanitarian aid (in the form of funding, workers and aid supplies) has rapidly increased, but there is no evidence that this surge was caused by a parallel surge in actual needs. The number of armed conflicts dropped after the Cold War and, despite a rising occurrence of disasters over the past twenty-five years, the total number of affected people has fluctuated without any clear upward trend. Even if the number and intensity of situations of armed violence that do not qualify as armed conflict have increased in several regions, such situations have not attracted much humanitarian aid. That said, the recent increase in the number of refugees and IDPs worldwide partly accounts for humanitarian market growth since 2012.

Ultimately, the humanitarian market boom of the 1990s and 2000s reflects the more prominent role of humanitarianism in global governance, next to a post-Cold War rise in peacekeeping operations. Humanitarian responses gained prominence as a foreign policy instrument, often used by default to compensate for the lack of political resolve and capacity to put an end to war crimes and crimes against humanity[95] in the face of domestic pressure to aid distant strangers whose suffering is brought home by instant media coverage. Such instant war and disaster coverage contributes not only to enhanced political pressure on donor states to respond to humanitarian crises, but also to a surge in private funding. In addition, emerging economies and other middle-income countries are displaying greater ability and willingness to deal with humanitarian crises at home and abroad.

Together with the expansion of the ideology of humanitarianism and the spreading of non-kin altruism beyond national boundaries, an issue that warrants further research is to what extent has the humanitarian market boom been supply driven? What has been the impact of the natural tendency of organizations to grow and expand into new areas (mission creep)? What has been the influence of more aggressive fundraising techniques in a competitive market? Humanitarian actors today provide a greater diversity of services directed at a broader range of target groups, whose plight was either neglected or simply ignored in the past. In 1990, there were hardly any aid programmes specifically targeted at the victims of sexual violence, nor at child soldiers and unaccompanied children, nor at the families of the missing. The range and quality of services has expanded, with expertise and activities in areas such as mental health, maternal care, HIV/AIDS, non-communicable disease, and water and sanitation in large urban centres.

Yet, more funding does not necessarily entail that better assistance and protection are provided to the vulnerable in difficult environments where it is most needed. Competitive bidding does not always minimize waste, especially when it is associated with longer supply chains and higher transaction costs. As aid programmes become more sophisticated, in particular in middle-income countries, they also become more costly. In this chapter's epigraph Nelson Mandela reminds us of a simple fact: those targeted by humanitarian action are best placed to judge its effectiveness. For the South African leader, the bad the ICRC prevented by visiting him in prison had been more important than the good it brought. Money and material resources are definitely not all that matter in the humanitarian marketplace.

3

WAR ECONOMICS

War in the preindustrial world was and still is more like a contest among crime families over who gets to control the rackets than a fight over principles.

If you're a modern, wealthy nation, however, war—even easy, victorious war—doesn't pay.

Paul Krugman, 2014[1]

During the Dot-Com or Internet Bubble of 1997–2000 investors poured billions of dollars into the information and communications technology (ICT) sector. New York's high-tech stock market peaked at a record high: the NASDAQ Composite index surged from below 2,000 points in 1998 to 5,000 points on 10 March 2000. As is often the case, the bubble's bursting was more spectacular than the boom: in just a year, the NASDAQ Composite was back below 2,000. The shockwave was neither limited to the US nor to capital markets. For instance, when connecting the dots, it appears that the investor frenzy and ensuing panic also had dire humanitarian repercussions in the Democratic Republic of the Congo (DRC).

War economy analysis helps to uncover how the ripple or 'butterfly' effects of an investment bubble in New York City can lead to a cholera outbreak in Kisangani. In this chapter, I first introduce the concept of war economy. I discuss war costs before turning to conflict finance and war profiteers. I examine in particular the role of aid and the variables that influence the capacity of humanitarian actors to conclude successful negotiations with armed groups. Humanitarian action may be provided in a neutral manner, but its distributional impact is not neutral. Like it or not, relief agencies are part of the political economy of war. Political economy analysis offers an avenue for humanitarians to address how their activities interact with war economies.

War Economy

In common parlance, the notion of a war economy often equates with Keynes' central topic in *How to Pay for the War*, which he published at the beginning of World War II.[2] Indeed, 'war economy' often refers to the generation, mobilization and allocation of resources to sustain a war effort.[3] This is somewhat artificially dissociated from economic activities undertaken by civilians who attempt to survive in the midst of wars and by relief agencies striving to assist them. This is why I adopt a broader definition of war economy, which includes a category of prime interest to humanitarian agencies: survival activities undertaken by people seeking to preserve their livelihoods. Examples of this include the case of tens of thousands of informal miners digging for gold and coltan in eastern DRC, and that of farmers growing poppies in Afghanistan where the opium economy generates not only huge profits, but also employment and income for tens of thousands of Afghans.

The contribution of Congolese miners or Afghan farmers to the war economy may be voluntary or coerced. In return, they usually benefit from an income and some degree of protection granted by those who thrive on their work. Virtually all profits accrue to armed groups, transnational criminal organizations, government officials and others who have a vested interest in the perpetuation of wars that instil a climate of impunity propitious to illegal activities. But the workers also face a greater risk of attack by opponents who wish to curtail the funding sources of the enemy or win an elusive war on drugs. Humanitarian action is part and parcel of contemporary war economies. It is of course primarily geared towards supporting coping mechanisms and survival strategies, or substituting for them when they fail. Yet, part of the resources brought to the field may end up benefiting warring parties, including human resources, as the kidnap-and-ransom industry tragically illustrates.

I posit that war economy comprises four categories that overlap and interact with each other: (i) conflict finance, or activities to fund and sustain the war effort; (ii) survival activities associated with coping mechanisms and strategies to avoid destitution; (iii) criminal and informal activities that flourish under a general climate of impunity generated by the war; and (iv) international trade and financial relations connecting the above three categories to the global marketplace. The latter obviously refers to trade in arms, ammunitions and security services, but also resource flows such as remittances sent back home by refugees or migrants working abroad.

Within this context, abrupt commodity price shocks on world markets can have a dire impact on armed conflicts and associated humanitarian situations, as illustrated by the Dot-Com Bubble's links with the boom and bust of coltan prices, and the attendant risk of a cholera outbreak in Kisangani. Since the mid-1990s, the DRC has been a significant producer of columbo-tantalite, a metallic ore known as coltan. When refined, coltan turns into tantalum that has many properties in its metallic form. It is heat resistant and can hold a large electric charge. It is used in the production of tantalum capacitors for electronic circuits in the production of many consumer electronics where size and weight matter, such as cell phones and laptops. Coltan is also used in the production of satellites, ballistic missiles and many other high-tech devices. The price of coltan mined in the eastern DRC followed a trajectory similar to that of the NASDAQ Composite index with a few months delay.[4] Coltan prices multiplied tenfold, from some $30 per pound in 1999 to $300 per pound by the end of 2000. A swift tenfold coltan price crash in 2001 followed as the bubble burst.

The coltan fever took place in the midst of the Second Congo War (1998–2003). The conflict—also referred to as Africa's World War or the Great African War—saw nine African countries sending troops to the DRC or supporting different Congolese armed factions.[5] Many of them fiercely competed to get a share of the country's extraordinary mineral wealth, including coltan, just one among many valuable extractive resources found in the country. The Dot-Com Bubble had dire repercussion in eastern DRC through different channels:

- As coltan prices skyrocketed, many workers moved into mining, including farmers from some of the most productive areas in the region (e.g. Masisi and Kalehe in North Kivu). As demand from mining areas increased while agricultural production declined, food prices reached new heights and food security deteriorated in the region.[6]
- Without any previous mining experience and no safety procedures in place, thousands of miners suffered accidents, including many children, while many more lost time and money in the pursuit of elusive quick gains.
- The commercialization of coltan became a highly lucrative venture for armed groups who fought over the control of mining sites and trading routes. These included militias backed by neighbouring Rwanda and Uganda, such as Bemba's Mouvement pour la Liberation du Congo (MLC) and the

Rassemblement Congolais pour la Démocratie (RCD) and its successive splinters: Wamba's RCD-Kisangani (RCD-K) and Ilunga's RCD-Goma (RCD-G). The RCD attempted to concentrate all coltan purchases under the Société Minière des Grands Lacs (SOMIGL) while processing and commercialization was allegedly in Rwandan hands. The 2001 coltan price drop put stress on RCD's finances. The armed groups turned to alternative funding sources with hardly any concern for the humanitarian consequences.

At the same time, the international community started to look more seriously into the murky business of conflict finance. The UN Security Council mandated a group named 'Panel of Experts on the Illegal Exploitation of Natural Resources and Other Forms of Wealth of the Democratic Republic of the Congo' to examine how mining in particular contributed to funding the various armed groups that committed war crimes and human rights abuses in the region. In its final report to the UN Security Council of October 2002, the Panel of Experts noted:

> Another strategy for raising revenue is to use RCD-Goma's public sector façade to requisition funds from public enterprises. On 21 November 2001 [just when coltan prices crashed], the Secretary General of RCD-Goma requisitioned by decree all revenues generated by public utilities and parastatals. On the following day the Secretary General annulled all existing collective agreements for workers in those enterprises. The decrees were applicable to all public enterprises, including the water utility, the airport authorities, the electricity utility ... Within a month, the water utility lacked sufficient funds to purchase water purification chemicals in Kisangani and Bukavu and power stations stopped functioning for lack of necessary repairs. The International Committee of the Red Cross has stepped in to provide 60 tons of chemicals for water purification and has financed costly repairs at Tshopo power station to avert a discontinuation of water supply in Kisangani and avert a cholera outbreak.[7]

Militias preyed on public utilities to make up for the losses ensuing from the collapse of global coltan prices. The International Committee of the Red Cross (ICRC) managed to keep Kisangani's water treatment plant operational. If the ICRC had not stepped in, much of the city's 600,000 inhabitants would likely have lost access to safe drinking water, increasing the risk of renewed cholera outbreaks.

When it released its first report on 12 April 2001, the UN Panel of Experts took the bold step of naming and shaming top political figures and multinational companies allegedly involved in the illegal exploitation of DRC's natural wealth, including Ugandan and Rwandan high-ranking officials and firms headquartered in Belgium and other Western countries.[8] The report spurred strong reactions in the Great Lakes region and beyond, reflecting how politically sensitive the issue of conflict finance is.

War's Costs and Losers

Over the past fifteen years, there has been a renewed interest in estimating the direct and indirect costs of armed conflict. Costing techniques involve a variety of approaches, from general equilibrium models to basic accounting methods. The estimation of total war costs often implies counterfactuals: researchers compare the actual post-war economic situation with how the situation would have evolved in a no-war scenario.[9]

The war cost literature generally looks at the consequences of armed conflict at a macro level, which is of little direct use to humanitarian practitioners. For example, various empirical studies find that civil wars tend to reduce the GDP growth of an average developing country by some 2 to 3 per cent a year, noting that the negative consequences can persist for years once the hostilities have ended. This is in part due to the legacy of civil war on social capital, trust and institutions, but also on the risk of renewed hostilities that tends to discourage investment.[10] A recent case study finds the costs of the Darfur conflict in Sudan reached, at a conservative estimate, $30bn between 2003–09. This amounts to 171 per cent of Sudan's 2003 GDP, which highlights a shameful fact: war costs amounted to some 13 per cent of GDP annually in a country that, over the past two or three decades, has barely invested 1.3 per cent of its budget on public health and even less on education.[11] While this provides an interesting insight into the contexts in which humanitarians operate, there is a macro-micro disconnect between the interests of economists and those of humanitarians in assessing the consequences of armed conflicts, save perhaps for a relatively recent wave of micro-level studies focusing on the livelihoods of affected individuals, households and communities.[12]

Since World War II came after a prolonged depression and was followed by three decades of unprecedented growth, at least in the industrialized world, many people tend to believe that war can boost the economy. It is true that armed conflict can stimulate economic activity in some sectors, and that fighting a war abroad without incurring destruction at home can benefit large segments of the economy. But what tends to be neglected is what would happen if the same resources mobilized for war were allocated to peaceful productive purposes while avoiding the destruction and pain (see the 'broken-window fallacy' argument in Chapter 5).[13] Economists resort to a combination of estimation techniques to calculate the costs of war:[14]

- *Accounting approaches* consist in identifying and adding up each individual direct and indirect cost of war. Direct costs typically include mobilization costs, expenditures required to equip and transport troops to the battle-field, to pay for arms and ammunition and to contract private military and security services. Direct costs also include any destruction of physical and human capital directly caused by armed violence. Indirect costs include the subsequent losses in industrial and agricultural productivity, and the costs associated with the breakdown of public institutions and services, including education, health services and the provision of safe drinking water. The costs accruing from the ensuing disease burden, disability and death are then added up. Indirect costs tend to be much larger than direct ones in contemporary civil wars. There are many methodological issues involved in such calculations, including the risk of recording the same cost twice (double counting) or of considering a range of expenditures as war costs that would be required under peaceful conditions anyway, such as national army and weaponry maintenance costs.

- *Economic modelling* involves diverse simulation techniques and counter-factual scenarios: war costs are typically calculated as the gap between the actual post-war situation and the situation that would prevail in a no-war scenario. War does not easily lend itself to lab experiments and getting ap-propriate counterfactuals is challenging. One method is to compare eco-nomic outcomes in different locations within the same country from the pre-conflict to the post-war periods, looking both at stocks and flows;[15] another is to compare economic performances in different locations that experienced different levels and types of violence. The latter was done in a study on the impact of the Rwandan Civil War of the early 1990s and on the 1994 genocide. Six years after the genocide, household consumption was generally substantially lower in zones that had been more severely hit by the civil war, hinting at a long-term negative impact of the armed conflict at the local level.[16] Other research strands focus on how armed violence influ-ences household-level activity choices including the adoption of different crop mixes,[17] or on how individual exposure to violence affects individual discount rates and risk-taking behaviour.[18]

- *Contingent valuation methods* serve to evaluate the costs of war in the ab-sence of market signals required to give a monetary value to the losses. They seek to identify how much people would be willing to pay for a lower risk of being affected by an armed conflict, or how much consumption they would forego in order to enjoy more peaceful and secure living conditions.

- *Event studies* examine, for example, the impact of war news on commodity prices and stock markets, such as the impact of the Iraq War on oil and stock prices,[19] or the effect of the civil war in the Ivory Coast on the cocoa market. A panel data study looked at the impact of the onset of armed conflict on market prices. Considering 101 intrastate and interstate conflicts between 1974 and 2004, the study found that in many instances war-related news has a significant impact on stock market indices, exchange rates, oil and other commodity prices. The study suggests that investors could exploit conflict information for lucrative investment strategies.[20] One of the main challenges associated with event data studies is to determine how much (and when) conflict news may have actually been anticipated by investors and speculators.

War costs appear to be generally more severe in cases of geographically pervasive conflicts where the state has lost its capacity to collect taxes and provide basic services. Where 'quasi-government structures' are able to maintain core functions, costs can be limited to a certain extent. Notwithstanding an expanding number of datasets related to war economies, data availability and reliability remain major constraints. Somalia is a case in point, with scant macroeconomic statistics over the past two decades. Researchers recently estimated the economic impact of the civil war in Somalia by looking at nighttime light emissions recorded by satellite images, taking electricity consumption as a proxy for disposable income in Somalia's cities. Interestingly, the armed conflict seems to particularly affect poorer households living in suburban areas when compared to their peers in more stable areas of Somalia, while more central 'business' districts fare better in spite of the war.[21] This suggests that the peace dividend would benefit the (suburban) poor in particular.

Despite the surge of 'big data' combined with the latest information technologies, accurately estimating the number of direct and indirect deaths and disabilities remains a challenge. The DRC controversy highlights this difficulty. Estimates by the International Rescue Committee (IRC) of 3.9 million excess deaths (that is, those deaths that would have been avoided in the absence of war) between 1998 and 2004[22] were later called into question by other studies.[23] Today, estimates range from half a million to more than five million Congolese dead because of the civil war, a tenfold gap depending on the source and methodology. Some researchers focus on estimates of numbers of violent deaths to ascertain the number of casualties directly attributable to conflict-related armed violence. Others seek to estimate excess mortality or excess deaths by comparing the actual mortality rate with what would have occurred in the absence of war. In the case of the DRC, whatever the exact number of deaths attributable to armed conflict, the dramatic human toll results mainly from the indirect effects of war: excess mortality from malnutrition and preventable diseases associated with large population displacement and the collapse of essential public services.[24]

In addition, macroeconomic data is not very reliable in low-income countries with weak statistical offices.[25] This applies in particular to fragile and conflict-ridden states where relevant data is simply missing or biased for political reasons. To compound the problem, the gross domestic product (GDP) benchmark is a flow indicator, which does not register changes in stock levels. In the short run, the massive destruction of physical, human and natural capital does not lower GDP, while a boom in military expenditures contributes to economic growth, making war a seemingly profitable enterprise.[26] Repairing destroyed infrastructure also increases GDP, pointing again to the broken-window fallacy argument.

Because of data availability and reliability, it is easier and safer to focus on industrialized nations waging distant wars. Indeed, there is a bias towards estimating the costs of war accruing to rich nations sending troops abroad rather than for war-torn countries in the developing world themselves. Plus, empirical studies often aim to inform and influence political debate in the North. One of the most notorious examples of war costing is Stiglitz and Bilmes' *Three Trillion Dollar War*. Their book, released in 2008, questions the Bush administration's misleading cost prediction of $50–60bn to overthrow Saddam Hussein and install a new Iraqi government. The authors estimate the eventual costs of the US military venture in Iraq to be in the thousands of billions of dollars when considering hidden and future costs,[27] ranging from $2.7 trillion in budgetary costs to $5 trillion in total economic costs. This goes beyond the direct costs reflected in US budgetary appropriations and those associated with American war casualties and disabled veterans' care. Estimating the indirect costs of the Iraq War rests on a number of assumptions, for instance: ascertaining the consequences of higher oil prices that can be attributed to the war,[28] or of productive labour losses, or the opportunity costs related to resources diverted to sustain the war.

Many consequences of civil war are intangible. To ascertain the overall costs of war, economists rely on specific concepts that serve to evaluate the monetary costs associated with battle-related deaths and injuries. They go well beyond estimating foregone earnings and productivity losses associated with population displacement, or evaluating the impact of infrastructure destruction and defence spending on capital formation.

Putting a Value on (the Quality of) Human Life

Putting a value on a lost life or the quality of life following an injury or traumatic war experience raises a number of theoretical, methodological and ethical issues. Calculating the so-called value of a statistical life is a standard economic approach for approximating the cost of war and terrorism fatalities (see Chapter 4, on terrorism economics). There is also much debate about estimating injury costs, which might involve calculating the present value of future treatment costs. Based on the notion of health-adjusted life years, the World Health Organization (WHO) has advanced the notion of disability-adjusted life years (DALYs) that captures the number of years of productive life lost due to disability and the number of potential lives lost due to premature mortality.[29] While there has been a serious attempt at costing death, injury and ensuing disability in the case of Western soldiers on 'stabilization missions' in the global South, the issues involved in war costing related to civilian war victims in so-called 'fragile states' largely remain unaddressed.

Information collected from subjective, self-reported life-satisfaction and happiness surveys has been used to evaluate the social cost of conflict.[30] But putting a monetary value on fear and psychological suffering, on the pain of mourning, or on witnessing the suffering of close relatives and friends can seem far-fetched, not least because traditional approaches relate to solvent demand that can be nil for war victims who have lost their savings and productive assets. To what extent does it offer a relevant approach for estimating the costs associated with post-traumatic stress disorder, prolonged fear from renewed attack, or sexual abuse against men, women and children? In eastern DRC, for example, families and communities often reject rape victims. In some cases, a raped woman may give birth to a child whose biological father is one of the rapists. If they are lucky, the mother and the child may find refuge in one of the hosting centres for victims of sexual abuse, as I have witnessed for instance in Bukavu, the capital of South Kivu. We may add the direct cost of hosting the victim and her new child in such a refuge. If we are interested in calculating long-term impacts, we may also add that the family that rejected a raped daughter lost a member who was involved in both agricultural and domestic activities. The cost may be estimated based on the average productivity of such activities in the region. But we have to make additional assumptions regarding the net present value of future costs and benefits associated with the child's education and the productivity of the mother and her grown-up child in Bukavu's evolving urban context.

Empirical studies generally assume that income increases wellbeing while violence and lost revenue reduce it. We must take a deeper look at such standard assumptions when considering the readiness of many to die for freedom, for the independence and glory of the homeland, or for religious and political ideals. As we shall see in the next chapter, suicide terrorism challenges such hypotheses.

In sum, the costing of armed conflict supports Paul Krugman's argument (in this chapter's epigraph): war doesn't pay in the case of a modern, wealthy nation. There is also mounting evidence that higher levels of lethal violence are associated with lower human development indices (HDI) and weaker development outcomes in poorer countries. If war is so costly in high and in lower-income countries, why does it remain the preferred option in so many instances? In a rational choice framework, the benefits must outweigh the costs, at least for those who favour going to war. As discussed in Chapter 1, rebels may seek to serve their own narrow interests or to spur progressive change in unequal societies that may end up benefiting the poor and marginalized. The government may seek to take advantage of a 'rally-around-the-flag' effect whereby large swathes of people rally around their leaders against a 'useful enemy'. This distracts the electorate from other ills such as a failing economy or rising inequality, at least in the short-to-medium term. President George W. Bush was, after all, re-elected for a second term after launching a costly venture into Iraq on dubious grounds. The economic interests and political support of the oil industry together with that of the military-industrial complex also weighed in the balance, reminding us of the speech that President Dwight D. Eisenhower delivered forty-four years earlier, just three days before stepping down in 1961: 'Only an alert and knowledgeable citizenry can compel the proper meshing of the huge industrial and military machinery of defense with our peaceful methods and goals, so that security and liberty may prosper together.'[31] Today, one must add to the equation the surge in private military and security companies whose business thrives in conflicts.

More broadly, it is essential to analyze conflict finance, war profiteers and peace spoilers in order to grasp how war economies evolve and interact with humanitarian action.

Conflict Finance and War Profiteers

In particular circumstances, the direct and indirect benefits of war may be both substantial and widespread. This was the case for Australia during World

War II. While the country did not suffer much destruction—save for a hundred air raids on Darwin and other northern towns and airfields—it benefited from strong foreign demand that gave a boost to its agricultural, mining and industrial sectors, so that it enjoyed near full employment. In contemporary civil wars, however, the majority suffer losses while profits accrue in particular to those involved in protection rackets, looting and illegal activities that flourish under conditions of impunity. At the global level, war means business for arms and ammunition manufacturers and dealers, private security and military service providers, transnational criminal organizations (TCOs) and—obviously involving different motives and at a lower magnitude—for the humanitarian, peace-building and reconstruction sectors.

The nature of the hostilities and the types of armed groups involved matter for humanitarian action. For aid practitioners, it is generally easier to deal with highly structured organizations involved in conventional warfare than with loose networks of fragmented groups involved in hit-and-run and criminal operations. In this context, conflict finance requires attention: the way armed groups finance themselves or seek to extract profits from war has a bearing not only on how the conflict evolves, but also on how warring parties behave vis-à-vis local communities and relief organizations. As suggested in Chapter 1, an armed group's inclination to grant access to humanitarian organizations or to respect international humanitarian law (IHL) often depends on a cost-benefit calculus involving military, economic and political considerations. The question is: why would a warring party change its behaviour or grant unimpeded access in response to humanitarian organizations' requests? Why, for instance, do some non-state armed groups commit to avoiding the use of anti-personnel mines, sexual violence or violence against children by signing the Deeds of Commitment of the non-profit organization Geneva Call?[32]

There are many variables beyond economic ones that explain the behaviour of an armed group, such as the group's identity, ideology, political agenda, positioning and communication. Economic agendas nonetheless shape the cost-benefit calculi of each warring party seeking at least to generate enough resources to cover the costs of mobilizing and maintaining its fighting capacity. This, in turn, requires considering the relative strength of the enemy and the extent of territorial control of the armed group. Let us take a closer look at these variables.

1. *Costs of mobilizing and maintaining fighting capability*

Mobilization and maintenance costs tend to be underestimated. At the end of the 1990s, the former DRC President, Laurent Désiré Kabila, boasted that it does not take much to run a rebellion: 'That's easy, ten thousand dollars and a satellite phone. The cash will buy you a small army. You use the phone to promote yourself to the world.'[33] Estimating the cost of putting together and maintaining an army of 1,000 combatants, Achim Wennmann found that, while the start-up costs can be as low as $65,000, maintenance costs oscillated between $2m and $35m per annum by the mid-2000s. This includes the costs of small arms and ammunition, logistics and the remuneration of combatants. The wide margin between $2m and $35m reflects the fact that maintenance costs increase significantly as an armed group moves up the ladder from relatively cheap hit-and-run operations to more expensive conventional armed confrontation. The cost further fluctuates with conflict intensity and the volatility of local prices for small arms and ammunitions.[34] In the absence of savings, an armed group must be able to generate regular revenues to pay for maintenance costs.

2. *Territorial control and the resources that a warring party is able to command*

Non-state armed groups typically receive funding from voluntary or coerced contributions from diasporas and domestic constituents, and from foreign allies.[35] An armed group will adapt its behaviour depending on how it feels with regard to its current financial situation and future funding prospects. To the extent that external funding is sufficient, the armed group does not need to extract more resources locally. Some scholars find that armed groups that do not depend on the backing of the local population tend to become indiscriminately violent more easily.[36] Humanitarian negotiators may have little leverage on an armed group that is financially self-sufficient, unless a powerful external sponsor agrees to push for behavioural change, for example by threatening to cut down its support in the case of renewed mass atrocities. When an armed group gets poorer or fears for its future financial viability, it may be more prone to engage humanitarian organizations in order to gain broader support and legitimacy. Conversely, however, as it becomes cash strapped an armed group may turn against civilians and relief organizations to extract resources required for its military and political survival.

As an armed group gains effective control over a territory and its population, it may shift from ad hoc predatory attacks involving looting and kidnapping to more permanent methods of extraction combined with a greater role in the local economy and stronger trade and financial relations. Full territorial control often leads to an armed group exercising de facto governmental functions, which include permanent taxation and the provision of security and quasi-public services.[37] When the rebels themselves originate from this very territory, they may display a greater interest in basic service delivery to the communities with whom they are closely related, and may also thereby muster political support from the host population. Strangers may have more incentives to exert violence as a way to spread fear among the population while striking selective deals with local criminal groups and political leaders. The examples below illustrate how territorial control and command over certain types and amounts of resources play out in humanitarian crises.

In Afghanistan, warring parties thrive notably on the drugs business as well as on the foreign aid enterprise. For example, the Taliban have been known to levy a 10 per cent tax on poppy production, as well as taxes on drug traffickers and protection rackets or 'protection services' more or less forcibly sold to international organizations and their Afghan partners.[38] How do protection rackets and extortion affect civilian welfare? A recent study on the effects of rebel taxation in Burundi first shows that extortion was widespread, with 30 per cent of the individuals in the sample having made at least one payment over the twelve years of civil war. Second, ad hoc extraction—for instance in the form of forced labour—had no beneficial impact on households, unlike more regular and institutionalized extraction, which significantly improved the welfare of 'tax payers'.[39] Another study, this time on Somalia, has a different conclusion: the multiple forms of taxation imposed by Al-Shabaab on the local population ended up weakening traditional redistribution processes and solidarity networks.[40]

The Fuerzas Armadas Revolucionarias de Colombia (FARC) developed ties with coca producers in the areas under their control as early as the 1980s but did not take an active role in the narcotics business (beyond taxing it) until the 1990s, when some elements of the armed group engaged in production and trade. Together with kidnap-and-ransom activities developed at a quasi-industrial scale, it managed to secure an annual income estimated at approximately $700m in the 2000s.[41] The FARC has been considered to be largely self-sufficient financially, which means humanitarian organizations have less leverage through third parties, but also means that the group may have an interest in mustering some support from host communities through a combination of welfare provision and restraint in the exercise of violence.

Once Indian support waned after the 1991 assassination of Rajiv Ghandi by a Tamil suicide bomber, the Liberation Tigers of Tamil Eelam (LTTE) relied increasingly on taxes levied among diaspora communities and in LTTE-controlled territory. The highest estimates put LTTE annual income at approximately $385m in the 2000s, a majority of which was generated through the Tamil diaspora.[42] Diaspora networks are usually too dispersed, divided and weak to be mobilized by humanitarian organizations hoping to wield influence on rebels. Following the December 2004 Indian Ocean Tsunami, there was a surge of humanitarian aid to Sri Lanka. This resulted in the LTTE strengthening its financial position by exerting some control over reconstruction funds in the areas under its command. This fact was arguably a major contributor in renewed hostilities, which led to all-out war and the eventual fall of the LTTE, with dramatic humanitarian consequences in northern Sri Lanka.

In the case of the Angolan Civil War, the Uniao Nacional para a Independência Total de Angola (UNITA) lost most of its foreign financial support in the 1990s. This resulted from a combination of the end of the Cold War, the demise of the Apartheid regime in South Africa, and the fall of the Mobutu regime in neighbouring Zaire. UNITA leader Jonas Savimba, who had maintained a dense network of backers and representatives with bank accounts in a dozen European countries and offshore centres, had to rely on diamond reserves to pay for weapons, logistics and patronage politics.[43] The rebels further suffered territorial losses in diamond-rich areas. As a result, UNITA's revenue may have fallen more than fivefold between 1997 and 2000, from $500m to 80m,[44] forcing the rebel group back into guerrilla warfare. The government seized the opportunity to intensify military offensives in 2000. People fled towards government-held enclaves while humanitarian agencies could not meaningfully operate in areas under UNITA's control. In parallel, the Angolan government received additional resources with the intensification of offshore oil production and upward oil prices as of 2000. This led to the eventual demise of the rebel group, which was unable to pay for the mounting mobilization costs required to withstand increasing pressure from the Angolan government forces.

3. *Economic agendas in war*

Whether economic activity is a means to support an armed struggle or is an end in itself can make a big difference in the conduct of hostilities, even if the boundary between these two scenarios is often blurred. When war spoils become the aim and violence is perpetuated to sustain profit rather than to challenge the political status quo, a non-state armed group may have less interest in adapting its behaviour to the laws of war, especially if the prime objective of violence is to maintain a climate of impunity for criminal activities to flourish. Calling on strictly profit-driven armed groups to respect human rights and IHL seems a priori hopeless, although there is hardly any evidence to sustain this assumption. In turn, designating and labelling an armed group as 'criminal' or 'terrorist' may further erode any concern it has with regard to its reputation and international legitimacy. In fact, stigmatization and international blacklisting reduces the opportunity cost of radicalization, and a stigmatized armed group may therefore feel that it has more to lose than to gain by engaging humanitarian organizations or more to gain than to lose by rejecting or grossly exploiting them.

To sum up, the costs of mobilizing and maintaining fighting capacity determine the amount of resources that an armed group must be able to generate to pay for the war. On that basis, three key variables related to conflict finance appear to exert a significant influence on the behaviour of armed groups with regard to humanitarian concerns and actors:

1. The economic agendas of armed groups over and above the sole objective to pay for the war, and the extent to which armed violence serves the purpose of maintaining a climate of impunity propitious to illegal activities.
2. The extent of an armed group's territorial control over people and resources, and in particular over natural resources that it can extract, trade and/or tax.
3. The type and amount of external resources that a warring party is able to command through foreign aid, third-party state support, diaspora networks and the like.

Following this logic, let us first explore the issue of illegal economic activities and organized crime before turning to natural resources and foreign aid in relation to conflict finance.

Organized Crime

Where to draw the line between politically motivated and criminal or profit-driven armed groups? The expansion of globalization has gone hand in hand with the partial privatization of armed violence. Armed conflicts are more often than not driven by hybrid motives in which the political and the criminal coalesce. Increasingly, warring parties cooperate, co-opt or merge with organized crime groups. The notion of organized criminal groups (OCGs) refers to a broad range of actors involved in illegal economic activities, from urban gangs to drug cartels.[45] Their activities involve the supply of illegal products and services, or bringing illegally onto the market other goods that are not in themselves illicit, such as the smuggling of cigarettes to avoid taxation. In theory, OCGs differ from political and terrorist organizations since they are purely profit-driven and do not pursue any political agenda. In practice, there has been an increasing politicization of such criminal groups while armed political groups cooperate with or even operate like OCGs, blurring the line between the two categories.

Transnational crime involves cross-border economic activities without formal authorization. The UN Convention against Transnational Organized Crime defines a transnational criminal organization (TCO) as 'a structured group of three or more persons that exists over a period of time, the members of which act in concert aiming at the commission of serious crimes in order to obtain a direct or indirect financial or other material benefit'.[46] OCGs and TCOs routinely lobby, bribe, collude with or simply eliminate state actors (political leaders, security forces, customs officials, etc.) and non-state actors who represent a potential obstacle to the expansion of their activities, or whose collaboration can be an asset. Weak states are particularly exposed as they are poorly equipped to enforce law and order and can be more easily infiltrated or co-opted by criminal organizations. Besides, since the end of the Cold War the spread of multiparty elections has been a conduit for TCOs to gain influence by funding political parties and supporting electoral campaigns. In Afghanistan, the onset of the 2014 presidential electoral campaign, for example, coincided with record opium production. The international fight against TCOs at times clashes with state sovereignty, which can be a serious obstacle in contexts where crime and the polity are strongly intertwined.

TCOs have proved as entrepreneurial and efficient on the global marketplace as well-established multinational corporations. They tend to have strong hierarchical structures at the very top, with loose, decentralized networks of affiliates and sub-contractors involved in transport, petty trade and money laundering, related to trafficking in a broad range of goods and services, from narcotics and counterfeited goods to small arms and light weapons, as well as humans and wildlife. Protected species have gained prominence in African conflicts, boosted by soaring demand from Asia. The Lord's Resistance Army (LRA), after losing much of Sudan's backing, intensified predatory practices including elephant poaching in northern DRC and southern Central African Republic (CAR). The simple correlation between LRA presence in an area and high numbers of elephant carcasses was clear by the time former President François Bozizé was ousted from power in March 2013.[47] This coincided with a steep increase in demand for elephant tusks in East Asia. 1 kg of raw ivory on the Chinese market rose from $750 in 2010 to $2,100 by mid-2014. The trade boosted links between warring parties and OCGs all the way from Central Africa to East Asia.[48]

The merging of criminal and political groups is particularly alarming in West Africa and the Sahel belt. Over 30 tons of cocaine was allegedly trafficked through the region in 2011 alone, generating some $900m in profit for criminal networks according to the United Nations Office on Drugs and Crime's (UNODC) World Drug Report 2012.[49] In June 2014 the West Africa Commission on Drugs reported that 'the work of traffickers is facilitated by a wide range of people, which can include business executives, politicians, members of the security forces and the judiciary, clergymen, traditional leaders and youth.'[50] As Paul Krugman stressed, many of today's richest states have their roots in 'contests among crime families over who gets to control the rackets',[51] with overlaps between what we would refer to today as criminal groups and the politico-economic elite. This may provide greater understanding of the current situation facing West Africa, but is no cause for optimism with regard to statebuilding perspectives. Guinea Bissau and Mali do not resemble Italian city-states of the fifteenth century. Collusion between armed and criminal groups combined with rivalries for the control of trafficking routes contributes more to hollowing out the state than to strengthening it.[52] In addition, civil wars in developing countries over the past three decades have been found to retard fiscal capacity as measured by tax revenue as a ratio of GDP, high-intensity conflicts being particularly harmful.[53] This finding differs from Charles Tilly's findings in his analysis of war's contribution to statebuilding in Western Europe over the last few centuries by, among other things, strengthening fiscal capacity.[54]

The violence exerted by criminal organizations and the security forces tasked with fighting them can have dramatic humanitarian consequences: take, for example, the number of people murdered, injured and kidnapped in Mexico over the past few years. The indirect effects can be even more severe, most notably through the weakening of public institutions and of the state's capacity to deliver security and basic social services. Compounded by the opacity surrounding organized criminal groups and the security and liability risks of engaging them, this shall remain a major challenge for humanitarian practitioners and researchers alike.

Natural Resources and War

The empirical literature on the aid-conflict nexus tends to consider aid, including humanitarian aid, as yet another resource that may fuel armed conflict. Against this background, let us consider first the relationship between natural resources and armed conflict in general, before looking at the interactions between foreign aid and conflict, with a particular emphasis on humanitarian action.

A conceptual distinction can be made between conflict resources and resource wars.[55] The former refers to the role of commodities in war economies, for example as a means to sustain rebel finance. The latter applies to armed conflicts that are fought for ownership of and access to strategic resources, often in relation to energy security concerns.[56] Oil, just like any other commodity, can be important in both cases. In the first half of 2014, the Islamic State in Iraq and Syria (ISIS) seized control of oil fields in northeast Syria and the semi-autonomous region of Iraqi Kurdistan. The group further controlled a portion of the oil pipeline linking Kirkuk to the Turkish port of Ceyhan. Selling oil well below market price, ISIS attracted traders from neighbouring regions and countries buying the oil and liquid gas that the group did not need for its own consumption. ISIS further benefits from well-established smuggling circuits that were consolidated during the UN embargo against Iraq in the 1990s. Some experts argued that the US eventually decided to strike ISIS positions from the air in order to prevent territorial gains when the group came to threaten the heart of Iraqi Kurdistan. Such concerns mounted as ISIS' artillery was capable of hitting Erbil, the capital city of a region that produces over 10 per cent of Iraq's oil output, about 370,000 barrels a day. While oil has become a conflict resource for ISIS, the US response arguably stems both from a concern over oil sales boosting ISIS' fighting capability and a wish to preserve Western oil interests in (northern) Iraq.

There is a rich and growing body of empirical literature on the influence of natural resources on interstate and intrastate war,[57] most of which is theoretically grounded on the contest model discussed in Chapter 1. Available evidence tends to confirm that there is no deterministic relationship between resources and conflict in general, although oil in particular has been highlighted as a powerful driver of armed conflict.[58] As usual, context matters, and there are of course more than just economic factors that fuel conflict.[59]

In general the evidence does not support the neo-Malthusian view that competition over scarce resources increases the probability of the outbreak or the duration of civil war.[60] On the contrary, it has prompted cooperation and collective action more often than armed confrontation. In the case of scarce water, for example, over 3,600 treaties on water have been signed between 1805 and 1984, while there have been only a handful of minor confrontations over the resource.[61] A recent study on the civil war in Darfur recognizes that competition over dwindling natural resources such as scarce grazing land has been a driver of conflict, but provides strong evidence that attacks by government-backed Janjaweed militias were primarily pursuing ethnic cleansing rather than access to resources.[62]

There is more evidence in support of the Cornucopians' view that resource abundance—or rather high dependence on non-renewable resources—may increase the probability of civil war. High resource dependence tends to be associated with weak institutions and rent seeking. But the impact of resource dependence on the onset, intensity and duration of civil war further depends on geography, history and the quality of institutions, and also on the specific characteristics of the commodity concerned.[63] Resources should not only be regarded as a (poisoned) gift from nature; they are embedded in global supply chains, shape social relations and are expressions thereof. As Philippe Le Billon puts it, they are complex objects produced by socio-natural processes as well as subjects influencing social relations.[64]

Schematically, natural resources can be categorized according to a few characteristics that have a potential bearing on armed conflict:

- Geography: resource extraction can be concentrated in one location (point resources) or spread over a large area (diffuse resources).
- Lootability: some resources can be easily looted and commercialized by individuals and small groups while others are much harder to divert and market outside formal channels.
- Factor intensity: extraction may require large capital investment and few human resources—such as oil extraction which tends to be capital-intensive—or labour-intensive, for example in the case of alluvial diamonds. Entry barriers are generally higher in capital-intensive sectors.

In each case, the conflict dynamics are different as are the implications for humanitarian action. Rebels may not have much incentive to topple the government and win the war when they draw profits from labour-intensive activities associated with the extraction of resources that are diffuse and relatively easy to loot, with low entry barriers, such as alluvial diamonds, coca, poppy or coltan. It is enough to exercise territorial control over the production area and main trading routes to extract profits from the natural bounty. This may render protracted civil war more likely, but may not necessarily make it more violent.[65] As a humanitarian practitioner in diverse civil war settings, I witnessed that low entry barriers to extract resources that are easy to loot tend to lead to weaker, more fragmented chains of command. Warlords and splinter groups can more easily secure access to conflict finance locally. This, in turn, renders humanitarian negotiations more complex. When seeking to secure safe access across resource-rich areas, humanitarians may have to strike deals with a greater number of armed groups with weaker command chains.

In the case of Colombia, price shocks affecting coffee and oil have had diverging effects on armed violence. Coffee cultivation is a labour-intensive, geographically diffuse activity, whereas oil production is more capital intensive and geographically concentrated. The sharp drop in coffee prices during the 1990s led to more violence in those municipalities growing more coffee. The lower wages of plantation workers meant lower opportunity costs of joining the rebellion. As prices have rebounded, the specific characteristics of the coffee sector and the relationships between entrepreneurs and other stakeholders in this sector have been conducive to lessening violence in Colombia.[66] On the other hand, higher oil prices did not lead to less, but to more violence in oil-producing regions by raising the gains from violent appropriation.[67]

Offshore oil exploitation is capital intensive and faces high barriers to entry. It is a point resource that is not easy to loot on a grand scale. Onshore oil can be slightly more easily diverted, as happens in the Niger Delta and, to a lesser extent, in the case of ISIS in Syria and Iraq. When located in the vicinity of the capital city or the main centres of power, oil may represent an incentive to stage a coup since oil revenues enhance the prize associated with state capture. But oil may also contribute to long-term regime survival as revenues provide the means to repress political opposition and reward clients, as witnessed in several autocratic rentier states. The situation differs when point resources are concentrated in remote areas where a minority group represents the majority of the local population. The risk of secessionist war is greater since partition becomes an attractive option.

This has been the case in Sudan with the eventual partition of the country. South Sudan became the fifty-fourth independent African state in 2011, and took about three quarters of the former Sudan's oil production. Oil discoveries in the 1970s were followed by intense exploration and construction work in

Unity State, which played a role in the resumption and intensification of hostilities between the North and the South. Two years after the introduction of a US trade embargo and asset freeze, the first Sudanese oil pipeline started operating in 1999, bringing oil from the Unity and Helglig fields in the south of the country to Port Sudan on the Red Sea. Exports to Asia rose to a commercial scale in 2000. When the Comprehensive Peace Agreement (CPA) entered into force five years later, the country was already producing about 380,000 barrels a day. The capacity was further raised to above half a million barrels a day once the pipeline linking the Upper Nile's oil fields to Port Sudan became operational in April 2006. Central to the economic agendas of the Khartoum government and the Sudanese People's Liberation Movement/ Army (SPLM/A), negotiations over oil led to the signing of a wealth-sharing agreement in which the parties agreed that half of the net oil revenue derived from oil wells located in Southern Sudan would be allocated to the Government of Southern Sudan and the other half to the National Government and States in Northern Sudan.[68]

The narrative was that peace would make the cake bigger for all parties and oil become an incentive for peace rather than a bone of contention leading to war. The CPA took a very optimistic stance over the oil production potential, stipulating that a 'Future Generation Fund' should be established once national oil production reaches two million barrels per day.[69] Implementation of the revenue-sharing agreement during the interim period from 2005 to 2011 was marred by a lack of transparency on oil production and sales figures. Khartoum nonetheless transferred a significant amount of funds to Juba, estimated at close to $12bn.[70] While the CPA had not settled the issue of oil ownership, the Government of South Sudan had agreed not to renege on existing concessions and contracts.

On independence day in July 2011, about three quarters of the former Sudan's total oil output ended up in Juba's hands. South Sudan became the world's most oil-dependent country. With some 350,000 barrels of oil exported daily to China and other Asian destinations via pipelines crossing north to the Red Sea, oil provided more than 98 per cent of government revenues and accounted for some 80 per cent of GDP. A row over oil transit fees levied by Khartoum led the South Sudanese government to shut down oil production in January 2012, with talks in Juba about building an alternative pipeline to the Kenyan port of Lamu to gain 'full oil independence' from Khartoum. This was followed by violent confrontation on various hot spots along the new international border. The price of imported basic necessities skyrocketed because of supply constraints together with a sharp depreciation of the South Sudanese pound (55 per cent in 2012 alone). The government asked for exceptional efforts from civil servants and drastically cut wages and social expenditures, while the prior oil bonanza had not been widely shared in a country where the overwhelming majority of the people depend on non-wage subsistence agriculture and pastoralism.

Managing the political and humanitarian consequences of such oil revenue volatility required immediate support from bilateral and multilateral donors as well as permanent adjustments from humanitarian organizations, including with regard to staff remuneration. Assistance shifted back from development to emergency aid, which was further reinforced as the country descended into civil war following the rupture between President Salva Kiir and Vice-President Riek Machar in 2013. In such a context, foreign aid in general, and humanitarian assistance in particular, can quickly shift from a very significant resource to a negligible input compared to other valuable assets and revenue flows. In the case of South Sudan, relief has come to represent a relatively marginal input compared to oil proceeds. In the 2012–13 budget, oil revenues were set around $3bn next to $1bn of development assistance and just $300m of humanitarian assistance.[71] Until the early 2000s, however, oil revenues were marginal and humanitarian assistance was a major stake, next to the agropastoral economy.

Various case studies illustrate the impact of natural resource exploitation on armed conflict. Should humanitarian and development aid be regarded as yet another resource that influences war duration and intensity?

Aid as a Resource in War

Much of the relevant academic literature indeed posits that aid, like other resources, can intensify and prolong conflict along a variety of conduits.[72] First, foreign aid may enhance the capacity of warring parties to wage the war because it can be diverted, taxed and looted, or simply because it can free up resources to pay for the war since aid is fungible. Second, just like oil or minerals, foreign aid represents a source of non-tax revenue that increases the prize associated with state capture[73] and spurs the same kind of rent-seeking behaviour as abundant natural resources.[74] Third, the high volatility of aid affects economic outcomes in low-income countries, akin to the volatility of commodity prices.[75] Negative aid shocks, or abrupt cuts in aid flows, have been found to increase the probability of civil war outbreak by weakening the government and motivating rebels to attack.[76] Fourth, foreign aid can reinforce grievances along identity lines when it lacks impartiality, or when it is perceived as biased in favour of specific groups irrespective of their actual requirement for assistance.[77] Fifth, evidence from field experiments in Afghanistan, Iraq and the Philippines hint at the fact that foreign aid used as a counterinsurgency instrument may expose the beneficiaries to increased insurgency attacks (see Chapter 4).

Afghanistan, a country that ranks at the very top of the world's official development assistance (ODA) recipients since 2003, sadly illustrates many of those ills. After the Taliban regime fell in 2002, the terms of engagement were biased from the outset as the CIA poured millions of dollars into the pockets of warlords and strongmen to buy peace and security.[78] Since then, the 'stabilization' and 'reconstruction' of the country are replete with egregious instances of protection racketeering on a grand scale, aid diversion and taxation by warlords and insurgents, fraught sub-contracting arrangements and widespread corruption that has enriched the Taliban, Afghan and foreign officials and business people, as well as private military and security contractors. This contributed to subverting state institutions at the expense of the vast majority of the Afghan people's security and wellbeing.[79] According to a UNODC survey, 52 per cent of Afghans reportedly paid bribes in 2009, the total amount of which may have surpassed $2.5bn, not far below the opium economy valued at $2.8bn the same year.[80] Compounded by a blurring of lines between military, statebuilding and humanitarian agendas, this eroded the legitimacy and acceptance of the aid enterprise as a whole. As the presence of international troops started to decline, armed groups turned to the humanitarian and development sectors to compensate for funding losses. In 2013 alone, an alarming 2,600 incidents targeted humanitarian workers in the country according to the Afghanistan NGO Safety Office.

On that basis, why do policy circles keep using ODA as a foreign policy tool in support of security, peacebuilding and statebuilding? Here, it is important to underline that there is no consensus on the aid-conflict nexus within the academic community. At the discursive level at least, foreign aid is seen as a means to improve the beneficiaries' wellbeing and strengthen state institutions, including security.[81] Some research findings support those claims. For example, a study on foreign aid in sub-Saharan Africa found aid to reduce conflict duration[82] while other studies highlighted that aid can contribute to reducing insurgent attacks, in particular when allocated to education. The reduction in attacks has, however, also been found to result from stronger counterinsurgency responses from the recipient government rather than from higher opportunity costs that would discourage better educated youths from joining the insurgency.[83]

The scholarly literature on the aid-conflict nexus suffers from various limitations when it comes to assessing the specific relationship between humanitarian action and armed conflict. Most empirical studies do not single out the specific role of humanitarian aid. They often take ODA figures as a proxy for foreign aid, thus mixing development with humanitarian assistance, which can account for a substantial portion of total ODA in war-torn countries. In line with underlying theoretical models, researchers routinely assume that foreign aid accrues directly and entirely to the recipient government. This is obviously not the case for large portions of humanitarian aid that is distributed directly to beneficiary communities, households and individuals. Empirical studies rarely seek to identify how much of the resources recorded as ODA—or as humanitarian aid—actually end up as resources made available in the recipient country. It would be necessary to subtract administrative and fundraising costs, headquarters and coordination expenditures, communications and the likes, which may represent over half of the total amount registered as humanitarian or development assistance.[84] As highlighted in the preceding chapter, food assistance data does not reflect the actual value of the food distributed.[85] Unlike the majority of development assistance, humanitarian aid data should not be equated with resources at the disposal of recipient governments.

To deepen one's understanding of this one should look at the modalities through which aid is distributed in the field. Let us consider the specific case of food aid to Somalia during the 2011–12 famine, as reported in a 2013 study by the Overseas Development Institute (ODI).[86] Over 250,000 Somalis are believed to have starved to death while Al-Shabaab, a Somali rebel group with alleged ties to al-Qaeda, controlled vast swathes of the territory, with the notable exception of the capital city, Mogadishu. The Islamist organization appointed local humanitarian coordination officers whose task was to regulate and monitor the activities of aid agencies. This included taxation: the group argued that, being the de facto government in the areas of operations of humanitarian agencies, it was responsible for the security of aid workers. This, in turn, required financial support from the humanitarians who 'required protection'. Initial registration fees could be as high as $10,000, followed by taxes on individual projects and on staff income. It seems that food and non-food items were subject to greater duties than medical assistance, food being more valuable and fungible in general than drugs and medical devices. Al-

Shabaab drew additional revenue from property rentals, logistics and transport. The diversion of food aid by Al-Shabaab was at times quite significant (up to two-thirds according to one source).[87]

A few organizations resisted aid diversion, insisting they distribute the food themselves directly to the beneficiaries they had selected. But some of them saw their goods eventually confiscated or destroyed by Al-Shabaab. Later, the UK Department for International Development (DFID) reported in its 2012–13 Report and Accounts, under its losses statement, that Al-Shabaab had confiscated £480,000 worth of UK-funded humanitarian supplies. This did not go unnoticed and provided ammunition to aid opponents.[88]

Negotiating better terms for famine victims required active, direct engagement with Al-Shabaab at different levels. However, counter-terrorism legislation governing donors outlaws engagement with Al-Shabaab and other organizations designated as terrorists. Humanitarians were left with a tough cost-benefit calculus: enter into negotiations and agree with the rebels on terms and conditions that might be unacceptable to donors in the hope of providing life-saving assistance, or withdraw from the area and let more children, elders, men and women starve to death. The ODI study importantly found that rigorous, structured engagement by some humanitarian actors with Al-Shabaab, from top commanders to local rank and files, succeeded in improving access and in retaining control over the design and delivery of aid projects in spite of the difficult environment.[89]

Aid diversion and fraught conditions for humanitarian engagement in Somalia are nothing new. Twenty-one years earlier, I was serving as a humanitarian worker in the region bordering Somalia and Ethiopia. The regime of Siad Barre, who had been in power since 1969, was collapsing. A Somali armed group looted our vehicle fleet. At the time, the Australian movie *Mad Max* was very popular, with Mel Gibson's role a source of inspiration for young Somalis. The rebels turned our former 4-wheel drives into combat vehicles with machine guns mounted at the top. They had apparent fun in mimicking shooting at us while looting the few remaining items in our pharmacy located in the Somali refugee camp of Hartisheikh, then one of the world's largest camps. Since it was in the midst of the month of Ramadan, we understood that intense khat chewing throughout the past few nights accounted for part of their aggressiveness. Yet, as a new humanitarian practitioner, I seriously wondered if it would not be wiser for the humanitarian community to leave and not come back before Somali group leaders agreed on renewed terms of engagement.[90] But already in 1990–91, this was not a realistic option for a fragmented humanitarian sector competing on the market. The payment of armed escorts rapidly became common practice throughout Somalia, turning into an industry in Mogadishu. More importantly, continued engagement in the field proved essential to save tens of thousands of civilians during the 1992 famine that hit central and southern Somalia.

Twenty-three years later MSF announced its sudden, full withdrawal from Somalia in August 2013, putting an end to decades of continuous operational presence in the country. This happened shortly after the liberation of two MSF workers who had been held hostage for more than twenty months in Somalia. MSF wanted to signal its discontent at the absence of minimal security granted to its staff and the lack of support from Somali elders and clan leaders in reducing violence against medical care providers.[91] This message was not heard as loud and clear as was expected (see Chapter 2). Yet another missed opportunity.

Several humanitarian organizations are striving to devise effective mechanisms to address aid diversion and other 'resource incidents' whereby goods and funds are simply wasted (e.g. kickbacks, overcharged goods and services, petty thefts) or, worse, end up fuelling violent conflict (e.g. extortion and aid diversion by warring parties). Often in response to donor pressure, many agencies have strengthened their monitoring and oversight processes and have provided their staff with training aimed at addressing corruption and reducing the likelihood of resource diversion. This does not happen by managerial decree but implies a corporate culture shift that promotes transparent, systematic reporting of—and learning from—critical incidents. It also depends on power relations. Yet, as long as competition prevails over cooperation in tough cases such as Somalia where remote management is widespread because of security constraints, individual humanitarian organizations remain in a weak position vis-à-vis armed groups who can play one organization off against the other. The growing variety of humanitarian actors on the market does not bode well for such cooperation.

Aid Fungibility

Aid diversion is conceptually straightforward, as is the operational response: it ought to be minimized. The issue of humanitarian aid fungibility is trickier, albeit nothing new.[92] The World Bank's Chief Economist Paul Rosenstein-Rodan reportedly said in 1947: 'When the World Bank thinks it is financing an electric power station, it is really financing a brothel.'[93] In other words, the recipient country can spare the expense on electrification, now financed by foreign aid, and can reallocate the domestic resources saved to pay for something that aid agencies would adamantly refuse to support, such as building a new presidential palace or buying weaponry. Humanitarian assistance can also free up resources that the recipient state would otherwise have to allocate to sustaining the livelihood of the citizenry. Think of the food aid granted by the World Food Programme (WFP) to Angola for decades.[94] In 1999–2000, the WFP allocated an operational budget of $207.7m to provide food to more than 1.5m people in government-controlled areas.[95] Generous food assistance may have allowed the government to spend more on its military campaign against UNITA while attracting civilians into state-controlled areas where food was being distributed. The strategy may have worked from a counterinsurgency perspective, but at a considerable human cost.

This unfolded while Angola was already the second largest oil producer in sub-Saharan Africa, behind Nigeria. Even if oil prices were relatively depressed, with a barrel of oil trading around $10, Angola was cashing in substantial oil receipts, most of which was however already committed to servicing oil-backed loans. The advocacy organization Global Witness published a groundbreaking report entitled 'A Crude Awakening' in December 1999, where it alleged that:

> A significant portion of Angola's oil derived wealth is being subverted for personal gain and to support the aspirations of elite individuals, at the centre of power around the Presidency. The war is generating vast profits for top level generals within the Angolan armed forces (FAA), as well as for international arms dealers, not to mention enormous suffering for the Angolan people.[96]

On 10 December 1999, the cover stories on Global Witness' Report by two weekly independent newspapers in Angola, *Folha 8* and *Agora*, were censored by order of the Angolan police. The order came just in time to remove the story, but too late to replace it with other news. The next morning, the cover of *Folha 8* kept the title of the news, but the next four pages were left blank except a few captionless photographs of oilrigs.[97] The blank pages generated more debate in Angola than the rest of the edition!

What would have happened if humanitarian organizations had refrained from distributing food assistance and pressed the state to care for its own people? Would the Angolan government have allocated a greater share of oil revenues to feed the hungry and to provide soldiers and police officers with allowances that would have rendered extortion unnecessary? Donors and humanitarian agencies may have discharged the authorities from their duty to support people's livelihoods in government-held enclaves, many of whom had been displaced because of the civil war. Yet, in the absence of a counterfactual, it is impossible to know how many more people would have starved to death without the provision of food assistance in 1999–2000. Given Angola's substantial oil proceeds, there was nonetheless a strong case in favour of pressing the authorities to fulfil their responsibility instead of standing in for them. That said, whose responsibility is it to exert pressure in favour of oil revenue transparency and accountability? It may arguably be that of oil companies, and is definitely more the remit of advocacy groups and states than of relief organizations. Besides, states and extractive industries have more clout and are better placed to exert such pressure.

The sections above highlight some of the dilemmas faced by humanitarian actors when integrating the issues of conflict finance, aid fungibility and the associated moral hazard[98] into their analyses. Beyond the Manichean approach to grant aid unconditionally or withhold aid altogether, the question for any humanitarian organization whose mission is to save lives and alleviate suffering is how to adapt aid programmes and delivery modalities with a view to minimizing the potential negative side effects. The next section illustrates how political economy analysis offers a useful analytical grid for identifying the relevant risks, and discusses how to reduce and manage these risks at the operational level—a due-diligence exercise regarding the interplay between humanitarian action and war economy dynamics.

The Political Economy of Humanitarian Action

Political economy analysis has been used and abused under various guises. It is understood and practiced differently by diverse professions and disciplines. Traditional economic theory assumes that individuals and firms behave opportunistically and seek to maximize utility or profits while, oddly in this framework, the state does not. Instead, the state is assumed to act as a benevolent entity that pursues maximum public welfare (the Pareto optimum for the society as a whole). *Modern political economy* departs from this assumption: it brings politics back into economic analysis by looking at the interests of state agents in policy making with a focus on the distribution of power and wealth.[99] It generally assumes that individuals behave in a rational and opportunistic manner, but take decisions on the basis of incomplete information and bounded rationality. Thus, when making decisions, people seek to satisfy rather than to maximize. The political economy of policymaking looks at how individual preferences take shape and are aggregated and channelled into political demands that, in turn, influence policymakers' preferences, depending on the demand and supply of political support. In sum, political economy analysis focuses on the interests, preferences, values and agency[100] of actors involved in decision-making processes.

The literature on the political economy of foreign aid broadly encompasses three main approaches. The dominant approach considers the donor and recipient countries as unitary actors pursuing their own interests. In such a macro approach, the donor designs its aid policy in the pursuit of economic, geopolitical, security, development and other objectives. The second approach focuses on a more micro-political level. It relaxes the unitary actor assumption and looks at the interactions between the executive and legislative branches within donor and recipient countries, factoring domestic interest groups into the analysis. A third and more recent approach draws on cooperative game theory to study aid allocation decisions as the outcomes of negotiations between donors and recipients pursuing divergent objectives.[101]

At a more operational level, development agencies have attempted to mainstream what they refer to as political economy analysis (PEA) into their operations. In the aftermath of the Cold War, the emphasis has been put on (good) governance: PEA was first approached primarily from a technical, capacity-building angle with a view to strengthening governance mechanisms and capabilities in recipient or 'partner' countries. Later on, some bilateral development agencies brought politics back into PEA by focusing on the institutional, structural and political variables that influence the behaviour and decisions of key stakeholders in partner countries.[102] The third and latest generation brought economics back into PEA with an emphasis on economic concepts and methods to analyze how (market) incentives shape behaviour and influence development outcomes. PEA has rightly been highlighted as a useful complement to (but is no substitute for) proper political analysis in international development cooperation.[103]

The standard political-economy approach to humanitarian crises and responses involves analyzing how war (or disaster) and humanitarian action redistribute wealth, income, power and agency in a given historical and institutional context.[104] Under PEA, humanitarian practitioners approach vulnerability and destitution in terms of exclusion, rights violations and powerlessness rather than as poverty or the mere lack of material and financial means. Conducting a PEA in a humanitarian crisis boils down to raising three key questions. First, who are the main actors involved? (This may be answered by studying a relief supply chain.) Second, who are the likely winners and losers of an aid intervention? And third, how do the belligerents finance the war, and how do humanitarian operations fit into this context? It also means looking more broadly at how a humanitarian crisis and aid transform social norms and institutions, as well as considering the economic functions of armed violence.

PEA can be particularly relevant when planning a relief operation, as a complement to traditional needs assessments. Humanitarians can usefully draw on PEA as part of a broader context analysis, for instance to reduce the risk of aid being diverted or instrumentalized, and to identify critical security issues and operational challenges along the relief supply chain. In the appendix I provide an example of how we applied PEA in the context of an emergency food aid and agricultural rehabilitation programme in Angola to identify, discuss and address security and operational issues.

What's in It for Humanitarian Studies and Practice?

As this chapter highlights, war economies lend themselves to standard economic inquiry, factoring into the analysis violent acquisitions and the economic functions of violence. Rational choice theory, with its focus on constrains and incentives, offers a framework for better understanding the behaviour of key actors in war, which can, for instance, inform humanitarian negotiations aimed at reducing IHL violations and securing field access. PEA can help humanitarians to identify and address potential security risks and resource incidents based on an examination of the interests of key stakeholders involved in, or affected by, war and relief operations. This can usefully complement (but not replace) broader context analysis, although neutral, impartial and independent actors need to be aware of a frequent anti-rebel bias in the empirical literature.

Humanitarians have started to pay greater attention to the multi-layered dynamics underlying war economies and factor them into their analyses, which is no easy task. The impact of the Dot-Com Bubble in the DRC illustrates the complex interactions between global (financial) markets, conflict finance and humanitarian consequences for local communities. Besides, war economy analysis must be handled carefully. Over a third of all journalists killed between 1992 and 2012 were reportedly covering issues related to organized crime and corruption.[105] Humanitarian organizations are rightly wary about being publicly associated with mounting global civil society pressure to closely monitor and report on conflict finance. Not that such pressure is a bad idea, but it can simply be too risky for relief organizations which have hundreds of staff on the ground.

Recent attempts to get solid empirical evidence on the causal links between aid and conflict remain inconclusive, although many of them point to disturbing facts that call for greater due diligence from relief agencies. As we have seen, ODA data, typically used as a proxy for aid in quantitative studies, is not appropriate for evaluating the specific impact of humanitarian aid. While existing models generally assume all aid to be up for capture by the recipient government, much official humanitarian assistance does not translate into actual resource flows into the field, and much of the rest does not transit via recipient countries' governments. Because of high fiduciary risks, relief agencies often favour aid projects over programmatic aid and seek to retain tight control over how funds are channelled to beneficiaries. As discussed above, this does not mean that project-based assistance is diversion immune. Valuable relief goods whose distribution implies heavy logistics, such as in-kind food distribution, are obviously more likely to help sustain the war economy than technical assistance geared to raising awareness on IHL. In this context, the gradual shift from in-kind to cash assistance deserves particular scrutiny since diversion may be either more difficult or easier to trace depending on where in the delivery chains it takes place (see Chapter 6). Another issue with ODA data is that several of its components do not translate into any actual resource transfers into war-torn recipient countries, for example debt write-off, headquarters expenditures and the hosting of asylum-seekers during the first year of residence in donor countries. Proxy indicators for poor macroeconomic data together with the increasing availability of geo-referenced data on both aid projects and violent incidents at sub-national level offer a promising opportunity to get a more refined picture of the aid-conflict nexus.[106]

Longstanding efforts to eradicate coca production in Colombia, poppy production in Afghanistan and elephant poaching for the ivory trade involving armed groups such as the Lord's Resistance Army show how difficult it is to get to grips with war economies. There is no quick fix. The US may have bought some quick wins in 2002 when it handed out millions to buy off Afghan warlords, but it instilled perverse incentives that rewarded violence, plaguing the relief enterprise. The analysis here suggests a need for stronger governance mechanisms combined with greater attention to how international aid, peacekeeping and peacebuilding ventures interact with war economies and can contribute to transforming them towards more sustainable foundations for peace.

4

TERRORISM ECONOMICS

We must address the root causes of terrorism ... I believe putting resources into improving the lives of poor people is a better strategy than spending it on guns.

Muhammad Yunus, 2006[1]

The terrorist attacks of 11 September 2001 and the subsequent launch of the Global War on Terror (GWOT) spurred renewed interest in terrorism research among social scientists, including economists. The latter have dealt with four broad sets of questions in particular. First, what are the political and socio-economic causes of terrorism? The emphasis has been on the costs, incentives, and rewards that shape the behaviour of individuals and groups who opt for terrorist attacks, typically on the assumption those individuals seek maximum impact under resource constraints.[2] Second, what are the economic consequences of terrorism? Third, how is terrorism financed? And fourth, how effective are different economic policies and measures aimed at addressing terrorism? An issue of particular interest has been the extent to which foreign aid can be an effective instrument in support of counterterrorism.

This chapter explores these questions. I briefly dwell on the definition of terrorism as well as on rational choice aspects of the phenomenon before addressing the economic consequences and the financing of terrorism, including kidnap for ransom. I then discuss policies and instruments devised to combat terrorism, looking in particular at economic sanctions and foreign aid in those situations of interest to humanitarians: armed conflicts. Indeed, humanitarian agencies have not been much concerned with domestic terrorism outside situations of armed conflict, save for prisoner visits by staff of the International Committee of the Red Cross (ICRC) and a few other organizations.

What Is Terrorism?

In the absence of a universal definition of terrorism, the label is attached to very different types of people and organizations. Humanitarian organizations increasingly operate in contexts where part of the territory is under the control of groups and individuals designated as 'terrorists' by the United Nations and major donor countries such as the US and the EU: Afghanistan, Colombia, Lebanon, Mali, Palestine, Somalia and Syria are a few such places. Consequently, the distinction between war economics and terrorism economics is largely artificial and certainly not clear-cut. Hence my decision to raise issues such as economic sanctions in this chapter, a topic that would also have fitted into Chapter 3 ('War Economics').

In contemporary asymmetric warfare, the weaker side often opts for terrorist tactics against the stronger in order to spread fear far beyond the limited population that such attacks can directly injure or kill. The increasing use of terrorist tactics in armed conflict raises daunting challenges for humanitarian organizations, as does the systematic labelling of armed groups as terrorists:

- Killing combatants may be lawful under international humanitarian law (IHL) in specific circumstances, but indiscriminate acts of terror are strictly prohibited, in both international and non-international armed conflicts. In addition, Article 3, common to the four Geneva Conventions of 1949, specifically prohibits murder and the taking of hostages, and requires humane treatment for all persons in enemy hands. Disseminating such basic IHL principles to groups that primarily resort to terrorist tactics means asking them to radically alter the way in which they operate, obviously an ambitious undertaking.
- Both counterterrorism legislation and economic sanctions seek to restrict resource flows to groups and individuals designated as terrorists. As is well documented in the case of Iraq, sanctions can have dire humanitarian consequences, for instance on the health status of the population at large. Coupled with counterterrorism laws and regulations, sanctions tend to impinge on the capacity of humanitarian organizations to effectively respond to the needs of affected communities.

There is no universal legal definition of terrorism. Each and every state retains the authority to define the term as it sees fit. And indeed, as a humanitarian worker, I cannot recall a single civil war where the political detainees or captured enemies where not labelled as 'terrorists' by the detaining authorities. During the civil war in El Salvador, for example, this practice greatly facilitated my task as an ICRC delegate of identifying and registering those detainees who were alleged guerrilla members or sympathizers of the Frente Farabundo Martí de Liberación nacional (FMLN): they were the only detainees on the prison registry recorded as 'D/T', which stood for 'Delincuentes/Terroristas' or Criminals/Terrorists.

A careful parsing of the dozen UN conventions addressing terrorism suggests that there is nonetheless an emerging consensus around an operational definition of terrorism. It revolves around the use of indiscriminate attacks intended to spread fear or terrorize a population through public media in support of a political cause. Large public-impact attacks such as 9/11 or the Madrid train bombing of 11 March 2004 give high worldwide visibility to the terrorist group. They tend to boost recruitment and thereby lower the cost structure of terrorist organizations. In a recent article on the new frontiers of terrorism research, Todd Sandler defines terrorism as 'the premeditated use or threat of use of violence by individuals or subnational groups to obtain a political or social objective through the intimidation of a large audience, beyond that of the immediate victim.'[3] Terrorist attacks tend to be perpetrated in a seemingly random manner to make as many people as possible feel that they, their relatives and their friends could also be targeted. The notion of state (-sponsored) terrorism has long been a sensitive issue, notwithstanding the fact that hardly anyone would deny that terrorist acts have been commissioned and carried out by states.[4]

Rational Choice Analysis of Terrorism

Dzhokhar and Tamerlan Tsarnaev, two US residents of Chechen descent, killed three people and injured over 250 more in the Boston Marathon Bombings of 15 April 2013. Following this deadly attack, the question was how on earth such a heinous crime could be committed or conceived. No one dared to publicly condone this act as rational. Yet, psychological profiling and socio-political research consistently finds that, in general, terrorists are neither psychopaths nor sociopaths. Empirical research on domestic terrorism tends not to support the idea that terrorists come from the poorest and least educated segments of society with little to lose, thus casting doubt on explanations that rest on the opportunity cost argument. In several instances terrorists are rather drawn from the ranks of the better educated, whose decision to join a terrorist group is motivated by political grievances,[5] which can be combined with a sense of frustration when legal channels to voice political protest are closed or seen as useless.

The analytical study of terrorism typically treats individuals perpetrating terrorist acts and the organizations commissioning them as rational actors. Economists indeed regard terrorists as rational, self-interested actors who behave opportunistically while operating under a set of constraints. The normative issue of how objectionable the terrorists' objectives are is another question. Just like other economic agents, they may take decisions on the basis of imperfect information and miscalculation. Terrorists are seen as resourceful in that they creatively adapt to changing circumstances and evaluate the outcome of alternative actions with a view to maximizing utility.[6] Terrorist organizations tend to rationally identify their targets, shifting targets and adopting different tactics in response to specific counterterrorist or 'deterrence' measures.

Suicide terrorism can be seen as the ultimate paradox: How can self-destruction be a self-interested act?[7] Suicide terrorism represents only a fraction of terrorist attacks, estimated between 6 and 8 per cent, but accounts for a larger share of fatalities (about a third). Research shows that, in economic parlance, the supply of suicide terrorists is relatively elastic[8] and abundant while, on the demand side, there are fewer terrorist organizations able to effectively channel volunteers to perform their deadly attacks. In 'An Economist Looks at Suicide Terrorism', Mark Harrison writes:

> From an economist's point of view suicide terrorism is the outcome of a contract between consenting parties. The suicide attacker and the militant faction enter voluntarily into this contract in the expectation of mutual benefit. Under the terms of the contract the volunteer agrees to trade life for identity. She will die to promote the faction's terrorist objectives. In return the faction endorses the volunteer's identity as a warrior martyr. As a result each party can achieve an objective that would be beyond the reach of either without this agreement.[9]

There remains a commitment problem. How can the suicide attacker be sure that the terrorist organization will give his or her sacrifice adequate recognition to reach the desired audience? Some researchers who have looked in particular at the case of Palestinian suicide bombers argue that the commitment problem has been solved by the organization promoting the martyr's deed while he or she is still alive. Prior to the fatal event, the volunteer records a 'statement of joy' on videos accompanied with photos and letters sent to family, friends and community members. Thereafter, the living martyr is considered, and sees him or herself, as already among the 'gloriously dead'.[10] There is no way back without losing face and self-respect.[11] Each party then has a strong incentive to implement the contract in full. Another aspect that has been taken into account in a rational choice framework is the influence of payments and in-kind assistance for the suicide terrorist's relatives by the organization commissioning the attack. The policy recommendations have consequently focused on weakening the organizations that recruit volunteers and plan the attacks.

By discussing suicide terrorism in terms of a commitment problem under contract theory, such an economic approach tends to disregard the political and emotional drivers. Territorial occupation has been identified among the top motivations for suicide attacks,[12] next to the lack of space for political contestation. Social anthropologists have focused more on the role of group dynamics and local networks of friends, schoolmates or kin who encourage each other to kill perfect strangers while committing suicide, sometimes without any well defined political agenda.[13] The implicit and explicit policy recommendations from empirical research can thus radically differ depending on the researchers' disciplinary perspective. Such recommendations range from opening up space for voicing discontent and influencing local-level group dynamics to destroying the leadership of organizations that stage suicide attacks and punishing the 'martyr's' relatives. Providing humanitarian aid and other forms of assistance may arguably help reduce terrorism by raising the opportunity cost and making terrorist attacks less attractive.[14] Instead of taking individual preferences for terrorism as given—a weakness of rational choice perspectives on terrorism—one should consider the possibility that significant humanitarian operations in the field may alter the preferences of potential recruits away from terrorism, which could also contribute to explaining why terrorist organizations sometimes target aid workers.

Terrorism research raises critical ethical questions. Some of the most relevant information is obtained by interviewing key informants (more or less loosely) associated with designated terrorist organizations. University ethics boards may refuse to give clearance for research that involves, for instance, interviewing prisoners who are suspected of terrorism and who may therefore be subjected to torture. As humanitarian practitioners are well aware, interviewing key informants further begs the question of how to protect information sources, and it is up for debate whether this even remains a realistic option in today's interconnected world infused with intrusive surveillance. Social scientists who conduct independent research on terrorism—even well-established scholars in top-tier US universities—have been subjected to in-depth searches on returning from the world's hottest trouble-spots, including the downloading of all data from their cell phones and laptops by US Homeland Security officers.[15] Another issue revolves around potential conflicts of interest when the research is funded by those governmental agencies that are directly involved in counterterrorism (for example by the US Department of Defence), or simply when research is made possible by security services granting privileged access to sensitive data. Those agencies funding research are obviously motivated by a keen interest in findings that can help to enhance the effectiveness of counterterrorism measures, or simply want external validation of their current policies and practices.

Finally, data quality and availability is of the essence. Two databases have been widely used for the economic analysis of terrorism and counterterrorism: the Global Terrorism Database (GTD) of the University of Maryland, and International Terrorism: Attributes of Terrorism Events (ITERATE) of Cornell University. Both datasets register terrorist incidents from media and news sources and other publicly available information. As a consequence, terrorist incidents may be underreported, in particular when it comes to minor incidents occurring in autocratic states with limited media freedom. The number of domestic terrorist events tends to be far greater than transnational ones, but domestic terrorism can spill over into transnational terrorism: the two should not be considered in isolation.

The Economic Impact of Terrorism

Studying the economic consequences of terrorism broadly follows the same logic as studying war costs. Macroeconomic analysis considers the direct and indirect impact of terrorism at national, regional and sectoral levels. It is no surprise that the overall impact of terrorism tends to be much smaller than that of civil war. A study of fifty-one African countries between 1970 and 2007 finds that the average GDP loss attributable to terrorist incidents is lower than 0.1 per cent, which is ten to twenty times less than in the case of civil war.[16] But the economic impact can still be significant in specific circumstances. A case study on Pakistan—one of the countries with the highest incidence of terrorism-related deaths in the 2000s—estimates that terrorism may cost up to 1 per cent of real GDP per capita annual growth,[17] which may be partly compensated by higher foreign military and development assistance granted with a view to supporting Pakistan's fight against terrorism.

Terrorism tends to hurt specific sectors such as transportation, which typically faces increasing security costs to address terrorist risks. The negative impact of terrorism on tourism is also well documented, as in the cases of Egypt and Spain, where the number of foreign visitors to the regions most affected and the ensuing revenues have dropped following terrorist attacks. Enders and Sandlers found that a terrorist attack by the Basque separatist organization Euskadi Ta Askatasuna (ETA) in the 1970s and 1980s typically scared away over 140,000 foreign tourists.[18] What happens once the terrorist threat disappears? A recent study finds that ETA's dissolution in 2011—after more than four decades of activity—had a positive impact on the number of Spanish visitors to the Basque Country, which experienced a 98.2 per cent increase in 2012, while domestic tourism dropped in other parts of Spain.[19]

Terrorism has been found to have a negative impact on private investment and a positive one on government expenditure, not least because of increased security expenditure in response to the threat of terrorism.[20] The security sector emerges as the big winner, in particular in countries that develop and export counterterrorism devices, technology and services. The insurance and reinsurance industry face both greater losses and the opportunity to develop the terrorism insurance market and increase premiums.[21] The 9/11 terrorist attacks in the US can be considered an outlier. Property losses have been estimated at up to $13bn, in addition to some $11bn for the clean-up operations. The overall insured losses amounted to $32.2bn. It was eventually decided to consider the destruction of the twin towers of the World Trade Center as two separate incidents, which had substantial consequences on insurance claims. The value of a statistical life (see below) was established at slightly below $7m, yielding a total loss of $40bn for 6,000 immediate and longer-term fatalities.

Rapid economic revival is often seen as a strategic reaction to terrorist attacks, as illustrated by a statement of the then Mayor of New York City Rudolph Giuliani on the day after 9/11: 'Go to restaurants, go shopping, do things, show that you're not afraid.'[22] In a highly resilient and diversified economy such as the US, the immediate economic shock of the terrorist attack was quickly absorbed. But the cost of the ensuing US military actions has been huge. In their book *The Three Trillion Dollar War*, Stiglitz and Bilmes estimate the cost of the ensuing US GWOT and the war in Iraq to be in the trillions of US dollars, diverting public funds away from other policy objectives and leaving the federal budget with a long-term burden.

Beyond the direct and indirect economic costs of terrorism, there are of course broader impacts including significant political and social outcomes over the long haul. Counterterrorism tends to impose tighter restrictions on individual freedoms and sets limits on privacy rights in liberal democracies, resulting in the securitization of public life, not to mention the legitimation and strengthening of autocratic regimes in North Africa, the Middle East and beyond. Terrorist attacks can further alter electoral outcomes, as was arguably the case in Spain right after the March 2004 Madrid train bombings with the electoral defeat of Prime Minister José María Aznar.

The Value of Life

In high-income countries, the value of a statistical life (VSL) often serves to ascertain the cost associated with war and terrorism fatalities. More generally, VSL is routinely used in cost-benefit analyses to determine how much to invest in public health and other public policies, or for insurance purposes. VSL measures trade-offs between death risk and money: it reflects how much people are willing to pay to reduce the probability of dying or, conversely, how much they are willing to accept against a higher risk of dying. The calculus is relatively simple. Imagine that someone wants to buy a new car and has the choice between two identical vehicles with only one difference: the cheaper one is less shock resistant. It costs $6,000 more to buy the car that implies a 0.1 per cent lower risk of dying in a fatal accident. If the buyer is willing (and able) to pay, the value of that buyer's statistical life is $6m, which is calculated as a willingness to pay $6,000 divided by a 0.001 lower risk of dying in a car accident.

In many real-life cases there is no market price to refer to. It is then impossible to obtain a VSL based on preferences revealed through market signals. Economists then turn to stated preferences and contingent valuation techniques, for instance in surveys where they ask individuals how much they would be willing to pay for a lower death risk. An alternative route is to resort to economic-forensic methods: this means for example estimating the net present value of future income streams that a young soldier would likely generate if he survived the war. VSL is highly sensitive to assumptions about how much to discount such future income flows.[23] In *The Three Trillion Dollar War*, Stiglitz and Bilmes consider a real discount rate of 4.5 per cent, which lies somewhere between the long-term real risk-free rate of 1 per cent and the 7 per cent historical real return on US equities. They reach a value of $7.2m for each US life lost in the Iraq War[24] (the VSL for US citizens typically ranges between $3m and $8m). Another study on the cost of the German participation in the Iraq and Afghan wars puts the VSL for German fatalities at €2.05m. Implying that a German soldier's life is worth less than half that of an American has caused outrage.[25] Overall, the net present value of the total costs of the German participation in the Afghan war has been tagged between €26bn and €47bn, with annual costs being between two and three times higher than the official figures released by the government.[26]

What would the VSL be for the countless Afghan and Iraqi fatalities? There is no readily available VSL for people in poorer countries. Lower per capita income should logically translate into lower VSL, depending on the income elasticity of VSL.[27] Simply put, poor people have less money available to pay to lower their risk of death. In economists' jargon, they display a lower 'willingness to pay' or a higher 'willingness to accept risk' than the rich. The 1948 Universal Declaration of Human Rights proclaimed that all human beings are born equal in dignity and rights. But nationality and residence make a huge difference to the VSL.

The technicalities involved in costing methods should not obscure the more fundamental theoretical and ethical issues. Value judgements should be made explicit, especially when they relate to valuating lives lost, disability and suffering across diverse geographies and temporalities. To begin, the rationale and purpose of estimating specific war and terrorism costs should be made explicit, since they often have a bearing on the precise causal relations, case studies and time periods deemed worth considering.[28] Besides, suicide terrorism challenges standard assumptions that associate greater income and lower risks with increased wellbeing, or that associate higher death risk with reduced life satisfaction. For suicide terrorist recruits, the prospect of sacrificing one's own life arguably increases current life satisfaction—or rather reduces the level of dissatisfaction.

Terrorism Finance

The vast literature on terrorism finance does a relatively good job of examining regulatory aspects of on-going efforts to counter the financing of terrorism, but does a poorer job of getting solid empirical evidence on the actual financing of terrorism.[29] To better grasp how different groups finance acts of terror, more research efforts should aim to get first-hand information from people who have been directly involved in terrorism finance. The same applies to evaluating the effectiveness of measures aimed to counter the financing of terrorism (CFT). De-listed individuals who have personally experienced targeted sanctions can obviously provide relevant insights on how they dealt with such measures.[30]

The financing of armed groups designated as terrorists does not radically differ from the financing of rebel groups in civil wars (discussed in the previous chapter). Terrorism finance may comprise informal taxation and protection rackets, as documented in the case of ETA for example. It may further include trade in illegal goods and—depending on the extent of territorial control over valuable resources—the direct exploitation and commercialization of agricultural and mineral products. At present, some of the most detailed and relevant information publicly available is found in the sanctions monitoring reports that are regularly submitted to the UN Security Council, such as the reports by the Analytical Support and Monitoring Team of the Al-Qaida Sanctions Committee.[31] In its 2014 Report, the Monitoring Team insists in particular on kidnap and ransom (K&R) as a source of terrorism finance and emphasizes that it is crucial to deter ransom payments to al-Qaeda and its affiliates:

> [A]n estimated $120 million in ransom payments was paid to terrorist groups between 2004 and 2012 ... A total of 1,283 kidnappings motivated by terrorism were reported in 2012, and a single hostage could deliver a seven-figure ransom into the hands of terrorists. AQIM [al-Qaeda in the Islamic Maghreb], with an estimated $15 million annual budget, received $5.4 million on average per hostage in 2012, an increase of nearly $1 million from 2011. Each ransom payment encourages further kidnappings, creating a vicious cycle of encouragement as well as funding for Al-Qaeda and its affiliates.[32]

The booming K&R market has become a significant funding source for several armed groups designated as terrorist and a major concern for those involved in the countering of terrorism finance. Instead of monetary ransom, demands can also include political concessions such as the release of prisoners, or a commitment to refrain from attacking specific locations over a given timespan.

Kidnap and Ransom

Kidnapping has arguably become the single biggest threat to humanitarian workers in the field. According to the Aid Worker Security Database,[33] the number of aid workers kidnapped (and not killed thereafter) has multiplied by eighteen in just a decade, from seven in 2003 to 128 in 2013. Even when adjusting for the increase in the number of humanitarian aid workers, there is a higher risk of being kidnapped while working in the field today than a few years ago. The incidence has increased from an annual average of thirteen for every 100,000 aid workers over the period of 2006–09 to seventeen for every 100,000 in 2010–12.[34] Kidnapping remains a low-probability, but can be a devastatingly high-impact event for individual humanitarian workers and their organizations:

Since 2009, kidnappings have become the most frequent means of violence against aid workers, showing the steepest and steadiest rise out of all tactics over the past decade. According to the data, the majority of kidnappings of aid workers (at least 85 per cent) do not end in the victim's death, but commonly with a negotiated release.[35]

Negotiated release may imply the direct or indirect payment of a ransom by the employer, the family or the home government of the victim. Relief agencies may be requested to refrain from exercising certain types of activities, such as female education in Afghanistan. In 2013, 85 per cent of kidnappings involved staff who were working in their home countries, as opposed to international staff working away from their home countries. This broadly reflects the ratio of national versus international staff involved in all security incidents. However, in proportion to their total number in the field, international staffers actually face a higher risk than their national colleagues. They represent relatively high-value targets as they tend to be given higher media attention and higher price tags.

This alarming increase in kidnapping reflects the reality of a booming K&R market in several regions around the globe. The K&R phenomenon has long been present in Latin American countries where it developed at an industrial scale in particular in Mexico, Colombia and Venezuela. I recall that, over lunch with members of a powerful business association in Bogotá a few years ago, Colombian businessmen entered into a verbal contest about who had the highest value on the domestic K&R market, many of them having experienced several kidnappings. Beyond Latin America, the K&R market has quickly expanded to parts of the Middle East, North Africa and Asia.

Estimating the market size is virtually impossible. Many incidents are not publicly reported and kidnappers often request that no one be informed outside those to be extorted for ransom.[36] By some estimates, the market would have reached half a billion dollars by 2010 at a time when the Somali piracy business reportedly peaked at $200m,[37] the majority of which was eventually covered by a rapidly growing K&R insurance industry.[38] A detailed breakdown of the figures provided by a specialized consultancy firm shows that NGOs as well as healthcare and education workers are among the most exposed, together with employees of energy and extractive firms and members of the security forces. Journalists accounted for 'only' 4 per cent of recorded cases in 2013–14. Estimates indicate that about two thirds of cases end with the payment of a ransom. The number of victims who have either been killed or managed to escape rose in the first semester of 2014, reaching 11 and 6 per cent of total cases respectively.[39]

The market involves a fluid mix of economically- and politically-motivated kidnappings. Aid workers and business employees kidnapped by Al Shabaab affiliates have been sold to other groups, including organized criminal groups. Syria is another case in point. By December 2014, the Islamic State in Iraq and Syria (ISIS) was believed to hold at least twenty-two foreign nationals captive in Aleppo in northern Syria. Negotiations were especially difficult because they involved a diverse range of home states and employers, each following different principles, policies and practices. ISIS had kidnapped some of the hostages directly, while it had bought or acquired others by force from other warring groups. ISIS had both political and financial demands, such as releasing prisoners in France and the United Kingdom and ransom payments. The video-recorded beheading of American and British captives in 2014 has arguably been associated with the fact that the US and the UK have not only adopted, but also implemented a strict policy not to pay any ransoms, which is not the case with many other states. In November 2014, the US administration began reviewing its policy on overseas terrorist-related hostage cases with regard to engagement with the hostage's family, intelligence collection and military engagement, while emphasizing that the ban on paying ransoms would not be reconsidered.[40]

The rationale for this policy is not only that it counters terrorism finance; it is also thought to remove the financial incentive to kidnap more nationals.[41] Drying up terrorist finance is a major counterterrorism policy objective. K&R is a low-cost tactic that can yield substantial financial return. If no ransoms were paid and no concessions granted, the market would dry up. Yet, given the human and political costs, most policymakers in democracies are not ready to implement such a policy. The US and the UK may be exceptions, but also enjoy a greater capacity to set up covert rescue operations. Besides, it is not easy for a state to prevent a family or a private company from paying a ransom for the release of a loved one or an employee, which may be all the more tempting when costs are covered by an ad hoc insurance policy.

Indeed, a whole industry has developed around the K&R problem. Specialized consultancy firms provide comprehensive service packages that range from risk monitoring to managing K&R crises, including handling relations between the hostage's family, the kidnappers and potential intermediaries.[42] The insurance industry has also become an important actor on the market. K&R insurance initially found its clientele among the US elite following a few highly publicized kidnappings such as the abduction and eventual murder of the baby-son of the aviator Charles Lindberg in 1932 or that of Patty Hearst in 1974. Worldwide, the market has grown significantly since 9/11. Insurance companies do not directly pay ransoms but typically reimburse the insured party for any ransom paid, as well as all the other related expenses, including fees paid to consultancy firms contracted to help manage the crisis.

K&R insurance is a surrealistic, Kafkaesque business filled with contradictions. First, an insured employee should not be informed about the insurance policy because of moral hazard. The insured could arguably behave in a more risky manner once aware of the coverage. Worse, he or she could co-organize a kidnapping in order to get a share of the ransom when reimbursed by the insurance. Second, kidnappers typically ask that no one be informed of the kidnapping except the employer or the family members to be extorted. Hence, informing the insurance company about the incident can put the hostage's life in danger. But the insurance company can turn down later reimbursement requests if it was not informed about the kidnapping event in a timely fashion. Third, selling K&R insurance goes against the stated policy of the US and many other countries and international organizations not to pay ransom fees to designated terrorist organizations. These ambiguities and difficulties result in rather convoluted statements by companies marketing their services, such as the following:

> At present, [K&R] is an extremely profitable coverage. But ... as more and more insurance companies see the potential for profits, loss ratios will go up as premium rates are minimized. A company that can most accurately forecast aggregate kidnapping activity and price policies accordingly stands to gain significant profits. The end goal, however, is to reduce the opportunities for kidnapping ... The insurance companies do not profit from the loss occurrences; they prevent their insureds from having to liquidate assets because of acts of terrorism. The policies align with the government goals of reducing terrorist activities.[43]

More broadly, such statements reflect the uneasiness of the international community of states when it comes to grappling with K&R. At a December 2012 meeting of the Global Counterterrorism Forum (GCTF),[44] ministers adopted the Algiers Memorandum on Good Practices on Preventing and Denying the Benefits of Kidnapping for Ransom by Terrorists. The Memorandum affirms that member countries should seek to 'Deny terrorists and terrorist organizations and their final beneficiaries the benefits of ransom—while seeking to secure the safe release of the hostage(s)—through financial, diplomatic, intelligence, law enforcement and other means and resources, as appropriate, not excluding use of force.'[45] Likewise, as the UN Security Council adopted Resolution 2133 in January 2014 calling on states to ask private sector entities not to pay ransoms in response to terrorist kidnapping, a state representative emphasized the need to strengthen measures to freeze and seize funds and other assets that are the products of hostage taking, but added that 'such measures should not undermine the possible payment of ransom for hostages'.[46] Denying terrorist organizations the benefit of ransoms while at the same time securing the safe release of hostages through financial means sounds like mission impossible.

The booming K&R market has dramatic consequences for the humanitarian sector in particular. Officially, all the major humanitarian agencies have adopted a straightforward policy: no ransoms whatsoever are to be paid.[47] For obvious reasons, it is impossible to know whether and how much third parties—often the home states of hostages—actually paid for the release of kidnapped nationals, or the arrangements struck between the different parties involved, including third parties closing the deals with the kidnappers. In any case, such incidents inflict terrible, long-lasting trauma on the victims and their families. They can also gravely affect the operational capacity of relief organizations. The risk of kidnapping may force humanitarian agencies to withdraw their staff and cut back their operations due to security concerns. The consequences can be dramatic for the vulnerable in conflict zones that end up bereft of any external humanitarian assistance and protection.

What can humanitarians do? The K&R market is set to further develop as long as the international community does not take more resolute and concerted action to dry it up. Relief organizations find themselves between a rock and a hard place, seeking to strike a balance between the need to preserve the lives of kidnapped colleagues today and the responsibility to reduce the risk of having many more staff kidnapped tomorrow. A first step is more collaboration and information exchange within the humanitarian sector itself. Aid agencies are reluctant to share information on K&R not only between different organizations, but also among different branches or sections of the same organization. Communication on K&R must obviously be done with extreme care, first and foremost to protect the victims and refrain from adding to the hostage market value. Yet, the sharing of information and best practices should not be left to private consultancy firms alone. After all, kidnappers readily exchange information about market conditions, helping each other to reach the best deals. Government intelligence services and private consultancy firms share information. Tighter cooperation and a more concerted response from the humanitarian sector are long overdue.

With respect to insurance, humanitarian organizations cover the major risks facing their staff, starting with standard travel accident insurance that excludes war risks. The latter are covered by specific war risk coverage policies sold by insurance companies such as Lloyd's of London. Kidnap, ransom and extortion coverage usually comes as another separate insurance policy that covers not only ransoms paid (or lost along the way), but often more importantly other expenses such as post-release medical care together with psychological and social rehabilitation, protection against legal liability and the advisory and crisis management support services sold by specialized firms. Despite the fact that this can make sense from a financial risk management perspective, humanitarian organizations should refrain from (or desist) contracting K&R insurance. Having such insurance makes the risk of kidnapping financially more acceptable. The resulting moral hazard provides a perverse incentive that contributes to sustaining the K&R market. There is no alternative beyond ceaselessly striving to open up and preserve a space for strictly impartial, neutral and independent humanitarian organizations to operate on the ground with the consent of warring groups, including those designated as terrorists. This, in turn, requires major donor states to grant humanitarian organizations the necessary space, including appropriate waivers in counter-terrorism legislation.

Countering Terrorism Finance

Close to 190 states are party to the International Convention for the Suppression of the Financing of Terrorism of 1999 that outlaws intentional support of terrorist acts, which makes it one of the most universal counterterrorism treaties. There is a broad consensus in research and policy circles that more stringent anti-money laundering measures and specific measures to counter the financing of terrorism implemented in the wake of 9/11 significantly deteriorated al-Qaeda and other terrorist organizations' capacities to finance their operations through formal financial institutions.

The US government gained privileged access to information on financial transactions across the globe through the database run by the Society for Worldwide Interbank Financial Telecommunication (SWIFT), a Belgian cooperative, whose back ups happened to be made on US territory. This has helped the US to track al-Qaeda finances and operatives and, more widely, to identify suspicious money transfers related not only to potential terrorist attacks, but for example also to tax evasion.[48] When made public by *The New York Times*, the wide access to confidential SWIFT data granted to the US Federal authorities sparked vivid concerns about privacy issues, particularly in Europe.[49]

CFT measures notably seek to prevent the formal financial sector from being used as a conduit in support of the commission of terrorist acts. The Financial Action Task Force (FATF)[50] has issued nine Special Recommendations against Terrorist Financing that complement forty recommendations on money laundering aimed at detecting, preventing and suppressing the financing of terrorist acts. The eighth recommendation relates to the humanitarian sector. It states that non-profit organizations should not be misused in the support of terrorism. The ensuing crack down on Islamic charities in particular has had broader implications in discouraging charitable giving to such organizations from potential donors who felt unable to carry out the required due diligence work themselves.

The CFT regime further includes the blacklisting of individuals and organizations as well as greater surveillance of informal money transfer systems (IMTS). Several IMTS firms and networks were shut down as a result. This has disrupted the financing of groups designated as terrorist organizations, but also hurt households and communities which largely depend on remittances sent via IMTS, be it in Afghanistan, Somalia or Sri Lanka. Following 9/11, the US Treasury closed down the overseas offices of the Somali informal money transfer or 'hawala' company, Al Barakaat, which equated with de facto comprehensive sanctions against Somalia. Millions of Somalis whose livelihoods depended on remittances suffered from the clampdown, while subsequent investigation could not establish any link between Al Barakaat and terrorism finance.

Sanctions and Humanitarian Exemptions: How Smart?

Counterterrorism comprises defensive measures such as strengthening the protection of potential targets and tightening the surveillance of suspects, as well as offensive measures including police, military and covert operations. In this context, economic sanctions seek to disrupt terrorism finance, as one of many instruments aimed at making terrorism costlier and less effective.[51]

More generally, imposing sanctions has been considered as an alternative to going to war, or as an option among a range of actions that can be taken against armed groups and belligerent countries. In this section, I thus consider economic sanctions beyond the sole case of counterterrorism. States have long used economic sanctions as a foreign policy instrument targeting states, or specific regions within a state, or specific groups, sectors, firms and individuals. Sanctions aim to signal the disapproval of the countries imposing the sanctions (this is the 'signalling effect'), to push for behavioural change ('coercion'), or simply to constrain and limit the target's agency. For example, the UN sanctions against al-Qaeda are intended to constrain the organization rather than to coerce its behaviour: no one expects economic sanctions to force the terrorist organization to surrender or abandon its fight. Indeed, sanctions appear in general more successful in constraining than in coercing the target's behaviour. Evidence on the effectiveness of targeted sanctions drawn from a database on UN sanctions highlights that sanction regimes have been successful in coercing change in only about 10 per cent of cases, while they have been more successful in signalling and constraining, with a success rate of 27 per cent.[52] In the third edition of *Economic Sanctions Reconsidered*, released in 2007, lead authors from the Peterson Institute for International Economics present findings based on the study of 204 sanctions over a century, with an emphasis on sanctions imposed by the US. They find that economic sanctions failed to achieve their foreign policy objectives in about two-thirds of the cases. In a third of them, sanctions at least partially achieved their initial aims. As expected, the success rate appears greater in the case of sanctions against democratic countries that have relatively dense trade and financial relations with the sender countries. The impact is weak when it comes to autocracies that had few trade and financial relations with sender countries before the sanctions.

The US was and remains a leading sender country, including comprehensive sanctions against Sudan and Iran, among others. Since the record of multilateral sanctions has improved over the past few years compared with unilateral sanctions, the US now tends to pursue sanctions more often in association with other sender countries and, in particular, the UN and the European Union (EU). The latter has been a strong proponent of targeted or so-called 'smart' sanctions instead of comprehensive ones.[53] Comprehensive sanctions inflict pain on the target country as a whole. The negative humanitarian consequences have generally been found to outweigh the political gains, leading to the conclusion that comprehensive sanctions are not a humane alternative to warfare. Because of the dire humanitarian consequences caused by such a blunt instrument, since the 1990s the UN, the EU and even the US have come to favour targeted sanctions. Although since then the UN has maintained some comprehensive sanction regimes, it has not imposed new comprehensive sanctions since 1994 (on Haiti).

Targeted sanctions have widely been referred to as 'smart': this normative labelling served as a slogan to help build a political consensus around sanctions reform. Implying that comprehensive sanctions are a somewhat 'stupid' instrument, sender countries started to replace them with 'smart' sanctions. The latter seek to reduce the adverse impact on the civilian population and cushion the pain inflicted to the vulnerable by hitting specific individuals and groups such as political leaders, rebels, companies and criminals. Yet, targeted sanctions sometimes target entire economic sectors or regions. In practice, the humanitarian consequences of targeted sanctions can be similar to those of comprehensive sanctions. This has been the case for instance with the widening of targeted sanctions against Iran since 2012 by the EU and others, including trade bans, oil embargoes and restrictions on financial flows.[54]

Several studies have focused on the humanitarian impact of sanctions over the past two decades, most notably the UN sanctions imposed on Iraq from 1990 to 2003. Isolating the specific effects of sanctions from those of other factors is highly challenging. Yet, the eventual impact on public health has repeatedly been found to be negative and substantial, even in the case of targeted sanctions. Since the end of the 1990s, humanitarian exemptions have become standard practice in UN Security Council resolutions imposing sanctions. Despite such exemptions, which allow trade in essential goods and services (food and medicines in particular), the long-term impact of sanctions on the health of the target country's population has often been significant. Financial sanctions in particular disrupt the inflow of remittances and cash assistance, and this is compounded by the withdrawal of development assistance and the gradual deterioration of healthcare education and knowledge as a consequence of long-term sanctions.

Besides, economic sanctions tend to have strong criminalizing effects. They often end up boosting the economic and political power of sanctions busters who circumvent trade and financial bans, as illustrated by the much-publicized UN oil-for-food scandal in the case of Iraq. The US Congress estimated that Iraqis with close ties to Saddam Hussein's regime earned more than $10bn illegally from smuggling oil and extorting kickbacks from firms trading through the UN's oil-for-food programme between 1997 and 2002.[55] These criminal networks do not 'evaporate' once the sanction regimes are lifted but continue to operate in the post-sanction, post-war period, which may adversely impact peacebuilding, statebuilding and reconstruction.

The criminal circuits established to circumvent the oil embargo on Iraq did not simply disappear after 2003, which made it more difficult for the new Iraqi government to capture all of the oil rent. A decade later, when ISIS gained full territorial control over parts of Northern Iraq and adjacent Syria, long-established oil smuggling circuits facilitated the illegal sales of oil that boosted the terrorist organization's war chest (see also Chapter 3).[56] ISIS gained control of a majority of oilfields in Syria and a few small fields in Iraq, giving it an estimated production capacity of up to 80,000 barrels of crude a day, some of which is processed in bootleg refineries. The group sold oil at a discounted price—allegedly between $25 and $40 a barrel while the international price was above $100. The middlemen included Iraqi, Syrian, Turkish and Iranian 'entrepreneurs' who had grown rich, connected and powerful during the earlier UN embargo against Iraq, and have revived their networks. International trading houses are wary of inadvertently commercializing crude extracted from ISIS-held oil fields. But unlike diamonds, oil is liquid: tracing its origin is difficult since it can readily be blended with crude from other origins.

The targeted sanctions imposed on Myanmar from 1997 onward illustrate the detrimental impact of 'smart' economic sanctions, but also the difficulty of identifying the impact of sanctions versus that of foreign investors' concerns, economic mismanagement and additional domestic policy variables. To start with, the abrupt withdrawal of Western Official Development Assistance (ODA) following the ban of non-humanitarian assistance to Myanmar by the EU and the US in 1996 affected the delivery of social services, primary healthcare and education in particular. Second, targeted sanctions included trade, financial, travel-related restrictions and an arms embargo. This impact was further aggravated by several domestic factors: ethnic discrimination and exclusion, civil war, the disaster caused by the May 2008 Cyclone Nargis, institutional fragility and weak infrastructure. The military regime responded by further reducing the share of total public expenditure allocated to social services, regardless of the fact that these sectors were particularly affected by the withdrawal of ODA, while it raised defence expenditures to maintain its military capability despite the arms embargo, which meant turning to alternative and more expensive sources.

The main issue here is that, except for very specific sanctions such as individual travel bans and asset freezes, the eventual cost of targeted sanctions can transfer onto the vulnerable. Just like foreign aid, sanctions are fungible. The sanctioned elite can transfer the burden onto weaker segments of society, for example by reducing social expenditures or preying on civilians to compensate for losses. In Iraq for instance, Saddam Hussein tended to channel the few resources available to support agricultural development in the Sunni heartland at the expense of Shia-dominated regions in the south of the country.

Sender countries have become aware of (some of) these pitfalls. They have inserted humanitarian exemptions into sanction regimes and counterterrorism legislation. At times, they have supported relief organizations precisely with the aim of cushioning civilians from the most severe humanitarian consequences of the sanctions, being concerned to render sanctions more acceptable to their own domestic constituencies. Yet, the same sender countries have made the cushioning of civilians from the humanitarian consequences of sanctions much harder through the enactment of counterterrorist legislation. Donor countries such as the US, the UK, Canada and Australia have adopted a battery of administrative, civil and criminal laws to ensure that no taxpayer money ends up in the hands of designated terrorist groups. Humanitarian organizations risk being fined or workers imprisoned for the inadvertent transfer of resources to terrorist actors, even if they had no intention whatsoever of supporting terrorist acts.[57]

In addition, donors have pushed for the inclusion of counterterrorism-related clauses in funding contracts. These require humanitarian organizations to exert due diligence, for example through careful screening of their staff and of implementing partner organizations against dozens of lists linking individuals and groups to terrorism suspects. Expanded due diligence may even require the screening of aid beneficiaries. Principled humanitarian organizations resist screening ultimate beneficiaries or denying them the right to assistance on the basis of potential sympathy for, or ties with, listed terrorist groups. This would go against the essential principle of impartiality. Besides, this could be perceived as evidence that humanitarian organizations lack independence and are not neutral. Finally, the withdrawal of medical assistance to individuals requiring healthcare on the basis of alleged ties to designated groups would violate medical ethics.

A 2013 study commissioned by the United Nations Office for the Coordination of Humanitarian Affairs (UNOCHA) and the Norwegian Refugee Council examined the impact of counterterrorism laws and donor measures in Somalia and the occupied Palestinian Territories. The combined effects at the structural, operational and administrative levels have been found to substantially reduce the acceptance, outreach and reactivity of humanitarian organizations, negatively affecting their capacity to respond to the needs for assistance and protection while increasing administrative costs and hurdles.[58] The authors conclude by calling on states and inter-governmental bodies to refrain from inhibiting on-the-ground engagement and negotiation with designated armed groups that de facto control territory and humanitarian access to the civilian population. Counterterrorism laws and regulations not only create many obstacles for the delivery of aid, but they also result in humanitarian agencies preferring self-restraint over taking the risk of providing assistance in murky circumstances where they may antagonize large donors and face unclear legal liability risks.

Some scholars have argued for shifting counterterrorism approaches towards relying more on carrots and less on sticks. The idea is to use foreign aid—together with other measures to reduce people's grievances—with a view to making peaceful alternatives more attractive to potential terrorist recruits, which increases the opportunity cost of joining or supporting terrorist organizations.[59]

Aid, Counterterrorism and Counterinsurgency

Humanitarian and development assistance is partly based on the assumption that aid can be an effective instrument to counter terrorism and insurgencies. For over a decade, the top recipients of ODA worldwide have included Afghanistan, Iraq, Pakistan and other contexts where designated terrorist groups operate. The precise causal pathways in which aid may reduce terrorism and support counterinsurgency largely remain to be theorized and better understood, notwithstanding a few empirical studies that support the argument that foreign aid can decrease terrorism.[60]

With foreign aid promoted as a recipe to fight terrorism, the US military in particular became progressively more involved in the delivery of assistance, for example by distributing relief goods directly to the local Afghan population in the context of hearts-and-minds campaigns to muster the support of local communities.[61] The 2006 US Army Counterinsurgency (COIN) Field Manual affirms that 'COIN programs for political, social, and economic well-being are essential to developing the local capacity that commands popular support.'[62] At an operational level, the US Commander's Emergency Response Programs (CERP) in Iraq and Afghanistan put over $6 billion into the hands of US Army brigade commanders, 'to respond with a nonlethal weapon to urgent, small-scale, humanitarian relief, and reconstruction projects and services that immediately assist the indigenous population and that the local population or government can sustain.'[63] Aid is expected to 'win the hearts and minds' of local community members: hearts through the provision of aid, and minds through economic opportunities that increase the opportunity costs of joining or supporting the rebellion. The mechanisms through which to achieve such results remain poorly specified and the empirical evidence displays mixed outcomes. The 2006 US Army COIN Manual draws some of its inspiration from anti-communist counterinsurgency warfare of the 1960s and 1970s. The civilian population is conceived of as uncommitted. The loyalty of local community members is thought to be up for grabs by one of the warring parties through the provision of superior goods and services, including security.[64] Such assumptions do not hold in many of today's armed conflicts fought along sectarian and ethnic lines, where individual decisions to side with the government or with the insurgents can hardly be dissociated from identity considerations.

A few recent quantitative and qualitative studies have sought to uncover if such aid programmes have led to more stability or more violence, with an emphasis on Iraq and Afghanistan. Interestingly, they do not reach the same conclusions. The quantitative studies, based on (quasi-)experimental research designs, are not all framed the same way but tend to share the same theoretical underpinnings. They are part of a welcome drive to use more robust impact evaluation methods to measure the effectiveness of aid interventions in humanitarian crises, including experimental identification methods (randomized controlled trials or RCTs) and quasi-experimental ones (e.g. regression discontinuity, difference in difference).[65]

Studies typically consider the interactions between three sets of actors: the insurgents or designated terrorists, the civilian population, and the government and its foreign allies. Foreign aid is conceived as a stake in a contest between the government and the insurgency: aid can improve the way the population perceives the state and provides an incentive to share strategic information or 'intelligence' with governmental and foreign allied forces. This in turn may lead to a drop in the number of attacks. The findings remain largely inconclusive, to say the least. Some find evidence in support of the hypothesis that aid reduces violence by weakening the insurgents' popular base. Others conclude that the instrumentalization of aid in hearts-and-minds campaigns leads the insurgents to intensify their attacks against the 'beneficiary' or recipient communities with a view to severing the ties between them and aid providers.

Let us consider research findings on aid effectiveness in winning the hearts and minds of Afghans. A majority of the quantitative studies match data on aid handouts with data on violent incidents. They find aid to have either a positive or a neutral impact with regard to lowering the level of violence and improving the attitude of Afghans towards their government:

- A randomized field experiment concluded that the Afghan National Solidarity Program (NSP)—a large-scale aid programme devised in 2002 to improve service delivery and infrastructure in rural areas while building participatory governance at local levels—has significantly improved the villagers' wellbeing as well as their attitude towards the government, at least in those districts where the initial level of violence was moderate. The researchers conclude that 'the findings provide general support for the strategy of winning "hearts and minds" through development projects',[66] most notably by increasing the opportunity cost of joining the rebellion.

- Another quantitative study found no clear impact on rebel violence associated with the NSP nor with the CERP.[67] The researcher questions, in particular, why CERP spending does not appear to be effective in Afghanistan, contrary to an earlier study that found CERP handouts have lowered the number of violent incidents in Iraq. The Iraq study found the population to accept sharing information in return for the provision of public goods.[68] In the Afghan case, the researcher finds anecdotal evidence that small-scale CERP projects, in which disbursements are less bureaucratic and subject to lower oversight, may have provided a tactical advantage when aid was made conditional on intelligence sharing. The study hence concludes: 'the importance of conditionality implies that future efforts to use reconstruction as a tool to increase stability could benefit from a greater emphasis or stronger guidelines about aid provision and community cooperation.'[69] However, a subsequent study revisited these findings by considering a much longer time frame and including broader geographical coverage and found no significant effect of CERP handouts on violence, be it the case of large- or small-scale projects.[70]

- Other researchers inquired into whether development assistance helped 'stabilize' Afghanistan by looking at the subjective perceptions of community members regarding security threats and attitudes towards foreign civilian and military actors. Based on a micro-level longitudinal study of eighty communities in relatively secure areas of northeast Afghanistan, they found no evidence that aid significantly impacted feelings of security or attitudes towards international actors. Aid may however have contributed to enhancing the government's legitimacy in a few instances. This is, in particular, the case for visible infrastructure projects perceived by the beneficiary population as significantly improving their livelihood, for example in the case of water and electricity provision projects.[71]

Intriguingly, qualitative field research covering the same time period and conducted in Kabul and five Afghan provinces reached radically more negative conclusions. Based on interviews and focus group discussions with community members and representatives of relevant institutions, it appears that a majority of Afghans have developed negative perceptions. The abuse, misuse and unfair allocation of aid have led to mistrust towards the government and the aid enterprise in Afghanistan. This had particularly destabilizing effects in highly contested areas where there was greater pressure to spend money quickly.[72] Afghans expressed more positive views on a few long-serving relief agencies that had built a strong relationship with communities. Echoing findings of other studies, tangible NSP projects in the infrastructure sector garnered some positive feedback. The researchers do not deny that 'winning hearts and minds' projects may have brought short-term benefits at the tactical level in a few instances where enhanced intelligence gathering had a positive outcome for the security of international forces. Yet, they add that 'there was little concrete evidence in any of the five provinces that aid projects were having more strategic level stabilization or security benefits such as winning populations away from insurgents, legitimizing the government, or reducing levels of violent conflict.'[73]

Comparing the findings above requires caution. The studies differ in their methodologies and timeframes. They consider different aid projects, security incidents and attitudes in different locations. Notwithstanding this, they produce somewhat contradictory recommendations. The question is then which ones exert the greatest influence on policymakers? One may assume that it is those quantitative studies that benefitted from privileged access to restricted information on the number and location of insurgency attacks and on foreign-funded aid programmes, since the policymakers who granted access to the researchers may obviously have a keen interest in the findings. It so happens that the studies with findings most supportive of, for instance, CERP in hearts-and-minds campaigns are those that benefited from funding and/or privileged access to data from institutions with a direct stake in CERP, such as the US Department of Defense.[74] This is not to imply that these studies lack scientific rigor. But it begs the question of whether policymakers only consider those studies that they supported or further factor in contradictory findings from other studies into their analysis. This, in turn, raises the question of what lessons they draw regarding the (mis)use of aid in counterinsurgency campaigns.

Other field experiments have started to be carried out on the impact of aid in the fight against listed terrorist organizations in contexts beyond Afghanistan and Iraq. Looking at a large community-driven development (CDD) programme in the Philippines, a 2014 study found that the prospect of the CDD programme mustering popular support for the government caused an increase in insurgent attacks in those municipalities that were slightly above the eligibility threshold and thus benefited from the CDD. No such increase was registered in the municipalities that were slightly below the eligibility threshold. The study concludes that insurgents sought to prevent the implementation of a state-sponsored aid package that could undermine their popular support base in CDD-eligible communities.[75] How can we expect local community members to react? In a rational choice framework, preferences for the CDD depend on the expected benefits accruing from the aid projects and on the costs associated with the risk of insurgent reprisals. Other factors need to be taken into account in addition to this basic cost-benefit calculus, such as whether insurgents originate from the very communities targeted by the CDD programme and thus have intimate links with the aid recipients.

The theory behind the design of empirical studies on aid effectiveness in counterinsurgency and counterterrorism campaigns needs to be revisited. For example, if aid recipients believe that the provision of assistance and security will only be temporary, it is rational not to change alignment to the extent that aid organizations and foreign military troops are soon expected to leave and the insurgency to return. The deterioration of the security situation and chaos that followed the withdrawal of massive foreign military support from Afghanistan, Libya and Iraq points to the fact that local communities may be better advised to play all sides. The situation would be different if local communities believed that the provision of welfare and security was a long-term commitment, providing an incentive to shift alignment away from the rebels. Preferences can also change with the introduction of an aid programme. A field experiment in post-conflict Liberia found that CDD succeeded in enhancing community cohesion over a short period of time in the reconstruction phase,[76] introducing new institutional dynamics. Empirically, research should further distinguish between aid programmes based on their stated and implicit aims, temporal horizons and supply chains.

Using aid as a soft weapon in war puts the 'aid beneficiaries' in a lose-lose situation. Time and again, experience shows that each warring party asks civilians to cooperate with them and to refrain from cooperating with the other, which often leaves civilians little choice but to play the dangerous game of playing both sides.

Concluding Remarks

Just as in the case of conflict analysis, rational actor models are relevant and useful for uncovering specific causal links in the case of terrorism, in conjunction with insights from other disciplines such as social anthropology and political science. Conceptual frameworks and empirical studies that narrowly focus on cost-benefit or 'sacrifice-reward' analysis to explain terrorist acts, discarding the role of emotions, identity, and political motivations, may lead to policy recommendations that overly emphasize deterrence to the detriment of addressing deeper root causes, and that favour tactical over strategic gains.

The track record of sanction regimes in combatting terrorism so far is poor. Successes have been registered with regard to curtailing terrorist finance via legal channels. But overall, sanctions have proved relatively ineffective in achieving their stated goals while often having adverse humanitarian impacts and strengthening criminal networks that cash in millions by circumventing the sanctions. Such networks pose a threat to post-conflict rebuilding. They can remain vibrant years after sanctions are lifted, as illustrated in Iraq and Syria in the case of oil and ISIS finance. Further research is required to understand how UN Security Council decisions in New York translate first into domestic legislation and administrative measures at the country level, and how they are then operationalized by firms and humanitarian agencies where compliance officers carry out careful due diligence work. Being risk averse, compliance officers may simply instruct not to engage where it is not possible to provide solid guarantees. On that basis, even targeted sanctions combined with humanitarian exemptions may de facto be tantamount to blind, comprehensive sanctions.

It is in the interest of humanitarian sector actors to join forces and argue firmly for lifting those provisions in counterterrorism regulations and sanction regimes that jeopardize impartial humanitarian action. The same applies to the need for more concerted and resolute action vis-à-vis K&R. Even if it appears reasonable from a financial risk management viewpoint, humanitarian organizations should resist contracting K&R insurance to avert the moral hazard and incentive to take on greater risks. For neutral, impartial and independent humanitarian organizations, the acceptance strategy remains the best chance to preserve a licence to operate in the most difficult environments. In the long run, such humanitarian engagement can have a positive transformative power.

Rigorous impact evaluation methods have started to be used more often in humanitarian settings. Yet, mixed evidence on the effectiveness of foreign aid and CDD programmes calls into question some of the theoretical underpinnings that guide empirical research on the impact of aid in combating listed terrorist organizations in the context of counterinsurgency campaigns. The opportunity-cost argument is not supported by available evidence, especially when looking beyond short-term tactical gains. Hearts-and-minds disbursements made conditional on the sharing of intelligence may actually antagonize civilians by putting them under greater risk of insurgent reprisal or—if they refuse to cooperate—of government reprisal for allegedly colluding with designated terrorist groups. Besides, the way host communities perceive the state and its foreign allies does not depend solely or even primarily on the provision of aid, but rather on other interventions such as poppy field eradication or repressive measures involving IHL violations. It is no surprise that the findings from subjective perception surveys do not conform to those from quantitative studies based on experimental research designs. How actor discourse is interpreted must of course be questioned, but no more than the quality and relevance of datasets on the intensity and location of violent incidents or of data on aid project funding. Against this backdrop, interdisciplinary research involving economists and so-called 'a-theoretical aborigines' (see Chapter 1) can help to address contradictory findings up front and combine insights from different approaches to challenge and revisit dubious hypotheses and enhance our theoretical framework.

5

DISASTER ECONOMICS

What is a cynic?
A man who knows the price of everything and the value of nothing.
And a sentimentalist ... is a man who sees an absurd value in everything, and doesn't
know the market price of any single thing.

Oscar Wilde, 1893[1]

Throughout history and across religious traditions, disasters have been equated with the wrath of God(s)—or the ire of Mother Nature herself. Faith and mourning rituals have helped survivors when seeking to make sense of the destruction and to heal from the trauma. Yet, it is not by divine design that the poor are significantly more exposed to disasters than the non-poor.[2] The death toll caused by natural hazards of comparable nature and intensity tends to be systematically higher in poor countries than in rich ones, even after controlling for demographic density, urbanization and other such variables. Inequality plays a central role in explaining how natural hazards turn into deadly disasters for specific groups within and across countries.[3] Besides, research shows that over half of the people affected by disasters between 2005 and 2009 were living in conflict-prone and fragile states,[4] suggesting a perverse cycle between war and disaster through weak institutions.

Disasters as a Socio-Economic Construct

Events such as earthquakes, storms, droughts and cyclones can be conceived of as natural hazards. The extent to which such hazards become disasters largely depends on the actions and preparedness of humans.[5] Many scholars have shown how quake- and weather-related disasters are socially constructed and determined,[6] just as Amartya Sen has shown how famine results from political and economic failures rather than a lack of food supply that can simply be imputed to adverse climatic events.[7] Disasters are by no means exogenous to the development process. They are embedded in social transformations and political economy interactions.[8]

Climate-related disasters are surging worldwide. But whether people suffer or not depends on where they live. Rising sea levels and ensuing flood risks affect the coastal plains of Bangladesh as much as they affect the Netherlands' lowlands or the Thames estuary. However, tidal flood risk exposure can be very high or minimal depending on whether you live in Chittagong, Amsterdam or London. The complex system of floodgates, barriers and dikes meant to protect London and Dutch towns from floods are the visible infrastructure that provides the British and the Dutch with greater protection than the Bangladeshis. Of course, the protective devices have to be fit for the purpose of resisting rare, extreme events. Dikes were not up to the job of preventing floods in New Orleans following Hurricane Katrina in 2005, nor could they avert the Fukushima nuclear accident following the 2012 Tohoku quake. In instances where protective measures fail to withstand the shock, the ensuing disaster tends to be worse than it would have been had the measures not been in place at all: the sense of protection provided by preventive infrastructure such as dikes encourages people to settle and invest in hazard-prone areas to a greater extent than in the absence of such infrastructure.

Institutions play a critical role in reducing vulnerability and increasing resilience over the long run. Let us take the example of storms that cut across the Hispaniola Island. Needless to say, the winds and rainfalls do not stop at the border between Haiti and the Dominican Republic that splits the island in two. Why then do Haitians typically incur greater mudslides and losses when a violent storm hits both sides of the border? A dense forest covers the Dominican Republic border in contrast to the bare hills in neighbouring Haiti. But forests or physical infrastructure are only a small part of the story. The institutional arrangements that support them are invisible but no less primordial. Compared with adjoining Haiti, which suffered decades of misrule, the Dominican Republic has developed an institutional framework more propitious to preserve the forest cover:

> Vibrant communities ensure that trees are not thoughtlessly felled and that saplings planted grow. Even if the interests of uplanders who cut the trees diverge from

those of the lowlanders who get the mud flows, communities bridge the difference and manage the fair use of the commons. Prosperity ultimately depends on rebuilding the trust and social capital that was lost even before the earthquake and hurricane struck.[9]

Unlike to the reconstruction of physical capital, there is no quick fix to (re) build institutions and social capital, as Bill Clinton found when he served as the UN Special Envoy to Haiti. Following the January 2010 earthquake, the grand design of 'Building Back Better' quickly faced the hard reality of weak state institutions, widespread insecurity and a sudden cholera outbreak for which the humanitarian community was ill-prepared, not to mention weaknesses embedded in the foreign aid system itself.[10]

This example highlights the central role of socially constructed institutions in determining the level of exposure or the vulnerability of a given population to disaster risks. Thus, the level of risk does not depend only on the occurrence and intensity of a natural hazard, but on the exposure or vulnerability to such risk, which can be summarized as:

$$Risk = f(hazard \times exposure)$$

The extent to which a natural hazard translates into a disaster is further mediated by the response capacity of those groups affected by the hazard, another social construct that is often equated with 'resilience'. This simple relationship can be formulated as follows:

$$Disaster = f\left(\frac{Hazard \times Vulnerability}{Resilience}\right)$$

The numerator, *Hazard x Vulnerability*, is somewhat similar to the notion of risk. It expresses the level of exposure to shocks and combines the frequency and intensity of natural hazards with the proportion of the population potentially affected. The latter depends on demographic density, type and quality of urban planning and buildings, location and quality of critical infrastructure, the level of poverty, inequality and social exclusion, and so forth. Vulnerability further depends on the type of decisions people make (or are forced into making): affluent people may have a strong preference for living on the coast to enjoy direct access to and a view of the sea. Urbanization and demographic growth may push the poor into marginal and more exposed areas. Farmers may seek to live and stay in flood plains or by river beds where water is abundant.[11] The denominator, *Resilience*, relates to the ability of a population to adapt to and recover from disasters. Chapter 7 discusses the burgeoning literature on the resilience paradigm in the context of humanitarian and development assistance. For now, suffice it to say that resilience captures the capacity of those hit by disasters to withstand and adapt to the shock and to bounce back in its aftermath.

Over the past decades, thousands of lives were saved through preventive measures, as in the case of the 1991 Mount Pinatubo volcanic eruption that affected a densely populated area in the Philippines. People living close to the volcano were evacuated in time and hundreds of millions of dollars in property saved thanks to timely forecasts by the Philippine Institute of Volcanology and Seismology together with the US Geological Survey. The fact that disasters are socially constructed and that 'natural disaster' is a misnomer is now widely acknowledged. Yet, 'natural disaster' keeps appearing in policy documents and remains widely used in common parlance. The concept of *natural* hazard itself has started to be contested. The increasing magnitude and frequency of weather-related hazards appears to be related to the anthropogenic nature of rapid climate change, even if scientific rigour calls for caution when associating particular events with human-induced global warming. Even the occurrence of geological hazards can be associated with economic activity such as drilling for geothermal energy, carbon sequestration, or shale gas and tight oil extraction. Several geothermal projects have been suspended in the past few years in the wake of quakes and aftershocks associated with drilling activities.

Economic Costs and Humanitarian Consequences

The vast literature on the consequences of disaster is very diverse in terms of theoretical and methodological underpinnings, methods, definitions and temporal horizons. Empirical studies usually distinguish between direct, immediate costs that can be attributed strictly to the occurrence of a disaster and the wider, longer-term consequences that encompass both direct and indirect effects. Cost-benefit analysis serves to compare the efficiency of investing in ex-ante preventive measures rather than in ex-post relief and recovery programmes.[12]

Assessing the direct consequences of disasters can be relatively straightforward in industrialized countries, less so in some developing countries where data can be more difficult to collect. The immediate effects are clearly negative. Assessing them involves the grim accounting of lives lost, people injured and displaced, houses and productive assets destroyed, supply of essential goods and services disrupted, and so on. Global estimates vary depending on their sources and actual coverage. Some studies exclude slow-onset disasters such as drought while others focus primarily on insured losses. In industrialized countries, insurance companies and the state are able to ascertain the overall total disaster costs in a relatively detailed manner since a substantial share of the losses are insured, which translate into claims and pay-outs. In developing countries, where most of the losses are not insured, disaster costs tend to be grossly underreported.

In their joint report entitled *Natural Hazard—Unnatural Disasters* (2010), the World Bank and the United Nations reported that 3.3 million people died from natural hazards between 1970 and 2008, with drought being the deadliest hazard. Over that period, drought took a toll of roughly one million people in Africa alone.[13] Yet, worldwide, Asia is the region with the greatest exposure to disaster risks. The Continent accounts for more than half of the global deaths from disasters over the last four decades.[14] As detailed in Chapter 2, regional disparities in terms of economic losses and human suffering are huge. For example, Hurricane Sandy, which hit the US East Coast in October 2012, took fifty-five lives in North America while it is not commonly known that the human toll was actually higher in the Caribbean, with an estimated seventy-one lives lost. A year later, Typhoon Hayan killed above 7,500 people in Southeast Asia, injuring another 27,000.[15]

The longer-term, overall impact of disaster is much more difficult to evaluate. It remains a controversial issue both from a theoretical and empirical viewpoint. Referring to the notion of creative destruction developed by the Austrian economist Joseph Schumpeter in the mid-twentieth century,[16] several scholars argue that disasters stimulate economic growth in the long run. Disaster precipitates the destruction of the old and thus makes way for the new faster than would otherwise be the case (see Chapter 7 on the transformative power of disasters). Based on a Schumpeterian model of endogenous growth, Aghion and Howitt find that disaster accelerates capital replacement associated with technological change, which increases productivity and generates a positive economic impact.[17] Under endogenous growth theory,[18] the destruction brought about by disasters can be seen as a form of accelerated capital depreciation that leads to the rapid adoption of new technology and infrastructure upgrading, which increases productivity. This is part of the theoretical foundations behind building back better (BBB).

Those who are more pessimistic about the consequences of disasters often invoke the 'broken window fallacy', which was described by the French economist and political figure Frédéric Bastiat in 1850.[19] He argued that seeing the overall impact on the economy as positive because reconstruction stimulates demand ignores the opportunity costs. As an illustration, let's say that a house owner has to replace a window after a hurricane. This will enhance the glazier's turnover, with a positive multiplier effect on the economy. But imagine that the house owner had planned to buy new shoes. He may have to postpone that expense to be able to pay for the window. This, in turn, is bad business for the shoemaker. At the end of the day, the house owner has a new window but must keep walking in worn-out shoes. Following a similar logic, Benson and Clay remark that public expenditure allocated to post-disaster relief and reconstruction cannot be allocated to the investments that were planned in the first place.[20] This is a critical argument in particular when considering disaster-affected states that are under tight budget constraints.

Similarly, in the case of foreign aid, donors may simply disburse at once the aid that was already budgeted over several years, reducing future development assistance flows to pay for immediate disaster response. A recent study analyzed how official development assistance (ODA) fluctuated after large disasters between 1970 and 2008. The findings show a median increase of 18 per cent in ODA after disasters (above the mean of thirty-one people killed per million inhabitants). This surge in aid typically covers no more than 3 per cent of total disaster losses, hinting at the need for disaster-hit countries to find alternative funding sources for recovery.[21] Several studies conclude that disasters produce clearly negative outcomes when factoring into the equation not only opportunity costs, but also the climate of uncertainty associated with the occurrence of frequent disasters, which tends to discourage investment.[22]

A devastating earthquake hit the Japanese port city of Kobe in 1995, killing 6,400, making some 300,000 homeless, and causing over $100bn-worth of damages. A few months later, many of the disaster scars had disappeared. Media reports hailed the astounding post-disaster recovery. Economic growth in the region surpassed expectations in the two years that followed the disaster.[23] However, a closer look at the Kobe recovery calls for caution. The city was running the sixth largest commercial port worldwide before the earthquake. Five years later, the port ranked at only number forty-seven in spite of massive investment in reconstruction.[24]

Empirically, identifying the long-term impact and indirect effects of disasters is much more challenging than simply accounting for the immediate effects. The lack of appropriate counterfactuals is an obstacle to figuring out how differently the situation would have evolved in the absence of disaster.

Besides, a majority of empirical studies rely on disaster cost data from insurance companies, which leads to estimation bias since disasters in low-income countries tend to be under-reported. Just as for costing the impact of war, the reliability of macroeconomic data in low-income countries is low, in particular in conflict- and disaster-affected countries in Africa.[25] With these caveats in mind, disaster losses have followed a steep ascending curve in recent decades (see Chapter 2). While disasters have received about a fifth of total humanitarian assistance, the damage from all natural hazards between 1970 and 2008 reached $2,300bn (in 2008 dollars), roughly equivalent to 0.23 per cent of cumulative world output.[26] For individual countries particularly exposed to disasters, losses can easily reach 3.5 per cent of GDP or more.[27]

Not all disasters affect the economy or sectors of the economy in the same way. The overall impact varies depending on the type, location and intensity of hazards. Severe quakes are relatively infrequent geological events that tend to be highly disruptive. As such, they may be more conducive to the Schumpeterian type of creative destruction and innovation discussed above. Weather-related events tend to hit highly exposed regions with greater frequency, which in turn can instil an atmosphere of uncertainty that discourages investment and slows down economic growth. A study comprising a large panel of countries over a period of forty-five years concludes that severe disasters, regardless of the type of hazards, have strong negative consequences on economic output. When it comes to disasters of lesser intensity, the impact can turn positive in the case of flooding, but not in the case of drought where the impact remains negative regardless of intensity.[28] At a more regional level, a study of the effects of disasters on GDP per capita and the debt-to-GDP ratio in twelve Caribbean countries over forty years finds that both storms and floods—whose prevalence is relatively high in the region—negatively affect growth while only floods increase the relative level of indebtedness.[29] When looking at the distribution of costs and benefits within disaster-affected societies, several large-N studies involving household surveys highlight that the poorest tend to suffer most. This is not surprising to the extent that more than half of the world's poorest depend on agricultural labour and are thus particularly exposed to extreme and chronic weather events[30] that may keep them trapped in poverty and indebtedness.[31]

A weakness of the empirical literature is that GDP growth generally serves as the dependent variable to ascertain the costs of disasters. As a flow indicator, GDP does not register the destruction of capital stocks, be it natural, physical or human capital. It only captures the impact of disaster on output. Environmental accounting offers alternative indicators that capture variations in capital stock levels, including natural capital. Putting a price on natural capital raises methodological and ethical issues, and several approaches have been developed to establish the shadow price of assets from which we derive many benefits that are not internalized by the market. For example, it has been calculated that maintaining the mangrove forests that had existed on India's East Coast in 1950 would have avoided 92 per cent of the approximately 1,000 deaths caused by the violent cyclone that hit the State of Odisha in 1999. When internalizing these costs, the value of a hectare of land with intact mangrove forests appears to be significantly higher than the market value of cleared land, even when adding the cost of mangrove regeneration on that land.[32] Empirical research on disaster costs should consider the impact on capital stock levels and could examine how a disaster affects genuine savings[33] over time. This would allow for variations in natural, physical and human capital stocks to be traced, thus taking into account the impact on sustainability—albeit to a limited extent since genuine saving is a weak sustainability indicator.[34]

Insuring Against Disaster Risks

When a disaster hits high-income economies, losses are often insured. When the rich are hit, health insurance pays for medical care and rehabilitation. Life insurance and social security schemes support surviving family members when the breadwinners have died or are incapacitated. Insurance pay-outs compensate for property losses (albeit less so in the case of earthquakes or acts of terrorism).[35] By contrast, insurance is a luxury that hardly anyone in low-income countries can afford. Back in 2008, virtually all of the losses caused by Cyclone Nargis in Myanmar were uninsured, and it seriously affected some 1.5m people, killing over 84,000. The same year, a mere 0.4 per cent of the losses incurred in neighbouring China as a result of the Great Sichuan Earthquake were insured, with insurance claims totalling approximately $300m against direct losses amounting to some $80bn.[36]

Humanity neither waited for insurance companies nor for aid organizations to address the risks associated with disasters. Solidarity mechanisms and mutual support have long played a central role in alleviating the plight of those community members facing extraordinary losses as a result of fire, flood, illness or death. Covering risks related to death has been a permanent concern throughout history. Researchers have found testimony of a Roman burial fund dating back from the early second century of our era.[37] The fund served as a collective saving instrument popular among the military and poorer segments of Roman society. The community members who contributed to the fund were then able to get financial support to cover the costs associated with burying their loved ones with dignity.

Yet, such mutual support mechanisms risk collapsing when a large-scale scourge hits the community as a whole, or if the damage is just too high. In the context of the expansion of world trade and the first industrial revolution, the insurance industry started developing at scale, including vis-à-vis natural hazard risks. Mutual insurance companies became common as a scaled-up version of mutual support schemes. Weather-related insurance already existed by the end of the eighteenth century, for example with hailstorm risk insurance in Mecklenburg.[38] Primary insurers soon faced difficulties as large-scale disasters affected growing urban centres: many insurance companies were overwhelmed by the scale of the disasters and simply went bankrupt. Today's largest reinsurance companies, Munich Re and Swiss Re, emerged in response to disastrous fires that ravaged Hamburg and the Swiss town of Glarus respectively. Reinsurance companies basically insure the risks borne by primary insurers. They cover a large universe of different risks and invest the premiums paid by primary insurers in global financial markets, spreading the risks globally into financial markets. The premiums, together with the return on financial investments, enable reinsurers to honour the claims made by their clients while making a profit.[39] The industry's longevity—over 150 years to date—bears witness to its success so far. Uninsurable risks, like nuclear accidents, are excluded from the insured universe.[40]

Insurance can be conceived of as spreading disaster losses over space and time in the form of premiums to be paid at regular intervals. To cover the insurance industry's running costs and generate a profit, insured people pay more in the form of premiums than the average amount of losses to be expected, since premiums collected by insurance companies must exceed future claims. Otherwise insurance is not commercially viable unless it gets support from governments or international organizations. As we shall see, public-private partnerships (PPPs) have multiplied to offer novel disaster insurance products in the developing world. This involves increasing cooperation between aid organizations and the insurance sector, but also increasing competition between the relief and insurance businesses.

According to Munich Re, annual disaster losses over the last ten years averaged $184bn. 30 per cent of the losses were insured,[41] which corresponds to some $45bn in annual insurance pay-outs to compensate for disaster losses. This global estimate must be considered with caution. As mentioned earlier, insured losses are accurately reported by the insurance industry while uninsured losses are not recorded in a systematic manner. Second, there are huge variations from country to country in the so-called insurance penetration rate, that is the share of total insurance premiums paid annually over GDP. In 2011, for example, insurance penetration reached 13 per cent in Holland against less than 2 per cent in Indonesia and 1 per cent in the Philippines. This is bound to change, knowing that Asia accounted for slightly more than half of the global death toll from disasters between 1970 and 2010 and suffered 40 per cent of the global economic losses.[42]

Despite adverse political economy dynamics that tend to discourage ex-ante investment in disaster risk prevention and management, insurance penetration is currently spreading in emerging economies under the combined impetus of economic growth (which means that there is more to lose) and urbanization (which means that there is a greater concentration of risks). Emerging middle classes are becoming more aware of disaster risks and insurance options. As countries in the Asia-Pacific region pursue strategies to better prepare for and respond to a variety of disaster risks while simultaneously transitioning to (upper)-middle income country status, the potential to adopt disaster insurance schemes is deemed high by industry experts. The South East Asia region is among the most exposed to natural hazards, with yearly losses estimated above $4.4bn.[43] The Association of Southeast Asian Nations (ASEAN) was instrumental in setting up the ASEAN Agreement on Disaster Management and Emergency Response (AADMER) that entered into force in December 2009. The agreement includes a regional framework for cooperation on disaster management that deals with issues such as funding, coordination and training as well as a binding instrument that relates to commitments taken under the Hyogo Framework of Action (HFA) to reduce disaster losses.[44]

In the following section, we discuss disaster insurance- and risk-linked securities (RLS), which are financial instruments whose value is not primarily driven by fluctuations on financial markets, but rather by the occurrence of disasters and the severity of the ensuing losses. Risk-linked securities can be defined as 'innovative financing devices that enable insurance risk to be sold in capital markets, raising funds that insurers and reinsurers can use to pay claims arising from mega-catastrophes and other loss events.'[45] Paradoxically, RLS spread at a time when the 2008 financial crisis made risk securitization highly unpopular.[46] As we shall see, catastrophic risk bonds or 'cat bonds' are one of the most prominent risk-linked securities. It is important to further distinguish between private insurance, for example contracted by individual homeowners, and governmental insurance schemes and risk transfer mechanisms that cover public and private asset losses.

The Surge in Disaster Risk Insurance and Risk-Linked Securities

'Compulsory earthquake insurance is our primary social responsibility.'[47] This quotation sounds like the perfect advert for a multinational insurance company, but actually features prominently on the homepage of the Turkish Catastrophe Insurance Pool (TCIP), a compulsory insurance scheme for Turkish house owners following a 1999 governmental decree.[48] The legislation determines the principles and procedures regarding the earthquake insurance that building owners or usufructuaries have to contract in order to ensure nation-wide coverage against quake-induced disaster risks, including tsunamis, landslides, fires and explosions. The stated objective is to reduce the financial liability of the Turkish government in the case of an earthquake: it can prevent a tax increase that the government would have to impose to pay for the reconstruction of uninsured private property. The premiums are meant to be affordable. On the flipside, the sum insured is limited to 150,000 Turkish Lira, or just above $70,000 (as of mid-2014). This may be enough to pay for the reconstruction of a modest accommodation in a rural area. But it would cover only a fraction of the losses incurred by a house-owner in a city that is highly exposed to quake risks such as Istanbul or Izmir.

When private insurance markets fail to provide affordable insurance, government subsidies or guarantees might be required if one wants disaster insurance to develop. Modern nation states are expected to serve as a last resort insurer in the event of a disaster. Based on the principle of national solidarity, the government is expected to compensate victims. If it is unable to do so, state legitimacy is at risk. When a cataclysmic event strikes, the state may run into large deficit and may have to drastically increase taxation. The global insurance industry claims to offer solutions that spread the risk and can transfer the disaster costs outside of the country. The same logic applies to so-called catastrophe bonds: 'cat bonds' appeared in the mid-1990s out of concern about the insurance industry hedging against catastrophic events. More than $40bn of cat bonds were issued over the decade preceding 2013. The amount of outstanding bonds increased from less than $3bn in 2002 to more than $19bn in 2013. According to estimates, about 80 per cent of cat bond buyers are pension funds and other institutional investors who find it attractive to diversify their portfolios. Cat bonds offer a reasonably high-yield asset class, dissociated from the vagaries of stock markets.

When designing a cat bond, a parametric trigger is established in relation to the intensity of a natural hazard, say wind speed, air pressure, rainfall or quake magnitude and location. Some cat bonds use industry loss triggers instead, activated when losses reach a certain level. When a catastrophic event crosses that threshold, the cat bond trigger is activated: the investors must then forgive the principal in part or in full. The issuing insurance or government entity can use the loan—turned into a grant—to pay for insurance claims or for emergency relief and rehabilitation. The financial return on cat bonds is higher than for normal bonds where the principal is not at risk. Cat bond yields can go as high as eleven points above the US Treasury bond yield. Cat bonds issued in 2013 with an average maturity of 3.3 years pay about 5.56 percentage points above short-term lending rates.[49] Parametric triggers reduce transaction costs since insurance claim experts do not need to ascertain the veracity and amount of alleged losses. In addition, index-based insurance products arguably reduce moral hazard since pay-outs are triggered by the observation of objective indicators that cannot be manipulated by the insured. In principle, the data provided by meteorological stations or seismographs suffice. But the availability and credibility of such information greatly varies from one country to another. For example, Japan had over 1000 seismographs scattered around the country by mid-2000 while Indonesia had less than 160 of them for the whole archipelago.[50] Actuaries need enough data to quantify the probability and amount of expected losses in order to determine the appropriate level of the bonds' yield or insurance premiums. This is obviously very difficult in the case of exceptional catastrophic events or in situations where there has not been enough data collected on the relevant parameters.

The case of Mexico provides a good illustration of how cat bonds have developed over the past decade. In 2005, Mexico budgeted about $50m for disaster recovery. It eventually had to pay $800m.[51] The Federal Government set up a Fund for National Disasters to be in a position to pay for emergency aid and post-disaster rebuilding. However, when several disasters strike in a row, the scheme remains largely underfunded. Besides, climate change, urbanization and economic growth all push disaster costs up. This prompted the Mexican government to issue earthquake cat bonds in 2006, followed by a 'multi-cat' securitization programme in 2009 that includes additional natural hazard risks such as hurricanes. In a detailed account of the Mexican cat-securitization programme design, Keucheyan[52] reports that the Mexican finance ministry worked together with the World Bank, Goldman Sachs and Swiss Re Capital Markets. A US catastrophe-modelling agency was tasked with defining the level and nature of the parametric triggers. When a quake or a hurricane hits Mexico, the modelling agency examines whether the relevant trigger has been activated or not. If it has not, the investor keeps the principal and keeps cashing hefty interest payments. In October 2013, *The Economist* reported that, out of a total of 200 bonds issued over fifteen years, only three cat bonds had been triggered.[53] The increased interest of capital markets for weather-index derivatives and cat bonds may be welcomed by the insurance industry... as long as the additional influx of liquidity on the disaster risk market does not depress insurance premiums and profits too much.

Since 2007, several catastrophe risk insurance pilot programmes have been launched with the support of the World Bank in particular. The case of Malawi provides an illustration of the recent catastrophe securitization boom that developed in disaster-prone countries. Malawi is chronically affected by weather events that regularly put food security at risk. The country launched two flagship risk transfer pilot programmes by the mid-2000s. Both are rainfall-indexed insurance schemes: a crop micro-insurance scheme for individual farmers and a sovereign derivative scheme for the government, said to be the first of its kind in Africa. Such derivatives transfer a portion of the risks out of the drought-affected country and into international financial markets, spreading the risk broadly and transferring disaster costs abroad. This allows for the reduction of not only the drain of an adverse weather shock on the domestic economy, but also foreign aid dependence.

Microinsurance has emerged over the past two decades as an alternative to traditional insurance for developing countries. Schematically, microinsurance comprises insurance products targeting the poor. The latter are not attractive clients for regular insurers since they do not have the means to buy standard insurance or have other more pressing spending priorities. The term 'micro' refers to the fact that the premiums and insured assets are limited enough to be affordable for the relatively poor. The number of people who have contracted microinsurance increased by more than 600 per cent between 2007 and 2012, reaching $500m for a market exceeding $40bn.[54] Since a substantial share of global output in the developing world is subject to the direct influence of weather events, weather-index insurance and derivatives are quickly expanding as additional disaster risk financing instruments, alongside sovereign cat bonds, contingency credits made available by international financial institutions, and the reserves that many developing countries have accumulated over recent years of budgetary and trade surpluses. Today, both weather-index micro-insurance and sovereign cat bond schemes are promoted in disaster-prone developing countries. However, the priority is to cover sovereign risks rather than to offer micro-insurance to individual farmers to the extent that the former entails smaller transaction costs and is easier to market at scale.

In May 2014, the African Union (AU) launched its first catastrophe sovereign risk pool insurance, backed by a dozen global reinsurers. As a specialized agency of the AU, the African Risk Capacity has issued policies to five countries covering severe drought risks (Kenya, Mauritania, Mozambique, Niger and Senegal). The pool fund provides early warnings from satellite-based rainfall data, triggering direct pay-outs to governments and communities.[55] From 2015 onwards, it is set to address floods and include additional countries such as Burkina Faso and Nigeria. The initial capitalization of $135m comprises $55m from the reinsurance market, with Germany, Britain, Sweden and the Rockefeller Foundation as major donors.

Challenges

There are many challenges to the expansion of disaster risk insurance and securitization, involving technical and institutional or 'cultural' obstacles. When the two Malawi pilots were launched, there were less than forty weather stations in the whole country, making weather index monitoring virtually impossible in certain locations. In principle, this can be overcome with satellite imagery. Yet, low resolution and dense clouds in critical growing periods often prevent the collection of the required data. Automated weather gauges can be used as an alternative unmanned device, as they are becoming cheaper and more reliable.[56] Technical barriers to the expansion of disaster risk insurance are receding but still hinder scalability in many instances.

Weather-indexed microinsurance is arguably tailored for 'the bottom of the pyramid'. Affordable premiums and low transaction costs are meant to target the poor. But just like microcredit, microinsurance is not an attractive option for the poorest; neither from the perspective of the insurer for whom demand is simply too low, nor for the insured, for whom there are obviously more urgent priorities and premiums are prohibitively high. Microinsurance is rather targeted at people just above the poverty line. It helps them to withstand adverse, recurrent shocks that would otherwise keep them in a poverty trap. For the industry, microinsurance further serves the purpose of 'educating the poor'. It contributes to raising awareness about risk and insurance. But such schemes are often not commercially viable. Premiums are too high, and pay-outs not frequent enough to become attractive to the poor. Research on contract renewal of health microinsurance in India finds that the dismal renewal rate stems from a poor understanding of the notion of insurance combined with insufficient information provided to allow subscribers to collect insurance payments when eligible.[57]

Several ASEAN countries have a large Muslim population for whom the consistency of insurance and other financial products with Sharia law is a concern. Insurance products do not appear to be Sharia compliant to the extent that they involve the payment of interests and that some contractual arrangements are deemed speculative because they involve risks and uncertainty.[58] The financial industry has developed a variety of instruments under the category of 'Islamic finance', which includes a number of principles such as the sharing of profits and losses. In Asia and the Middle East in particular, the insurance industry has worked with Islamic scholars to design a Sharia compliant version of conventional insurance based on a cooperative system of contributions and payments in case of disaster losses called 'tafakul'. It is premised on the principles of mutual assistance and voluntary contributions: a group of participants is pooled together and voluntarily shares the risks and surpluses from a mutual pool. The reinsurance industry has also developed Sharia compliant products. With the help of a Sharia advisory board, Swiss Re launched a Sharia compliant version of reinsurance in the Middle East in 2006, called 'retafakul'. The company acquired a licence to set up retafakul operations in Malaysia three years later, noting that the Islamic-finance insurance segment had grown by 25 per cent annually between 2004 and 2007, well above the 10 per cent for conventional insurance.[59]

The share of disaster losses covered by formal insurance remains marginal in many developing countries. Even if the market is developing quickly, life and health insurance typically come well ahead of disaster risk insurance.[60] To overcome some of the obstacles, insurance companies are teaming up with development banks, philanthropists and aid agencies in the context of Public-Private Partnerships (PPPs), discussed in the following section. Major aid organizations see great potential for PPPs to strengthen disaster risk governance, increase disaster risk insurance coverage and promote microinsurance products in developing countries.

Public-Private Partnerships

In a 2012 report entitled 'Advancing Disaster Risk Financing and Insurance in ASEAN Member States', the World Bank and the Global Facility for Disaster Reduction and Recovery (GFDRR)[61] lament that the penetration rate of property catastrophe insurance, agricultural insurance and disaster microinsurance remains very low in South East Asia. The report insists that greater insurance coverage would provide additional resources for timely relief and rehabilitation. This requires overcoming supply-side constraints by broadening the marketing channels and the technical capacity of the different stakeholders involved. To ease constraints on the demand side, the report recommends enhancing insurance education and risk exposure awareness among the authorities and the wider public, and improving the legal and regulatory systems.[62] ASEAN member states may be able to mobilize sufficient funding for immediate response to 'regular' disasters. But additional resources are often required to pay for early recovery, in particular in poorer member states like Cambodia, Laos and Myanmar. The report calls for developing disaster risk financing and insurance in the ASEAN region not only with national governments, but also with sub-national state entities that face great budget volatility risks associated with disasters. To ensure that the funding made available matches post-disaster requirements, the report finally suggests blending public contingency budgets and the build-up of reserves with private insurance, cat bonds and contingency credits by international financial institutions.[63]

Typhoon Hayan hit the Philippines in October 2013, providing an opportunity to push these recommendations ahead. A few months after the typhoon killed over 6,000 people and destroyed more than 1.5m homes, the United Nations International Strategy for Disaster Reduction (UNISDR) teamed up with Munich Re and Willis Re to present members of the Senate in Manila with a new product: the Philippines Risk and Insurance Scheme for Municipalities (PRISM). PRISM is a high-yield, state-subsidized cat bond that the municipalities sell to private investors, who would forgive the principal if a catastrophic event were to reach the predetermined threshold.[64] In a statement issued in January 2014, the head of UNISDR claimed: 'In order to be successful, it will require mandatory take-up by local government units, but it will make them masters of their own destiny when it comes to responding to relief and recovery needs in the wake of a major disaster event'.[65] The UNISDR person in charge of outreach and advocacy in Manila added, 'the number of people dying in disasters is going down, but the real challenge is economic losses. Insurance is a means of shifting the focus from saving lives to also saving money.'[66] She went on to express her wish 'to see the Philippines lead the world on this kind of innovation.' Franklin Drilon, the Philippine Senate President, tempered the enthusiasm, noting that such a novel approach is not a silver bullet for disaster risk management and requires 'a paradigm shift' that will take time,[67] next to a concern over costs.

Insurers increasingly team up with governments and international organizations to insure against risks that most of the people exposed could not afford on a commercial basis. The public sector brings in its regulatory power and political clout to establish the institutional framework for the insurance market to flourish. The private sector brings in technical expertise and financial resources. The international aid community plays a critical role by bringing into the partnership its convening power and a legitimacy that helps market new products in developing countries, together with subsidies for pilot programmes that are not (yet) commercially viable or are simply too risky. Launched in 2007, the Caribbean Catastrophe Risk Insurance Facility (CCRIF) was the first catastrophe insurance pool for governments, providing insurance coverage to sixteen countries in a region swept by frequent storms and hurricanes.[68] This innovative way to engage in pre-disaster planning was developed under the World Bank's leadership and with financial support from Japan. The CCRIF was capitalized through contributions from Canada, the European Union and many other donors plus membership fees paid by participating states. This was followed by other similar schemes supported by the World Bank, such as the Pacific Catastrophe Risk Insurance pilot programme that also seeks to help small island states that are highly exposed to weather-related hazards to access the international catastrophe risk insurance market. The Mongolian Index-based Livestock Insurance is another pilot designed by the World Bank with Japanese and Swiss funding to protect Mongolian herders' productive assets against adverse weather and other events. Again, portions of the risks facing the cattle are transferred outside of the country to the global financial market.[69]

Political Economy Constraints

The typical collective action, moral hazard, asymmetric information problems that discourage ex-ante investment in disaster risk prevention are well known, but remain difficult to overcome.[70] The provision of free relief and rehabilitation and of government guarantees and subsidies are all subject to moral hazard that reduces the incentive to invest in disaster prevention and preparedness. Based on a narrow cost-benefit calculus, foreign aid remains the preferred option in many disaster-prone countries, which reduces the incentive to invest in prevention. A recent study shows that the anticipation of external assistance has a strong explanatory power on the low demand for disaster risk insurance even in the case of the French Overseas Departments, which are hazard-prone territories where the supply of insurance products is strong.[71] Along the same lines, evidence from a field experiment conducted in Pakistan after extensive flooding in 2010 provides interesting insights: while overall demand for flood micro-insurance increased among those who suffered direct losses, demand remained significantly lower among those households who benefited from free post-disaster assistance to rebuild their homes or to replace productive assets such as livestock. Yet, in those cases where such assistance compensated only for the loss of less valuable assets, the negative impact on demand for flood micro-insurance appeared much more limited.[72] In other words, the experience of direct flood loss significantly raises demand for micro-insurance only in the absence of substantial compensation by relief agencies. This reflects an ambiguous relationship between the aid and insurance sectors: both sides call for building partnerships, as reaffirmed in the Sendai Framework for Disaster Risk Reduction approved in March 2015. At the same time, the generous provision of relief reduces the incentive to buy insurance among disaster-prone states and communities. Conversely, widespread insurance coverage tends to render post-disaster reconstruction interventions by the aid industry superfluous, as often witnessed in industrialized countries.

The case of subsidized insurance raises specific issues. In the aftermath of Hurricane Sandy, which hit the US East Coast in October 2011, the Texan Republican senator Ron Paul criticized the moral hazard embedded in federal subsidies to the National Flood Insurance Program (NFIP), which makes it cheaper for people to settle, build and rebuild their homes in flood-prone areas. The senator wrote: 'NFIP disguises the real cost of flood insurance in flood-prone areas, which influences homebuilding and sales in such areas ... The obvious and expected outcome is more danger to life and limb when disaster strikes'.[73] Soon thereafter, the US Congress passed a Flood Insurance Reform Act in an attempt to reduce moral hazard. Public subsidy cuts were set to increase NFIP premiums. Less than two years later, as mid-term elections in the US were approaching, both the House of Representatives and the Senate overwhelmingly voted in favour of removing the 2012 provisions that made property insurance more costly. Expressing support for this 2014 Homeowner Flood Insurance Affordability Act, a senator hailed the fact that 'we have averted the manmade perfect storm that would have crushed thousands of families under the weight of skyrocketing flood insurance rates, forced many from their homes, plummeted property values and destroyed entire communities.'[74] Politics obviously prevails over moral hazard concerns. This leaves open the question of who should be held accountable if a 'perfect storm' crushes the lives of those families who can afford to stay or settle in risky locations as a result of the 2014 Act.

The Political Economy of Prevention

Mr Kotaku Wamura was the long-time mayor of Fudai, a little town on the north-eastern coast of Japan. He was considered a fool when he decided in the late 1960s to build a 51-foot (15.5 metres) high floodgate to protect his community from the next tsunami. Building the floodgate and adjacent wall between two mountainsides took about fifteen years. The cost exceeded $30m (in 2011 dollars). In March 2011, when the Tohoku quake wreaked havoc on the entire region, he was, posthumously, hailed as a hero. The device saved the lives and homes of the Fudai residents who would otherwise have faced the deadly fate of neighbouring communities.[75] Worldwide, such costly preventive investments are luxurious outliers. The political economy of disaster prevention provides strong incentives to underinvest in ex-ante, preventive measures starting with building the capacity to identify and monitor risks. Economists typically resort to cost-benefit analysis to demonstrate that prevention is more cost effective than ex-post responses. Insights from behavioural economics hint at a seemingly innate tendency to misforecast the effects of high-impact, low-probability disaster risks, compounded by the fact that the poor tend to attribute a very low value to future losses (that is, they are subject to hyperbolic temporal discounting of the future).

In spite of a widely shared narrative that ex-ante investment in disaster prevention and preparedness is the best way to save lives and money, political will remains weak and action sluggish.[76] In disaster-prone countries, those holding power stand to lose political support if they decide to increase taxes or divert public expenditures to pay for disaster prevention. Forced displacement is even less popular. Relocating the communities most exposed out of villages close to Yogyakarta, an Indonesian city that lies under the threatening shadow of the Merapi Volcano, simply appears not to be an option given the strong attachment that binds people to their land. Even temporary evacuation when the alert is raised to the top level proves very difficult. Conversely, political leaders can reap significant gains when responding effectively to disasters, showing compassion and directing life-saving operations in the media spotlight. In addition, massive influx of foreign aid sometimes compensates for all the costs, and may even produce a surplus.

Disaster prevention has not been much more popular with the international aid community than with states, and foreign aid faces the same political economy hurdles that hamper adequate public investment in disaster reduction and preparedness. Less than 0.5 per cent of total ODA has been allocated to disaster prevention and preparedness over the past twenty years.[77] Most of the funds came from the humanitarian sector, which however does not even account for 4 per cent of official humanitarian assistance. As in the case of underinvestment in other public goods, the lack of investment in disaster risk prevention results from collective action problems, moral hazard, asymmetric information[78] and a tendency towards myopic behaviour. Moral hazard refers to the tendency to take higher risks knowing that we won't bear (all) the costs if and when such risks materialize. Moral hazard associated with foreign aid and insurance can discourage states, firms and households from investing in prevention and preparedness.

The majority of surveys and experiments that examine individual and collective attitudes towards risk consistently reveal a tendency to ignore high-intensity, low-probability risks. Myopic behaviour refers to our tendency towards wilfully ignoring certain risks and discounting the future (that is, putting a low net present value on future disaster costs).[79] In practice, in the majority of poor countries most people face a much higher risk of dying from an easily preventable disease or from a road accident than from natural hazard. Investing scarce resources in public heath or in road safety consequently appears economically more rational than investing in disaster prevention. This raises the question of who actually suffers from myopia among research subjects and experts.

It has been calculated that approximately 60,000 people die each year in disasters, first and foremost because of collapsing buildings as quakes hit developing countries.[80] The vast majority of these deaths could be avoided by investing in quakeproof construction at an additional cost of roughly 10 per cent of total building costs.[81] So why do house owners not simply pay to make their families safer? Information dissymmetry between the house owner (principal) and constructor (agent) provides part of the explanation.[82] Knowing that the principal has neither the expertise in construction nor the ability to exert tight oversight, the agent shall rationally decide to reduce costs by lowering the quality of building materials and finish. Conversely, the principal may rationally expect that investing in quakeproof construction will be useless to the extent that the building might be less resistant than agreed and paid for. Besides, the intensity of future quakes remains uncertain. Investing in prevention will be money wasted unless the house is resistant enough to withstand the shock intensity.[83]

Another issue revolves around collective action and free-riding problems, well known in the context of international negotiations over climate change mitigation. At a more micro-level, collective action issues can arise, for example in quake-prone locations when a landowner wishes to build a new house where adjoining buildings risk collapsing over his property in the event of a quake. The landowner would be ill-advised to invest in quake-proof construction if the neighbours don't.

The construction and infrastructure sector is known for being particularly exposed to corruption and bribery, which increases the price and lowers the quality of preventive and post-disaster reconstruction programmes. In the case of Aceh in Indonesia, for instance, village heads monitoring construction work funded by the World Bank after the December 2004 tsunami reportedly sold material worth about a quarter of the total budget illegally.[84] Corruption discourages investment in prevention, since investors suspect that part of the money will end up in offshore bank accounts rather than being used for disaster prevention. While these arguments are valid, corruption can also make prevention more attractive for corrupt politicians. Even if a portion of the investment is lost along the way, prevention can still be more cost-effective than the massive disaster response required in the absence of preventive action. In addition, there is no evidence that prevention is more prone to corruption than disaster response. On the contrary, it may be easier to keep bribery under a certain threshold under the normal circumstances than during the hectic conditions under which disaster response takes place.

In theory, one way to encourage investment in disaster prevention would be to 'put the incentives right' by rewarding effective preventive measures when they successfully prevent destruction during shocks. But in practice, would taxpayers accept ODA being used to reward people after non-disasters? Certainly not. In the case of the Tohoku quake, the Fudai residents who suffered minimal loss thanks to the floodgate built by their former mayor would be rewarded while the victims of failed prevention would be punished for not having invested the same amount in prevention by the withholding of life-saving assistance: a non-starter! Anecdotal evidence indicates, however, that the demand for prevention increases among the population hit by disasters. Two years after the 2004 Indian Ocean tsunami, the risk of social unrest and civil society pressure pushed through the adoption of a new Indonesian Disaster Management Law,[85] which made prevention a priority. Preventive measures have gained momentum in particular in a few urban centres where wealth and productive assets are concentrated.[86]

Enhanced Cooperation, Tougher Competition

A catastrophic event often causes substantial resource transfers over a short time span. The evolving mix between insured and uninsured losses—or between international and domestic relief—affects how the disaster costs and benefits are eventually distributed. Resources may flow from insurance companies to homeowners, or from foreign taxpayers to aid organizations, down to international and local contractors, who in turn may sub-contract the execution of reconstruction projects. In the case of cat bonds, resources typically flow from foreign institutional investors to (re)insurance companies or, in the case of sovereign cat bonds, to central and local governments in disaster-hit countries.

Since the turn of the millennium the disaster risk market has grown, with disaster risk insurance, cat bonds and risk-linked derivatives set to expand quickly in the developing world, especially in South East Asia. This is perceived as an opportunity by some disaster-prone countries, wary of massive foreign interference after a sudden large disaster, to reduce aid dependency and further assert national sovereignty. So far, the implementation of pilot projects suggests that many disaster risk-linked financial products are not (yet) commercially viable in low-income and lower-middle income countries. Many projects are thus developed in the context of public-private partnerships that seek to draw on the comparative advantage of the insurance industry and international development cooperation agencies.

This may lead to both increased cooperation and enhanced competition between the humanitarian sector and the insurance industry. Disaster-hit countries and communities prefer getting free ex-post assistance to having to pay ex-ante disaster risk insurance premiums or interests on cat bonds. Conversely, the needs for relief and recovery assistance diminish as a greater share of the losses are insured. The merit of insurance and derivative products is that they transfer disaster costs abroad irrespective of the humanitarian response or lack thereof. That said, foreign aid remains the default option in many developing countries, in particular in the case of rare, extreme events.

6

SURVIVAL ECONOMICS

If the potential victims have the incomes with which to buy food, then markets and railways can work to get food to the affected people.

Amartya Sen, 2001[1]

Theory Meets Practice?

The popular uprising that broke out during the spring of 2011 in Syria rapidly degenerated into a brutal civil war with dire humanitarian consequences. By November 2014, the conflict had taken an estimated 200,000 lives. About 6.5 million Syrians were internally displaced while more than three million fled abroad. The magnitude, cost and complexity of the crisis has put the humanitarian sector under great stress, leading the UN to launch its largest ever funding appeal for a single crisis, asking donors for $6.5bn to fund its 2014 operations related to Syria. Neighbouring countries host the bulk of the refugee caseload, Lebanon ranking first. In November 2014, the country hosted more than 1.1 million Syrians registered with the United Nations High Commissioner for Refugees (UNHCR), next to more than 400,000 Palestinian refugees registered with the United Nations Relief and Works Agency (UNRWA), and many other unregistered refugees, making up well over a quarter of the total resident population.[2]

Assessing the resulting vulnerability and need for humanitarian assistance of both the refugee and host populations is particularly challenging for several reasons:

- Lebanon at first adopted an open door, no camp policy: for more than three years, Syrians have been able to seek refuge in Lebanon, but not to settle in camps. As a result, refugees live in more than 1,500 locations across Lebanon, in individual rented apartments, collective shelters, unfinished buildings or informal tented settlements, among others. The prevailing economic, social and political conditions vary greatly from place to place, including with regard to access to shelter and health facilities.

- Despite the fact that Lebanon has not ratified the 1951 Refugee Convention, Syrians have been authorized to stay for twelve months following entry. Renewal has been subject to a $200 fee per person, which is unaffordable for many impoverished refugee households. Syrians who entered the country illegally or who are unable to renew their entry permit risk being arrested, which limits their freedom of movement and access to essential services. Tighter restrictions were introduced in January 2015, with Syrians requiring visas for entry—an unprecedented move by the Lebanese government to control the influx of previously unrestricted refugee entry.

- While some refugees have no income whatsoever, others receive financial support from family members working abroad or earn an income, often from precarious seasonal work in the informal sector, estimated to represent a third of total economic output in Lebanon.

- Since a large share of humanitarian funding appeals have not been met by donor contributions, relief agencies have had to identify and select aid recipients among the most vulnerable Syrian refugees. Lebanese host communities have become increasingly hostile towards refugees, making it imperative to extend aid to vulnerable Lebanese households with a view to containing mounting resentment and compensating for the negative effects of the crisis on host communities' livelihoods.

- Lebanon is classified as an upper middle-income country (MIC) with an average income per capita of $9,870 in 2013. Yet, Lebanon is far from a developmental state: it has been portrayed as a merchant republic flourishing under a sectarian regime.[3] A study conducted prior to the Syrian crisis showed that 'each sect's share of public expenditures bears a striking resemblance to the sectarian distribution of the country.'[4] The allocation of public social expenditure in Lebanon has been at best blind to disparities in education and health or, at worst, has reinforced such disparities by using a sectarian rather than a needs-based rationale. State institutions have developed on the basis of a liberal, sectarian compromise[5] and the provision of basic services largely rests in private hands.

In this chapter, I focus on how scholars and practitioners assess the impact of humanitarian crises at the micro level. I look at how individuals, households and communities attempt to cope and survive in the midst of crises, and how humanitarian organizations assess the vulnerability and needs for assistance of crisis-affected people accordingly. The impact of the Syrian crisis in Lebanon serves as a case study to illustrate the complexity of assessing the needs for humanitarian assistance in a MIC where the vulnerable live primarily in urban settings. This case study is particularly relevant to the extent that the humanitarian sector is set to operate increasingly in urban contexts and in countries that have graduated from low-income country (LIC) to MIC status. Insights from the Lebanese case study may thus prefigure several of the forthcoming challenges facing the relief sector. That being said, humanitarian crises will also continue to affect vulnerable people in rural areas of LICs such as South Sudan or the Democratic Republic of Congo for years to come. The relevant issues in such diverse contexts are obviously very different.

In the next section, I discuss needs assessment concepts and approaches before turning to aid responses. In the case of Lebanon, cash assistance has emerged as a preferred aid modality among the beneficiaries and various humanitarian organizations. Multi-sector cash assistance programmes cover not just food needs, but also housing, education, transport, heating, water and other requirements. Cash assistance is by no means a silver bullet, but is nonetheless a game changer: it challenges long-established aid modalities and sectoral boundaries, pushes transaction costs down and can contribute to giving the beneficiaries greater agency.

Assessing the Impact of Crises at the Micro Level

Economists have long emphasized macro-level consequences of armed conflict, looking at war costs in terms of economic output losses, foreign and domestic investment drops, average income per capita reduction and so on. This is of little help to humanitarians, as it does not say much about the vulnerabilities and aid requirements of specific groups of people. Besides, large swathes of economic activity go unrecorded in war-torn countries where the informal sector is pervasive. In summer 1999 I conducted an economic-security assessment in Kinshasa to assess the potential for a food crisis if Congolese rebels were to cut off the capital city from its hinterland. Since official data put income per capita at a level that was much lower than the cost of a basic food basket in Kinshasa, I first concluded that the vast majority of the population was already food insecure. Yet, an income and expenditure survey carried out in one of Kinshasa's poorest suburban areas showed that households had developed a remarkably diversified portfolio of informal resource-generating activities, resulting in actual income per capita being three times higher than the official data indicated.

Assessing the needs for humanitarian assistance requires shifting the focus to the vulnerabilities, livelihoods and capacities of individuals, households and communities. The household level is often the most relevant unit for livelihood analysis since household members share resources to satisfy basic needs. A household can be defined as a group of people with different needs and abilities who share resources (income, assets, food production, etc.) to cover their food and non-food requirements. Depending on the context, a household can be limited to the nuclear family or comprise extended family members and beyond. The vulnerable have a low capacity to anticipate, cope with and recover from the impact of war or disaster. Vulnerability thus refers to the level of exposure and sensitivity to a potential shock—as determined by politico-institutional, economic, physical, social and environmental factors—mediated by the capacity to cope with that shock. Coping strategies reduce vulnerability in that they encompass all the options that people are capable of mobilizing to reduce the negative impact of a shock and to maintain or restore their livelihoods. The concept of livelihood, in turn, refers to the capabilities, resources and strategies that people can mobilize to make a living.

Since household income in crisis-affected settings tends to be difficult to measure, relief organizations have increasingly used proxy means testing (PMT) as a method to assess livelihood levels. The idea behind PMT is to use indicators that require information that can be relatively rapidly and easily collected, or simply observed. The indicators that most correlate with livelihood levels can be identified through regressions, and weighed accordingly. PMT methods typically involve surveys where enumerators register indications on proxy indicators such as demographic data (e.g. number and age of household members), human capital (e.g. year of education, professional skills), physical capital (e.g. housing, consumer goods, vehicles) and productive capital (e.g. tools, agricultural land).

The ultimate objective is to determine whether a household lies below or above a given cut-off point and thus whether it is eligible for a social protection or humanitarian aid programme or not. PMT has not been developed to identify the vulnerable in crisis situations, but instead to target social protection programmes on the poor in developing economies under 'normal circumstances'. Poverty does not necessarily equate with vulnerability. Hence, when it comes to targeting humanitarian programmes on the vulnerable in chronic crises, PMT must be adapted to account for the impact of the crisis on powerlessness, lack of agency and social exclusion.

The starting point of humanitarian needs assessment is often a baseline scenario, which provides information on people's livelihood under normal circumstances. The baseline serves as a reference to assess how a humanitarian crisis affects people's livelihoods. The generalization of Living Standard Measurement Study (LSMS) surveys spearheaded in the 1980s by the World Bank in developing countries can offer valuable baseline information to humanitarian organizations that intervene in the event of a crisis. Yet, such surveys carried out for development purposes tend to ignore conflict-related issues since LSMS surveys are geared towards informing development policy and programmes. In addition, they typically focus on poverty,[6] which does not equate with vulnerability. The poor may actually be less vulnerable to a crisis than those who are wealthier. This was, for example, the case in Peru following the economic crisis and structural adjustment shock of the 1980s. Severe child malnutrition increased more in middle-class quarters of Lima than in poorer suburbs of the capital city. Prior to the crisis, the poor were typically active in the informal sector and derived income from a relatively large portfolio of activities. The livelihood of middle-class civil servants or company employees involved a much narrower portfolio of resource-generating activities. As the crisis broke out, impoverished middle-class workers were adamant on staying in middle-class neighbourhoods where rent was relatively expensive and access to informal activities was limited, even at the expense of properly feeding their own children. By contrast, the poor were able to mobilize a greater portfolio of potential resource-generating activities and continue to more adequately feed their children. LSMS surveys seldom provide findings by livelihood groups, which is the usual entry point of many vulnerability assessments. Another limitation of LSMS surveys is that they tend to relate to administrative entities at the sub-national level, which often do not fit the spatial delineation of conflict-affected areas.

In emergency situations, time is of the essence: for humanitarian agencies, it is better to get a timely yet imperfect picture of needs rather than a comprehensive picture but too late. Rapid or 'good-enough' assessment methods seek to inform aid interventions to save lives before it is too late. Many emergencies tend to turn into protracted crises. In such cases, rapid assessments must swiftly be complemented or substituted by more in-depth, rigorous needs assessments. Purely life-saving activities tend to be the exception rather than the norm, especially in chronic crises, and the humanitarian sector strives to intervene to support the livelihoods of people before they fall destitute and risk imminent death. In recent years, the humanitarian sector has invested a lot of energy in improving needs assessment methods, both in specific sectors such as water and sanitation, health, food and shelter as well as at the multi-sector level, across clusters.[7] The next section turns precisely to needs assessment methods, with an emphasis on food and economic security.

Needs Assessments

The principle of impartiality dictates that humanitarian action responds to the most pressing needs for assistance as a matter of priority irrespective of political, ethnic, religious and other interests. For humanitarian organizations, correctly assessing the urgency and intensity of the needs for assistance is thus a pre-condition for the impartial delivery of aid.

Relief agencies have developed specific socio-economic needs assessment methods that fit their domain of expertise and activity, without much interaction with academic work on the consequences of humanitarian crises. Nonetheless, a few scholarly contributions exerted a major influence on humanitarian needs assessments. The vast literature on household economics shed light on micro-level decisions regarding savings, consumption, labour and intra-household transfers.[8] More importantly perhaps, the capabilities approach elaborated by Amartya Sen in the 1970s and 1980s greatly influenced the design of contemporary humanitarian needs assessments. Sen's insights on famine[9] altered the way humanitarians approach food crises by shifting the emphasis from a lack of food availability on the market to people's lack of access to food. At the operational level, the focus shifted away from heavy logistical operations involving the shipment of food surpluses from abroad, towards enhancing households' capability to produce, buy or otherwise obtain sufficient and adequate food, with the aim of preserving or restoring food security. The latter is a multidimensional concept that refers to a situation where people can cover their dietary needs to live a healthy and active life in a sustainable manner.[10]

The concept of entitlement is central to this approach. Sen defined entitlement as 'the set of alternative commodity bundles that a person can command in a society using the totality of rights and opportunities that he or she faces'.[11] The underlying observation is that individuals can command varying amounts of goods and services depending on their ability to produce them or buy them.

Sen's conceptualization of famine and relatively narrow definition of entitlements raised a series of critiques and suggestions for improvements. In conflict settings, there is a need to include extra-legal acquisitions and losses, broadening Sen's notion of legally-based or lawful claims to goods and services supplied by the market or derived from one's own production.[12] Beyond private entitlements, public and civil entitlements need to be factored into the equation to account for access to public services, communal resources, solidarity networks, humanitarian aid, and welfare functions fulfilled by non-state armed groups.

It took years before Sen's insights trickled down into needs assessment methods. Anthropometric measures of nutritional status (e.g. mid-upper arm circumference, height-for-age, weight-for-height) were complemented by dynamic household economy and market analysis to examine how humanitarian crises affect people's food security and, more broadly, economic security. As Alain Mourey, a pioneering nutritionist, used to say to new recruits of the International Committee of the Red Cross (ICRC) in the 1990s, 'we humans are not just digestive tubes'.[13] Food hardly ever represents more than three quarters of households' compulsory expenditures. More often, and increasingly in MICs, food accounts for less than half of the expenses of crisis-affected households, next to shelter, health, transport, heating and so on.

To account for food and non-food requirements, the Household Economy Approach (HEA), developed in the 1990s by Save the Children Fund (SCF) in cooperation with the Food and Agriculture Organization (FAO), focuses on the economic security of households. Under this approach, a household economy is defined as 'the sum of ways in which the household gets its income, its savings and asset holdings, and its consumption of food and non-food items.'[14] The HEA follows the logic of first identifying a baseline scenario, referring to how people live under 'normal' circumstances, and then assessing how a crisis and aid intervention affect different groups of vulnerable households that share similar livelihood patterns.

The ICRC adopted the economic security approach at the end of the 1990s. The objective is to assist conflict-affected households to cover their basic needs in a sustainable manner, as defined by their biology, environment and cultural standards. No one denies that environmental variables such as cold winters impact compulsory expenses (e.g. stove, fuel, blankets). Factoring cultural standards into needs assessment can be more controversial. Of course, food aid has to be culturally appropriate. But to design more generous aid packages for Syrians than for Central Africans on the basis that cultural standards in MICs are associated with higher living standards than in low-income countries (LICs) arguably contradicts the principle of impartiality, even if it is true that living costs tend to be higher in MICs' urban areas than in LICs' rural ones.

Figure 13 illustrates the underlying logic of needs assessment approaches that focus on household economic security. The main point is to understand to what extent households are able to cover their basic needs by mobilizing a diversity of resources including their own productive capital, labour, savings, and the totality of transfers from public and private sources, domestic or foreign. Preserving or restoring productive capital is essential to avert destitution and enable households to cover their basic needs in a sustainable manner. When the resources generated by productive capital do not suffice to satisfy basic needs, households can use their savings, sell their assets and get loans, which is not sustainable over the long run. Local solidarity networks, social protection schemes, remittances and foreign aid can all be critical to avert destitution and maintain or restore economic security during crises.

As we can see from Figure 13, market analysis is critical when carrying out economic security assessments. It means looking at supply chains as well as at monetary transactions and barter trade in contexts where monetized exchanges remain marginal. Price fluctuations provide signals that can be highly relevant to assess the evolution of households' livelihoods and level of vulnerability. Properly interpreting price fluctuations is of the essence. For example, I am reminded of two distinct contexts where armed conflict caused meat prices to plunge: in the first case because of excess supply in South Sudan as herders and cattle growers who were falling destitute had no option but to sell their animals to survive; in the other case because of lower demand as consumers in Brazzaville adapted their diet to lower incomes by eating less meat. The same applied to drops in local gold prices: during the Second Intifada in the Palestinian Territories households tapped into their savings by selling their jewellery on the local market to pay for essential goods and services, below the world price for gold; in another instance the gold price drop resulted from the strategy of an armed group to gain full control over the local gold market and bar competitors from purchasing gold at higher, international prices. Such examples highlight the fact that price fluctuations can offer valuable insights into the evolving economic insecurity of different household groups in conflict settings, provided price variations are correctly interpreted.

Several humanitarian organizations have increasingly included market analysis in needs assessments and turned to market-based programming,

13. Household economy

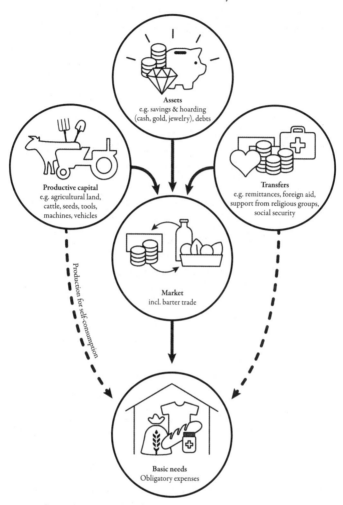

meaning that aid interventions work through and in support of local mar-kets,[15] as we shall see in the case of the World Food Programme (WFP) food e-vouchers programme allowing Syrian refugees to buy food in local shops throughout Lebanon. Market analysis includes tools such as the Emergency Market Mapping and Assessment (EMMA) and the Market Information and Food Insecurity Response Analysis (MIFIRA). EMMA focuses on specific markets deemed essential for supplying goods and services to, or generating incomes for, crisis-affected people. It follows a good-enough assessment approach and primarily consists of the rapid collection of qualitative data. MIFIRA goes deeper into quantitative analysis, looking at key indicators related to the food market in order to inform decisions such as whether to address food insecurity via in-kind food aid, vouchers, or cash assistance depending on specific market conditions.[16] Building on these tools, the International Movement of the Red Cross and Red Crescent has developed a Rapid Analysis of Markets (RAM) and a Market Analysis Guidance (MAG) that seek to enable a wide pool of non-specialized staff to contribute to market analysis in humanitarian crises, at least with regard to data collection.

The first challenge is for humanitarian organizations to gain sufficient expertise to collect the right data and correctly interpret it. Local capacities can be built in situations of chronic crisis, as in Darfur where the Feinstein International Center (Tufts University) supported a Sudanese NGO in managing a community-based market-monitoring network. The aim is to identify how to support livelihoods, economic activities and peaceful relations through trade based on a better understanding of shifting trade patterns and market dynamics.[17] The second challenge is to capture power relations in market analyses, for these largely determine households' market access and vulnerability. Market-based assessment tools such as EMMA generally raise only a few questions with regard to market controls and power relations. They should be complemented with deeper political economy analysis to grasp how issues such as monopolistic rents, patronage networks and extra-legal acquisitions influence the success or failure of humanitarian market-based programming. More broadly, carrying out assessments in conflict settings raises specific methodological and ethical questions that deserve particular attention.

– Methodological and Ethical Issues

Humanitarian agencies used to rely on qualitative field research methods that typically involve semi-structured interviews with key informants, focus group discussions, direct observation and, increasingly, market analysis. In emergencies, rapid assessments are generally based on small and non-representative samples. This does not allow for extrapolation and, to get a better picture, requires efforts to triangulate the data with other information sources. For such assessments to be useful to other humanitarian organizations, full transparency must be provided with regard to baseline data, sampling and extrapolation. Sample bias may result from constrained field access. For example, the vast majority of vulnerability surveys performed in 2013 and 2014 in the

Central African Republic were carried out in and around the capital city Bangui, neglecting more insecure rural areas where needs and vulnerability to armed violence could be higher. Besides, access constraints and quickly evolving environments limit opportunities to crosscheck data and gather more evidence. Thanks to satellite imagery and new information and communications technologies, data collection methods have diversified and now include, for instance, geo-referenced data on the location of critical infrastructure and movements of population.

Further bias results from the fact that in conflict-torn areas, respondents may not faithfully report the truth because of a fear of retaliation, distrust of the interviewers, not recalling facts associated with traumatic events, or simply because of inappropriate questions. Conducting surveys in sensitive contexts requires solid research ethics. Both humanitarian workers and researchers must prioritize the safety and wellbeing of the respondents over the imperative to collect the data and the wish to complete surveys as initially planned on time. A prime concern must also be the security of local enumerators hired to collect information in the field. Assessments must therefore be framed on the basis of strong research ethics and must avoid providing perverse incentives that may put the security of interviewees and enumerators at risk.

Finally, the lack of data sharing and assessment coordination among humanitarian organizations combined with a natural tendency for each agency to trust only its own assessments leads to many overlaps involving the same questions put to the same conflict-affected communities. This spurs not only assessment fatigue, but also resentment when repeated visits and assessments do not translate into any tangible benefit for the interviewees. The drive towards more cooperation in multi-sector, multi-agency assessments is welcome, as is the sharing of findings with all other interested humanitarian organizations. Yet, without solid preparedness and political resolve, it remains virtually impossible to conduct a rapid multi-agency assessment in a sudden-onset emergency. In the case of Lebanon, discussed in the following section, it took more than a half a year to agree on a vulnerability assessment questionnaire within the multi-agency Targeting Working Group.

The Syrian Crisis in Lebanon

As argued above, the Syrian refugee crisis is relevant to highlight the complexity of needs assessment—albeit it is a specific case study that is not representative of other humanitarian crises such as those affecting South Sudan or the Central African Republic. A majority of Syrian (and Palestinian) refugees have settled in the poorest areas of Lebanon such as the north and the Bekaa Valley. A majority of both the Syrian refugees and vulnerable Lebanese live side-by-side in hundreds of locations where local authorities are typically understaffed.[18] Syrians have only limited access to education, healthcare, energy, water and sanitation provided by a dysfunctional Lebanese public sector. To gain a better understanding of the living conditions of the Syrian refugees and to take informed decisions on designing and targeting aid programmes for the vulnerable, the WFP, together with UNHCR and UNICEF, designed and oversaw two Vulnerability Assessment of Syrian Refugees (VASyR) surveys in 2013 and 2014.[19] The 2013 survey comprised interviews with a representative sample of 1,400 Syrian households selected in a two-stage cluster of random selection proportional to population size, with an additional criteria related to refugee registration date. This income and expenditure survey involved many local enumerators visiting and interviewing refugee households across Lebanon.

Average monthly expenditure per household was found to be $774, nearly half of which was for food and a quarter for accommodation rent, as reported in Table 1.

Table 1: Average monthly expenditure per household

Food	370
Rent	194
Health	70
Alcohol	37
Transport	34
Soap	23
Electricity	22
Water	12
Other	7
Education	5
Agricultural Inputs	0
Toral	774

Source: VASyR 2013, p. 20.

On the income side, 57 per cent of the refugees reported that their primary livelihood source depends on employment—casual labour in the non-agricultural sector ranking first—while 30 per cent reported different types of assistance including food vouchers, cash assistance, gifts and remittances as their primary livelihood source. Unsustainable coping strategies involve asset sales (or dissaving) and buying food on credit resulting in greater indebtedness. About half of the interviewees reported that they had to turn to less preferred food, to reduce meal frequency and portion size as well as essential non-food expenditures. About 70 per cent of households were found to be vulnerable or unable to meet all of their basic food and non-food requirements, warranting continued food and non-food assistance. 12 per cent of the refugees were categorized as severely vulnerable in that they were found to be unable to meet their basic food expenses even without considering non-food requirements. The assessment also addressed education. Rather than attending school, many Syrian children have to work. The impact of the crisis will be felt over the long-term: hundreds of thousands of school-aged Syrians are simply left out of already overcrowded public schools in Lebanon, while transport costs and tuition fees for semi-private schools have discouraged many families from sending their children to private school.

Other needs assessment surveys tap into the pool of expertise available at Lebanese universities and research centres—which possess the relevant skills and in-depth knowledge of the local context—to design and carry out solid vulnerability assessments. For example, Oxfam commissioned the Beirut Research and Innovation Center (BRIC) in 2013 to conduct a countrywide household survey and interview key Lebanese officials in charge of service provision to Syrian refugees. The study found significant variations in the individual situations of Syrian refugees. For example, some of them brought substantial savings with them while others arrived empty handed. Like the VASyR, the BRIC study highlighted a significant gap between the average Syrian household income and expenditures, even after including cash assistance by the UNHCR and WFP's food vouchers.[20] In addition, the study provides very rough approximations of several potential coping mechanisms. Looking at savings for example, it was estimated that Syrian refugees had brought assets worth at least $100m into Lebanon by mid-2013.[21] In addition, jewellery in general, and gold in particular, represent a major form of family savings, the precise amount of which is impossible to estimate. Mutual support between the refugees was frequently reported, but many respondents lamented not being able to provide more generous support to fellow Syrian refugees.

Contrary to support from family members and neighbours, there was little mention of assistance from local authorities (government, political and religious figures). On their part, Lebanese officials at the municipal level lamented that they received no mandate or direction from the central government beyond an informal invitation to record statistics on refugees and beef-up security measures. Local officials nonetheless represent an important source of information to refugees, along with exchanges with fellow Syrians about aid opportunities and aid cuts, so that word of mouth takes precedence over briefings by aid agencies about aid programmes.

A second VASyR was carried out in 2014 with the aims of assessing the impact of the rapid increase in the number of refugees and of targeting aid on the (most) vulnerable. The number of Syrian refugees had increased from 423,495 to more than one million between the two assessments. Based on interviews with 1,750 households, the 2014 VASyR highlighted that the relationship between Syrian refugees and the Lebanese host communities had seriously deteriorated. For example, two-thirds of the interviewees reported that they suffered from restricted movement mainly out of serious security concerns with host communities. Host communities played a significant role in assisting Syrian refugees, in particular at the beginning of the crisis. As the crisis dragged on, social cohesion has been put to the test. Foreign aid has targeted first and foremost the refugees, which has spurred resentment among the host population. As the political and sectarian violence that tears Syria apart makes way into Lebanon, for example in the Sunni enclave of Arsal, north of Baalbek towards the Syrian border, the pressure to close the border has intensified, leading to Syrians being denied access to Lebanon. A study by researchers at the American University of Beirut in 2014 reported that the great majority of Lebanese interviewed in the Bekaa and Akkar (north) wished their government would effectively close its border with Syria and forbid refugees all access to work.[22] Indeed, in early 2015, Lebanon imposed tight visa restrictions on Syrians entering the country.

– Baseline and Impact on Lebanon

Assessing the impact of the Syrian crisis in Lebanon requires looking at the situation prior to the crisis. The Lebanese polity rests on a power-sharing system between different sectarian communities where religious affiliation serves as a basis for representation. Sectarian-based political parties further fulfil key security and welfare functions for their own supporters and constituents. At times, some political parties expand the provision of welfare across religious boundaries, which has been the case in particular with Hezbollah in southern Lebanon during and after the Israeli military occupation. Sunni Muslim, Shia Muslim and Christian political parties all play a critical role in substituting for or complementing public services including basic health care, education, and social protection. This serves to cement intra-confessional solidarity, muster political support and strengthen militia groups. Sectarianism, just like social welfare, entails a process of inclusion and exclusion.[23] In an in-depth case study of welfare and sectarianism in Lebanon, Melani Cammett found that political parties that face harsh competition within their own religious group tend to limit the provision of social services to closely affiliated in-group members, while parties that enjoy a dominant position within their own religious group have a greater propensity to inclusive distribution that may even reach out to selected out-group members.

More concretely, the author finds that while Hezbollah offers services primarily in Shi'a neighbourhoods, its welfare institutions tend to service members of other confessional origins as well. The Sunni Muslim Future Movement of Saad Hariri has extended services relatively broadly (in particular after 2005), unlike Christian political parties, which focus more narrowly on their support base within Christian communities. At the same time, these religious parties share executive power and ministerial positions. The Lebanese administration at the sub-national level is organized around eight regional governorates or *mohafazat*, under the responsibility of a governor or *mohafiz* appointed by the cabinet to implement national policies and liaise with the twenty-six districts and 985 municipalities, many of which have very little resources and hardly any employees.[24]

After the Israeli military intervention of 2006, the Lebanese economy had grown by a remarkable yearly average of 9 per cent in 2007–10. The growth rate came down to less than 2 per cent in 2011–13, just as the Syrian crisis broke out. According to the Global Humanitarian Assistance 2014 Report (GHA 2014), remittances represent the major resource inflow in Lebanon (with an estimated total of $7.3bn in 2012), followed by foreign direct investment ($3.7bn). Humanitarian and development aid are relatively marginal in comparison, coming to $404m and $489m respectively. Based on 2012 data, foreign aid together with international peacekeeping ($525m) is not even equivalent to 10 per cent of total government expenditures ($13.3bn).[25]

The overall impact of the Syrian crisis on the Lebanese economy has repeatedly been singled out as negative outright. The World Bank estimated that the crisis cost 2.9 per cent of GDP per year between 2012 and 2014, with the tourism sector and investor confidence being particularly impacted. The debt-to-GDP ratio was 134 per cent in 2012 and the fiscal deficit close to 9 per cent of GDP. With government revenue decreasing by $1.5bn and public expenditure increasing by $1.1bn in 2013 to respond to enhanced demand for public services as a result of the Syrian refugee influx, the quality of and access to essential services is set to diminish for both the refugee and Lebanese population. The Director of the National Poverty Targeting Programme noted that the majority of the Syrian refugees had settled in host communities that had the greatest incidence of poverty and the poorest infrastructure before the crisis, estimating that 1.2 million Lebanese had been directly or indirectly affected by the refugee influx.[26]

Based on a 2007 UN Development Programme (UNDP) survey, a quarter of the Lebanese population lived below the national poverty line of $4 a day, with large spatial disparities. The Syrian crisis may have pushed an additional 170,000 into poverty and multiplied unemployment by two so that it reached about 20 per cent of the population. The country's infrastructure, badly in need of repair and new investment before the crisis, was simply not prepared to cope with the sudden surge in demand associated with the refugee influx. About 80 per cent of Lebanese had access to an inefficient water network and 93 per cent to the electricity network. Power cuts are very frequent, which nurtures a juicy business for those sectarian leaders involved in the sale of fuel and generators.

There have been very few studies on the economic benefits from the refugee influx. Various sectors and groups profit from the ensuing windfall. Landlords and landowners draw higher rents, as reflected by a 44 per cent rental price hike between June 2012 and June 2013 alone. The massive aid influx stimulated demand for goods and services in relatively underserved areas, offering business opportunities to Lebanese suppliers. By November 2014, the WFP food e-voucher programme (described below) had injected about $800m into the economies of Syria's neighbouring countries hosting refugees. In Lebanon, about 400 shops are involved in the food aid programme while local banks deal with the distribution of cash and electronic vouchers to the refugees via ATM cards.

In 2013, labour supply in Lebanon had increased by an estimated 30 per cent. The agriculture, construction and service sectors have benefited from an abundant supply of cheap labour to increase profit margins. The BRIC study confirmed that domestic businesses hired Syrians who accept jobs for lower daily remuneration than the Lebanese, about $6 instead of $15 a day in rural areas,[27] resulting in wages being halved over two years in the agricultural sector. Daily labourers, shop keepers and sex workers were also cited as making lower incomes.[28] Even if some argue that Syrians take up jobs that Lebanese are not willing to perform, there is a widespread sense that Syrians take jobs away from the Lebanese, especially among the unemployed Lebanese youth. As in any other country experiencing a large influx of migrants, this has prompted mixed feelings and the refugees sometimes serve as scapegoats for Lebanese political, security and economic woes. In response to popular pressure, the government has started to crack down on Syrian-operated shops and barred refugees from opening new businesses in 2014. This results in refugees depending more on humanitarian aid, frustrating breadwinners who are no longer able to fulfil their role. Yet, given the sheer scale of the rapid migratory inflow, many Lebanese host communities deserve to be praised for welcoming a high number of refugees despite very limited resources. By early 2015, Lebanon had come under serious strain, still bearing deep scars from the civil war that tore the country apart between 1975 and 1990. The large influx of Syrian refugees, mainly Sunni Muslims, strains the delicate balance between demography and political representation. This is a very sensitive issue, which explains why there has not been any country-wide demographic census since 1932 to ascertain the size of each Lebanese community.

In sum, the humanitarian sector in Lebanon shifted from rapid needs assessment to more in-depth household economy analyses in order to design and adapt aid programmes accordingly. Such analyses provide a reference for targeting aid to those deemed more vulnerable, notably in response to funding shortfalls. Humanitarian aid has played a role in cushioning the shock associated with the refugee influx, not least thanks to cash-based assistance that allows refugees to cover some of their needs across sectors. Yet, the aid system is also facing mounting constraints. As the crisis drags on and humanitarian funding is limited, more attention is given to the capacity of the Lebanese state to address the needs of vulnerable refugees and nationals alike. The next section turns to aid funding and programming, with an emphasis on cash assistance.

Humanitarian Aid in Lebanon

Schematically, one may distinguish between a traditional, Western-led humanitarian response under the leadership of the UN, and humanitarian aid by so-called non-traditional donors. The second consists of Gulf and other Arab states as well as national Red Crescent societies and Islamic charities from the Gulf region. Within the UN humanitarian system, the UNHCR is playing a lead role: in addition to its mission of registering and protecting refugees, the UNHCR is the lead coordinating agency and is a major donor for dozens of non-governmental organizations that implement aid programmes in the field. The UNHCR budget skyrocketed from $13.5m prior to the crisis in 2010 to funding requirements of $557m in 2015. This includes a budget for the partial reimbursement of refugees' healthcare expenditure with the support of GlobeMed Lebanon, a private healthcare benefits management company whose primary role is to review the cases of refugees needing hospitalization and possibly subsidized care.[29] As for non-traditional donors, despite lip-service paid to coordination, it is close to impossible to ascertain the aid volume because of a lack of transparent reporting and the difficulty of tracing the channels through which the aid reaches Syrian refugees. In 2013, Kuwait, the United Arab Emirates and Saudi Arabia reportedly contributed 13.4 per cent of total international humanitarian assistance to Lebanon.[30] There are rumours of humanitarian aid totalling $100m from the countries of the Gulf Cooperation Council channelled via Lebanese sectarian groups between 2011 and 2013.[31]

International humanitarian aid pledging conferences brought together traditional and non-traditional donors as well as official and private actors in Kuwait in January 2013 and 2014. Despite substantial pledges, large shares of the funding appeals for Lebanon remain unmet.[32] Faced with increasing funding constraints, the UNHCR and the WFP have started to target the vulnerable. The VASyR surveys conducted in 2013 and 2014 pointed to a great heterogeneity in the refugees' livelihoods and served to establish selection criteria for identifying the vulnerable who should be entitled to humanitarian assistance. The underlying logic is to rely on proxy means testing to assess the extent to which households are able to generate resources required to cover compulsory expenditures. The exact formula to select aid beneficiaries has been kept confidential to reduce the risk of biased responses in needs assessment surveys.

The selection criteria include demographic data regarding household size and characteristics (e.g. female-headed, high dependency ratio, disabled household members) as well as socio-economic data regarding assets, employment, remittances and other income sources. It was decided that 10 per cent of the refugees would automatically receive aid based on demographic data alone. Yet, discarding economic variables may lead to inconsistencies where, say, a female-headed household with a disabled child receives aid regardless of the fact that it may benefit from regular remittances from close relatives working in the Gulf. The 2014 VASyR found 29 per cent of the sample population not to have the means to cover basic food requirements. Aware that food expenses represent only a portion of obligatory expenses, the WFP opted for providing food assistance to 70 per cent of the refugees in 2014, set to go down to 55 per cent in 2015. Anticipating funding gaps, in its 2015 plan the UNHCR included the possibility of securing access to Lebanese primary health-care facilities for only half of the Syrian refugees and referrals to secondary and tertiary medical care for less than a quarter of them.[33] In the case of a large cash shortfall, the UNHCR plans to prioritize child education and projects that help maintain peaceful coexistence with the local host communities by targeting support to Lebanese institutions and communities most affected by the presence of the refugees.[34]

The impact of the Syrian crisis in Lebanon is regarded by some humanitarian and development agencies as an opportunity to improve the provision of basic services in Lebanon, including water and electricity, primary healthcare and education, much of which is in private hands. Yet, donors have not met funding requests for the Lebanese government. Because of political instability and a weak, fragmented state, Lebanon has been unable to design and implement a national plan to respond to the crisis. The donor community, notwithstanding a consensual rhetoric to coordinate and implement aid programmes with the host state, has shown great reluctance to support state institutions and a systematic preference for bypassing them. This is motivated by fear of corruption,[35] low trust in an arguably dysfunctional political system and the presence of Hezbollah ministers in the cabinet.[36] The latter is of particular concern to the US, which is by far the largest humanitarian aid donor to Lebanon. Hezbollah has featured on the US State Department list of foreign terrorist organizations since 1997 and counter-terrorist legislation dictates that no US taxpayer money benefits such organizations and their members (see Chapters 4 and 7).

Cash and Voucher Assistance

Cash assistance is nothing new. The direct provision of cash to the poor has long been a favoured form of social protection in industrialized and developing countries. More recently, conditional cash transfer programmes in Latin America have been hailed for successfully combating poverty, whereby poor households receive regular cash allowances provided that they meet specific conditions, such as their children attending school or healthcare and vaccination campaigns. In the humanitarian sector, too, cash assistance is nothing new. Cash-for-work projects have been implemented in many protracted crises. Yet, there is no such thing as a statistical aggregate that would sum up on-going cash-based programmes. Reporting is complex since aid interventions often combine cash with other aid modalities. Hence the total amount of humanitarian cash-based assistance cannot be established with certainty. Estimates indicate that it accounted for a mere 1.5 per cent of total humanitarian funding between 2009 and 2013,[37] but is set to grow.

In Lebanon, multilateral and bilateral aid agencies as well as NGOs have embraced cash-based programming. Markets are deemed sufficiently efficient for supply to respond swiftly to any surge in demand without causing any significant price increase. Starting with the 'winterization programme' in 2013–14, the UNHCR shifted from sector-specific to multi-sector, unconditional cash grants. It distributed ATM cards to the Syrian refugees, who can withdraw their cash monthly aid allowances directly from cash machines throughout Lebanon. The project runs in partnership with CSC bank, a domestic financial institution active in the card and electronic payment process sector. The beneficiaries can freely choose how to spend cash grants according to their own needs and preferences. By enabling the recipients to cover any unmet requirements—food, shelter, transport, education, healthcare or otherwise—multi-sector cash assistance bypasses the boundaries that preside over organizational mandates and that drive turf battles in the humanitarian sector.

The WFP began shifting from paper food vouchers to electronic vouchers in September 2013. A year later, the WFP assisted over 90 per cent of the 880,000 Syrian refugees with e-vouchers. The programme involves seven implementing INGOs and a partnership with the Bank Libano-Française. It further benefits from Mastercard's technical support. The e-cards are automatically uploaded with $30 per person each month and can then be redeemed in some 400 small and medium-sized shops across the country. Instead of having to pay for transport to go to a typically overcrowded food distribution point every month, beneficiaries can purchase food items of their choice in the amount and frequency they wish. By the autumn of 2014, WFP was planning to provide monthly assistance to 75 per cent of the total registered refugee population through the provision of e-cards, depending on adequate funding. On 1 December 2014, the WFP publicly announced that it was forced to suspend its food voucher programme to 1.7 million Syrian refugees in Lebanon, Turkey, Jordan, Iraq and Egypt. Unlike complex logistical operations associated with food distribution in-kind, the food e-voucher programme can be flexibly suspended and restarted as soon as donor money gets in—which was the case a few days after the WFP announcement. The aid programme can be resumed by simply recharging the beneficiaries' cards. Instead of falling on WFP logistics, the inconvenience of unexpectedly stopping and restarting the programme is passed on to the private shops, traders and suppliers involved in the food supply chain and, of course, ultimately to the 'beneficiaries' whose assistance is withheld.

The following quotation from a participatory study on the impact of the Syrian crisis on Lebanon three years down the road is revealing about the great potential of cash-based programming for donor and humanitarian agencies:

> Humanitarian partners are planning to expand and harmonize cash assistance programmes, with the aim of delivering a multi-sectoral and comprehensive package of assistance through a single ATM card. Given the wide dispersal of the displaced population, the move from in-kind distribution to unconditional cash assistance is expected to bring cost efficiencies. First, cash will empower beneficiaries to use assistance in a way that best meets their needs. Second, it also increases operational efficiency as it entails less administrative costs especially given the responsiveness of the commodities market ... Third, it injects resources into the local economy ... As for the vulnerable host communities ... [i]t would build on a government national safety net and can include transfer of tools and knowledge.[38]

The participatory study praises cash assistance as a means of addressing the basic needs of the vulnerable across sectors in a cost-effective manner, as facilitated by technological innovations. Unconditional cash assistance is further hailed for boosting the local economy and possibly leading the Lebanese state to envisage supporting vulnerable people among the refugees and host communities alike. To the extent that markets are highly responsive and suppliers able and willing to respond to higher demand in remote areas, the inflationary pressure of cash assistance is expected to remain limited. Conversely, cash assistance averts the risk of pushing down domestic agricultural prices, a well-known issue associated with the distribution of imported food.

– The Pros and Cons of Cash-based Assistance

In addition to contributing to a rich literature on food aid[39] and cash assistance,[40] economists have long debated the pros and cons of providing cash instead of food in kind.[41] The debate has been particularly heated when it comes to food versus voucher or cash assistance in developing countries.[42] First, the relative effectiveness of each aid modality depends on contextual variables. Shifting from in-kind food to cash assistance requires well-functioning markets for grains and other foodstuffs; where such markets exist there are strong arguments in favour of cash aid. Countless case studies show that cash assistance reduces transaction costs as aid organizations can spare high transport, storage and delivery costs. Injecting cash stimulates the local economy, softens the negative economic impact of conflict and can support post-war recovery. Cash aid further tends to generate the largest welfare gains as it gives beneficiaries greater freedom on how to allocate aid between food and non-food requirements including agricultural tools and fertilizers, housing, transport, education, health and so forth. Lastly, cash is perceived as less stigmatizing for the beneficiaries to the extent that its delivery is less publicly visible than in-kind distribution. Overall, cash thus appears as a more dignifying mode of assistance.

The flipside is that distributing cash instead of food makes self-selection less likely. Food distribution being potentially more stigmatizing, only those who require assistance may eventually actively seek to get food aid (self-selection). Cash may thus be less appropriate in cases when selecting the beneficiaries would be overly time-consuming and costly.[43] In addition, cash transfers require the formal identification of beneficiaries while food aid is often granted on the basis of lists provided by communities or authorities, which include names and household sizes but lack any requirement to check each beneficiary against an identity document. In the case of cash assistance, the need for individual beneficiary identification to avoid fraud and multiple registrations can entail a time-consuming, costly process and eventually exclude marginalized people devoid of an appropriate proof of identity. The rapid spread of new biometric identification technologies can contribute to overcoming some of these barriers in the near future.

Cash aid is not suited to contexts where food supply is constrained and suppliers cannot be expected to efficiently match increasing demand. In this context, importing and distributing food instead of giving cash protects both the beneficiary and non-beneficiary populations against food price hikes. Another, more paternalist, argument relates to the assumption that in-kind or voucher food aid results in greater marginal propensity to consume food than is the case with cash assistance. In other words, aid recipients would tend to sell a lower portion of the food they get in kind than the share of the cash assistance that they would otherwise allocate to non-food items. In-kind food assistance would thus be a superior aid modality when the prime objective is to boost recipients' food intake. Indeed, in-kind food aid has been found more effective in achieving the objective of restoring or improving the quality of diets and the nutritional status of recipients. Food vouchers—a form of cash transfer—can also serve to achieve such nutritional outcomes.

In conflict settings, cash assistance is inappropriate when transferring money is simply too risky or when there is no distribution network to operate in an efficient and secure mode. The last argument against cash is that it can easily be diverted. Yet, as discussed in Chapter 3, this is also true of in-kind assistance. In addition, cash-based relief programmes have been relatively successfully implemented in low-income countries and fragile environments, including Somalia, a country that heavily relies on imported food but features a dynamic trader community and competitive markets. Recurrent famines tend to result from entitlement failures rather than from the mere lack of food availability. A group of humanitarian organizations joined hands in implementing cash and voucher-based responses to the 2011 famine (see Chapter 3). The ex-post evaluation indicated that the informal *hawala* money transfer system and private traders contributed to successful implementation, channelling the cash and vouchers to the beneficiaries and responding to the ensuing demand by satisfactorily supplying the market, with no evidence of inflation in spite of more than 100,000 households receiving regular cash transfers for more than six months to buy food.[44]

However, there are very few rigorous impact evaluations that empirically test the propositions above, and even fewer that examine the impact and cost-effectiveness of cash versus in-kind assistance in chronic crises.[45] The effectiveness and efficiency of different aid modalities should be benchmarked against the cash alternative to the extent that cash appears to be more cost-effective. A WFP-International Food Policy Research Institute (IFPRI) study assessed the performance of different transfer modalities on household food security in Ecuador, Niger, Uganda and Yemen using an experimental design with transfer modalities randomly assigned at the level of localities. The effectiveness of different aid modalities is found to depend largely on contextual variables such as the functioning of food markets. But in all four cases, the cost of cash transfers is found to be lower than that of in-kind distribution. In the case of Ecuador, for instance, it is four times lower, and about 10 per cent lower than in the case of food vouchers. A shift from food to cash thus permits increasing the number of beneficiaries by 12 per cent without increasing the WFP budget in Ecuador.[46] These findings may be valid when aid programmes involve repeated transfers. Due to lower start-up costs however, in-kind food assistance may still be more efficient in the case of a one-off distribution.

Another randomized study evaluated the impact of a winter cash transfer programme for Syrian refugees in Lebanon. The UNHCR and partner organizations granted $575 to each of 87,700 refugees from November 2013 to April 2014. The objective was to help refugees keep warm and dry during the winter, but there were no conditions regarding cash allocation. Only those refugees residing over 500 metres above the sea level were eligible. The evaluation compared a treatment group of beneficiaries living slightly above 500 metres with a control group of non-beneficiaries residing slightly below that altitude. Both the treatment and control groups were thus deemed to share similar characteristics prior to the programme implementation. The divergences observed between the two groups at the end of the programme could thus be attributed to the cash intervention.[47]

The impact evaluation found that the cash intervention had improved Syrian children's access to school and reduced child labour. It had increased solidarity support mechanisms within the beneficiary communities and reduced intra-household tensions. There was no evidence of fund diversion by intermediaries and no reports of fund 'misuse' by beneficiaries who might have increased alcohol or tobacco consumption. A majority of the cash was spent on basic needs, food and water in particular, but not so much on winter items. Finally, the programme's multiplier effect on the local economy was estimated at $2.15 for each dollar of cash assistance, with no evidence of significant price increases in consumer goods on local markets. This is an impressive success, even if this winterization programme did not serve to buy blankets, stoves, fuel and other items as initially planned, which is not surprising since the evaluation focused on households living just above the 500m threshold and the 2013–14 winter was mild. This does not preclude the possibility that beneficiaries residing above 1000m allocated a greater share of the cash to withstand the cold. In a nutshell, the findings were outright positive on all fronts. This came as a surprise to the extent that the preparatory phase of the cash programme had been too short to allow the programme managers to follow best practices in cash programme design. For example, no comprehensive market assessment was carried out to anticipate the likely impact of a large cash inflow on local markets.[48]

– Phasing Out Cash Assistance

Phasing out a cash assistance programme is more problematic than phasing out food aid. Once food recipients are able to meet their own food requirements, it makes sense to stop distributing food for free in order to avoid aid dependency and avert the negative impact of free food distribution on local markets, particularly if the food is imported. Under the same logic, beneficiaries of unconditional, multi-sector cash assistance should not graduate from the aid programme until they are able to cover all their basic needs on their own. Considering the Syrian refugee crisis in Lebanon, this is wishful thinking. Until the refugees can safely return home, graduation will depend on the capacity to link the current humanitarian response to long-term multi-dimensional development programmes in which Lebanon will have to play a leading role.

The World Bank and the UN tabled a 'Lebanon Roadmap of Priority Interventions for Stabilization from the Syrian Conflict'[49] in November 2013. The roadmap's objective is to restore and expand economic and livelihood opportunities for both the host and refugee populations and 'build resiliency in equitable access to and quality of sustainable basic public services; and strengthen social cohesion.' The roadmap claims to view development priorities with humanitarian needs in parallel for the first time, as both are directly linked to access to essential services, to economic opportunities and the ability of vulnerable communities to cope with the protracted crisis. The implementation of such a roadmap implies a transformational agenda that would deeply affect the prevailing social and political order. Social vulnerability is one of the ingredients that cements the sectarian Lebanese polity, which has proved remarkably resilient over the past decades. The maintenance of social insecurity together with the provision of social protection through sectarian, family leadership serves as an instrument of governance, authority and public action.[50] Responding to the Syrian crisis may offer an opportunity for the foreign aid community to provide financial incentives and put political pressure on Lebanon to reconsider the welfare function of the state at central and local levels vis-à-vis sectarian dynamics. Empowering central and sub-national state institutions to take a leadership role in assisting the vulnerable among the refugee and Lebanese populations may however quickly face political resistance from deeply-entrenched sectarian dynamics and interests. One should certainly resist adopting an essentialist view of sectarian identity, recognizing that individual identities evolve over time and are broader than narrow sectarian categories. That said, the Syrian crisis challenges long-established institutional arrangements and the delicate balance between demography and political representation, which is felt as politically threatening by several communities.

Wrapping up, the insights from the on-going refugee crisis in Lebanon illustrate some of the challenges of assessing the needs for assistance in complex urban, MIC settings. They highlight three major trends: increased reliance on proxy means tests to identify and select aid beneficiaries; increasing use of market analysis in vulnerability assessments; and a move to addressing needs through multi-sector cash-based programming when and where appropriate. These trends have a serious bearing not only on the humanitarian sector itself, but also on the way the sector relates to the host states and the private sector.

Concluding Remarks

Rapid needs assessment techniques serve to design life-saving responses in emergencies. In protracted crises, where the majority of humanitarian action takes place, they must be complemented with more detailed and rigorous assessments. Increasingly, relief agencies resort to proxy means testing (PMT) to identify and select the beneficiaries entitled to humanitarian aid, often in response to funding constraints that render aid targeting necessary. Such approaches are inherently inaccurate because of sampling errors, enumerators' subjective judgements, inappropriate weighing of indicators and the like. Instead of promoting impartiality in aid distribution, PMT may lead to the arbitrary selection of aid recipients. Too often, it ultimately serves as a simple rationing tool to adjust the number of beneficiaries to funding constraints or, in other words, to match the supply of humanitarian assistance with donor demand (see Chapter 2). Besides, means testing methods have been designed to target the poor in social protection programmes, which does not necessarily equate with targeting the vulnerable in a humanitarian crisis. Such methods tend to neglect critical political economy issues related to the way crises redistribute power, wealth, income and destitution, which deserve greater scrutiny when it comes to humanitarian needs assessments in general, and in urban settings in particular.

As the Lebanese case study illustrates, cash assistance is set to grow in the near future. Smart cards, mobile money, biometric recognition and other technological innovations offer opportunities to expand cash-based assistance in crisis contexts and areas where it was previously simply not feasible. It fits well with the current aid agenda and resilience paradigm that favour market-based solutions. The economic literature raises many arguments in support of cash-based programming and a few against it. Cash assistance is no silver bullet. Its adequacy depends on a host of context-specific variables such as the degree of financial inclusion, the potential linkages with social programmes that also rely on cash transfers, nutritional objectives, and recipients' preferences for food versus cash assistance. In any case, cash programming is a game changer that affects the relationship between aid providers and recipients. It also impacts the demand for certain skills and services on the humanitarian market and contributes to challenging entrenched sectoral boundaries often related to humanitarian organizations' institutional mandates.

Cash aid gives beneficiaries a greater say over how to allocate aid according to their needs. It generally cuts down transaction costs compared to in-kind distribution and reduces ensuing grievances. But in some instances, bringing trucks and moving goods into remote areas is important to reduce isolation and reinforce passive protection of conflict-affected communities through greater physical presence. In conflict-ridden areas, it is necessary to go beyond cost-benefit analysis and consider the symbolic dimension of heavy logistics and physical field presence of humanitarian agencies via warehouses, distribution sites, local offices and the likes. At the same time, cash assistance does not mean leaving beneficiaries to their ATM cash machines: nothing prevents humanitarian agencies from using the time and resources saved to increase proximity and field presence with more staff spending time with communities at risk. Last but not least, a shift to cash aid bears the risk that some donors may reduce their overall contributions since cash provides them with less visibility than food bags stamped with donors' logos, not to mention the lost opportunity for donor countries to get rid of food surpluses. These issues deserve further inquiry.

Historical evidence suggests that aid granted to refugees in protracted crises tends to influence the expectations of host communities regarding the type, quality and quantity of services that can be expected from the state. Over time, humanitarian assistance can affect the authority and legitimacy of the state, raising the bar against which domestic constituencies gauge their government's performance. Large-scale and long-term cash assistance in favour of hundreds of thousands of Syrian refugees in Lebanon pushes the host state to step in and harmonize the support provided to vulnerable Lebanese with that granted to refugees. This may conflict with the welfare function traditionally fulfilled by sectarian parties seeking greater support and authority in return.

A major challenge identified in the vulnerability assessments conducted in 2014 is to address the mounting tensions between Syrian refugees and Lebanese host communities. The UNHCR has suggested assisting refugees in developing 'self-resilience' and in sharing quality time with host communities. The UNDP, together with UNHCR, spearheaded a Regional Refugee and Resilience Plan, presented as 'a global first for the UN in the terms of its response to crises ... [an] inclusive model for delivering an effective and coordinated response which addresses, through national plans, immediate vulnerability, strengthens social cohesion, and builds the resilience of people, communities and national systems.'[51] The next chapter focuses precisely on the resilience paradigm and the transformative power of humanitarian crises and responses.

THE TRANSFORMATIVE POWER
OF HUMANITARIAN CRISES

I always tried to turn every disaster into an opportunity

John D. Rockefeller[1]

As the American oil tycoon John D. Rockefeller put it, disasters can be conceived as opportunities to advance specific interests and agendas. Crises are powerful vectors of change that produce winners and losers over space and time. They can be seized as opportunities to instil reforms that would otherwise be difficult or impossible to implement.[2] Humanitarian crises represent critical junctures that can radically alter long-term development trajectories. Wars and disasters do not only redistribute the cards—at least those left on the table after the crisis—but they can also alter the rules of the game. Indeed, civil wars may occur precisely because people want change.

Nowadays, the dominant transformative agendas spearheaded by the global aid community revolve around stabilization, peacebuilding and statebuilding in conflict-ridden or so-called 'fragile states', or around disaster risk management (DRM) and building back better (BBB) with reference to disaster settings. Central to these agendas is the resilience paradigm, which pursues the expansion of a specific form of governmentality[3] associated with liberal democratic peace. This may fit the transformative agenda of the international development aid enterprise, but less so the more conservative and limited agenda of the humanitarian sector. The key question for humanitarian organizations deemed impartial, neutral and independent is the degree to which they associate themselves with transformative endeavours that pursue changes in value systems, institutions, regulatory frameworks, technological systems and power structures.[4] The response to this question has a direct bearing on the way humanitarians operate on the ground, in particular on how they interact with a growing variety of actors involved in relief and recovery as drivers of change rather than as impartial aid providers.[5]

Stabilization, DRM and BBB remain fuzzy concepts. They refer to a wide set of discourses, policies and practices. This brings humanitarians closer to a broad diversity of actors who intervene in humanitarian crises with different objectives and agendas, such as private contractors, multinational and domestic corporations, military coalitions and regional inter-governmental organizations. The intensification of cross-sector collaborations and multi-stakeholder partnerships may help humanitarians prevent and respond to humanitarian crises more effectively. But collaborative arrangements can also put the humanitarian space in jeopardy through the politicization and instrumentalization of humanitarian aid in the pursuit of objectives that go well beyond saving lives, alleviating suffering and protecting human dignity.

Following 9/11, Afghanistan and Iraq have become the top recipients of foreign aid in terms of money and personnel.[6] Several bilateral and multilateral development organizations have sought to reposition themselves as relevant partners in stabilization, partly as a way to muster renewed political support for aid budgets and to (re)gain a stronger voice at inter-ministerial and inter-agency levels. More broadly, humanitarian and development aid actors increasingly work in the same contexts where stabilization and BBB prevail at the discursive, strategic and operational levels. Humanitarians tend to refer to such contexts as 'chronic crises' while development actors refer to 'fragile states', thus providing different justifications for operating in the same areas. The progressive blurring of lines between humanitarian action, development assistance and military interventions has revived divisions between relief and development as well as within the humanitarian community itself. A few humanitarian organizations have opted to stay clear of broader economic and political agendas. Many others were happily co-opted under the humanitarian umbrella of comprehensive approaches linking aid with security and diplomatic undertakings.

In this chapter, I first look at the transformative impact of humanitarian crises. I then examine the tensions embedded in comprehensive approaches that combine political, security, development and humanitarian objectives. Drawing on previous chapters, I focus on stabilization in war and BBB in disaster settings, and question how the rise of the resilience paradigm impacts the humanitarian sector. Since an expanding web of collaborative arrangements and a growing variety of actors have come to characterize the humanitarian marketplace, the last section discusses the issue of partnerships, with a particular emphasis on the business-humanitarian nexus.

Crises as Critical Junctures for Development Trajectories

The Black Plague can be considered the largest disaster ever to have hit Europe in terms of the proportion of the total population that died over a few years: the scourge wiped out a good third of the European population, peaking between 1348 and 1350. In *Economic Behavior in Adversity*,[7] Jack Hirshleifer gives a fascinating account of the transformational impact of the Black Death, which raged from Sicily to the North Sea and from Portugal to Russia. The immediate effect was a dramatic fall in total economic output. In the longer-term, the pandemic radically altered the balance between factors of production. Labour became scarcer and land relatively more abundant. This abrupt alteration in the capital-to-labour ratio strengthened the bargaining power of serfs vis-à-vis landlords. Nominal wages of agricultural labourers increased substantially while the income of landowners suffered from a lower rent value associated with relatively more abundant agricultural land. Serfs were able to challenge the ties that bound them to their lords' estates. As labour supply had plummeted, those tenants who survived were allowed greater mobility and bargained for more favourable labour conditions. This eroded medieval institutions and contributed to giving rise to more modern contractual arrangements between capital owners and the labour force.

While this may hold true for England in particular and Western Europe in general, the reverse actually unfolded in Eastern Europe. In *Why Nations Fail*, Acemoglu and Robinson underline that the East European landed aristocracy, wary of losing its power over serfdom, tightened its grip over the serfs, for instance prohibiting them from leaving their lord's property on pain of death. As a result, medieval institutions were firmly reinstated in Eastern Europe whereas they had been seriously eroded in the West.[8] The authors argue that this deviation in responding to the plague represents a critical juncture that accentuated minor differences and explains diverging development trajectories over centuries, with earlier industrialization and stronger growth in Western than in Eastern Europe. This example highlights that major disasters can give rise to progressive change or increased repression that preserves the status quo, depending on the institutional context and the outcome of power struggles.

Let us consider another of the worst deadly pandemics: the so-called Spanish Flu swept across the globe at the end of World War I, killing up to 100 million people,[9] more than the total battle-related deaths during the war. The immediate impact was a drop in global economic output. But the longer-term effect on per capita income turned positive in several countries, as was the case in the US during the 1920s, again thanks to an abrupt alteration in the capital-to-labour ratio.[10] More recently, a spatial evaluation of the impact of Hurricane Katrina in Louisiana, Alabama and Mississippi revealed that specific disaster-hit areas became a 'doughnut hole' of unemployment and low income surrounded by a ring of higher growth in neighbouring regions that benefited from the reconstruction activities.[11] As is often the case, politics provides part of the explanation. Since the city of New Orleans was expected to remain firmly in the Democrat camp, it was less attractive to provide relief there compared to other spots where relief could serve the purpose of rewarding allies or winning over the votes of disaster victims.[12]

Financial and economic crises also represent critical junctures for change. Milton Friedman, one of the most influential economists of the second half of the twentieth century, released a new edition of *Capitalism and Freedom* in 1982. This coincided with the outburst of the Mexican debt crisis that was about to spread to Latin America and the whole developing world, spurring a wave of neoliberal reforms associated with aid conditionality. Prophetically, Friedman wrote in his preface:

> Only a crisis—actual or perceived—produces real change. When that crisis occurs, the actions that are taken depend on the ideas that are lying around. That, I believe, is our basic function: to develop alternatives to existing policies, to keep them alive and available until the politically impossible becomes politically inevitable.[13]

In *The Shock Doctrine: The Rise of Disaster Capitalism*, Naomi Klein illustrated this process with a series of cases showing how the powerful seize the opportunities created by wars and disasters to impose drastic reforms that would otherwise be inconceivable. Such reforms are made possible by the public's disorientation in the midst of large collective shocks.[14]

Stabilization and the Securitization of Aid[15]

Conceiving of foreign aid as an instrument to advance security objectives is nothing new. Since its inception, official development assistance (ODA) has largely been driven by the security and geostrategic concerns of donor countries.[16] The Marshall Plan represents a well-known early case of a reconstruction and stabilization package. The American contribution was immense, amounting to $13.2bn from 1948 to 1951, equivalent to 2.5% of the recipients' GDP, or approximately $110bn in 2014 US dollars. Yet, the major contribution to European recovery was not financial aid itself, but rather the conditions attached to the Marshall Plan. The plan strongly encouraged recipient governments to deregulate the post-war economy, promote regional integration and rely more heavily on market mechanisms. Massive aid contributed to cushioning the population against the social costs of adjustment to these reforms. Aid was granted on the condition that recipient governments committed to keeping budgets and inflation under control.[17] As the Cold War intensified, the objective of containing the spread of communism became increasingly central to the plan. Subsequently, ODA became a foreign policy instrument often used to support and reward allies in the Third World during the Cold War.[18]

Today, the security-development nexus has once again assumed prominence under 'stabilization', all the way from Colombia to Afghanistan via the Sahel region, Kenya, Somalia, Sri Lanka and Pakistan. Defining the concept is problematic since stabilization refers to a broad agenda and to operational approaches that carry different meanings for different actors under the shared stated objective of promoting peace, security and democracy. Civil servants and diplomats refer to stabilization with the purpose of enhancing domestic policy coherence and overall consistency in their dealings with war-torn states in the context of whole-of-government or comprehensive approaches aimed at ensuring a 'unity of purpose' across government agencies and departments. In many of the traditional aid donor countries, this has translated into the adoption of a '3D approach' that combines defence with diplomacy and development objectives.

Canada, Denmark, Germany, Italy, the Netherlands, the UK and the US have all adopted versions of the 3D approach. A quick look at the resources allocated to defence versus humanitarian and development budgets shows that the relationship between each of the three Ds is highly skewed. For example, in 2009 the combined military budgets of Development Assistance Committee (DAC) members were 8.5 times higher than their foreign aid budgets. There are very significant variations from one donor country to another, as illustrated in Figure 14, which shows the ratio of ODA to military expenses in 2013.[19] It is not surprising that defence tends to prevail over development and humanitarian objectives, even if the aid voice may have more weight in countries where ODA amounts to at least 60 per cent of military expenditure (e.g. Denmark and Norway) than in countries where it is below 30 per cent (e.g. Australia, Canada and France), not to mention the US where ODA is less than 5 per cent of military expenditure.

Under the banner of stabilization and statebuilding, international aid and military actors join hands with host states in activities ranging from counter-insurgency operations to the provision of relief and development assistance to local communities. The objective is to give the state greater legitimacy and weaken the insurgency by winning people's hearts and minds, enhancing intelligence gathering by turning community members into informants.[20] With the blurring of lines between military, development and humanitarian remits and actors, it is not surprising that insurgent groups have reacted by attacking humanitarian aid workers, who represent the softest targets among potential 'stabilizers' to the extent that they operate in the field without armed protection. Since 2006, the majority of attacks committed against humanitarian workers are concentrated in countries targeted by stabilization like Afghanistan, Pakistan, Iraq, Sudan, Chad and Somalia, with over 270 workers killed, abducted or severely injured in those places in 2010 alone. In 2013, the total number of workers (national and international) abducted, killed or wounded amounted to 461.[21] In a vicious cycle, insecurity pushes aid agencies to seek

14. ODA in % of military expenditure, 2013

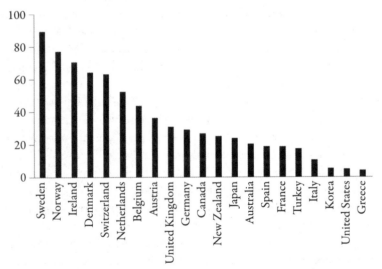

Source: ODA data from DAC and military expenditure from SIPRI.

military protection, further adding to the blurring of lines between humanitarian, development and military actors as perceived by host communities.

Managing Disaster Risks and Building Back Better

Compared to war settings, disaster situations may seem more propitious for close collaboration between humanitarian and other actors in general, and the military in particular. There is a tendency to think of post-disaster environments as apolitical spaces where compassionate actors come from all walks of life to help 'innocent' victims; a blank page where history can be written anew. This is obviously far from field reality. First, post-disaster situations can be suffused with power struggles and social tensions inherited from the past, which are exacerbated by the dislocation caused by the disaster and the ensuing struggle to capture part of the aid package. Second, disasters are often associated with episodes of armed violence, which often justifies military intervention with the stated aim to put an end to looting and restore law and order. Over half of the people affected by disasters between 2005 and 2009 were reported to live in conflict-prone and fragile states.[22] Theoretical arguments and rudimentary empirical evidence hint at a perverse cycle between disaster, weak institutions and war. For example, drought episodes are characterized by higher mortality rates when hitting war-torn countries.

This does not mean that disaster causes armed conflict. Since the end of the Cold War, the increased frequency and intensity of climate-related disasters has not been paralleled by a surge in the number of armed conflicts. Recent findings from panel data analysis actually contradict the growing concern over the climate-conflict nexus: countries affected by a higher incidence of climate-related disasters face a lower probability of civil war.[23] Further research is required to better identify causal links and the role of specific contextual variables. Even in the absence of an established causal relationship between disaster and armed conflict, organizations that want to be perceived as strictly impartial, neutral and independent humanitarian actors have good reasons to envisage civil-military cooperation in post-disaster contexts on a cautious case-by-case basis.

The global aid community has embraced DRM as an overarching agenda that includes disaster risk reduction (DRR), the mitigation of existing risks, and disaster preparedness and disaster response. DRR is geared towards identifying and reducing the causal factors of disaster risks, including those caused by natural hazards such as floods, droughts, cyclones and earthquakes. In practice, DRR involves a range of preventive activities, such as the retrofitting of critical social facilities and infrastructure. This may, for example, imply rendering health facilities quake-proof, promoting environmental recovery through reforestation to reduce landslide risks, or implementing corrective actions after a disaster such as relocating people out of highly-exposed areas or rebuilding quake-resistant houses.[24]

In the context of disaster response, the catch-all concept of BBB has gained great traction among disaster-prone states and international organizations. In practice, it includes a wide array of programmes and activities aimed at reducing exposure to risks and enhancing 'resilience' (see next section and Chapter 5). Just like stabilization, BBB does not pursue a neutral agenda restricted to technical fixes, but involves a process of rapid political and social transformation that is perceived positively by some and negatively by others. It is hard to argue against BBB: as Lilianne Fan puts it, 'who would want to build *worse* or reinstate conditions of inequality, poverty and vulnerability if the chance of something better was at hand?'[25] However, the variety of relief and reconstruction activities initiated under BBB has a substantial impact on how different stakeholders understand the role and scope of humanitarian action.

By way of example, let us consider post-disaster reconstruction in the Province of Aceh, Indonesia following the December 2014 tsunami. The disaster that hit the conflict-torn province killed an estimated 165,000 there and destroyed vast chunks of the southern and eastern coastal areas. An unprecedented worldwide mobilization made about $8bn available for relief and reconstruction. BBB as a concept became so popular that it made its entry into the recovery plan as a separate budgetary line that accounted for a quarter of the total of $8bn.[26] The Indonesian government established a special agency to oversee the relief operations. The president appointed Kuntoro Mangkusubroto—a former minister of mining known for his integrity—to establish and conduct the Agency for the Rehabilitation and Reconstruction of Aceh and Nias, known under its Indonesian acronym BRR, for Badan Rehabilitasi dan Rekonstruksi. Enjoying high respect and credibility, Mr Mangkusubroto was adamant that BRR be established as a fully autonomous agency equipped with an anti-corruption unit—quite an innovation in Indonesia at the time! Beyond Aceh, the ambition was to seize the opportunity of the disaster to instil governance reform in Indonesia. However, the outpouring of foreign aid was quickly followed by accusations of corruption in several BRR-managed projects.[27]

The tsunami drew international attention to the civil war that had started almost three decades earlier, pitting the Indonesian government against the

Free Aceh Movement (known as the Gerakan Aceh Merdeka or GAM) fighting for the independence of the oil-rich province. A few months after the tsunami, the peace agreement was eventually signed on 15 August 2005. BRR sought to push for reforms with a view to lifting post-conflict Aceh 'out of isolation'. From the outset, Bill Clinton, who had been appointed UN Special Envoy for Tsunami Recovery in Southeast Asia, included the promotion of entrepreneurship accompanied by market-based reforms in his ten key BBB propositions. A decade later, can we say that BBB successfully turned Aceh into an open neoliberal playground, echoing Naomi Klein's 'disaster capitalism' argument? As so often, the reality is more complicated. The post-tsunami provincial leadership, largely originating from the ranks of GAM, prioritized the restoration of sovereignty and the right to self-governance and autonomous development.[28] The BBB agenda clashed with that of former GAM leaders, who came into power after the 2006 elections. Aceh's criminal war economy quickly turned into a post-conflict economy driven by rent seeking and clientelism. Top figures among GAM commanders shifted from combatants to contractors, enticed by juicy post-disaster construction contracts where political connections and corruption often determined who was contracted and at what price.[29] Other GAM figures became provincial political leaders and civil servants.[30] The provincial authorities strengthened the application of Sharia law,[31] including vis-à-vis non-Muslims,[32] and infuriated Jakarta by introducing a provincial tax on mining activities requiring extractive industries to pay between 2.2 and 6.6 per cent of their product-selling price to the Acehnese administration.[33] Overall, local and regional political economy interactions combined with diverging 'ideas that were lying around'—to paraphrase Milton Friedman—to undermine the BBB, liberal grand design.

Again, in the aftermath of the January 2010 earthquake in Haiti, BBB dominated the discourse within a resilience agenda. This raised expectations among Haitians, soon followed by a deep sense of frustration as recovery stalled and the promise of a better future did not materialize for the majority of Haitians despite billions of aid dollars pledged. BBB arguably diverted resources and energy away from responding effectively to urgent needs, most notably saving lives when an unexpected cholera outbreak took thousands more Haitian lives just nine months after the earthquake.[34] Some humanitarian practitioners argued that BBB, as an overarching strategy focusing on recovery and resilience, contributed to the failure of the aid enterprise in the case of Haiti: it raised expectations too high with regard to the speed and extent of the post-earthquake recovery, causing resentment among Haitians as their expectations were left unmet.

BBB, like stabilization, emphasizes the role of humanitarian and development assistance in enhancing the resilience of crisis-affected states. But what is resilience, and what does it mean, in particular for the humanitarian sector in its interactions with the state?

Resilience

The international humanitarian and development fields are awash with buzzwords. Resilience has been consecrated as a new catchword in recent academic and practitioner literature, while donors have increasingly targeted funding towards humanitarian programmes tagged with a 'resilience' label. There is very little consensus on the concept of resilience; it encompasses a broad diversity of understandings, from a focus on the inner ability of individuals to withstand natural hazards and other adverse shocks to an emphasis on the dynamic relationship between individuals and their social and natural environments in the context of complex adaptive systems. The resilience paradigm is often perceived as a response (in the context of neoliberal critiques of aid concerned with aid dependence) to the fact that ODA would arguably neglect and erode the capacity of aid recipients to absorb and adapt to shocks.[35] However, as noted by David Chandler, the distinction between resilience proponents and opponents is not so clear-cut:

> While some work is critical of the concept of resilience—predominantly by asserting that it is a framework for neoliberal understanding—for many radical or critical thinkers ambiguity seems to dominate, arguing that resilience is problematic when used by hegemonic power but that understandings of adaptive complexity can be useful tools of oppositional critique.[36]

Initially conceptualized in particular in psychology, engineering and ecology, resilience more recently gained traction in the fields of climate change adaptation and DRR. Different definitions have been advanced depending on the disciplinary perspective as well as on the field of study or practice.[37] The constitutive elements of most definitions include the ability to absorb, adapt to and recover from the impact of a shock associated with a sudden change in the environment. The concept is applied all the way from individuals and communities to entire societies and the planet.[38] Resilience is not so much about preservation or returning to a state of equilibrium. Many definitions relate to the capacity to adapt and transform rather than to resist change.

From a normative viewpoint, resilience can be positive as much as it can be negative. For example, warlords in Afghanistan have proven remarkably resilient in resisting peacebuilding pressure and in keeping the criminal economy bustling, a kind of resilience that the international donor community has not hailed as positive.

Development actors embraced resilience as a key objective in the 2000s, in addition to poverty reduction and economic growth. Just like vulnerability, resilience does not reduce to poverty levels. The poor can sometimes be more resilient to adverse shocks than the wealthy, since under normal circumstances the former must draw on a greater diversity of coping mechanisms to make a living than the latter. There can even be a trade-off between resilience and wellbeing when individuals who become destitute adapt their preferences and lower their expectations to adjust to a new adverse reality. Such adaptive preferences may strengthen resilience at the cost of greater poverty or inequality.[39] Likewise, in the humanitarian field there can be a tension between reducing vulnerability and pursuing greater resilience. Adopting a vulnerability approach implies dealing with social and political dynamics. A resilience approach tends to place more emphasis on the capacity of systems to absorb shocks and recover without necessarily paying much attention to social exclusion and power relations within the system, which risks drawing attention to technical fixes only. In war and disaster settings in particular, social and political economy dynamics should lie at the heart of any resilience agenda pursued by humanitarian actors. On that basis, the resilience paradigm can help situate vulnerability in the context of complex adaptive systems, which allows for better capturing of systemic interactions and feedback loops.

Traditional needs assessments tend to focus on weaknesses, deficits and failures. A resilience approach puts more emphasis on the ability of individuals, communities and institutions to adapt and reorganize. It draws attention to existing strengths, flexibility and systemic interactions involving transformations and innovations. This can be particularly relevant in conflict zones where political hybridity prevails, such as northern Iraq, the Kivus or South Sudan. Hybrid political orders underscore the fact that the state is not necessarily the only provider of security, welfare and representation. It shares authority, legitimacy and the capacity to provide security and welfare with a variety of formal and informal networks, strongmen, traditional leaders and institutions,[40] each with conflicting claims to economic resources and political legitimacy. Hybrid political orders may offer a modicum of stability, redistribution and inclusivity, all of which are potential vectors of resilience worth considering,[41] at least from a humanitarian standpoint. Where essential public services have never been effectively provided or have broken down as a result of civil war, local public or private institutions may represent pockets of effectiveness worth supporting, be it in the health, water and sanitation or agriculture sectors. A resilience approach may be conducive to identifying and supporting rather than circumventing such institutions, which may be reasonably effective in 'serving some conception of the public good despite operating in an environment in which most public organizations are ineffective and subject to serious predation [or] patronage'.[42] This is nothing new. Often unwittingly, humanitarian pragmatism has contributed to bottom-up statebuilding by supporting the capacity of sub-national and quasi-state entities to extend essential services to community members. Depending on the circumstances, this can coincide with—or run counter to—top-down statebuilding strategies pursued under the stabilization agenda inspired by a Weberian conception of modern statehood.

Resilience can serve as a collective heuristic device to stimulate collaboration between researchers from different disciplines and aid workers from different agencies around innovative research and operational approaches in situations of chronic crisis. This challenges the traditional humanitarian/development divide between the conservative agenda of neutral and impartial life-saving operations and the more transformative ambitions of the development agenda. The resilience paradigm, by bringing humanitarian actors deeper into cross-sector collaborations, can erode the legitimacy and acceptance of humanitarian action in the field. Collaborative arrangements must be carefully crafted with regard to legitimacy issues, weighing the risks and opportunities involved. The case of partnerships between humanitarian and business actors illustrates many of the issues involved.

Business-Humanitarian Partnerships[43]

The rebalancing of power between the state and the market together with the partial privatization and outsourcing of humanitarian operations has led to greater private sector involvement in humanitarian crises and responses. And as the humanitarian sector grows larger and professionalizes, it borrows from business in terms of management philosophy, corporate culture and the conscientious pursuit of innovation. The business world exerts an increasing influence on the humanitarian sector, as is evident from the insurance industry's involvement in disaster risk management (see Chapter 5) and the information and communications technology sector's partnerships with humanitarian organizations (see below).

Different companies can play various roles in humanitarian crises, from perpetrating international humanitarian law (IHL) violations to being victims of such violations; from contributing to disasters to supplying humanitarian organizations with relevant goods and services to address the plight of those hit by disasters; or from providing direct assistance in the field to spurring innovations indirectly. Such roles largely hinge upon the characteristics of the economic sector in which a company operates, its ownership and organizational structure, its corporate culture as well as the type of humanitarian crisis in which it operates. Beyond multinational companies, the contributions of domestic companies are worth exploring further as they develop greater relationships with humanitarian agencies in crisis-prone environments, for example in the transport, logistics and banking sectors. Doing away with the unitary-actor assumption about the business sector allows a more nuanced appreciation of the various impacts of different business entities in humanitarian crises, and the ensuing risks and entry points for aid agencies.

The funding share of the business sector in total humanitarian assistance remains limited. Private companies and corporations donated an estimated $1.1bn between 2008 and 2012 to humanitarian NGOs, the International Movement of the Red Cross and Red Crescent and UN agencies,[44] or slightly less than 1 per cent of total humanitarian assistance. But the contributions from businesses are not limited to cash donations. Beyond funding and traditional client-supplier relations, humanitarian organizations have increasingly engaged private companies for other purposes such as in-kind donations of goods and services, the transfer of specific skills and know-how, or the introduction of innovations in humanitarian operations. Some humanitarian actors have also engaged in public advocacy campaigns and lobbying activities, for example targeted at the pharmaceutical sector.

Even if the issue may seem obvious, the motives for business-humanitarian collaborations stir much debate. To start, private firms obviously do not pursue the same objectives as humanitarian organizations and cannot be labelled 'humanitarian actors'. The business of business is business: corporations pursue profit and shareholder-value maximization. This does not preclude individual company executives or employees from sharing at times genuine humanitarian concerns, for instance when the staff of an extractive industry working on an oil rig in the Mediterranean Sea decide to rescue Africans and Syrians floating adrift as they attempt to seek refuge in Europe.[45] At a corporate level, there are several drivers for business-humanitarian partnerships (BHPs). First, associating a company's brand with a humanitarian cause can be a cost-effective way to manage reputational risks and bolster public image. Second, a BHP can help preserve the company's license to operate in difficult environments and protect the long-term viability of investments in such contexts. Third, engaging humanitarian organizations can give partner companies a first-mover advantage in crisis zones, providing a competitive edge in so-called 'frontier markets' over competitors during the reconstruction phase, as the corporate partner has already established a presence during the crisis. And fourth, BHPs can enhance employee satisfaction and help a company to attract and retain the best talents while contributing to a distinct corporate culture that can pride itself on supporting relief operations in response to major humanitarian crises.[46]

As for humanitarian organizations, the motives to partner with private companies include: (i) getting financial support and diversifying funding sources, (ii) tapping into the technical expertise, skills and innovation potential of companies with a view to enhancing operational capacity, (iii) promoting greater respect for IHL and human rights—with an emphasis on the 'negative' responsibility of firms to do no harm—and (iv) enhancing humanitarian outreach, which emphasizes the 'positive' corporate responsibility to do good and tap into the political outreach of the business world, a contentious issue worth exploring further.

In sum, BHPs can strengthen the operational capacity of humanitarian agencies, but also entail risks in terms of reputation, legitimacy and licence to operate in war-torn countries. Indeed, humanitarian organizations evolve in an arena of internal and external normative scrutiny and deliberation involving multiple audiences such as armed groups, donor states, advocacy NGOs as well as the staff and associated members of relief organizations. The legitimacy of collaborative arrangements between the humanitarian and business sectors can be contested by different audiences. For the humanitarian partner in a BHP, associating its brand or image with that of a multinational company can have a serious impact on how it is perceived by key stakeholders, which can put its reputation at risk. Yet, there is no inherent incompatibility between humanitarian organizations and profit-driven entities. Much depends on the behaviour, activities and reputation of the corporate partner.

Establishing the legitimacy of BHPs can be considered as an iterative process embedded in the specific normative context of humanitarianism. Based on a detailed study of the principles and guidelines adopted over time by major humanitarian organizations with regard to BHPs,[47] my colleague Liliana Andonova and I found out that legitimation strategies rest to a large extent on normative fit, institutional integrity and comparative worth.[48] First, there is a need to ensure the normative fit or moral acceptability of partnerships to avoid violations of widely shared moral standards as well as blatant discrepancies between the values and mission of the humanitarian organization and the behaviour and activities of its corporate partner. Humanitarian organizations such as UNICEF and the International Movement of the Red Cross and the Red Crescent have adopted principles on selecting 'appropriate' corporate partners, which for example excludes firms that manufacture arms and ammunitions or whose activities are materially deleterious to health. Second, the institutional integrity of BHPs must be warranted through internal procedures that ensure adequate transparency, accountability and oversight. This includes due diligence in screening companies against the principles mentioned above, together with transparent decision-making procedures. Third, outcome legitimacy relies on the eventual positive humanitarian impact of business-humanitarian partnerships. This remains the Achilles heel of legitimating strategies: the capacity of humanitarian organizations to rigorously assess the comparative worth of a partnership, or to evaluate its humanitarian outcome, remains extremely weak. Singling out the specific impact of BHPs is methodologically challenging and remains under-researched.

Many BHPs involve companies active in the information and communications technology (ICT) sector. Even outside of any partnership framework, the ICT sector illustrates how an industry can alter the way humanitarian action is carried out. The advent of geospatial data and GIS mapping, mobile communication, open-data systems, and satellite imagery affects early warning, crisis mapping, needs assessment and humanitarian coordination. Mobile-phone money transfer systems allow SMS-based giving and the design of mobile e-vouchers and cash-transfer programmes. ICT innovations further gave rise to web-based fundraising and the leveraging of global volunteer networks, as well as the expansion of social media in crisis-affected environments, providing affected people with the opportunity to voice concerns and hold humanitarian agencies to account. Conversely, relief organizations can seek greater beneficiary participation in programme design and evaluation through ICTs.

Most such technologies have not been developed with the purpose of supporting relief operations. Rather, the ICT sector is an engine of technological advances that commercial actors have adapted to the specific market features prevailing in humanitarian crises. Some of these adaptations end up impacting relief work and offering opportunities for collaboration between ICT firms and humanitarians. This is not risk free. The interface between new technologies, accountability and confidentiality raises serious challenges. The digital divide remains a significant obstacle and dual-use products are a risk. Confidentiality and privacy breaches can have major implications for the protection of key informants and beneficiaries in conflict zones. Connectivity can increase the vulnerability of humanitarian workers to attacks by providing real-time information on field movements and activities. Similarly, it raises the suspicion of warring parties regarding humanitarian workers more or less unwittingly providing intelligence to 'the enemy', which pushes rebels to shun contacts with humanitarian actors or to scare them away. The emergence of volunteer and technical networks of 'digital humanitarians' unfamiliar with the principles of neutrality, impartiality and independence is another source of concern. Organizations whose objectives are strictly humanitarian must carefully weigh the risks and opportunities of partnering with other actors who, like John D. Rockefeller, seek to turn every disaster into an opportunity.

Wrapping Up

Both humanitarian and development aid organizations invest much of their resources in the same contexts—labelled 'chronic crises' or 'fragile states'. They often share common objectives, such as reducing malnutrition and child mortality or providing drinking water to vulnerable communities. The traditional relief/development divide based on emergency versus long-term interventions, or externally- versus domestically-driven aid programmes, has largely faded. The divide is being reconfigured along a tension between a conservative humanitarian agenda and the transformative projects pursued by the development aid and peacebuilding communities who see crises as critical junctures for advancing a liberal and democratic peace project. Resilience—a concept with both conservative and transformative features—can serve as a common heuristic tool to stimulate debates and research involving different operational actors and scientific disciplines, in particular with regard to hybrid political orders and bottom-up statebuilding processes.

The stabilization and BBB agendas involve an increasing range of collaborative arrangements between humanitarian and other actors, including private companies. For the relief agencies involved, cross-sector collaborations can enhance humanitarian outcomes but require paying careful attention to legitimacy issues, including the normative fit, institutional integrity and comparative worth of partnerships. Such a framework, outlined above for business-humanitarian partnerships, can be applied to other types of collaborative arrangements that are shaping new modes of governance in the humanitarian marketplace.

CONCLUSION

Knowledge speaks, but wisdom listens.

Attributed to Jimi Hendrix[1]

The emergence of modern humanitarianism in the second half of the nineteenth century coincided with that of neoclassical economics. The former emphasized human life and dignity in war, including that of wounded enemies on the battlefield. The latter grew on methodological individualism and its emphasis on the preferences and actions of individuals in shaping social reality. Yet, it is only in recent decades that economics expanded outside its traditional precinct to study humanitarian crises, which had long interested other social sciences. The low level or lack of engagement of (some) economists with other disciplines (save for political science, to an extent) has raised controversy over economics imperialism and concerns regarding the impact of potentially biased policy advice based on findings that consider only portions of a fragmented social reality. That said, it was high time to devote greater attention to the economics and political economy of disaster, civil war and humanitarian response.

Linking theory, research and practice, this book highlights how humanitarian economics can contribute to addressing some of today's thorniest humanitarian challenges. Humanitarian economics can help enhance our understanding of humanitarian crises and of the difficulty of adequately preventing and responding to them; it can further strengthen the humanitarian sector's ability to assess and address the needs of affected people as well as to evaluate the impact and side-effects of aid policies and interventions. This book thus examines the contributions of economists and other social scientists to enhancing our understanding of the economics and political economy of humanitarian crises. It further looks at the economics of humanitarianism understood not only as a set of ideals and principles, but also as a booming aid industry and a global movement involving scores of relief organizations employing hundreds of thousands of professionals.

I started by discussing fundamental epistemological issues involved in the study of armed conflict, disaster and humanitarian action. I considered in particular whether and how altruism, emotions and humanitarian principles challenge or fit into a utility-maximizing, rational choice framework. I then examined the humanitarian marketplace and how supply and demand as well as 'needs' and supply chains evolved over the past twenty-five years. The central part of the book dealt with the contributions of war economics, terrorism economics and disaster economics to our understanding of humanitarian crises and responses. In each of the three chapters I delved into distributional issues, starting with costs and humanitarian consequences, followed by finance and profits, and then exploring how foreign aid is embedded in contemporary disaster and war economies. I then turned to how individuals, households and communities seek to survive in the midst of humanitarian crises and how aid agencies assess and respond to the ensuing needs for assistance. The impact of the Syrian crisis in Lebanon served as a case study to illustrate the complexity of intervening in an urban, middle-income country environment. Looking at the transformative power of humanitarian crises, the final chapter situated these issues in the context of broader political and economic agendas involving an increasing web of cross-sector collaborations. As an illustration, I discussed the varying roles of private companies in humanitarian crises and the risks and opportunities associated with business-humanitarian partnerships.

In this short conclusion, I do not attempt to summarize or expand on the major arguments of each chapter. Instead, I elaborate on selected topics that cut across the whole book, from theoretical and methodological issues to the major contributions of humanitarian economics to humanitarian studies and practice, and highlight three avenues for future research.

Data, Methods and Ethics

The field of humanitarian economics has emerged in the context of a global trend for more evidence-based interventions in humanitarian crises. Empirical evidence refers to research findings based on sound research methods and trustworthy data that are fit for the specific purpose of the study. Empirical research in economics depends on the availability and quality of quantitative data, which can be particularly poor in the specific circumstances of war and disaster. This can be compounded by the lack of baseline information and adequate counterfactuals. The increasing availability and precision of geospatial data and satellite imaging techniques, together with the 'big data' revolution and better datasets on violent events and disasters, allow for more creativity in conducting quantitative research on topics and contexts where this was simply not an option a few years back. The introduction of technological innovations, often in partnership with commercial firms, contributes to the generation of new pools of data, as in the case of electronic food vouchers through ATM cards that allow for the tracking of consumption decisions of millions of refugees over several years.

Relief agencies generate an increasingly large pool of data through more systematic monitoring and evaluation, and also through large-scale needs assessments. Programme and project evaluation is one of the most advanced sectors of humanitarian studies for the purpose of generating evidence.[2] Natural experiments and randomized controlled trials (RCTs) in humanitarian crises remain exceptions to the norm, albeit their number has been increasing in the past few years,[3] as discussed for example in the case of impact evaluations of cash assistance programmes in Lebanon. Data on humanitarian demand and supply is being collected in a more systematic manner. In short, there are more opportunities than ever before for quantitative studies on humanitarian crises.

At the same time, this raises important ethical issues to the extent that such studies can have a direct bearing on the security and integrity of research subjects. Many of those ethical issues are well known in medicine and public health, but tend to be less well known in economics where there is no such thing as a Hippocratic Oath to 'do no harm'. As is obvious from the preceding chapters, much of the economic literature on humanitarian crises does not look at war or disaster from a humanitarian perspective or out of an explicit humanitarian concern. Conducting research for the sole purpose of enhancing our understanding of war, terrorism and disaster is of course welcome. Yet, lacking sensitivity for humanitarian issues when conducting research in humanitarian crises can have grave consequences.

First, protecting the physical integrity and dignity of informants and local research partners is a priority, which requires putting researchers' incentives in line with high ethical standards all the way from initial research design to disseminating findings and recommendations, as discussed in the case of needs assessments in Lebanon. Second, the neutrality and do-no-harm principles that (should) preside over humanitarian action should ideally also apply to academic research on humanitarian crises.[4] For example, the literature on civil war economies presents a frequent anti-rebel bias in that it questions the economic agendas, greed and criminal activities of non-state armed actors, but not those of ruling elites. Such a bias risks reinforcing a tendency to dismiss rebels as mere criminals while possibly condoning repressive regimes prone to denying non-state armed actors any of the rights and protections that they would be entitled to as parties to a non-international armed conflict. A third concern is that information and communications technologies offer considerable scope for innovation in the humanitarian sector, but also raise serious concerns with regard to confidentiality, localization and security[5] in relation to the risk of inadvertently contributing to gathering intelligence for one of the warring parties. A fourth issue that deserves further inquiry is how to valuate lives lost and impaired, in particular in poorer countries. Establishing the value of a statistical life for people bereft of solvent demand raises methodological and ethical issues (Chapter 5) similar to those humanitarians face when considering the notion of 'cultural standards' in needs assessments and aid programming (Chapter 6). Additional concerns relate to the sensitivities involved in collecting information from interviewees living under crisis conditions, and to assessment fatigue generated by repeated interviews that are not followed by any tangible benefit for the interviewees.

As with any other research topic, possible conflicts of interest must be properly managed when dealing with humanitarian crises, for example in cases where research is funded or facilitated by one party to the conflict. The economic profession is known for its distinct taste and ability for research-policy transfer.[6] Research on sensitive issues, such as the effectiveness of hearts-and-minds campaigns in Afghanistan and Iraq, are likely to have a bearing on local communities targeted by those campaigns. Impact evaluations of aid as a foreign policy instrument in stabilization and counterinsurgency contexts typically equate aid effectiveness with short-term tactical gains in reducing the occurrence of violent events (Chapter 4).[7] Qualitative field research on similar issues in the same locations reaches different conclusions when looking at strategic outcomes in terms of winning or losing 'hearts and minds'. Confronting those studies calls for revisiting a few core assumptions, such as the opportunity cost argument. Further cross-disciplinary research would broaden our understanding of the realities experienced by local communities that are courted, and threatened, by opposing armed groups in different war settings. More broadly, disciplinary boundaries tend to fragment the complex social reality that prevails in humanitarian crises. Reconstructing and understanding that reality in all its complexity requires strong interdisciplinary engagement.

What Humanitarian Economics Brings In

The field of humanitarian economics offers an already rich but still largely untapped resource, which may greatly contribute to supporting evidence-based humanitarian policy and practice at a time when the sector faces both an unprecedented boom and a deep crisis: too often, it fails to adequately address acute needs for assistance and protection in the heart of armed conflicts.

Humanitarian organizations have displayed renewed interest in strengthening their negotiations capabilities, notably to obtain improved field access, stronger security guarantees, and greater international humanitarian law-compliance from warring parties. Training manuals implicitly build on rational choice theory. They emphasize interests, costs and benefits and other such issues beyond legal and normative considerations. As discussed in Chapters 1 and 3, drawing on conflict theory and political economy analysis (PEA) can greatly contribute to understanding how key stakeholders interact in war economies, including humanitarians themselves. Critical factors worth considering comprise extent of territorial control, access to resources and trading routes, as well as mobilization and opportunity costs. They also encompass economic agendas in war, where the boundary between organized political and criminal groups is increasingly blurred.[8] These factors, in turn, provide a wealth of insights not only on the functions of and rationale for violence, but also on potential incentives, levers and entry points in humanitarian negotiations. PEA may further contribute to identifying aid diversion and security risks and revising delivery modes and supply chains accordingly.

More broadly, we have seen various ways in which humanitarian economics can support and inform humanitarian policies and action. Humanitarian economics contributes to more robust needs assessment approaches, which are required under the essential principle of impartiality. This principle dictates the targeting of assistance and protection on the sole basis of urgency and intensity of needs. Recent attempts to bridge the micro-macro divide and to intensify micro-level analysis of armed violence should be pursued further to inform humanitarian responses, together with greater emphasis on local market dynamics and links to global markets. Several livelihood and needs assessment techniques build on household economics and an expanded version of Sen's notion of entitlements. Proxy means tests increasingly serve to identify and select those entitled to humanitarian assistance. In this context, market analysis and price monitoring becomes the daily bread of aid workers, as in the case of cash-based assistance that has expanded from pilot projects to large-scale humanitarian operations in middle-income countries and, more and more, in so-called fragile states as well.

By raising moral hazard, collective action and asymmetric information problems, PEA contributes to better understanding the risks and opportunities for effective disaster prevention and risk management. As illustrated in the context of food aid during the Angolan Civil War, PEA can also greatly contribute to proper context analysis and due diligence in humanitarian programming under a do-no-harm approach. With its focus on distributional issues, it can inform debates on frequent operational dilemmas such as balancing the opportunity of saving lives with the risk of feeding not just the hungry but also the war chest of those responsible for the famine in the first place. As discussed in Chapter 4, economic analysis can also ascertain the humanitarian impact of trade and financial sanctions—including 'smart' ones—even if it remains highly challenging to disentangle the specific impact of sanctions from humanitarian outcomes that result from other factors. Embargoes and sanction regimes often prove relatively ineffective in the face of widespread informal activities, weak judicial systems and low enforcement capacity or political will. Their long-term criminogenic influence on war economies deserves further research, as it can have a significant bearing on the transition from war to peace.

The role and influence of the business sector in humanitarian crises and responses is another transversal topic raised in this book, including with regard to motives and legitimacy issues surrounding business-humanitarian partnerships. Humanitarian organizations have emulated businesses in adopting result-based management, performance indicators and the active pursuit of innovation, while companies partner with humanitarian agencies for varying motives. The case of the insurance industry illustrates the multifaceted interactions between the business and humanitarian sectors. The rise of kidnap-and-ransom insurance to cover heightened kidnapping risks in several parts of the world raises moral hazard problems and risks fuelling the market. In this case, humanitarian organizations (and others) should stay clear of buying such insurance even if it makes sense from a financial risk management viewpoint. The sector has developed disaster risk insurance products tailored for the developing world and middle-income countries in particular, including Sharia-compliant versions for Muslim countries. Insurance firms have teamed up with multilateral and regional organizations to market catastrophe bonds and a micro-insurance scheme that can involve weather-related parametric triggers, contributing to lower transaction costs. Disaster insurance and risk-linked securities offer an opportunity for disaster-prone but sovereignty-assertive states to pass part of the disaster costs on to global financial markets and reduce dependency on (volatile) foreign aid when hit by a disaster. The impact of enhanced insurance market penetration deserves more scrutiny as it results in increased cooperation between aid agencies and insurance companies, but also in increased competition.

Tensions between cooperation and competition prevail also in the humanitarian sector itself. Further research can shed light on instances where competition stimulates enhanced humanitarian outcomes and others where it produces adverse effects. We have seen that increased fragmentation and fierce competition in the humanitarian marketplace may weaken the sector's position vis-à-vis warring parties, donors and others who can be quick to play one organization off against another. This renders coordinated responses illusory even in the following three instances where stakes are high for the humanitarian sector as a whole: removing counterterrorist provisions that jeopardize the exercise of impartial humanitarian action; putting pressure on all potential leverage points to resolve kidnapping cases and reduce their occurrence; and redressing the terms of engagement with power holders and brokers in contexts where the balance between humanitarian outcomes and adverse side-effects turns negative.

These few examples illustrate that the contributions of humanitarian economics are wide-ranging, from capturing how costs and benefits are generated and distributed in disaster and war to how this affects warring party behaviour and the livelihoods of affected people. Humanitarian economics can greatly enrich humanitarian studies and practice, provided we stave off Hirshleifer's prediction that economists shall brush aside so-called 'a-theoretical aborigines' as we enter this field.[9]

Concluding Thoughts and Future Research

In the previous chapters, I discussed a range of issues that deserve greater scrutiny and further research. Here I return to three problem areas and outline avenues for cross-disciplinary, cross-sector research collaborations.

Alfred Marshall wrote that '[neoclassical e]conomics is a study of mankind in the ordinary business of life.'[10] Humanitarian economics is a study of mankind in crisis situations. Studying the economics of war, disaster and humanitarian action raises with particular saliency some of the well-known criticisms of rational-choice theory models. It begs the question of the roles of emotions and altruism in explaining the behaviour of combatants, terrorist recruits, humanitarian aid workers and disaster victims. As we have seen, the assumption that reason underlies decision-making processes does not preclude economic theory from integrating cooperation and reciprocity in a game-theoretical framework, imperfect information and limited ability to predict outcomes under bounded rationality, the symbolic dimension of material transactions, or the role of institutions and uncertainty. Some rational choice explanations of suicide terrorism—arguably the ultimate paradox for maximizing individuals—focus on the role of identity, as traded for life under contract theory (Chapter 4). Further research involving recent advances in behavioural economics and neuroscience together with contributions from social psychology and anthropology can improve our understanding of humanitarian crises and interactions between diverse factors that shape the behaviour of key stakeholders in a variety of war and disaster settings.

As many seasoned humanitarian practitioners argue, successful humanitarian negotiations rest not only on informed cost-benefit analysis, but also on emotional intelligence. For some, a capacity for empathy bred by active field presence and proximity with the vulnerable (and the perpetrators of violence) is part of the humanitarian's DNA. Chapter 1 focuses on non-kin altruism as both an innate trait and the product of socialization that fuels the initial impetus for humanitarian response. The principles of impartiality, neutrality and independence can then be seen as beacons in the rationalization process that channels this impulse towards effective humanitarian outcomes, notably by helping to create trust with key actors.

Yet, as discussed in various chapters, the definition and interpretation of humanitarian principles and key concepts such as vulnerability, resilience and humanitarian action itself remain contested. Scholarly work has long been biased toward humanitarianism's European and Christian heritage. Exploring the evolving understandings of these concepts across geographies and temporalities provides an opportunity for research involving scholars and practitioners from the North and South. The growing ability and resolve of emerging economies and other middle-income countries to deal with humanitarian crises at home and abroad calls for more attention to humanitarian expressions under different religious and secular traditions.

Humanitarian crises can be seen as critical junctures for change, as they are by major aid donors who have adopted comprehensive approaches combining defence with diplomacy and development in the context of stabilization and building-back-better agendas. Not surprisingly, this has resulted in tensions between the conservative agenda of neutral, impartial and independent humanitarian actors and the diverse transformative projects pursued by other actors in the global aid market. When the US Department of State released its first Quadrennial Diplomacy and Development Review in December 2010 under the title *Leading through Civilian Power*, then US Secretary of State Hillary Clinton declared: 'Leading through civilian power saves lives and money [...] Where we must work side by side with our military partners in places like Afghanistan and Iraq and in other fragile states around the world, we can be the partner that our military needs and deserves.'[11] For the world's largest donor, marketing foreign aid as an efficient instrument to pursue security objectives may be a means to muster short-term domestic support for aid budgets. This may however be shortsighted and subject to backlash both domestically and abroad. The pursuit of other objectives than humanitarian and development goals further reduces aid effectiveness, which provides ammunition to aid sceptics keen to challenge aid budgets in donor countries. As for recipient countries, insurgents and other powerful actors may reject the liberal peacebuilding and development enterprise altogether, staging violent attacks against aid workers. It is in the interest of the development enterprise to stand for poverty reduction in and of itself—just as saving lives, alleviating suffering and protecting human dignity should remain legitimate humanitarian objectives in and of themselves.

Findings on the role of foreign aid in supporting counterinsurgency and stabilization enterprises or in reducing terrorist acts remain inconclusive and produce mixed recommendations. Some studies hail aid as successfully altering the cost-benefit calculus of potential insurgent recruits and supporters while others question the opportunity cost argument, for example on the basis that those commissioned to perform terrorist acts often come from the more educated and better off. Humanitarian economics can shed more light on the broader impact of foreign aid on local communities caught up in armed conflict beyond impacts on livelihoods, health and nutrition, or the number and intensity of violent events. It can further contribute to a better understanding of how different aid modalities affect the position of aid 'beneficiaries' vis-à-vis armed actors and how aid plays out with top-down and bottom-up state-building dynamics.

* * *

Coming back to this book's preface and my first humanitarian field assignments twenty-five year ago in Ethiopia, Iraq and Sri Lanka, I remember trying to apply a few conceptual and methodological tools that I had just acquired as a fresh graduate in economics to help me make sense of the situation and respond accordingly. I admit that I felt rather lost at the time but had the intuition—and later developed the strong conviction—that it was an undertaking worth pursuing. As the book's bibliography bears witness to, hundreds of academics, researchers and practitioners have expanded on the work of a few pioneers, contributing a great wealth of knowledge on the economics and political economy of humanitarian crises and action. It is on that basis that I started writing *Humanitarian Economics*. I hope that this book will contribute to invigorating research, education, debates and reflective practice in this field, as well as fruitful collaborations with neighbouring ones. I hope that this can in turn contribute to supporting the humanitarian enterprise in its efforts to protect the rights and meet the expectations of millions of people whose lives are deeply impacted by humanitarian crises.

APPENDIX TO CHAPTER 3

PEA: THE EXAMPLE OF FOOD AID IN ANGOLA

Food aid has consistently been highlighted as particularly prone to diversion and political instrumentalization. As an illustration of the applicability and relevance of political economy analysis (PEA) in the humanitarian sector, I provide in this appendix a concrete example of PEA being carried out in the context of a large-scale emergency food assistance and agricultural rehabilitation programme in Angola.

When hostilities resumed between the Government of President Dos Santos and the Uniao Nacional para a Independência Total de Angola (UNITA) in December 1998, the country witnessed a surge of internally displaced people (IDPs) fleeing rural areas towards government-held enclaves such as Huambo and Kuito on the Planoalto. The 1999 spring harvest had been very poor, not least because farmers opted for premature harvesting to avoid the risk of later plunder by warring parties. In August 1999, the incidence of acute malnutrition surged to an alarming rate of 40 per cent, which was comparable to what was registered in Somalia during the deadly 1992 famine. The International Committee of the Red Cross (ICRC) and the World Food Programme (WFP) coordinated their airlifted food aid operations, the former servicing some 330,000 beneficiaries in Huambo and its outskirts. In less than a year, acute malnutrition dropped to 3 per cent.

At the end of 1999 I was asked to assist the ICRC nutritionist and agronomist in assessing the adequacy of the relief operation from a socioeconomic viewpoint. We carried out a political economy analysis: for each phase of the food aid operation we examined the interests, objectives and potential strategy of the major stakeholders involved and how the ICRC should address them. This analysis is summarized in Table 1, where each row refers to one stage in

Table 1: Relief Access Mapping—Food Aid in Angola (1999–2000)

Stages of the relief operation	Main stakeholders involved	Stakeholders' interests and likely strategies	Risks from a humanitarian point of view	Preventive and corrective measures by relief agencies
Initial need assessment	Central and local government officials	Avoid a food crisis and ensuing turmoil, yet without having to mobilize domestic resources	Aid fungibility	Independent rigorous need assessment, cross-checking with local traders
		Get political reward for getting food distributed	Discharging the authorities from their obligation vis-à-vis the civilian population	Persuade the authorities to protect and assist the civilians
	Beneficiaries	Get continued food assistance	Aid dependence, negative spin-off for local farmers	One-off, simultaneous distribution of food with seeds, tools and fertilizers
	Rebels	Attack convoys to stop and divert food aid	Security of staff and facilities	Airlifted operation, planes spiralling up & down on landing strips in enclaves Parallel food distribution in rebel-held area?

Table continued

Stages of the relief operation	Main stakeholders involved	Stakeholders' interests and likely strategies	Risks from a humanitarian point of view	Preventive and corrective measures by relief agencies
Funding (cash & kind)	Donors	Get rid of food surpluses; promote the marketing of GM (genetically modified) maize seeds	GMO (genetically modified organisms) unwillingly disseminated; dependence on imported seed varieties	Milling the imported maize for consumption; buying local maize seed varieties for planting
Beneficiary selection and food distribution modalities	Government	Select beneficiaries among 'sympathisers'. Get political reward for the distribution	Fraught targeting, not based on actual needs	Independent selection of beneficiary list. Direct distribution to individual beneficiaries
	Security forces	Looting part of the food distributed for own consumption and monetization	Security risks and nutritional status of the beneficiaries	Escorting beneficiaries back home; advocating for adequate wages to be paid to security forces
Procurement, logistics, recruitment, sub-contracting	Local labour	Competition to get access to jobs	Unbalanced recruitment antagonizing groups against each other or against relief organizations	Context-sensitive recruitment procedures, under expatriate responsibility

Table continued

Stages of the relief operation	Main stakeholders involved	Stakeholders' interests and likely strategies	Risks from a humanitarian point of view	Preventive and corrective measures by relief agencies
	Traders and locals businesses	Gaining new market opportunities, not losing existing ones	Security risks	Dialogue with business people; corroborate if need assessment is validated by market signals
	Monopolists (often a coalition of political and economic elites)	Preserving monopoly rent (e.g. microcredit scheme for buying seed and fertilizers)	Security risks for humanitarian workers	Careful monitoring and communication with key actors (e.g. this is a one-off distribution)
Project monitoring and evaluation	Farmers	Keep getting free seeds and fertilizers while keeping food prices high	Discouraging farmers from planting as a result of depressed food prices	Close monitoring of evolving nutritional situation and access to food. Agricultural rehabilitation programme
	Logistics providers	Continued business		
	Traders	Continued business and/ or stepping in to import the food once free distribution ends	Coalition of actors pushing for protracted assistance and renewed food aid	Monitoring and evaluation of the humanitarian, economic and political-economy effects of the relief operation

the relief operation and the columns address the interests and strategies of the key actors as well as the preventive and corrective measures that relief agencies could take. Such a Relief Access Mapping (RAM) table permits humanitarian workers to collectively explore the political economy of an aid project both within field offices and in interactions with headquarters. It further offers a relatively simple yet powerful tool for highlighting potential security risks.[1]

Table 1 presents the RAM that summarizes the main issues raised as part of our PEA related to the 1999–2000 food aid operation in Angola

The issues raised in Table 1 are self-explanatory, with four issues that deserve further elaboration:

- *Funding*: since the food to be distributed was primarily maize shipped from the United States, we discussed the risk of recipients keeping some of the maize beans for planting instead of eating, and the ensuing risk of disseminating genetically-modified (GM) maize on the Angolan Planoalto. The decision was taken to mill all the imported maize in order to distribute only *fuba* or maize flower for consumption, even if this slightly delayed the distribution and made the operation costlier. At the same time, the ICRC purchased local maize seed varieties to be distributed with agricultural tools and fertilizers for the next planting season.

- *Distribution*: some food recipients reported that they were the victims of extortion at checkpoints when heading home from distribution sites. The first reaction was to have ICRC expatriates escort them through the checkpoints, which ensured safe passage. Yet, some food recipients later reported that local security forces intruded at night to levy dues directly from their homes or shelters, with serious security risks for the recipients' families. It became obvious that the security forces would continue to loot as long as they did not get properly paid by the state to sustain themselves and their families. This prompted the ICRC to intervene directly in the capital city, Luanda, with the relevant ministries. The government released its decision a few months later to significantly increase the remuneration of the security forces.

- *Procurement/Logistics*: from the initial need assessment phase to the final ex-post evaluation, regular exchanges with local business people provided particularly useful insights. The latter started by expressing outright support for the free distribution of imported food into the government-held enclaves on the basis that the food recipients were not among their potential clients. In other words, they were not solvent. Distributing food for free would thus not compete with local business interests. This reinforced our conviction that food distribution was needed. Local business people insisted that we keep paying our staff in US dollars. As aid agencies were the largest employer in town, this was critical to sustain the demand for the consumer goods that local traders imported into the enclaves. The only reservation came from the local politico-economic elite involved in (micro)credit institutions. Some of them were used to extending loans to farmers allowing them to purchase agricultural inputs before the planting season. They were also involved in selling seeds. Explaining that the free distribution of seeds, tools and fertilizers was a one-off donation to restart agricultural activities helped to ease the tensions and avert potential attempts to derail the seed distribution programme.

- *Monitoring and evaluation*: we distinguished between three categories of outcomes when putting the monitoring and evaluation system in place:[2] (i) the humanitarian effects of distributing food rations related to the evolving rate of acute and moderate malnutrition; (ii) the economic effects related to the local price fluctuations of maize and *fuba* together with that of other staple foods. We also thought it useful to monitor any potential surge in transport and warehousing prices as well as changes in wages in specific labour market segments such as daily labourers; and (iii) the political-economy effects as detailed in Table 1.

NOTES

INTRODUCTION

1. William Shakespeare, *Henry V*, Act 4, Scene 6.
2. The woman was known to the Lebanese security services. She was released from a Syrian government prison a few months earlier, along with more than 140 other women, as part of a prisoner swap involving the release of thirteen nuns by Jabhat al-Nusra, an al-Qaeda affiliate in Syria. See Martin Chulov, 'Wife and Child of Islamic State Leader Baghdadi Held in Lebanon', *The Guardian*, 2 December 2014, *http://www.theguardian.com/world/2014/dec/02/al-baghdadi-wife-son-arrest-lebanon-fake-passport*, last accessed 9 January 2015.
3. Thomas Wyke, 'Lebanese Hostage Executed by Al-Qaeda Linked Group in Syira', *International Business Times*, http://www.ibtimes.co.uk/lebanese-hostage-executed-by-al-qaeda-linked-group-syria-1478352, last accessed 9 January 2015.
4. Alessandria Masi, 'ISIS Leader's Ex-Wife, ISIS Commander Wife Released in Lebanon', *International Business Times*, http://www.ibtimes.com/isis-leaders-ex-wife-isis-commander-wife-released-lebanon-1745166, last accessed 9 January 2015.
5. Bruno Frey and Heinz Buhofer, 'Prisoners and Property Rights', *Journal of Law and Economics* 31, 1 (1988), pp. 19–46, p. 21.
6. Theodor Meron, 'International Humanitarian Law from Agincourt to Rome', *International Law Studies* 75 (1999), pp. 301–311.
7. In medieval times, the ruler often reserved the right to negotiate and receive the ransom for the most valuable prisoners, but had first to reward the captors to benefit from the property right transfer.
8. English knights refused to execute Henry V's order to kill the prisoners so the king had to order his archers to do the dirty work. The knights not only repudiated such an un-chivalrous task, they also did not want to lose the benefit of future ransoms by killing 'their' prisoners.
9. Henry Dunant, *A Memory of Solferino*, reprinted in Geneva: ICRC, 1862/1959, p. 122.

213

10. Frey and Buhofer, 1988, op. cit., pp. 19–46.

11. This figure was later revised. See GHA Report 2015, Global Humanitarian Assistance, Bristol (UK): Development Initiatives, 2015.

12. Sean Healy and Sandrine Tiller, *Where is Everyone? Responding to Emergencies in the Most Difficult Places*, Geneva: MSF, 2014.

13. Ben Parker, 'Humanitarian Besieged,' *Humanitarian Exchange* 59, November 2013, p. 5.

14. There are a very few academic references to humanitarian economics. A thesis was presented under that title in 1978 at the Piraeus Graduate School of Industrial Studies by Lazaros Houmanidis, wherein the concept of humanitarian economics referred to a political economy model in which 'the state must serve the entire nation', under a social economics rather than humanitarian perspective.

15. See e.g. Abhijit Banerjee and Esther Duflo, *Poor Economics: A Radical Rethinking of the Way to Fight Global Poverty*, New York: Perseus Books, 2011; Pranab Bardhan and Christopher Udry, *Development Microeconomics*, Oxford: Oxford University Press, 1999; see also the Abdul Latif Jameel Poverty Action Lab (J-PAL) website: http://www.povertyactionlab.org/, last accessed 20 April 2015.

1. REASON, EMOTION AND COMPASSION

1. H. D. Mahoney (ed), *Edmund Burke, Reflections on the French Revolution*, New York: Macmillan, 1955, p. 86.

2. Since the turn of the millennium, there has been a revival in the literature on the role of emotions in international relations, with authors considering, for example, resentment, anger, revenge and humiliation; see Brent Sasley, 'Emotions in International Relations', *E-International Relations*, http://www.e-ir.info/2013/06/12/emotions-in-international-relations/, last accessed on 16 September 2014.

3. Joe Krishnan, 'Panic as Deadly Ebola Virus Spreads Across West Africa,' *The Independent*, http://www.independent.co.uk/news/world/africa/panic-as-deadly-ebola-virus-spreads-across-west-africa-9241155.html, last accessed 16 September 2014.

4. While Max Weber associated the process of modernization with that of rationalization, he underscored that social action was determined by a diversity of drivers. Beyond rational cost-benefit calculus, they include emotions, moral values and tradition. In daily life, our actions are often determined by effects and emotions as well as by values. Those values can be related to ethical, religious or political imperatives to which we may feel committed regardless of the anticipated consequences. Besides, sheer habit and imitation determine many actions devoid of subjective meaning or purpose. As discussed in this chapter, empirical evidence from behavioural economics and evolutionary biology challenges the standard social science assumption of selfish, utility-maximizing individuals as the sole anthropological reference for analysing and predicting decisions.

5. Since the late nineteenth century, neoclassical economics has dominated main-

stream (micro)economics. It was first coined in relation to Alfred Marshall and the Austrian School and was later associated with the marginalist revolution spearheaded by Leon Walras, Carl Menger, and William Jevons.

6. François Jean and Jean-Christophe Rufin, *Economie des Guerres Civiles*, Paris: Hachette, 1996.

7. See for example Marshall Sahlins, *Stone Age Economics*, Chicago: Aldine, 1972; Harold Schneider, *Economic Man*, New York: Free Press, 1974.

8. Even if this debate is somewhat dated, it continues to attract interest under different guises. For example, in 2011 David Graeber highlighted the fact that debts (and gifts) actually preceded barter trade and monetary exchanges. See David Graeber, *Debt: The First 5000 Years*, Brooklyn: Melville House, 2011; Chris Hann and Keith Hart, *Economic Anthropology: History, Ethnography, Critique*, Cambridge: Polity, 2011.

9. The Pareto optimum (named after the nineteenth century Italian economist Vilfredo Pareto) refers to the optimal allocation of resources from a societal point of view where, in a fixed group of actors, no one can be better off without making somebody else worse off. Interestingly, Jean Pictet, in his famous 1979 *Commentary* on humanitarian principles, wrote that '[h]umanitarianism works toward the establishment of a social order which should be as advantageous as possible for the largest possible number of people' (Jean Pictet, *The Fundamental Principles of the Red Cross: Commentary*, Geneva: ICRC, 1979, p. 18). Contrary to the pursuit of a Pareto social optimum, however, humanitarianism is clearly geared towards assisting and protecting the most vulnerable on an impartial basis, with a focus on powerlessness and distributional issues.

10. Alfred Marshall, *Principles of Economics*, London: Macmillan, 1890.

11. Jack Hirshleifer, *The Dark Side of the Force: Economic Foundations of Conflict Theory*, Cambridge: Cambridge University Press, 2001.

12. Major writings on economic issues related to World Wars I and II include John M. Keynes, *The Economic Consequences of Peace*, New York: Harcourt, Brace, and Howe, Inc., 1919; *How to Pay for the War*, New York: Harcourt, Brace, and Howe, Inc., 1940; and Arthur Cecil Pigou, *Political Economy of War*, London: Macmillan and Co., 1921.

13. Charles Anderton and John Carter, *Principles of Conflict Economics: A Primer for Social Scientists*, New York: Cambridge University Press, 2009, p. 2.

14. Original quote in: Gordon Tullock, *The Vote Motive*, London: Institute for Economic Affairs, 1976; as quoted in Jane Mansbridge, *Beyond Self-Interest*, Chicago: University of Chicago Press, 1990, p. 12.

15. For a historical account, see Edmund Silberner, *La Guerre et la Paix Dans l'Histoire des Doctrines Economiques*, Paris: Sirey, 1957. For a review of the recent literature, see Christopher Blattman and Edward Miguel, 'Civil War', *Journal of Economic Literature* 48, 1 (2010), pp. 3–57.

16. See for example: James Fearon, 'Rationalist Explanations for War', *International Organizations* 49, 39 (1995), pp. 379–414; Michelle Garfinkel and Stergios Skaperdas, 'Economic Perspectives on Peace and Conflict' in Michelle Garfinkel and Stergios Skaperdas (eds), *The Oxford Handbook of the Economics of Peace and Conflict*, New York: Oxford University Press, 2012, pp. 3–19; Stergios Skaperdas, 'An Economic Approach to Analyzing Civil Wars', *Economics of Governance* 9, 1 (2008), pp. 25–44.

17. Christopher Cramer, *Civil War is Not a Stupid Thing: Accounting for Violence in Developing Countries*, London: Hurst, 2006.

18. Paul Collier *et al.*, *Breaking the Conflict Trap: Civil War and Development Policy*, Washington: The World Bank and Oxford University Press, 2003, pp. 13–32.

19. Charles Tilly, 'War Making and State Making as Organized Crime' in Peter Evans *et al.* (eds), *Bringing the State Back In*, Cambridge: Cambridge University Press, 1985, pp. 169–186. The great Arab historian Ibn Khaldun already highlighted the centrality of war in the rise and fall of empires in the fourteenth century. See also Peter Turchin, *War and Peace and War: The Rise and Fall of Empires*, New York: Plume, 2006.

20. The 1991 US intervention in Iraq arguably served the purpose of boosting demand and reviving the US military industry as the post-Cold War peace dividend had started to affect the sector. See also Vijay Mehta, *The Economics of Killing: How the West Fuels War and Poverty in the Developing World*, London: Pluto Press, 2012.

21. Daniel Kahneman and Amos Tversky, 'Prospect Theory: An Analysis of Decisions and Risk', *Econometrica* 47, 2 (1979), pp. 263–291.

22. The rank-dependent expected utility model accounts for the fact that individuals tend to overweight low-probability events associated with very substantial outcomes, be it extraordinary gains or losses.

23. See for example Robert Powell, 'War as a Commitment Problem', *International Organization* 60, 1 (2006) pp. 169–203.

24. Thomas Shelling, *The Strategy of Conflict*, Cambridge: Harvard University Press, 1960.

25. See for example Thomas Shelling, *Arms and Influence*, New Haven: Yale University Press, 1966.

26. Trygve Haavelmo, *A Study of the Theory of Economic Evolution*, Amsterdam: North Holland, 1954.

27. See Jack Hirshleifer, 'The Analytics of Continuing Conflict', *Synthese* 76, 2 (1988), pp. 201–33; 'The Dark Side of Force: Western Economic Association International 1993 Presidential Address', *Economic Inquiry* 32, 1 (1994), pp. 1–10; and 'Conflict and Rent Seeking Success Functions: Ration vs. Difference Models of Relative Success', *Public Choice* 63, 2 (1989), pp. 101–112. See also Michelle Garfinkel, 'Arming as a Strategic Investment in a Cooperative Equilibrium', *American*

Economic Review 21, 1 (1980), pp. 43–68; and Stergios Skaperdas, 'Cooperation, Conflict and Power in the Absence of Property Rights', *American Economic Review* 82, 4 (1992), pp. 720–739.

28. See for example Paul Collier, and Anke Hoeffler, 'Greed and Grievance in Civil War', *Oxford Economic Papers* 56, 4 (2004), pp. 563–595; Herschel Grossman, 'A General Equilibrium Model of Insurrections', *American Economic Review* 81, 4 (1991), pp. 912–921. The 'greed' argument has often been opposed to the 'grievance' approach, which posits that a failure to peacefully address political grievances is a prime motivation for rebellion, especially when grievances can be mobilized along identity lines (such as ethnicity and religion). See Ted Gurr, *Why Men Rebel*, Princeton: Princeton University Press, 1970; Roger Petersen, *Understanding Ethnic Violence: Fear, Hatred, Resentment in Twentieth Century Eastern Europe*, New York: Cambridge University Press, 2002.

29. But this does not explain why civil war is highly persistent in quite a few middle-income and high-income countries.

30. James Fearon, 'Rationalist Explanations for War', *International Organization* 49, 3 (1995), pp. 379–414.

31. Charles Anderton, 'Killing Civilians as an Inferior Input in a Rational Choice Model of Genocide and Mass Killing', *Peace Economics, Peace Science and Public Policy* 20, 2 (2014), pp. 327–346. This dataset, funded by the US government, is compiled by collecting information from a number of international sources to document incidents of deliberate killing of civilians in situations of political conflict around the world. Multiple indicators are used to ascertain whether a civilian has been deliberately killed, including whether the non-combatant status of the victim is asserted or not, whether this status was contested or not, and whether the intent of the perpetrator is established, among many others. For a description of all indicators and the most recent dataset from January 2013 to the present, see: Political Instability Task Force Worldwide Atrocities Dataset, http://eventdata. parusanalytics.com/data.dir/atrocities.html, last accessed 12 September 2014.

32. This argument may not only hold true for insurgents and non-state armed groups, but also for Western industrialized states, currently waging war under the banner of the so-called 'war on terror'. A recent study conducted by Stanford University and New York University found that out of every fifty civilians killed, only one terrorist was killed, resulting in 98 per cent collateral damage: http://www.daily-mail.co.uk/news/article-2208307/Americas-deadly-double-tap-drone-attacks-killing-49-people-known-terrorist-Pakistan.html, last accessed 26 January 2015.

33. David Keen, *Useful Enemies: When Waging Wars is More Important than Winning Them*, New Haven: Yale University Press, 2012.

34. Anderton and Carter, 2009, op. cit., p. 2.

35. Such feelings and emotions could be conceptualized as interpersonal externalities in the preferences of adversaries. See Michelle Garfinkel and Stergios Skaperdas, 2012, op. cit.

36. A recent study looked at citation patterns in flagship journals between 2000 and 2009: articles in the *American Political Science Review* cite articles published in the top twenty-five economics journals over six times more often than political science journals are cited in the *American Economic Review*. The asymmetry is even starker in the case of cross-citations between economics and sociology journals. See Marion Fourcade, Etienne Ollion and Yann Algan, 'The Superiority of Economists', *Journal of Economic Perspectives*, forthcoming (2015).

37. Hirshleifer, 2001, op. cit., p. 11. In a footnote, Hirshleifer concedes that researchers from other discipline may sometimes do good work on conflict analysis... when they're actually doing economics!

38. An example is the World Bank's research conducted under Paul Collier, which inquires into the causes of rebellion without putting rational, opportunistic oppressors in governments under similar scrutiny.

39. Daniel Rothenberg (ed.), *Memory of Silence: The Guatemalan Truth Commission Report*, New York: Palgrave Macmillan, 2012.

40. Mancur Olsen, *Power and Prosperity: Outgrowing Communist and Capitalist Dictatorships*, New York: Basic Books, 2000.

41. Cameron Thies, 'State Building, Interstate and Intrastate Rivalry: A Study of Post-Colonial Developing Country Extractive Efforts, 1975–2000', *International Studies Quarterly* 48, 1 (2004), pp. 53–72; Richard Snyder, and Bhavnani Ravi, 'Diamonds, Blood and Taxes: A Revenue-Centered Framework for Explaining Political Order', *Journal of Conflict Resolution* 49, 4 (2005), pp. 563–597.

42. For a critical review of the so-called shrinking of the humanitarian space, see Sarah Collinson and Samir Elhawari, 'Humanitarian Space: A Review of Trends and Issues', London: ODI/HPG, 2012.

43. Deborah Mancini-Griffoli and Andre Picot, 'Humanitarian Negotiation: A Handbook for Securing Access, Assistance and Protection for Civilians in Armed Conflict', Geneva: Centre for Humanitarian Dialogue, 2004.

44. Gerard McHugh and Manuel Bessler, *Humanitarian Negotiations with Armed Groups: A Manual for Practitioners*, New York: OCHA, 2006.

45. Mancini-Griffoli and Picot, 2004, op. cit., p. 67.

46. Ibid.

47. Claire Magone, Michael Neuman and Fabrice Weissmann, *Humanitarian Negotiations Revealed: The MSF Experience*, London: Hurst, 2011.

48. Ibid.

49. Rebecca Solnit, *A Paradise Built in Hell: The Extraordinary Communities that Arise in Disaster*, New York: Viking/Penguin, 2009.

50. Szalavitz, Maia, '"Paradise Built in Hell:" How Disaster Brings Out the Best in People', *Time*, http://healthland.time.com/2011/03/22/a-paradise-built-in-hell-how-disaster-brings-out-the-best-in-people/, last accessed 15 September 2014.

51. Gestures meant to save lives and alleviate suffering are also found among several

other species, see for example Victoria Horner *et al.*, 'Spontaneous Prosocial Choice by Chimpanzees', *Proceedings of the National Academy of Sciences*, 108, 33 (2011), pp. 13847–13851.

52. See Philippe Ryfman, *La question humanitaire*, Paris: Ellipses, 1999. In 1812, the US Congress approved an emergency aid package for Venezuela after an earthquake that affected the people of Caracas. In 1860, the French Government decided to deliver aid to the Maronite community suffering from repression in Lebanon. Neither humanitarian venture was devoid of geopolitical considerations.

53. These principles were first proclaimed in 1965 at the twentieth International Conference of the Red Cross and Red Crescent Movement in Vienna. Three additional principles are geared more specifically towards the International Movement of the Red Cross and Red Crescent: voluntary service, unity and universality.

54. Jean Pictet, *The Fundamental Principles of the Red Cross, Commentary*, Geneva: ICRC, 1979, p. 22.

55. John Rawls, *A Theory of Justice*, Cambridge: Harvard University Press, 1971.

56. Jean Pictet, 1979, op. cit., p. 51.

57. 'Voluntary service', International Federation of Red Cross and Red Crescent Societies (IFRC), http://www.ifrc.org/en/who-we-are/vision-and-mission/the-seven-fundamental-principles/voluntary-service/, last accessed on 16 September 2014. The contemporary concept of volunteering derives from the military. In the nineteenth century, a volunteer often referred to someone offering himself for military service without being conscripted. After 1945, the term came to be used in civilian rather than military contexts.

58. This is also the case in German with the concept of *Freiwilligenarbeit*.

59. Caroline Brassard *et al.*, 'Emerging Perspectives on International Volunteerism in Asia', IVCO 2010 Forum Research Paper, http://www.sif.org.sg/files/ivco2010_emerging_perspectives.pdf, last accessed 16 September 2010.

60. Auguste Comte, *Catéchisme Positiviste (1852)*, Editions du Sandre, Paris: 2009.

61. Daniel Batson, *The Altruism Question: Toward a Social Psychological Answer*, Hillsdale: Lawrence Erlbaum Associates, 1991, pp. 6–7.

62. Jacob Neusner and Bruce Chilton (eds), *Altruism in World Religions*, Washington: Georgetown University Press, 2005.

63. Robert L. Trivers, 'The Evolution of Reciprocal Altruism', *The Quarterly Review of Biology* 46, 1 (1971), pp. 35–57.

64. Ibid.

65. Robert Axelrod and William Hamilton, 'The Evolution of Cooperation', *Science* 211, 4489 (1981), pp. 1390–1396. It must be noted that, at least in theory, the same individuals do not have to meet again for reciprocity to evolve. Indirect reciprocity, one could call it reciprocity by proxy, can develop based on others perceiving a person to be an altruist, which will help that person to benefit from altruistic actions from others in return.

66. Serge-Christophe Kolm, 'Introduction to the Economics of Altruism, Giving, and Reciprocity', in Serge-Christophe Kolm and Jean Mercier Ythier (eds), *Handbook of Economics of Giving, Altruism and Reciprocity*, Amsterdam: North-Holland, 2006, 1, pp. 1–122, p. 44.

67. See for instance Kenneth Arrow, *The Limits of Organization*, New York: Norton, 1974.

68. For the purposes of this book, 'aid workers' refers to both national and international employees of not-for-profit organizations that provide assistance in humanitarian crises, including those agencies that provide both relief and development aid. This definition excludes employees of organizations pursuing strictly political, security, peacebuilding, religious or advocacy agendas (for example, human rights organizations or UN peacekeepers).

69. Peter Walker and Catherine Russ, 'Professionalising the Humanitarian Sector: A Scoping Study', report commissioned by Enhancing Learning & Research for Humanitarian Assistance, 2010, p. 21.

70. 'Voluntary Service' IFRC, op. cit.

71. Weber contrasted an ethics of conviction—where people convinced to fight for the good cause aren't willing to compromise—with an ethics of responsibility, under which political leaders weigh the motives of a decision against the consequences.

72. Ernst Fehr and Bettina Rockenbach, 'Human Altruism: Economic, Neural, and Evolutionary Perspectives', *Current Opinion in Neurobiology* 14 (2004), pp. 784–790.

73. Steven Pinker, *The Better Angels of Our Nature: The Decline of Violence in History and Its Causes*, New York: Viking Books, 2011.

74. Richard Dawkins, *The Selfish Gene*, Oxford: Oxford University Press, 1976; Terry Burnham and Dominic Johnson, 'The Biological and Evolutionary Logic of Human Cooperation', *Analyse & Kritik* 27 (2005), pp. 113–135. Religion has also been subject to recent work in biology and cognitive psychology focusing on the role of natural selection in the emergence and variety of religious thoughts and practices (see Pascal Boyer and Brian Bergstrom, 'Evolutionary Perspectives on Religion', *Annual Review of Anthropology* 37 (2008), pp. 111–130).

75. 'Group selection' provides a competing explanation: some groups would have gained an evolutionary edge over competing groups thanks to a stronger tendency towards altruistic behaviour between their members. This explanation remains highly contested. See Ali Arbia and Gilles Carbonnier, 'Human Nature and Development Aid: IR and the Biology of Altruism', *Journal of International Relations and Development* (Forthcoming, 2015).

76. Knud Haakonssen (ed.), *Adam Smith: The Theory of Moral Sentiments*, New York: Cambridge University Press, 2002, pp. 11–12.

77. Ibid, p. 12.

78. Frans de Waal, 'Putting the Altruism Back into Altruism: The Evolution of Empathy', *Annual Review of Psychology* 59 (2008), pp. 279–300.

79. Giacomo Rizzolatti *et al.*, *Mirrors in the Brain: How Our Minds Share Actions, Emotions, and Experience*, Oxford: Oxford University Press, 2008. In the case of gustatory pleasures and pains for instance, the mirror systems of individuals who evaluate themselves as more empathic than others tend to be more activated by facial emotions expressed by others, both in the case of disgust and pleasure (see Mbemba Jabbi *et al.*, 'Empathy for positive and negative emotions in the gustatory cortex', *NeuroImage* 34, 4 (2007), pp. 1744–1753).

80. Michael Koenigs *et al.*, 'Damage to the prefrontal cortex increases utilitarian moral judgements', *Nature* 446, 7138 (2007), pp. 908–911.

81. Simon Baron-Cohen, *Zero Degrees of Empathy: A New Theory of Human Cruelty*, London: Penguin/Allen Lane, 2011.

82. Gerald Marwell and Ruth Ames, 'Economists Free Ride, Does Anyone Else?', *Journal of Public Economics* 15, 3 (1981), pp. 295–310.

83. To be fair, economists were slightly higher in terms of number of hours they reported spending in volunteer activities. See R.H. Frank *et al.*, 'Does Studying Economics Inhibit Cooperation?', *Journal of Economic Perspectives* 7, 2 (1993), pp. 159–171.

84. Ibid, pp. 170–171.

85. Alain Cohn, Ernst Fehr and Michel Maréchal, 'Business Culture and Dishonesty in the Banking Industry', *Nature*, 2014, advanced online publication.

86. Researchers recently found evidence linking the spread of norms with the spread of breadth and width of market interactions and, to a lesser but still significant extent, with the diffusion of religion. See Joseph Henrich *et al.*, 'Markets, Religion, Community Size, and the Evolution of Fairness and Punishment', *Science* 327, 5972 (2010), pp. 1480–1484.

87. This is now widely integrated in current models of expected utility. See also Robert Axelrod, *The Evolution of Cooperation* (Revised ed.), New York: Perseus Books Group, 2006.

88. Daniel Kahneman, *Thinking, Fast and Slow*, London: Allen Lane, 2011.

89. Richard Dawkins, *The Selfish Gene* (30th Anniversary Edition), Oxford: Oxford University Press, 2006, p. ix.

90. See for example Eran Halperin *et al.*, 'Emotion Regulation and the Cultivation of Political Tolerance', *Journal of Conflict Resolution* 58, 6 (2014), pp. 1110–1138.

91. Abraham Maslow, 'A Theory of Human Motivation', *Psychological Review* 50, 4 (1943), pp. 370–96.

92. The Report highlights three main principles guiding human decision making: first, people think fast and rely more on their intuition than on careful analysis; second, mental models are rooted in different cultures, which influence our thinking, thus, human behaviour and judgment is highly contextual; and third, institutions and social norms motivate people's behaviour.

93. Jeffrey Carpenter and Caitlin M. Meyers, 'Why Volunteer? Evidence on the Role of Altruism, Image and Incentives', *Journal of Public Economics* 94, 11–12 (2010), pp. 911–920.

94. Richard Titmuss, *The Gift Relationship: From Human Blood to Social Policy*, London: George Allen and Unwin, 1970.

95. Benjamin E. Hippen, 'Organ Sales and Moral Travails: Lessons from the Living Kidney Vendor Program in Iran', *Policy Analysis* 614, Washington: Cato Institute, 2008.

96. One strain of research deals with moral dilemmas, as in the web-based Moral Sense Test from the Cognitive Evolution Laboratory of Harvard University. The results, combined with more classical research design outcomes, so far hint at a general sense for some norms, but not for others. People tend to answer certain questions in consistent ways despite a wide variety of justifications and a lack of internal logic for these justifications. Yet the nature of a web-based test bears the risk of obvious biases and has therefore to be taken with a grain of salt.

97. Urs Luterbacher and Carmen Sandi, 'Breaking the Dynamics of Emotions and Fear in Conflict and Reconstruction', *Peace Economics, Peace Science and Public Policy* 20, 3 (2014), p. 489.

98. Pictet remarks that 'Some philosophers maintain that the moral value of an act of charity depends upon the nobility of purpose of the one who performs it. Possibly so, but for the Red Cross what counts is that it be effective, that it be beneficial to those who suffer ... It does not matter a great deal, after all, in what spirit the act is performed.' Jean Pictet, 1979, op. cit., p. 16.

99. Ibid., p. 31.

100. Indeed, people from various origins and cultural backgrounds tend to come to the same conclusion in international experiments when solving moral dilemmas, albeit they provide a great variety of motivations for their decisions. See Bryce Huebner and Marc Hauser, 'Moral judgments about altruistic self-sacrifice: when philosophical and folk intuitions clash', *Philosophical Psychology* 24, 1 (2011), pp. 73–94.

101. Jane Piliavin, 'Altruism and Helping: The Evolution of a Field: The 2008 Cooley-Mead Presentation', *Social Psychology Quarterly* 72, 3 (2009), pp. 209–225.

102. Gilles Carbonnier, 'Security Management and the Political Economy of War', *Humanitarian Exchange* 47 (2010), pp. 18–21.

2. THE HUMANITARIAN MARKET

1. Nelson Mandela, quoted in *Deprived of Freedom*, Geneva: ICRC, 2002, p. 30.

2. Albert Schweitzer, French theologian, musician and medical missionary, quoted in: Surabhi Ranganathan, 'Reconceptualizing the Boundaries of "Humanitarian" Assistance: "What's in a Name" or "The Importance of Being Earnest"', *John Marshall Law Review* 40, 1 (2006), footnote 1.

3. Vaclav Havel, 'Moi Aussi Je Me Sens Albanais', *Le Monde*, 29 April 1999.

4. 'ARSIC-N and ANA Travel Outside Boundaries to Deliver Aid', *International Security Assistance Force*, http://www.nato.int/isaf/docu/news/2007/12-december/071220b.html.accessed 27 October 2014.

5. ICJ, *Military and Paramilitary Activities in and against Nicaragua (Nicaragua v. United States of America)*, Judgment, 27 June 1986, paras 242–3.

6. DAC members further agree on best practices and regularly review their policies and practices among peers. As of 2014, the DAC consisted of the European Union and twenty-eight donor states: Australia, Austria, Belgium, Canada, the Czech Republic, Denmark, Finland, France, Germany, Greece, Iceland, Ireland, Italy, Japan, Korea, Luxembourg, The Netherlands, New Zealand, Norway, Poland, Portugal, Slovak Republic, Slovenia, Spain, Sweden, Switzerland, the United Kingdom and the United States.

7. The definition was largely inspired by the work of the Good Humanitarian Donorship Initiative. See: 'Good Humanitarian Donorship', http://www.goodhumanitariandonorship.org, last accessed 23 October 2014.

8. Importantly, activities to protect the security of persons or property through the use or display of force are excluded. Humanitarian aid includes aid to refugees in developing countries, but not to those in donor countries: 'Glossary', *OECD*, http://www.oecd.org/site/dacsmpd11/glossary.htm#H, last accessed 23 October 2014.

9. Riccardo Bocco, Pierre Harrison and Lucas Oesch, 'Recovery', in Vincent Chetail (ed.), *Post-conflict Peacebuilding—A Lexicon*, Oxford: Oxford University Press, 2009, pp. 268–279.

10. 'About FTS', FTS, http://fts.unocha.org/pageloader.aspx?page=AboutFTS-uctr-lAboutFTS, last accessed 23 October 2014.

11. The Programme is run by Development Initiatives, an independent organization funded by Canada, the Netherlands, Sweden and the United Kingdom. See: 'About GHA', GHA, http://www.globalhumanitarianassistance.org/about-gha, last accessed 23 October 2014.

12. The response of the Philippine authorities and local communities to Typhoon Haiyan provides further evidence of the prominent role of the domestic response in middle-income countries in terms of resources and leadership. See GHA Report 2014, Global Humanitarian Assistance, Bristol (UK): Development Initiatives, 2014.

13. Through its 'query wizard for international development statistics', the DAC provides statistics on aid commitments for the humanitarian aid grouping, which comprises four categories: humanitarian aid, emergency response, reconstruction relief and rehabilitation, and disaster prevention and preparedness. For definitions, see the 'DAC Glossary of Key Terms and Concepts', OECD, http://www.oecd.org/dac/dac-glossary.htm, last accessed 23 October 2014. A pledge is defined

as a political announcement of intent on behalf of a donor to contribute a certain amount to a certain area; a commitment is a firm obligation, expressed in writing and backed by the necessary funds; a disbursement is the release of funds to or the purchase of goods or services for a recipient—by extension, the amount thus spent. Disbursements record the actual international transfer of financial resources, or of goods or services valued at the cost to the donor. Note that there can be important discrepancies between commitments and actual disbursements, and that it can take several years to disburse a commitment.

14. Time series in current or nominal dollars are adjusted for inflation in the donor's currency and fluctuations in the exchange rate between that currency and the United States dollar. The data is then presented in dollars, in constant prices with regard to a reference year, reflecting the purchasing power that nominal dollars would have in the reference year.

15. According to GHA estimates, private voluntary contributions reached new heights at $5.6bn in 2013, about a third of the size of government contributions that year. See GHA Report 2014, op. cit.

16. This is how the Global Humanitarian Assistance (GHA) Programme estimates the volume of private funding: ibid, p. 121.

17. Ibid.

18. 'International Financial Report 2013', *MSF*, 2013.

19. This is not surprising to the extent that states signatory to the Geneva Conventions have entrusted the ICRC with the mandate to guard international humanitarian law: 'Financial & Funding Information Overview', *ICRC Annual Report 2013*, Geneva: ICRC, 2014.

20. GHA Report 2014, op. cit., p. 37.

21. Ibid., pp. 34–35.

22. Romilly Greenhill, 'Real Aid 2: Making Technical Assistance Work', ActionAid, 2006; Gilles Carbonnier *et al.*, 'Effets Economiques de l'Aide Publique au Développement en Suisse', Geneva: IHEID, 2012.

23. 'World Development Indicators: Aid Dependency', World Bank, http://wdi.worldbank.org/table/6.11, last accessed 23 October 2014.

24. ODA captures aid flows directed at more than 150 developing countries and territories. It does not comprise aid granted to industrialized countries, such as emergency assistance to Japan after the 2011 Tohoku earthquake and tsunami, or to the US in response to the 2005 Hurricane Katrina.

25. Gilles Carbonnier, 'Humanitarian and Development Aid in the Context of Stabilization: Blurring the Lines and Broadening the Gap' in Robert Muggah (ed.), *Stabilization Operations, Security and Development*, New York: Routledge, 2014, pp. 35–55.

26. GHA Report 2014, op. cit, p. 10.

27. Ibid, p. 16.

28. United Nations, 'Overview of Global Humanitarian Response 2014', Geneva: OCHA, 2013, p. 6.

29. In 2012 for example, two-third of official humanitarian assistance was directed to protracted crises: GHA Report 2014, op. cit.

30. Ibid., p. 89.

31. Ibid., p. 3.

32. Maslen Casey-Stuart (ed.), *The War Report 2012*, Oxford: Oxford University Press, 2013. The report finds that most of the 95,000 people killed by belligerents in 2012 were civilians. Almost 35,000 were killed in the context of indiscriminate use of weapons in populated areas, with over ninety per cent of the casualties thought to have been civilians.

33. Michel Wieviorka, *La Violence*, Paris: Balland, 2004. Wieviorka distinguishes, among others, between infra-political violence associated with the partial privatization of violence and meta-political violence often found in reaction to feelings of threatened identity associated with globalization.

34. Modern-day armed conflicts are often difficult to categorize given, for instance, the unidentifiable nature of some parties involved or spill-overs into neighbouring states. In Syria, some non-state armed groups may be fighting independently, others with or alongside government forces, or under the *de facto* control of another state.

35. The International Criminal Tribunal for the former Yugoslavia (ICTY) has set out criteria for such situations whereby the conflict must require a certain degree of intensity and organization of the armed groups: see: ICTY, *The Prosecutor v. Ramush Haradinaj, Idriz Balaj and Lahi Brahimaj (Haradinaj et al.)*, Trial Chamber Judgement, 3 April 2008, Case No. IT-04-84-T, paras 49 and 60. Although the situation of violence in Mexico would likely fulfill the IHL criteria of intensity of violence, the drug gangs and cartels would need to fulfill a second criteria of being considered 'organized', in which case the IHL rules of non-international armed conflict apply.

36. IHL rules apply to situations of non-international armed conflict in several circumstances. Common Article 3 to the four Geneva Conventions provides a minimum set of guarantees but does not offer a clear definition. Additional Protocol II (APII) applies in the case of non-international armed conflict, but only to those states who are parties to the treaty. In any case, Common Article 3 may still apply, even in situations where fighting occurs only between non-state armed groups,

37. E.g. the Heidelberg Institute for International Conflict Research (HIIK—Heidelberg University), the Center for International and Conflict Management (CIDCM—Maryland University), and the UCDP.

38. Battle-related deaths occur as a result of traditional battlefield fighting, guerrilla activities and bombardments. Military and civilian deaths are counted as battle-related deaths. See 'Definitions', Uppsala University Department of Peace and

Conflict Research, http://www.pcr.uu.se/research/ucdp/definitions/, last accessed 23 October 2014.

39. Tilman Brück, Patricia Justino, Philip Verwimp and Andrew Tedesco, 'Measuring Conflict Exposure in Micro-Level Surveys' HiCN Working Paper 153 (2013), p. 20.

40. Monty Marshall and Ted Robert Gurr, 'Peace and Conflict', Center for International Development and Conflict Management, University of Maryland, 2005, p. 11.

41. Empirical evidence tends to support the assumption that media reporting on disasters is positively correlated with funding and disaster severity, as reported in Oscar Becerra, Eduardo Cavallo and Ilan Noy, 'Foreign Aid in the Aftermath of Large Natural Disasters', *Review of Development Economics* 18, 3 (2014), pp 445–460.

42. Marshall and Gurr, 2005, op.cit., p. 12.

43. Sebastian Abuja *et al.*, 'Global Overview 2014: People Internally Displaced by Conflict and Violence', Geneva: Norwegian Refugee Council/Internal Displacement Monitoring Center, 2014.

44. The World Health Organization (WHO) defines collective violence as the instrumental use of violence by people who identify themselves as members of a group against another group, in relation to a feeling of group identity that can be transitory or permanent: 'Collective violence', WHO, http://www.who.int/violence_injury_prevention/violence/world_report/factsheets/en/collectiveviolfacts.pdf, last accessed 23 October 2014.

45. In the 2004–09 period, El Salvador ranked first, followed by Iraq, Jamaica, Honduras, Colombia and Venezuela. See 'Geneva Declaration on Armed Violence and Development', http://www.genevadeclaration.org/home.html, last accessed 23 October 2014.

46. The Geneva Declaration has decided to group countries with populations lower than 100,000 together (e.g. in the Caribbean, these are grouped as 'Lesser Antilles'; in Oceania, as 'Micronesia') to avoid—at least to some degree—skewing the ranking with the presence of very small states that have high rates but small incidence of violence (e.g. small islands can have rates over 50 because of one or two homicides.

47. In this book, I do not consider technological disasters such as oil spills, nuclear incidents or hazardous material transportation incidents that generally do not trigger an international humanitarian response.

48. Debarati Guha-Sapir and Philippe Hoyois, 'Measuring the Human and Economic Impact of Disasters', Report produced for the Government Office of Science, Foresight project, 'Reducing Risks of Future Disasters: Priorities for Decision Makers', 27 November 2012, pp. 6–13.

49. 'Glossary', EM-DAT, http://www.emdat.be/glossary/9, last accessed 23 October 2014. EM-DAT focuses on the occurrence and effects of mass disasters across the

globe since 1900. It provides data on the human impacts of disasters (deaths, injuries, homelessness and people otherwise affected), the economic losses and international relief efforts. EM-DAT is based on data provided by UN agencies, non-governmental organizations, insurance companies, research institutes and press agencies. A disaster is registered in EM-DAT when at least one of the following criteria is met: ten or more individuals are reported killed, at least 100 people have been affected, a state of emergency has been declared, or a call for international assistance has been emitted.

50. Biological disasters result from exposure of living organisms to germs and toxic substances, for example cholera or Ebola epidemics, animal stampedes or insect infestation. Geophysical events include earthquakes and volcano eruptions, while floods, landslides and avalanches fall under hydrological events. Meteorological and climatological events include storms, cyclones, droughts and wildfires. The CRED also considers man-made disasters such as industrial accidents.

51. MunichRe maintains the NatCatSERVICE loss database: http://www.munichre.com/natcatservice, last accessed 23 October 2014. SwissRe's Sigma database provides detailed accounting of insured losses and further seeks to cover uninsured losses: http://www.swissre.com/sigma/, last accessed 23 October 2014. SwissRe and MunichRe grant their clients privileged access to full information packages, but also release publicly available reports on a regular basis.

52. Access to the Lloyd's Casualty Weekly Reports and customized information requires paying a subscription fee.

53. Guha-Sapir and Hoyois, 2012, op. cit., pp. 29–31.

54. In EM-DAT, deaths include all the people confirmed dead and those missing and presumed dead. People affected are those deemed to require assistance during an emergency such as food, water, shelter, sanitation and immediate medical assistance. The total number of people affected further include those reported injured or homeless. Debarati Guha-Sapir, Philippe Hoyois and Regina Below, 'Annual Disaster Statistical Review 2013', Brussels: CRED, 2013, p. 9.

55. Guha-Sapir and Hoyois, 2012, op. cit., pp. 32–3.

56. Interpreting the downward trend of disasters since the mid-2000s is fraught with ambiguities and requires disaggregating the data by examining the evolution of different types of disasters in different locations.

57. Guha-Sapir and Hoyois, 2012, op. cit. In addition, CRED data indicates that, since the mid-2000s, geophysical events have oscillated around the figure of thirty.

58. UN and World Bank, 'Natural Hazards Unnatural Disasters: the Economics of Effective Prevention', Washington: The World Bank, 2010, p. 2.

59. In EM-DAT, the registered figure corresponds to the estimated value of the direct damage occasioned by the event, expressed in current US dollars and, in this report, was converted into 2013 dollar values for easier comparison. Estimates of disaster damages must be treated with caution, because of (a) the financial value of

infrastructures, which is much higher in high-income countries than in middle- and low-income countries; and (b) the low reporting rates of direct losses, which is better for large disasters.

60. If we were to add data from national disaster databases, it has been estimated that direct disaster losses may be at least 50 per cent higher than internationally reported disasters (UNISDR, 'Global Assessment Report on Disaster Risk Reduction', 2013). The insurance penetration rate being lower in developing countries, losses are not systematically recorded nor properly valued.

61. Guha-Sapir and Hoyois, 2012, op. cit., p. 26.

62. Economic costs expressed in constant US dollars of 2011: author's calculations based on CRED EM-DAT data as reported in ibid., p. 25.

63. CRED experts stress that 'the current state of scientific research on the differential impact of disasters on prepared and un-prepared communities does not allow for such causal associations. Drawing such a conclusion would require studies with quasi–experimental design where villages with and without interventions are compared.' See Guha-Sapir and Hoyois, 2012, op. cit., p. 22.

64. UN humanitarian agencies are those pertaining to the Inter-Agency Standing Committee on Humanitarian Affairs (IASC) that include FAO, OCHA, UNDP, UNFPA, UNHCR, UNICEF, WFP and WHO, in addition to UNRWA and the IOM.

65. E.g. World Vision, Save the Children Fund, CARE, Action against Hunger, Caritas, Oxfam, MSF and Médecins du Monde.

66. The ICRC, the International Federation of Red Cross and Red Crescent Societies (IFRC), and the individual national societies.

67. Dennis Dijkzeul and Zeynep Sezgin (eds), *The New Humanitarians: Principles and Practice*, London: Routledge, forthcoming.

68. Thomas Weiss, *Humanitarian Business*, Malden: Polity Press, 2013, pp. 44–45; Gilles Carbonnier, 'Privatisation and Outsourcing in Wartime: the Humanitarian Challenges', *Disasters* 30, 4 (2006), pp. 402–16.

69. See e.g. Ronald Coase, 'The Nature of the Firm', *Economica* 4, 16 (1937), pp. 386–405.

70. Patrick Daly and Caroline Brassard, 'Aid Accountability and Participatory Approaches in Post-Disaster Housing Reconstruction', *Asian Journal of Social Science* 39, 4 (2011) pp. 508–533, p. 530.

71. Glyn Taylor *et al.*, 'The State of the Humanitarian System', *ALNAP*, London: Overseas Development Institute, 2012.

72. The remaining 19 percent is reported as 'unknown'.

73. When considering both humanitarian and development assistance, World Vision International is the largest aid NGO in terms of budget; Glyn Taylor *et al.*, 2012, op. cit., pp. 27–8.

74. Thomas Richard Davies, 'The Transformation of International NGOs and Their

Impact on Development Aid', *International Development Policy/Revue internationale de politique de développement*, 3, 2012.

75. GHA Report 2014, op. cit.

76. Inter-Agency Standing Committee, 'IASC Guidelines on Mental Health and Psychosocial Support in Emergency Settings', 2007, p. 72.

77. Christina Maslach and Michael Leiter 'Early Predictors of Job Burnout and Engagement', *Journal of Applied Psychology*, 93, 3 (2008), pp. 498–512.

78. Stuart Carr *et al.*, 'Humanitarian Work Psychology: Concepts to Contributions', White Paper Series, International Affairs Committee of the Society for Industrial and Organizational Psychology, 2013.

79. Quoted in Peter Redfield, *Life in Crisis: The Ethical Journey of Doctors without Borders*, Los Angeles: University of California Press, 2013, p. 136.

80. Alexandra Meierhans, Victor Bresch and Sabina Voicu, 'Expatriate Taxation and the Evolution of the Humanitarian Sector', MIMEO, Geneva: The Graduate Institute, 2012.

81. Alexander Cooley and James Ron, 'The NGO Scramble: Organizational Insecurity and the Political Economy of Transnational Action', *International Security* 27, 1 (2002), pp. 5–39, p. 36.

82. Fiona Terry, 'The Impact of MSF's Withdrawal from Somalia in 2013: MSF's Medical Care under Fire Project', Geneva: MSF, April 2014, p. 24.

83. The relationship between humanitarian NGOs and their home states has been ambiguous from the outset. Save the Children Fund (SCF) and Oxfam came into being out of a resolve from British citizens to circumvent embargoes imposed by their own government in order to alleviate the plight of civilians suffering from the consequences of these sanctions, in Germany at the end of World War I and in Greece during World War II, respectively. By contrast, the creation of CARE at the end of World War II was much more aligned with US foreign policy and with the Marshall Plan in particular. See Philippe Ryfman, *Une histoire de l'humanitaire*, Paris: La Découverte, 2008.

84. UNGA, 'Strengthening of the Coordination of Humanitarian Emergency Assistance of the United Nations', UNGA, UN Doc. A/RES/46/182, 78th plenary meeting, 19 December 1991. The Resolution further stresses that 'Contributions for humanitarian assistance should be provided in a way which is not to the detriment of resources made available for international cooperation for development.' (Art 9).

85. Peter Walker and Daniel Maxwell, *Shaping the Humanitarian World*, London: Routledge, 2009, pp. 121–4.

86. Sarah Collinson, Samir Elhawary and Robert Muggah, 'States of Fragility: Stabilisation and its Implications for Humanitarian Action,' *Disasters* 34, 3 (2010), pp. 275–96. The Solidarists' stance against exclusion can be seen to be in line with the requirement of impartiality that demands responses tailored to actual needs,

avoiding discrimination between aid darlings and orphans. Dunantists would, however, regard it as risky for their operational capacity to advocate for greater gender equality in Afghanistan or for better political representation of ethnic minorities in Myanmar.

87. Philipp Fountain, 'Religion and Disaster Relief: Rethinking their Relationship in Asia'. Paper presented at a seminar on Religious Studies, Victoria University of Wellington, March 2014.

88. Martin Riesebrodt, *The Promise of Salvation: A Theory of Religion*, Chicago: University of Chicago Press, 2010, p. 89.

89. Michael Barnett, *Empire of Humanity: A History of Humanitarianism*, Ithaca: Cornell University Press, 2011.

90. Ibid.

91. 'The Code of Conduct for the International Red Cross and Red Crescent Movement and NGOs in Disaster Relief', IFRC, Principle 3, p. 2.

92. Max Weber, *From Max Weber: Essays in Sociology*, New York: Oxford University Press, 1946, p. 155.

93. Gilles Carbonnier, 'Reconsidering the Secular as the Norm', *International Development Policy—Religion & Development* 4 (2013), pp. 7–12.

94. Didier Fassin, *Humanitarian Reason: A Moral History of the Present*, Berkeley: University of California Press, 2012, p. 249.

95. Samantha Power, *A Problem from Hell: America and the Age of Genocide*, New York: Basic Books, 2013.

3. WAR ECONOMICS

1. Paul Krugman, 'Why We Fight Wars', *International New York Times*, http://www.nytimes.com/2014/08/18/opinion/paul-krugman-why-we-fight.html?smid=nytcore-iphone-hare&smprod=nytcore-iphone, last accessed 17 November 2014.

2. John Maynard Keynes, *How to Pay for the War*, Macmillan: London, 1940; Keynes argued for compulsory saving rather than deficit spending to contain domestic demand and inflation during WWII. Workers later withdrawing their savings would contribute to post-war recovery.

3. The study of war economies has been greatly enriched by literature on defence economics. See e.g. Ron Smith, *Military Economics*, London: Palgrave, 2009; Charles Anderton and John Carter, *Principles of Conflict Economics: A Primer for Social Scientists*, Cambridge: Cambridge University Press, 2009; Jurgen Brauer and Paul Dunne, *Peace Economics: A Macroeconomic Primer for Violence-Afflicted States*, Washington: US Institute of Peace, 2012. Another reference on war economies is: Michael Pugh, Neil Cooper and Jonathan Goodhand, *War Economies in a Regional Context: Challenges of Transformation*, Boulder, CO: Lynne Rienner, 2004.

4. Demand was also high for specific videogame appliances such as Sony's PlayStation 2.

5. Angola, Namibia and Zimbabwe intervened in support of the DRC government together with the Central African Republic, Chad and Sudan, while Burundi, Rwanda and Uganda supported rebel groups.

6. Stephen Jackson, 'Fortunes of War: The Coltan Trade in the Kivus', background research for HPG Report 13, London: ODI, 2003, p. 16.

7. United Nations Security Council (UNSC), 'Letter dated 15 October 2002 from the Secretary-General Addressed to the President of the Security Council', UN Doc. S/2002/1146, 16 October 2002, para. 88.

8. UNSC, 'Report of the Panel of Experts on the Illegal Exploitation of Natural Resources and Other Forms of Wealth of the Democratic Republic of the Congo', UN Doc. S/2001/357, 12 April 2001. Just two weeks after the report's publication, on 26 April 2001, six ICRC workers were killed in the vicinity of Bunia, in North-East DRC. A week later, the President of the UN Security Council opened the session devoted to the examination of the first Expert Panel Report by expressing sadness and outrage over these murders.

9. For a survey of the different methods used in calculating the costs of war, see Javier Gardeazabal, 'Methods for Measuring Aggregate Cost of Conflict' in Michelle Garfinkel and Stergios Skaperdas (eds), *Handbook of the Economics of Peace and Conflict*, New York: Oxford University Press, 2012, pp. 227–251.

10. Robert Bates, *When Things Fell Apart: State Failure in Late Century Africa*, Cambridge: Cambridge University Press, 2008. The economies of post-World War II Japan and West Germany bounced back unusually rapidly, not so much as the result of generous reconstruction packages, but rather based on strong social cohesion and the quality of institutions and human capital.

11. Hamid Ali, 'Estimate of the Economic Cost of Armed Conflict: A Case Study From Darfur', *Defence and Peace Economics* 24, 6 (2013), pp. 503–519.

12. For example, the 'Households in Conflict Network' (HiCN: www.hicn.org): See HiCN Working Paper 153 of August 2013, and Chapter 6 of this book.

13. This is akin to the broken window fallacy argument advanced by Frédéric Bastiat in the mid-nineteenth century, as discussed in Chapter 5 in the context of estimating the economic consequences of disasters.

14. Geneva Declaration on Armed Violence and Development, *Global Burden of Armed Violence*, 2008, Chapter 5, pp. 89–108.

15. Patricia Justino, Tilman Bruck and Philip Verwimp (eds), *A Micro-level Perspective on the Dynamics of Conflict, Violence, and Development*, Oxford: Oxford University Press, 2013.

16. The study focuses in particular on the impact of human capital destruction. It looks at labour and agricultural productivity. See: Pieter Serneels and Marijke Verpoorten, 'The Impact of Armed Conflict on Economic Performance: Evidence from Rwanda', *Journal of Conflict Resolution* (December 2013).

231

17. Mohammad Badiuzzaman, John Cameron and Syed Mansoob Murshed, 'Household Decision-Making Under Threat of Violence: A Micro Level Study in the Chittagong Hill Tracts of Bangladesh', Working Paper 39, Brighton: MICRO-CON, 2011; Carlos Bozzoli and Tilman Brück, 'Agriculture, poverty, and postwar reconstruction: micro-level evidence from Northern Mozambique', *Journal of Peace Research* 46, 3 (2009), pp. 377–397.

18. Maarten Voors *et al.*, 'Does Conflict affect Preferences? Results from Field Experiments in Burundi', Working Paper 71, Brighton: Households in Conflict Network, 2010.

19. Justin Wolfers and Eric Zitzewitz, 'Using Markets to Inform Policy. The Case of the Iraq War', *Econometrica* 76, 302 (2009), pp. 225–250.

20. Massimo Guidolin and Eliana La Ferrara, 'The economic effects of violent conflict: Evidence from asset market reactions', *Journal of Peace Research* 47, 6 (2010), pp. 671–684.

21. Anja Shortland, Katerina Christopoulou and Charalampos Makatsoris, 'War and Famine, Peace and Light? The Economic Dynamics of Conflict in Somalia 1993–2009', *Journal of Peace Research* 50, 5 (2014), pp. 545–561.

22. Benjamin Coghlan *et al.*, 'Mortality in the Democratic Republic of Congo', *Lancet* 367, 9504 (2006), pp. 44–51.

23. See e.g. Andrew Mack, 'Armed Conflicts', in Bjorn Lomborg (ed.), *Global Problems, Smart Solutions: Costs and Benefits*, Cambridge: Cambridge University Press, 2013, pp. 62–71.

24. For an analysis of the methodological issues involved in the DRC case, see Michael Spagat, 'Estimating the Human Costs of War: the Sample Survey Approach' in Garfinkel and Skaperdas (eds), 2012, op. cit., pp. 318–340.

25. Morten Jerven, *Poor Numbers*, Ithaca: Cornell University Press, 2013.

26. Under that logic, the destruction of the historical centre of Dresden and the bombing of its baroque palaces and churches during the Allied air raid of 13–14 February 1945 did not affect German GDP, while it contributed to growth in the UK and the US.

27. Joseph Stiglitz and Linada Bilmes, *The Three Trillion Dollar War: The True Cost of the Iraq Conflict*, London: Allen Lane/Penguin Books, 2008.

28. In 2002 economic analysts predicted that a successful war to topple Saddam Hussein would keep the price of oil around $20 a barrel and give a boost to the world economy. See Andrew Stephen, 'Iraq: the hidden cost of the war' *New Statesman*, http://www.newstatesman.com/world-affairs/2007/03/iraq-war-wounded-bilmes-cost, last accessed on 17 November 2014. Six years later, oil prices were way above $100 a barrel.

29. WHO, 'Health statistics and information systems', http://www.who.int/health-info/global_burden_disease/metrics_daly/en/, last accessed 17 November 2014.

30. Heinz Welsch, 'The Social Cost of Civil Conflict: Evidence from Surveys of Happiness', *Kyklos* 61, 2 (2008), pp. 320–340.

31. Dwight Einsenhower, 'Farewell Radio and Television Address to the American People, January 17th, 1961', Eisenhowever Archives, http://www.eisenhower. archives.gov/all_about_ike/speeches/farewell_address.pdf, last accessed 17 November 2014; and 'Military-Industrial Complex Speech, Dwight D. Eisenhower, 1961', Public papers of the Presidents, Dwight D. Eisenhower, 1960, pp. 1035–1040, http://coursesa.matrix.msu.edu/~hst306/documents/indust. html, last accessed 17 November 2014.

32. 'Deed of Commitment', Geneva Call, http://www.genevacall.org/how-we-work/ deed-of-commitment/, last accessed 20 November 2014. Some of the insights that follow are drawn from Paul Chick, Daniel Slomka and Seo Young So, 'Negotiating a Change of Behavior with Non-State Armed Groups', Applied Research Project for Geneva Call, MIMEO, The Graduate Institute, Geneva, 2012.

33. Aidan Hartley, 'The Art of Darkness', *The Spectator*, 27 January 2001, http:// archive.spectator.co.uk/article/27th-january-2001/22/the-art-of-darkness, last accessed 17 November 2014. Laurent Désiré Kabila was arguably well placed to comment on this issue based on his alleged long experience of guerrilla warfare, including exchanges with Ernesto 'Che' Guevara in Tanzania in the mid-1960s.

34. Achim Wennmann, 'Grasping the Financing and Mobilization Cost of Armed Groups: A New Perspective on Conflict Dynamics', *Contemporary Security Policy* 30, 2 (2009), pp. 265–280.

35. Examination of eighty-nine conflicts involving non-state armed groups shows that insurgencies supported by foreign states eventually won their wars in more than half of the cases, whereas insurgencies without external support won in just three out of a total of eighteen cases. See Ben Connable, and Martin C. Libicki, *How Insurgencies End*, Santa Monica: Rand, 2010.

36. See e.g. Jeremy Weinstein, *Inside Rebellion: The Politics of Insurgent Violence*, Cambridge: Cambridge University Press, 2006; Stathis Kalyvas, *The Logic of Violence in Civil War*, Cambridge: Cambridge University Press, 2006.

37. Mancur Olson, 'Dictatorship, Democracy, and Development', *The American Political Science Review* 87, 3 (1993), pp. 567–576.

38. United Nations Office on Drugs and Crime (UNODC), 'Afghanistan Opium Survey 2012', 2013, pp. 18–19.

39. Rachel Sabates-Wheeler and Philip Verwimp, 'Extortion with Protection. Understanding the Effect of Rebel Taxation on Civilian Welfare in Burundi', *Journal of Conflict Resolution* 58, 8 (2014), pp. 1474–1499.

40. Daniel Maxwell and Nisar Majid, 'Another Humanitarian Crisis in Somalia? Learning from the 2011 Famine', *Feinstein International Center*, Tufts University, 2014.

41. Paul Collier, 'Economic Causes of Civil Conflict and Their Implications for Policy' in Crocket, Chester *et al.*, *Leashing the Dogs of War Conflict Management in a Divided World*, Washington: USIP, 2007, pp. 197–218.

42. Christopher Corley, 'The Liberation Tigers of Tamil Eelam,' in Michael Freeman

(ed.), *Financing Terrorism: Case Studies*, Surrey: Ashgate Publishing, 2012. In addition, evidence hints at the fact that diaspora funding tended to diminish in importance during peace episodes as the LTTE turned more to local taxation.

43. Christian Dietrich, 'UNITA's Diamond Mining and Exporting Capacity', in Jakkie Cilliers and Christian Dietrich (eds), *Angola's War Economy: The Role of Oil and Diamonds*, Pretoria: Institute for Security Studies, 2000, pp. 275–294.

44. Alex Vines, 'Angola: Forty Years of War', in Peter Batchelor and Kingma Kees (eds), *Demilitarisation and Peace-Building in Southern Africa—Volume II: National and Regional Experiences*, Aldershott: Ashgate, 2004, p. 87; Achim Wennmann, 'Economic Dimensions of Armed Groups: Profiling the Financing, Costs, and Agendas and their Implications for Mediated Engagements', *International Review of the Red Cross* 93, 882 (2011), p. 333–352.

45. Achim Wennmann, 'Negotiated Exits from Organized Crime? Building Peace in Conflict and Crime-affected Contexts', *Negotiation Journal*, 2014, pp. 255–273.

46. UNODC, *United Nations Convention against Transnational Organized Crime*, Article 2, 2000.

47. Notably around two national parks (Garamba and Okapi).

48. See: 'Price of Ivory in China Triples', *The Guardian*, http://www.theguardian.com/environment/2014/jul/03/price-ivory-china-triples-elephant, last accessed 17 November 2014; Krista Larson, 'Central African Republic Elephant Poaching Rises After Government is Overthrown', Huffington Post, http://www.huffingtonpost.com/2013/04/25/central-african-republic-elephant-poaching_n_3155923.html, last accessed 17 November 2014; UNSC, 'Letter dated 26 June 2014 from Panel of Experts on the Central African Republic Established Pursuant to the Security Council Resolution 2127 (2013) Addressed to the President of the Security Council', UN Doc. S/2014/452, 1 July 2014.

49. UNODC, 'World Drug Report 2012', Vienna, 2012.

50. 'Not Just in Transit: Drugs, the State and Society in West Africa', Independent Report of the West Africa Commission on Drugs, 2014, pp. 20–22.

51. Paul Krugman, *New York Times*, op. cit.

52. Kwesi Aning and John Pokoo, 'Understanding the Nature and Threats of Drug Trafficking to National and Regional Security in West Africa', *Stability* 3, 1 (2014), pp. 1–13.

53. Abdur Chowdhury and Syed Mansoob Murshed, 'Conflict and Fiscal Capacity', *Defence and Peace Economics* DOI: 10.1080/10242694.2014.948700 (2014).

54. Charles Tilly, *Coercion, Capital and European States, AD 990–1992*, Cambridge: Blackwell, 1992.

55. Philippe Le Billon, *Wars of Plunder: Conflicts, Profits and the Politics of Resources*. London/New York: Hurst/Columbia University Press, 2012.

56. Michael Klare, *Resource Wars*, New York: Holt, Henry & Co, Inc., 2002.

57. For a recent literature review, see: Vally Koubi *et al.*, 'Do Natural Resources Mat-

ter for Interstate and Intrastate Armed Conflict?', *Journal of Peace Research* 51, 2, (2014), pp. 227–243.

58. See, for instance: Michael Ross, 'Blood Barrels: Why Oil Wealth Fuels Conflict', *Foreign Affairs*, May/June 2008, http://www.foreignaffairs.com/articles/63396/michael-l-ross/blood-barrels, last accessed 17 November 2014, and Jeff Colgan, *Petro-Aggression: When Oil Causes War*, Cambridge: Cambridge University Press, 2013.

59. In the case of the civil war in Sierra Leone, diamonds have been singled out as a major conflict driver. Yet experts on the Mano River region insist on the centrality of other factors, in particular a crisis of modernity, whereby young people rebelled against traditional institutions; another factor is the influence of an imported revolutionary ideology among the intellectual elite. See Paul Richards, 'The Political Economy of Internal Conflict in Sierra Leone', Working Paper 21, Working Paper Series, Netherlands Institute of International Relations, 2003; John Hirsch, *Sierra Leone: Diamonds and the Struggle for Democracy*, Boulder: Lynne Rienner, 2001.

60. Thomas Homer-Dixon, *Environment, Scarcity, and Violence*. Princeton: Princeton University Press, 1999.

61. The Worldwatch Institute, 'State of the World 2005—Redefining Global Security', p. 84. See also the Special Symposium on Water Conflicts in the *Economists for Peace and Security Journal* 2, 2 (2007).

62. Ola Olssen and Eyerusalem Siba, 'Ethnic Cleansing or Resource Struggle in Darfur? An Empirical Analysis', *Journal of Development Economics* 103, C (2013), pp. 299–312.

63. Another factor is state capacity and institutional quality, both of which tend to be negatively affected by high dependence on natural resources. Another perspective claims that an increase in non-tax revenue is associated with more political stability, both in dictatorships and democracies and regardless of the non-tax revenue source, be it oil, minerals or foreign aid, see: Kevin Morisson, 'Oil, Nontax Revenue, and the Redistributional Foundations of Regime Stability', *International Organization* 63, 1 (2009), pp. 107–138.

64. Philippe Le Billon, 2012, op. cit., p. 10.

65. See ibid., and David Keen, *Useful Enemies: When Waging Wars is More Important than Winning Them*, New Haven: Yale University Press, 2012; Päivi Lujala, 'Deadly Combat over Natural Resources', *Journal of Conflict Resolution* 53, 1 (2009), pp. 50–71.

66. Angelika Rettberg *et al.*, 'Entrepreneurial Activity and Civil War in Colombia', Working Paper 06, UNU-WIDER (2010).

67. Oeindrila Dube and Juan Vargas, 'Commodity Price Shocks and Civil Conflict: Evidence from Colombia', *Review of Economic Studies* 80 (2013), pp. 1384–1421. Another question is to what extent the commodity price shocks are perceived as

transitory. In dynamic models, the decision to fight does not depend so much on current gains, but rather on the discounted present value of longer-term gains. If the drop in coffee price is perceived to be part of a long-term downward trend, it is not just the opportunity cost of joining the rebellion that decreases, but also the discounted present value of controlling the coffee trade.

68. Agreement on Wealth Sharing During the Pre-Interim Period between the Government of the Republic of Sudan and the Sudan People's Liberation Movement, 10 January 2004, Articles 5.4 to 5.6, p. 54.

69. Experts affirm that oil production peaked in 2010 and will rapidly dwindle in the coming decades. In terms of reserves, BP's 2013 Statistical Review reports that South Sudan was holding some 3.5bn barrels and Sudan was holding around 1.5bn barrels. Most of this oil is located in the Melut and Muglad oil basins that extend across the border into the two countries.

70. 'Oil and Peace in Sudan', *The Guardian*, http://www.theguardian.com/global-development/poverty-matters/2011/jan/07/sudan-referendum-oil-sharing-agreement, last accessed 17 November 2014.

71. 'South Sudan Overview', *World Bank*, http://www.worldbank.org/en/country/southsudan/overview, last accessed 17 November 2014.

72. Nathan Nunn and Nancy Qian, 'US Food Aid and Civil Conflict', *American Economic Review* 104, 6 (2014), pp. 1630–66; Milton Esman and Ronald Herring, *Carrots, Sticks, and Ethnic Conflict: Rethinking Development Assistance*, Ann Arbour: University of Michigan Press, 2003; Linda Polman, *The Crisis Caravan: What's Wrong with Humanitarian Aid?*, New York: Metropolitan Books, 2010; David Bryer and Edmund Cairns, 'For Better? For Worse? Humanitarian Aid in Conflict', *Development in Practice* 7, 4 (1997), pp. 363–374.

73. Herschel Grossman, 'Foreign Aid and Insurrection', *Defense Economics* 3, 4 (1992), pp. 275–288.

74. Simeon Djankov, José Montalvo and Marta Reynal-Querol, 'The Curse of Aid', *Journal of Economic Growth* 13, 3 (2008), pp. 169–194. Based on a study involving a large panel of data, the authors conclude that aid flows can actually represent a greater 'resource curse' than oil revenues, in particular regarding the detrimental impact of aid on political institutions.

75. Claudio Raddatz, 'Are External Shocks Responsible for the Instability of Output in Low Income Countries?', *Journal of Development Economics* 84, 1 (2007), pp. 155–187.

76. Richard Nielson *et al.*, 'Foreign Aid Shocks as a Cause of Violent Armed Conflict', *American Journal of Political Science* 55, 1 (2011), pp. 219–232.

77. As is well documented, rebel leaders can mobilize people by harnessing their socio-economic and political grievances, and their perceptions of discrimination. Impartiality in the design and delivery of humanitarian assistance can help avert such grievances if it is perceived as impartial by beneficiaries and non-beneficiaries alike.

78. Matthew Rosenberg, 'With bags of Cash, C.I.A. Seeks influence in Afghanistan', *New York Times*, http://www.nytimes.com/2013/04/29/world/asia/cia-delivers-cash-to-afghan-leaders-office.html?pagewanted=all, last accessed 15 January 2015.

79. For an account of such practices, see e.g. Kathleen Hughs and Steve Zyck, 'The Relationship between Aid, Insurgency, and Security: Part One and Two', *Civil-Military Fusion Center Monthly Report on Afghanistan*, 2011.

80. Joseph Carter, 'Aiding Afghanistan: How Corruption and Western Aid Hinder Afghanistan Development', *Foreign Policy Journal*, 18 June 2013, pp. 107–124. p. 108.

81. World Bank, *World Development Report 2011: Conflict, Security, and Development*, Washington: The World Bank, 2012; Paul Collier and Anke Hoeffler, 'Aid, Policy, and Peace: Reducing the Risks of Civil Conflict' *Defense and Peace Economics* 13, 6 (2002), pp. 435–450.

82. Jopper De Ree and Elenonora Nillesen, 'Aiding Violence or Peace? The Impact of Foreign Aid on the Risk of Civil Conflict in sub-Saharan Africa', *Journal of Development Economics* 88, 2 (2009), pp. 301–313.

83. Jean-Paul Azam and Veronique Thelen, 'Foreign Aid Versus Military Intervention in the War on Terror', *Journal of Conflict Resolution* 54 (2010) pp. 237–261. The authors further find that US military interventions tend to be counterproductive in oil exporting countries but seem effective in reducing the supply of insurgent and terrorist attacks in non-oil-exporting countries.

84. Romilly Greenhill, 'Real Aid: Making technical assistance work', Action Aid, 2006.

85. A recent study considers a much more robust indicator: the volume of food aid (wheat) shipped from the US to developing countries in thousands of metric tons. The findings show that US food aid tends to increase the incidence and duration of civil war in recipient countries, but has no robust effect on international armed conflict. See Nathan Nunn and Nancy Qian, 'US Food Aid and Civil Conflict', *American Economic Review* 104, 6 (2014), pp. 1630–66.

86. Ashley Jackson and Abdi Aynte, 'Talking to the other side: Humanitarian negotiations with Al-Shabaab in Somali', ODI HPG Working Paper, 2013, p. 18.

87. Ibid., p. 18.

88. See note on p. 208 of 'Annual Reports and Accounts 2012–2013', UK Department for International Development, https://www.gov.uk/government/uploads/system/uploads/attachment_data/file/209330/DFID_Annual_Report.pdf, last accessed on 17 November 2014.

89. Jackson and Aynte, 2013, op. cit., p. 21.

90. In addition, a colleague had been killed in a tragic ambush a few weeks earlier in the region.

91. See: 'MSF forced to withdraw from Somali—in depth interview', Youtube, https://www.youtube.com/watch?v=ZXfx0-Y-VM, last accessed on 17 November 2014.

92. There is a vast literature on aid fungibility. See e.g. Stephan Leiderer, 'Fungibility

and the Choice of Aid Modalities—The Red Herring Revisited', Working Paper 68, UNU-WIDER, 2012; Tarhan Feyzioglu, Vinaya Swaroop and Min Zhu, 'A Panel Data Analysis of the Fungibility of Foreign Aid,' *World Bank Economic Review* 12, 1 (1998), pp. 29–58. Some forms of aid are obviously more fungible than others. Developmental food aid programmes, in vogue a few decades ago, were precisely grounded on the fungibility of aid. They were geared towards supporting the recipient country's balance of payments and easing budgetary constraints by allowing the government to sell the food on the domestic market (monetization). By the same token, some donors could get rid of their agricultural surpluses.

93. Go Devarajan *et al.*, 'What does Aid to Africa Finance?', Development Research Group, Washington: The World Bank, 1999, p. 1.

94. 'After 30 years, WFP ends food aid to Angola', *World Food Programme*, http://www.wfp.org/news/news-release/after-30-years-wfp-ends-food-aid-angola, last accessed 17 November 2014.

95. 'Angola: Emergency food stocks running low' IRIN, http://www.irinnews.org/report/15671/angola-emergency-food-stocks-running-low, last accessed 17 November 2014.

96. Global Witness, *A Crude Awakening: The role of the oil and banking industries in Angola's civil war and the plunder of state assets*, London: Global Witness, 1999, p. 2.

97. 'At a glance: Angola', *Media Institute of Southern Africa*, http://www.ifex.org/angola/1999/12/13/newspapers_censore/, last accessed 18 November 2014.

98. 'Moral hazard' refers to people's tendency to take higher risks when they know they won't bear (all) the costs if and when such costs materialize. Moral hazard associated with foreign aid and insurance can discourage states, firms and households from investing in prevention and preparedness. Government guarantees and subsidized insurance are also subject to moral hazard (See Chapter 7).

99. Bruno Frey, *Modern Political Economy*, New York: Halsted Press, 1978.

100. 'Agency' refers to the freedom that people have to make decisions about their own lives, even in the midst of a crisis. It can be defined as the capacity of individuals or groups to make their own choices based on their ability to deliberate, mobilize and act in pursuit of their own interests and objectives.

101. Raymond Hopkins, 'The Political Economy of Foreign Aid' in Finn Tarp (ed.), *Foreign Aid and Development: Lessons Learnt and Directions for the Future*, London: Routledge, 2000.

102. An example is DFID's 'Drivers of Change' approach, which focuses on structures, agents and institutions, and examines the interactions between economic, social and political factors that impede or favour poverty reduction and inclusive development.

103. David Hudson and Andrian Leftwich, 'From Political Economy to Political Analysis', Research Paper 25, Development Leadership Program, June 2014, pp. 8–9.

104. Philippe Le Billon, 'The Political Economy of War: What Relief Workers Need to Know,' Humanitarian Practice Network Paper no. 33, ODI, London, July 2000.

105. According to the Committee to Protect Journalists, 35 per cent of journalists killed worldwide since 1992 were covering crime and corruption, see: 'Organized Crime and Corruption', Committee to Protect Journalists, http://cpj.org/reports/2012/04/organized-crime-and-corruption.php, last accessed on 10 August 2014.

106. See for example Michael Findley *et al.*, 'The Localized Geography of Foreign Aid: A New Dataset and Application to Violent Armed Conflict', *World Development* 39, 11 (2011), pp. 1995–2009.

4. TERRORISM ECONOMICS

1. Karl Ritter and Doug Mellgren, 'Nobel Laureate: Poverty Fight Essential', Associated Press, http://web.archive.org/web/20061212170635/news.yahoo.com/s/ap/20061210/ap_on_re_eu/nobel_prizes, last accessed 20 January 2015.

2. Theoretical papers typically rely on game theory, for example to analyze bargaining in hostage crises. Recent advances allow adding more iterations or stages to the game. One party can for instance make choices while attempting to anticipate their opponent's response and factoring into their analysis the likelihood that their opponent will attempt a parallel anticipation.

3. Todd Sandler, 'New Frontiers of Terrorism Research: An Introduction', *Journal of Peace Research* 248, 3 (2011), pp. 279–286, p. 280.

4. A well-known example is the bombing of Pan Am Flight 103 that crashed near Lockerbie in Scotland in December 1988. The regime of the former Libyan leader Muammar Gaddafi was accused of involvement, and thus of state-sponsored terrorism. Besides, several states draw their origins from what would nowadays be regarded as terrorist acts.

5. Alan Krueger, 'What Makes a Homegrown Terrorist? Human Capital and Participation in Domestic Islamic Terrorist Groups in the U.S.A.', *Economics Letters* (Elsevier) 101, 3 (2008), pp. 293–296.

6. Bruno Frey, *Dealing with Terrorism—Stick or Carrots?*, Cheltenham: Edward Elgar, 2004.

7. Mark Harrison, 'An Economist Looks at Suicide Terrorism', *World Economics* 7, 3 (2006), pp. 1–15.

8. Alan Krueger, *What Makes a Terrorist? Economics and the Roots of Terrorism*, Princeton: Princeton University Press, 2007, p. 41.

9. Mark Harrison, 2006, op. cit.

10. Ariel Merari, 'The Readiness to Kill and Die: Suicidal Terrorism in the Middle East.' In Reich, Walter (ed.), *Origins of Terrorism: Psychologies, Ideologies, Theolo-*

gies, States of Mind, Second edition, Washington: Woodrow Wilson Center and Johns Hopkins University Press, 1998, pp. 192–207.

11. Bob Simon, 'Mind of the Suicide Bomber', http://www.cbsnews.com/news/mind-of-the-suicide-bomber/, accessed 27 November 2014.

12. Robert Pape, *Dying to Win: The Strategic Logic of Suicide Terrorism*, New York: Random House, 2005.

13. Scott Atran, *Talking to the Enemy: Faith, Brotherhood, and the (Un)Making of Terrorists*, New York: HarperCollins, 2010.

14. Bruno Frey and Simon Luechinger, 'How to Fight Terrorism: Alternatives to Deterrence', *Defence and Peace Economics* 14, 4 (2003), pp. 237–249; Charles Anderton and John Carter, 'On Rational Choice Theory and the Study of Terrorism', *Defence and Peace Economics* 16, 4 (2005) pp. 275–282.

15. Personal communications with US researchers working in Afghanistan and Sudan.

16. Khusrav Gaibulloev and Todd Sandler, 'The Adverse Effect of Transnational and Domestic Terrorism on Growth in Africa', *Journal of Peace Research* 48, 3 (2011), pp. 355–371.

17. Sultan Mehmood, 'Terrorism and the Macroeconomy: Evidence from Pakistan', *Defence and Peace Economics*, 25, 5 (2014), pp. 509–534.

18. Walter Enders and Todd Sandler, 'Causality Between Transnational Terrorism and Tourism: The Case of Spain', *Terrorism* 14, 1 (1991), pp. 49–58.

19. Augusto Voltes-Dorta, Juan Luis Jiménez and Ancor Suárez-Alemán, 'The Impact of ETA's Dissolution on Domestic Tourism in Spain', *Defence and Peace Economics* (2015), DOI:10.1080/10242694.2015.1025485.

20. Giorgios Skaperdas, 'The Cost of Organized Violence: A Review of the Evidence', *Economic of Governance* 12, 1 (2011), pp. 1–23, p. 14.

21. For a review of the literature on terrorism economics see Friedrich Schneider, Tilman Brück and Daniel Meierrieks, 'The Economics of Terrorism and Counter-Terrorism: A Survey (Part I and II)', Economics of Security Working Paper 44 and 45, European Security Economics (EUSECON), 2011.

22. Fred Kaplan, 'In Crisis, N.Y. Mayor Giuliani's Image Transformed, *Boston Globe*, 14 September 2001, http://www.boston.com/news/packages/underattack/globe_stories/0914/In_crisis_Giuliani_s_image_transformed+.shtml, last accessed 20 April 2015.

23. Kip Viscusi and Joseph Aldy, 'The Value of a Statistical Life: A Critical Review of Market Estimates Throughout the World' *Journal of Risk and Uncertainty* 27, 1 (2003), pp. 5–76. The discount rate serves to calculate the present value of a future income or loss. It generally reflects the average interest rate or return on investment. The higher the discount rate, the lower the present value of future incomes or losses.

24. Joseph Stiglitz and Linda Bilmes, *The Three Trillion Dollar War*, New York: W.W. Norton & Co., 2008. On the issue of using VSL to assess the cost of war,

see also Ron Smith, 'The Economic Cost of Military Conflict', *Journal of Peace Research* 51, 2 (2014), pp. 245–256, p. 253. The author critically underlines that 'while the productivity of capital may justify discounting future commodities, it does not seem to justify discounting future lives.'

25. Tilman Brück, Olaf De Groot and Friedrich Schneider, 'The Economic Costs of the German Participation in the Afghanistan War', *Journal of Peace Research* 48, 6 (2011), pp. 793–805.

26. The wide margin reflects the fact that several of the assumptions required to quantify all costs in monetary terms are uncertain. See ibid.

27. Ron Smith, 2014, op. cit., p. 252.

28. Ibid. When the aim is to stir up the US domestic political debate, the emphasis is naturally on the US economy rather than on that of Iraq or Afghanistan. The costs of the wars in Iraq and Afghanistan on the US economy have been extensively debated on the basis of Stiglitz and Bilmes' estimates, as well as reports examined within the US Congress Joint Economic Committee. See also Linda Bilmes, 'The Financial Legacy of Iraq and Afghanistan', Harvard Kennedy School Working Paper, RWP13–006, March 2013; Charles Schumer and Carolyn Maloney, 'War at any price: Total Economic Costs of the War Beyond the Federal Budget', A Report by the Joint Economic Committee of Majority Staff Chairman, November 2007.

29. Thomas Biestecker, 'Trends in Terrorist Financing—A Review of the Literature', Booz, Allen & Hamilton Consultants, Washington DC, August 2011. There are a few exceptions, including a series of more recent and detailed case studies. See e.g. Michael Freeman (ed.), *Financing Terrorism. Case studies*, Surrey: Ashgate Publishing, 2012. See also: Scott Atran, 2010, op. cit.

30. Thomas Biersteker, ibid.

31. Pursuant to the UNSC [United Nations Security Council] Resolution S/RES/1267 (1999), 15 October 1999.

32. UNSC, 'Letter Dated 22 January 2014 from the Chair of the Security Council Committee Pursuant to Resolutions 1267 (1999) and 1989 (2011) Concerning Al-Qaida and Associated Individuals and Entities Addressed to the President of the Security Council', UN Doc. S/2014/41, 23 January 2014, p. 14.

33. 'Humanitarian Outcomes', Aid Worker Security Database, https://aidworkersecurity.org/, last accessed on 25 November 2014. The data is collated through the systematic analysis of publicly available information supplemented by regular exchanges with relevant relief agencies. In 2013 the total number of national and international aid workers abducted, killed or wounded was 461.

34. 'Humanitarian Outcomes', *Aid Worker Security Report 2012*, 2013, pp. 4–5.

35. Ibid., p. 2.

36. In Mexico, for example, relatives of victims hesitate to report events to the police for fear of collusion between gangs and security forces. In several emerging econ-

omies, kidnapping for ransom has become a mass market hitting the emerging lower-middle class. The Mexican federal police have reported ransoms as low as $250. See Dudley Althaus, 'Even the 99 percent get kidnapped in Mexico', http://www.globalpost.com/dispatch/news/regions/americas/mexico/140411/kidnapping-mexico, last accessed 27 November 2014.

37. NYA International, 'Global Kidnap for Ransom Update—June 2014', 2014.
38. Thomas Kostigen, 'When should you consider kidnap insurance?', Marketwatch, http://www.marketwatch.com/story/when-should-you-consider-kidnap-insurance-2011–07–29, last accessed on 27 November 2014. This is far from insignificant in the face of an overall premium base for political risks estimated around $1.4bn for 2012 according to Willis' *Marketplace Realities 2013*. Since there is a strong relationship between drops in fisheries' production value and increases in piracy, there is a suggestion in favour of working towards enhancing labour opportunities among potential pirate recruits rather than relying solely on protective and repressive measures.
39. NYA International, 2014, op. cit.
40. Rick Gladstone, 'U.S. Agencies Review Policies on Hostages', *New York Times*, 19 November 2014, http://www.nytimes.com/2014/11/19/world/middleeast/isis-hostages-us-reviews-policies.html, last accessed 16 December 2014.
41. Rukmini Callimachi, 'Before Beheading: Hostages Endured Torture and Dashed Hopes, Freed Cellmates Says', *New York Times*, 26 October 2014, http://www.nytimes.com/2014/10/26/world/middleeast/horror-before-the-beheadings-what-isis-hostages-endured-in-syria.html?hp&action=click&pgtype=Homepage&version=HpHedLargeMediaSubhedSum&module=photo-spot-region&region=top-news&WT.nav=top-news, last accessed 27 November 2014.
42. As one example among many, the 'Crisis Prevention and Response' services of an international consultancy firm includes training and advice together with regular updates on K&R worldwide. See 'About NYA International', http://www.nyainternational.com/index.php?lang=en, last accessed on 27 November 2014.
43. Michael Henk, 'Pirates, Kidnappings, and Ransom: The Business of K&R Indemnity Policies', Milliman, http://www.milliman.com/insight/2013/Pirates-kidnappings-and-ransom-The-business-of-KR-indemnity-policies/, last accessed 27 November 2014.
44. GCTF is an informal platform launched by then US Secretary of State Hillary Clinton on 22 September 2011 in an attempt to move beyond the obstacle of agreeing on a definition of terrorism in multilateral institutions.
45. 'Algiers Memorandum on Good Practices on Preventing and Denying the Benefits of Kidnapping for Ransomby Terrorists', Global Counterterrorism Forum, http://www.thegctf.org/documents/10162/36031/Algiers+Memorandum+on+Good+Practices+on+Preventing+and+Denying+the+Benefits+of+KFR+by+Terrorists-English, last accessed 27 November 2014.

46. 'Security Council Adopts Resolution 2133 (2014), Calling upon States to keep Ransom Payments, Political Concessions from Benefiting Terrorist', UN, http://www.un.org/News/Press/docs/2014/sc11262.doc.htm, last accessed 27 November 2014.

47. As reported by IRIN on the cases of Save the Children and Oxfam, and confirmed in March 2013: 'Aid Worker Kidnappings Rise Fuelling Debate Over Ransom', IRIN, http://www.irinnews.org/report/97697/aid-worker-kidnappings-rise-fuelling-debate-over-ransom, last accessed 3 December 2014.

48. Eric Lichtblau and James Risen, 'Bank Data is Sifted by US in Secret to Block Terror', *New York Times*, http://www.nytimes.com/2006/06/23/washington/23intel.html?hp&ex=1151121600&en=18f9ed2cf37511d5&ei=5094&partner=homepage&_r=0, last accessed 27 November 2014.

49. Ibid.

50. The FATF is an inter-governmental body established in 1989 with the objectives to set standards and promote the implementation of legal, regulatory and operational measures for combating money laundering and terrorist financing. The taskforce had thirty-six members as of November 2014. See: 'FATF Members and Observers', FATF, http://www.fatf-gafi.org/pages/aboutus/membersandobservers/#d.en.3147, last accessed 27 November 2014.

51. Frey Bruno and Simon Lüchinger, 'Countering Terrorism: Beyond Deterrence', in Matthew Morgan (ed.), *The Impact of 9/11 on Politics and War: The Day that Changed Everything?*, London: Palgrave Macmillan, 2009, pp. 131–9.

52. Thomas Biersteker, Sue Eckert and Marcos Tourinho (eds), *Targeting Sanctions: The Impacts and Effectiveness of UN Action*, Cambridge: Cambridge University Press, forthcoming (2015).

53. Gary Hufbauer, Jeffrey Schott, Kimberly Elliott and Barbara Oegg, *Economic Sanctions Reconsidered*, Third Edition, Washington: The Peterson Institute of International Economics, 2007.

54. Erica Moret, 'Humanitarian Impacts of Economic Sanctions on Iran and Syria', *European Security* 26 (February 2014), pp. 1–21.

55. Peter Andreas, 'Criminalizing Consequences of Sanctions: Embargo Busting and its Legacy', *International Studies Quarterly* 49, 2 (2005), pp. 353–360.

56. Borzou Daragahi and Erika Solomon, 'Fuelling Isis Inc', *Financial Times*, 21 September 2014, http://www.ft.com/intl/cms/s/2/34e874ac-3dad-11e4-b782-00144feabdc0.html#axzz3EJKiMhVM, last accessed 27 November 2014.

57. Counterterrorism and Humanitarian Engagement Project, 'An Analysis of Contemporary Counterterrorism-related Clauses in Humanitarian Grant and Partnership Agreement Contracts', Research and Policy Paper, May 2014.

58. Kate Mackintosh and Patrick Duplat, 'Executive Summary' in 'Study of the Impact of Donor Counter-Terrorism Measures on Principled Humanitarian Action', OCHA and Norwegian Refugee Council, July 2013.

59. Bruno Frey 2004, op. cit.
60. This is arguably the case when aid is allocated to specific sectors such as health, education and conflict prevention. See Joseph Young and Michael Findley, 'Can Peace be Purchased? A Sectoral-Level Analysis of Aid's Influence on Transnational Terrorism', *Public Choice* 149 3/4 (2011), pp. 365–381.
61. This is not a new phenomenon. It was already prominent during twentieth-century armed conflicts such as the Vietnam war.
62. The U.S. Army/Marine Corps, *Counterinsurgency Field Manual*, Chicago: University of Chicago Press, 2007.
63. 'Commander's Emergency Response Program', US Army Combined Arms Center, http://usacac.army.mil/cac2/call/docs/09–27/ch-4.asp, last accessed 30 September 2014. CERP funds amounted to $2.8bn in Iraq and $3.44bn in Afghanistan (as of March 2012), see: 'Iraq: Money as Weapon', *Washington Post*, http://www.washingtonpost.com/wp-srv/business/cerp/, last accessed 30 September 2014; Anthony Cordesman, 'The Cost of the Afghan War: FY2002—FY2013', CSIS, 2012, http://csis.org/files/publication/120515_US_Spending_Afghan_War_SIGAR.pdf, last accessed 30 September 2014.
64. Stathis Kalyvas, 'Review of The New *U.S. Army/Marine Corps Counterinsurgency Field Manual*', *Perspectives on Politics* 6, 2 (2008), pp. 351–353.
65. For a discussion of different impact evaluation methods in humanitarian settings, see Jyotsna Puri, Anastasia Aladysheva, Vegard Iversen, Yashodhan Ghorpade and Tilman Brück, 'What Methods May be Used in Impact Evaluations of Humanitarian Assistance?' IZA Discussion Paper No. 8755, Bonn: Institute for the Study of Labour (2015).
66. Andrew Beath, Christia Fotini and Ruben Enikolopov, 'Winning Hearts and Minds through Development: Evidence from a Field Experiment in Afghanistan', MIT Political Science Department, Working Paper No. 2011 (2012), p. 22.
67. Tiffany Chou, 'Does development assistance reduce violence? Evidence from Afghanistan', *The Economics of Peace and Security Journal* 7, 2 (2012), pp. 5–13. The study further considers a third aid programme, which is a community development programme run by USAID. The data on violent events comes from the U.S. Military's Combined Information Data Network Exchange (CIDNE), which records geo-referenced data on security incidents in Afghanistan. The data on aid projects comes from NATO/ISAF's Afghanistan Country Stability Picture Database (ACSPD), which includes inputs from various sources (the Afghan Government, Provincial Reconstructions Teams, international organizations and NGOs, etc.). The ACSP database is part of the so-called INDURE portal, which requires an invitation to join but contains no classified information, see: 'Afghan Country Stability Picture', Ronna, https://ronna.apan.org/Pages/ACSP.aspx#database, last accessed 1 October 2014.
68. Eli Berman, Jacob Shapiro and Joseph Felter, 'Can Hearts and Minds Be Bought?

The Economics of Counterinsurgency in Iraq', *Journal of Political Economy* 199, 4 (2011), pp. 766–819.

69. Tiffany Chou, 2012, op. cit., p. 9.

70. Travers Child, 'Hearts and Minds Cannot be Bought: Ineffective Reconstruction in Afghanistan', *The Economics of Peace and Security Journal* 9, 2 (2014), pp. 43–9.

71. Jan-Rasmus Böhne and Christoph Zürcher, 'Aid, Minds and Hearts: The Impact of Aid in Conflict Zones', *Conflict Management and Peace Science* 30, 5 (2010), pp. 411–32.

72. Paul Fishtein and Andrew Wilder, 'Winning Hearts and Minds? Examining the Relationship between Aid and Security in Afghanistan', Feinstein International Center, Tufts University, 2012.

73. Ibid, p. 3.

74. Tiffany Chou, 2012, op. cit. benefited from access to the U.S Military's CIDNE database; Berman *et al.*, 2011, op. cit. received a grant from the US Department of Defence and the US Department of Homeland Security, while the authors acknowledge critical support throughout the duration of the research project from the US Military Academy.

75. Benjamin Crost, Joseph Felter and Patrick Johnston, 'Aid Under Fire: Development Projects and Civil Conflict', *American Economic Review* 104, 6 (2014), pp. 1833–56.

76. James Fearon, Humphreys Macartan and Jeremy Weinstein, 'Can Development Aid Contribute to Social Cohesion after Civil War? Evidence from a Field Experiment in Post-conflict Liberia', *American Economic Review: Papers & Proceedings* 99, 2 (2009), pp. 287–91.

5. DISASTER ECONOMICS

1. Oscar Wilde, *Lady Windermere's Fan*. Act III.

2. Namsuk finds that the poor are about twice as exposed to disasters than the non-poor, based on country-level data on the number of people affected by disasters involving 208 countries over four decades: Kim Namsuk, 'How much more exposed are the poor to natural disasters? Global and regional measurement', *Disasters* 26, 2 (2012), pp. 195–211.

3. Fikret Adaman, 'Power Inequalities in Explaining the Link Between Natural Hazards and Unnatural Disasters', *Development and Change* 43, 1 (2012), pp. 395–407.

4. Jan Kellett and Dan Sparks, 'Disaster Risk Reduction: Spending where it should count', Briefing Paper 1, 2012, p. 31.

5. The World Bank and the United Nations, *Natural Hazards, Unnatural disasters: the Economics of Effective Prevention*, Washington: The World Bank, 2010.

6. Phil O'Keefe, Ken Westgate and Ben Wisner, 'Taking the Naturalness out of Natural Disasters', *Nature* 260 (1976), pp. 566–567; Terry Cannon, 'Reducing Peo-

ple's Vulnerability to Natural Hazards: Communities and Resilience', Wider Research Paper 2008/34, UNU-Wider (2008).

7. Amartya Sen, *Poverty and Famines: An Essay on Entitlement and Deprivation*, Oxford: Clarendon Press, 1981.

8. For earlier contributions on the disaster-development nexus, see Kenneth Hewitt (ed.), *Interpretations of Calamity*, London: Allen and Unwin, 1983; and Piers Blaikie *et al.*, *At Risk: Natural Hazards, People's Vulnerability, and Disasters*, London: Routledge, 1994.

9. The World Bank and the United Nations, 2010, op. cit., p. 8.

10. Lilianne Fan, 'Disaster as Opportunity? Building Back Better in Aceh, Myanmar and Haiti', HPG Working Paper, London: ODI, 2013.

11. Ajaz Chhibber and Rachid Laajaj, 'The Interlinkages between Natural Disasters and Economic Development', in Debarati Guha-Sapir and Indhira Santos (eds), *The Economic Impacts of Natural Disasters*, Oxford: Oxford University Press, 2013.

12. Micro-level studies tend to focus on households, communities and firms while macroeconomic analyses contemplate variations in output, investment, saving, government income and expenditure, and other aggregates. The former tend to favour case studies while the later often involve large-N studies—surveys that encompass a large number of observations, interviewees or cases. Small-N studies focus on smaller samples with a limited number of cases or observations. There is a trade-off between generalization and the pursuit of external validity: large-N studies make generalization easier but external validity harder to verify; small-N studies go into more depth for a few cases but make generalizing harder.

13. The World Bank and the United Nations, 2010, op. cit., p. 10.

14. Asian Development Bank, 'From Aceh to Tacloban: Lessons from a Decade of Disaster', Development Asia, 2014, p. 10. The report further stresses that Asia has double the global average annual deaths by disaster, or about one person per 1,000 square km.

15. Swiss Re, 'Natural Catastrophes and Man-Made Disasters in 2013: Large Losses From Floods and Hail: Haiyan hits Philippines', *Sigma* 1 (2014).

16. The notion of creative destruction refers to the fact that entrepreneurs, by bringing innovations in the pursuit of new economic opportunities, destroy competing economic activities but, at the same time, create new ones and move the entire economy forward. See Joseph Schumpeter, *Capitalism, Socialism and Democracy*, New York: Harper, 1947.

17. See Chhibber and Laajaj, 2013, op. cit. These findings are consistent with earlier work by Jose-Miguel Albala-Bertrand in *The Political Economy of Large Natural Disasters*, Oxford: Clarendon Press, 1993.

18. Paul Romer, 'The Origins of Endogenous Growth', *Journal of Economic Perspectives*, 8, 1 (1994), pp. 3–22.

19. Frédéric Bastiat, *Ce qu'on voit et ce qu'on ne voit pas: Choix de sophismes et de pamphlets économiques*, Paris: Romillat, 1850/2005.

20. Charlotte Benson and Edward Clay, 'Understanding the Economic and Financial Impacts of Natural Disasters', World Bank Disaster Risk Management Series, 4 (2004).

21. Oscar Becerra, Eduardo Cavallo and Ilan Noy, 'Foreign Aid in the Aftermath of Large Natural Disasters', *Review of Development Economics* 18, 3 (2014), pp. 445–460.

22. Guha-Sapir and Santos, 2013, op. cit.; Benson and Clay, 2004, op. cit.

23. James Surowiecki, 'Creative Destruction: Cost of Natural Disasters?', *New Yorker*, 28 March 2011.

24. 'Global Assessment Report on Disaster Risk Reduction', UNISDR, 2013.

25. Morton Jerven, *Poor Numbers: How We are Misled by African Development Statistics and What to do About It*, Ithaca: Cornell University Press, 2013.

26. World Bank and UN, 2010, op. cit., p. 10.

27. Benson and Clay 2004, op. cit.

28. Norman Loayza, *et al.*, 'Natural Disasters and Growth—Going Beyond the Averages', World Bank Policy Research Working Paper 4980, Washington: The World Bank, 2009.

29. Sebastian Acevedo, 'Debt, Growth and Natural Disasters: A Caribeean Trilogy', IMF Working Paper 14, 125 (2014).

30. Shaohua Chen and Martin Ravallion, 'Absolute Poverty Measures for the Developing World, 1981–2004', World Bank, Policy Research Working Paper Series 4211 (2007).

31. Debarati Guha-Sapir and Indhira Santos, 'The Increasing Costs and Frequency of Natural Disasters' in Guha-Sapir and Santos, 2013, op. cit.

32. Asian Development Bank 2014, op. cit., p. 47; Saudamini Das, 'Storm Protection by the Mangroves in Orissa: An Analysis of the 1999 Super Cyclone', SANDEE Working Paper 25–07, South Asian Network of Development and Environmental Economics (2007).

33. Gilles Carbonnier and Natascha Wagner, 'Resource Dependence and Armed Violence: Impact on Sustainability in Developing Countries', *Defence and Peace Economics* 25, 6 (2013), pp. 1–18; Kirk Hamilton, 'Accounting for Sustainability. Measuring Sustainable Development: Integrated Economic Environmental and Social Frameworks', Paris: OECD, 2014.

34. Genuine saving is referred to as a weak sustainability indicator in the sense that it assumes that natural capital can be fully substituted by human and physical capital, which is obviously not the case if we are serious about human survival. But environmental destruction is at least recorded as a negative, unlike GDP, which goes unaffected (in the first year).

35. Earthquake losses are often not insured. For example, only about 11 per cent of homes in California are insured against earthquakes. Acts of terrorism are often excluded from insurance coverage. In the case of severe flooding, the coverage var-

ies, depending in particular on the socioeconomic status of those who suffer the losses.

36. Angelika Wirtz, 'Natural Disasters and the Insurance Industry', in Guha-Sapir and Santos (eds), 2013, op. cit. 11.

37. Craig Churchill, 'Protecting the Poor: A Microinsurance Compendium', Geneva: ILO, 2006.

38. Angelika Wirtz, 2013, op. cit.

39. We distinguish between the underwriting and investment sides, which insurance industry accounting rules keep separate. While the underwriting side generally generates only a small profit on insurance proper, larger profits come from investing the cash flow or 'surplus' built by the accumulation of investment income and a small amount from profits on underwriting. Any losses on the underwriting side, when claims exceed premiums and expenses, are typically covered by such surplus.

40. Risks are not insurable if the premium would have to be set too high in order to cover the potential claims, if the nature of the loss cannot be clearly defined and financially set, or if the loss is not random in nature because of the risk of adverse selection.

41. 'Overall Picture of Natural Catastrophes in 2013 Dominated by Weather Extremes in Europe and Supertyphoon Haiyan', Munich Re, http://www.munichre.com/en/media-relations/publications/press-releases/2014/2014–01–07-press-release/index.html, last accessed 14 October 2014.

42. Asian Development Bank, 2014, op. cit., p. 17.

43. 'ASEAN—Disaster Risk Financing and Insurance in ASEAN Member States: Framework and Options for Implementation', World Bank & GFDRR, Washington: The World Bank, 2012.

44. 'ASEAN Agreement on Disaster Management and Emergency Response (AADMER) Work Programme 2010–2015', ASEAN, http://www.asean.org/resources/publications/asean-publications/item/asean-agreement-on-disaster-management-and-emergency-response-aadmer-work-programme-2010–2015–4th-reprint, last accessed 14 October 2014.

45. J. David Cummins, 'CAT Bonds and Other Risk-Linked Securities: State of the Market and Recent Developments', *Risk Management and Insurance Review* 11, 1 (2008), pp. 23–47, p. 23.

46. This boom happened while hitherto unknown acronyms such as CDO (collateralized debt obligation), CDS (credit default swap) and MBS (mortgage backed securities) became headline news as the 2008 financial crisis unfolded.

47. 'Natural Disaster Insurance Institution', http://www.tcip.gov.tr/hakkinda.html, last accessed 14 October 2014. TCIP enjoys a privileged position, offering its services in response to the Turkish governmental decree rendering earthquake insurance compulsory. Yet, it is run as a private entity with no support from the government, except in exceptional cases where losses would exceed TCIP claim payment capacity.

48. Eugene Gurenko *et al.*, 'Earthquake Insurance in Turkey', Washington: The World Bank, 2006.

49. Noah Buhayar and Charles Mead, 'Drooling Cat-Bond Investors Overlook Risk, Montross Says', *Bloomberg*, http://www.bloomberg.com/news/2013–06–06/drooling-cat-bond-investors-overlook-risk-montross-says.html, last accessed 14 October 2014.

50. Yuli Suwarni, 'After Japan Disaster, Government "Urged to Revise Mitigation" System', *The Jakarta Post*, http://www.thejakartapost.com/news/2011/03/23/after-japan-disaster-government-urged-revise-mitigation-system.html, last accessed 26 April 2014.

51. E. Michel-Kerjan *et al.*, 'Catastrophe Financing for Governments: Learning from the 2009–2012 MultiCat Program in Mexico', OECD Working Papers on Finance, Insurance and Private Pensions, 9, Paris: OECD, 2011, p. 24.

52. Razmig Keucheyan, *La nature est un champ de bataille: Essai d'écologie politique*, Paris: Zones, 2014.

53. 'Catastrophe Bonds: Perilous Paper', *The Economist*, 5 October 2013.

54. Craig Churchill and Michal Matul (eds), 'Protecting the Poor: A Microinsurance Compendium', Vol. II, Geneva: ILO, 2012.

55. 'Africa Investment: Africa Assumes Onus on Disaster Relief With Catastrophe Insurance Pool', *Reuters*, http://www.reuters.com/article/2014/05/15/africa-investment-idUSL6N0O05JJ20140515, last accessed on 14 October 2014.

56. Angelika Wirtz, 2013, op. cit. 36.

57. Jean-Philippe Platteau and Darwin Ontiveros, 'Understanding and Information Failure in Insurance: Evidence from India', Working Paper 1301, Department of Economics, University of Namur, 2014.

58. In the case of Pakistan, however, empirical evidence shows that the growth in demand for flood micro-insurance among the victims of the severe 2010 flood has not been significantly affected by potential concerns over the compatibility of the insurance product with Sharia law. See Ginger Turner, Farah Said and Uzma Afzal, 'Microinsurance Demand After a Rare Flood Event: Evidence from a Field Experiment in Pakistan', The Geneva Papers on Risk and Insurance 39 (2014), pp. 201–223.

59. 'Insurance in the emerging markets: Overview and prospects for Islamic Insurance', *Sigma* No. 3, Zurich: Swiss Re, 2008.

60. Insurance penetration varies greatly even within individual sub-regions. For example, 54 per cent of respondents in Hanoi reported having health insurance against 31 per cent in Manila and only 10 per cent in Jakarta; see 'Urban Poverty and Health In Asia', Asian Trends Monitoring Bulletin No. 22, Lee Kuan Yew School of Public Policy, National University of Singapore, 2013.

61. GFDRR is a partnership involving states and international organizations. Established in 2006, its mission is to 'mainstream disaster risk reduction and climate

change adaptation in country development strategies': 'GFDRR', http://www.
gfdrr.org/sites/gfdrr/files/urban-floods/RR.html, last accessed 14 October 2014.

62. The World Bank and GFDRR 2012, op. cit., p. 2.

63. By mid-2011, the World Bank granted a $500m contingent credit to the Philippines for natural catastrophes, which was already drawn down by December the same year following the devastation caused by the Tropical Storm Sendong.

64. Razmig Keucheyan, 'Privatised Catastrophe', *Le Monde Diplomatique*, 4 March 2014, pp. 4–5.

65. 'Typhoon Haiyan losses trigger major new proposal on catastrophe insurance for the Philippines', UNISDR, http://www.unisdr.org/archive/36205, last accessed 14 October 2014.

66. Imelda Abano, 'Philippines Mulls Disaster Risk Insurance for Local Governments', Thomson Reuters Foundation, http://www.trust.org/item/20140122150502-gcd5q/, last accessed 14 October 2014.

67. Ibid.

68. 'About us', CCRIF, http://www.ccrif.org/content/about-us, last accessed 14 October 2014.

69. Jerry Skees, Barry Barnett and Anne Murphy, 'Creating Insurance Markets for Natural Disaster Risk in Lower Income Countries: the Potential Role for Securitization', *Agricultural Finance Review* 68, 1 (2008), pp. 151–167.

70. Charles Cohen and Eric Werker, 'The Political Economy of 'Natural' Disasters', Harvard Business School Working Paper, 08–040, 21 November 2008.

71. Céline Grislain-Letrémy, 'Natural Disasters: Exposure and Underinsurance', *INSEE*, Série des documents de travail de la Direction des Études et Synthèses Économiques, G2013/12, 2013.

72. Ginger, *et al.*, 2014, op. cit.

73. Ron Paul, 'The Economics of Disaster—And Who Should Pay?' The Hill, http://thehill.com/blogs/congress-blog/economy-a-budget/265961-the-economics-of-disaster-and-who-should-pay, last accessed 26 April 2014.

74. 'Senate approves bill to curb flood insurance hikes', Insurance Journal, http://www.insurancejournal.com/news/national/2014/03/13/323273.htm, last accessed 14 October 2014.

75. Tomoko Hosaka, 'How Fudai, Japan Defied The Tsunami Devastation', *Huffington Post*, http://www.huffingtonpost.com/2011/05/13/fudai-japan-tsunami-_n_861534.html, last accessed on 8 April 2014.

76. Howard Kunreuther and Erwann Michel-Kerjan, 'Natural Disasters', Copenhagen Consensus Center, 2012.

77. 'Saving Lives Today and Tomorrow: Managing the Risk of Humanitarian Crises', OCHA, 2014, p. 3.

78. While neoclassical economics assumes that parties to an exchange have perfect information, asymmetric information in contract theory focuses on the power imbalances that result when one party enjoys better information than the other.

79. Eric Neumayer, Thomas Plümper and Fabian Barthel, 'The Political Economy of Natural Disaster Damage', *Global Environmental Change* 24, 1 (2013), pp. 8–19.

80. Chares Kenny, 'Disaster Risk Reduction in Developing Countries: Costs, Benefits and Institutions', *Disasters* 36, 4, (2012), pp. 559–88.

81. Chares Kenny, 'Why do People Die in Earthquakes? The Costs, Benefits and Institutions of Disaster Risk Reduction in Development Countries', Working Paper 4823, Washington: The World Bank, 2009.

82. George Akerlof, 'The Market for "Lemons": Quality Uncertainty and the Market Mechanism', *The Quarterly Journal of Economics*, 84, 3 (1970), pp. 488–500.

83. Neumayer, Plümper and Barthel, 2013, op. cit.

84. Benjamin Olken (2004), cited in Chares Kenny, 2012, op. cit., p. 574.

85. *Law of the Republic of Indonesia Concerning Disaster Management*, Law 24, 26 April 2007.

86. Gareth Williams, 'Study on Disaster Risk Reduction, Decentralization and Political Economy', The Political Economy of Disaster Risk Reduction, Analysis Prepared as UNDP's Contribution to the GAR 2011, March 2011, http://www.preventionweb.net/english/hyogo/gar/2011/en/bgdocs/Williams_2011.pdf, last accessed 14 October 2014.

6. SURVIVAL ECONOMICS

1. Amartya Sen, 'Apocalypse Then', *New York Times*, 18 February 2001, http://www.nytimes.com/books/01/02/18/reviews/010218.18senlt.html, last accessed 16 December 2014.

2. Unless otherwise specified, the data provided in this chapter originates from four sources: my own research in Lebanon in November and December 2014; the (Syrian) Strategic Needs Analysis Project (SNAP); reports of the Assessment Capacity Project (ACAPS); and the World Bank's 'Lebanon: Economic and Social Impact Assessment of the Syrian Conflict' of September 2013.

3. Carolyne Gates, *The Merchant Republic of Lebanon: Rise of an Open Economy*, Oxford and London: Center for Lebanese Studies and I. B. Tauris, 1998.

4. Nisreen Salti and Jad Chaaban, 'The Role of Sectarianism in the Allocation of Public Expenditure in Postwar Lebanon', *International Journal of Middle East Studies* 42, 4 (2010), pp 637–655, p. 652.

5. Myriam Catusse, 'La question sociale aux marges des soulèvements arabes: Leçons libanaises et marocaines', *Critique internationale* 61 (2013/14), pp. 19–34.

6. Poverty is a multi-dimensional concept that involves many elements that are relevant to vulnerability analysis. In practice, however, poverty is too often reduced to the monetary benchmark related to the international poverty lines of $1.25 per capita/day (for extreme poverty, at purchasing power parity, 2005) and $2 per capita/day. National poverty lines vary between countries and tend to be higher in middle-income than in low-income countries. In Lebanon, an upper middle-income

country, the poverty line is set at \$4 while those living on less than \$2.4 a day are considered extremely poor in that they are not able to meet their basic food and non-food requirements without external assistance.

7. The Inter-Agency Standing Committee (IASC) Needs Assessments Task Force has developed the so-called Multi-Cluster/Sector Initial Rapid Assessment (MIRA) to improve coordination across sectors and agencies. See: IASC, 'Multi-Cluster/Sector Initial Rapid Assessment (MIRA)', 2012. OCHA is expected to release a new version in 2015.

8. Based on the pioneering work of Gary Becker and Jacob Mincer under New Home Economics.

9. Amartya Sen, *Poverty and Famines: An Essay on Entitlement and Deprivation*, Oxford: Clarendon Press, 1981.

10. Measuring food security requires considering indicators beyond traditional anthropomorphic measures of nutritional status. See e.g. Christopher Barrett, 'Measuring Food Insecurity', *Science* 327, 5967 (2010), pp. 825–8.

11. Amartya Sen, *Resources, Values and Development*, Oxford: Basil Blackwell, 1984, p. 497.

12. Stephen Devereux, 'Sen's Entitlement Approach: Critiques and Counter-critiques', *Oxford Development Studies* 29, 3 (2001), pp. 245–63.

13. Alain Mourey, *Nutrition Manual for Humanitarian Action*, Geneva, ICRC, 2008.

14. SCF, 'Household Economy Approach: A Resource Manual for Practitioners', Save the Children, Development Manual No. 6, 2000, p. 7.

15. Oxfam and WFP, 'Executive Brief: Engaging with Markets in Humanitarian Response', 10 July 2013.

16. WFP, 'Comparative Review of Market Assessments Methods, Tools, Approaches and Findings', September 2013. An EMMA assessment was conducted in 2013 in Lebanon to assess the capacity of the agriculture, construction and services markets to absorb additional workers from the host and Syrian refugee population.

17. See: Margie Buchanan-Smith, 'Markets and Trade in Darfur', *Feinstein International Center*, http://fic.tufts.edu/research-item/markets-and-trade-in-darfur/, last accessed on 16 December 2014.

18. The Swiss Agency for Development and Cooperation (SDC), 'Responding to the Impact of the Syrian Crisis on Lebanon', 2014, p. 36

19. WFP, UNHCR, and UNICEF, 'Vulnerability Assessment of Syrian Refugees in Lebanon', 2013; WFP, UNHCR, and UNICEF, 'Vulnerability Assessment of Syrian Refugees in Lebanon', 2014.

20. Beirut Research and Innovation Center (BRIC), 'Survey on the Livelihoods of Syrian Refugees in Lebanon, Research Report', November 2013.

21. Ibid., p. 21.

22. Charles Harb and Rim Saab, 'Social Cohesion and Intergroup Relations: Syrian Refugees and Lebanese National in the Bekaa and Akkar', American University of Beirut and Save the Children, 2014.

23. Melani Cammett, *Compassionate Communalism: Welfare and Sectarianism in Lebanon*, Ithaca: Cornell University Press, 2014.

24. Rabih Shibli, 'Reconfiguring Relief Mechanisms: The Syrian Refugee Crisis in Lebanon', Issam Fares Institute, American University of Beirut (February 2014), p. 10.

25. Chloe Stirk, 'Humanitarian Assistance From Non-State Donors: What is it Worth?', GHA, Briefing Paper, 2014, p. 133.

26. BRIC, 2013, op. cit., p. 37.

27. Ibid., p. 40.

28. Oliver Holmes, 'Syrian Refugees Burden and Benefit for Lebanese Economy', *Reuters*, http://www.reuters.com/article/2013/04/17/us-crisis-lebanon-refugees-idUSBRE93G0MW20130417, last accessed 16 December 2014.

29. Amnesty International, 'Agonizing Choices: Syrian Refugees in Need of Health care in Lebanon', London: Amnesty International, 2014.

30. Based on data from the Financial Tracking Service (FTS—UNOCHA), the GHA 2014 Report estimated that Kuwait contributed $79m, the United Arab Emirates $29m and Saudi Arabia $20m in 2013.

31. Dalya Mitri, 'Challenges of Aid Coordination in a Complex Crisis: An Overview of Funding Policies and Conditions Regarding Aid Provision to Syrian Refugees in Lebanon', Civil Society Knowledge Center, Lebanon Support, 23 May 2014, pp. 11–12.

32. In 2013, just over half of the funding requirements of the fifth Regional Response Plan were met. The sixth Syria Regional Response Plan (RRP), presented in 2014, was one of the largest funding appeals ever for a refugee crisis. Less than half of it may end up funded with regard to Lebanon.

33. The UNHCR refunds up to 75 per cent of healthcare costs for life-saving emergency care.

34. UNHCR, 'UNHCR Global Appeal 2015: Lebanon', 2014.

35. Corruption in Lebanon is known to be pervasive. In 2012, the country ranked 128 out of a total of 176 countries on the Transparency International Corruption Perception index.

36. Rabih Shibli, 2014, op. cit., p. 7.

37. Stirk, 2014, op. cit., p. 75.

38. SDC, 2014, op. cit., p. 35.

39. For a review, see e.g. Christopher Barrett and Daniel Maxwell, *Food Aid After Fifty Years: Recasting its Role*, New York: Routledge, 2005.

40. See e.g. Ariel Fiszbein and Norbert Shady, 'Conditional Cash Transfers: Reducing Present and Future Poverty', World Bank Policy Research Report 47603, Washington, DC: The World Bank, 2009.

41. For a brief survey of the literature see Melissa Hidrobo *et al.*, 'Cash, Food, or Vouchers? Evidence from a Randomized Experiment in Northern Ecuador', *Journal of Development Economics* 107, C (2014), pp. 144–56, pp. 144–5.

42. Michael Devereux, 'Cash transfers and social protection', paper presented at the Regional Workshop on 'Cash transfer activities in southern Africa', Johannesburg: SARPN, 9–10 October 2006.

43. See Charles Blackorby and David Donaldson, 'Cash Versus Kind, Self-Selection, and Efficient Transfers', *American Economic Review* 78, 4, (1998), pp. 691–700.

44. Sophia Dunn, Mike Brewin and Aues Scek, 'Cash and Voucher Monitoring Group: Final monitoring report of the Somalia cash and voucher transfer programme', ODI, 2013.

45. Jenny Aker, 'Cash or Coupons? Testing the Impact of Cash Versus Vouchers in the Democratic Republic of Congo', Center for Global Development, Working Paper 320 (2013); Manohar Sharma, 'An Assessment of the Effects of the Cash Transfer Pilot Project on Household Consumption Patents in Tsunami-Affected Areas of Sri Lanka', Washington: IFPRI, 2006. See also the Cash Learning Partnership (CaLP) website: http://www.cashlearning.org/

46. Melissa Hidrobo, *et al.*, 2014, op. cit., p. 154.

47. International Rescue Committee, 'Emergency Economies: The Impact of Cash Assistance in Lebanon', August 2014.

48. Danish Refugee Council Lebanon, 'Unconditional Cash Assistance via E-Transfer: Implementation Lessons Learned. Winterization Support via CSC Bank ATM Card', February 2014.

49. The World Bank, 'Lebanon Roadmap of Priority Interventions for Stabilization: Strategy for Mitigating the Impact of the Syrian Conflict,' Washington: The World Bank, 15 November 2013, p. 3.

50. Myriam Catusse, 2013/14, op. cit., pp. 19–34.

51. UNDP, '3RP: Regional Refugee and Resilience Plan', http://arabstates.undp.org/content/rbas/en/home/ourwork/SyriaCrisis/projects/3rp/, accessed 19 December 2014.

7. THE TRANSFORMATIVE POWER OF HUMANITARIAN CRISES

1. As quoted in: Peter Collier and David Horowitz, *The Rockefellers: An American Dynasty*, New York: Holt, Rindhart and Winston, 1976.

2. Mark Skidmore and Hideki Toya, 'Do Economic Disasters Create Long-Run Growth?', *Economic Inquiry*, 40, 4 (2002), pp. 664–687.

3. Foucauldian concept referring to the art of government broadly defined, including and going beyond the state.

4. 'Climate Change 2014: Impacts, Adaptation, and Vulnerability' IPCC Working Group II, http://ipcc-wg2.gov/AR5/report/final-drafts/, last accessed 29 September 2014.

5. See e.g. Mark Duffield, *Development, Security and Unending War: Governing the World of Peoples*, Cambridge: Polity, 2007.

6. According to the official development assistance (ODA) statistics released by the Development Assistance Committee (DAC) of the OECD, http://www.oecd.org/dac/stats/data.htm, last accessed on 30 September 2014.

7. Jack Hirshleifer, *Economic Behavior in Adversity*, Chicago: University of Chicago Press, 1987.

8. Daron Acemoglu and James Robinson, *Why Nations Fail: The Origins of Power, Prosperity and Poverty*, USA: Crown Business, 2012.

9. The most conservative estimates put this figure around 30 million.

10. Elizabeth Brainerd and Mark V. Siegler, 'The Economic Effects of the 1918 Influenza Epidemic', CEPR Discussion Paper No. 3791, 2003.

11. Yu Xiao and Uttara Nilawar, 'Winners and Losers: Analysing Post-Disaster Spatial Economic Demand Shift', *Disasters* 77, 4 (2013), pp. 646–668.

12. Ibid; Eric Boehlert, 'The Politics of Hurricane Relief', Salon, 5 September 2005, http://www.salon.com/2005/09/05/hurricane_track_record/, last accessed 6 October 2014.

13. Milton Friedman, *Capitalism and Freedom*, Chicago: University of Chicago Press, 1982, p. ix. Since then, the political feasibility of implementing structural adjustment programmes has been questioned because such programmes repeatedly went off-track (see e.g. Stephan Haggard, Jean-Dominique Lafay and Christian Morrisson, *The Political Feasibility of Adjustment in Developing Countries*, Paris: OECD Development Centre, 1995).

14. Naomi Klein, *The Shock Doctrine: The Rise of Disaster Capitalism*, New York: Picador, 2007. Klein argues that those shocks serve the purpose of advancing the neoliberal agenda and the interests of the rich and powerful to the detriment of those bearing the brunt of the disaster costs.

15. This section draws from sections of: Gilles Carbonnier, 'Humanitarian and Development Aid in the Context of Stabilization: Blurring the Lines and Broadening the Gap' in Robert Muggah (ed.), *Stabilization Operations, Security and Development—States of Fragility*, New York: Routledge (2014), pp. 35–55.

16. For a review of the empirical evidence, see Subhayu Bandyopadhyay and Katarina Vermann, 'Donor Motives for Foreign Aid', *Federal Reserve Bank of St. Louis Review* (July/August 2013).

17. Bradford J. De Long and Barry Eichengreen, 'The Marshall Plan: History's Most Successful Structural Adjustment Program', NBER Working Paper No. 3899, Cambridge, MA: National Bureau of Economic Research, 1991; Gilles Carbonnier, 'Conflict, Postwar Rebuilding and the Economy: A Critical Review of the Literature', War-torn Societies Project—Occasional Paper, 2, Geneva: UNRISD, 1997.

18. Roger Riddell, *Does Foreign Aid Really Work?*, Oxford: Oxford University Press, 2007.

19. The picture would be different if one looked at military expenditures for overseas

activities only, excluding domestic defence spending. Data on military expenditures for Figure 14 comes from SIPRI Military Expenditure Database, http://www.sipri.org/research/armaments/milex/milex_database, last accessed 30 September 2014. The aid data comes from the OECD QWIDS, http://stats.oecd.org/qwids/, last accessed 13 October 2014.

20. Robert Muggah, 'Introduction', in Robert Muggah (ed.), *Stabilization Operations, Security and Development—States of Fragility*, New York: Routledge, 2014, pp. 1–14.

21. Aid Security Database, https://aidworkersecurity.org/index.php, last accessed 30 September 2014.

22. Jan Kellet and Dan Sparks, 'Disaster Risk Reduction: Spending Where it Should Count', Global Humanitarian Assistance Briefing Paper, 2012, p. 31. More broadly on the relation between disasters and civil wars, see: Philip Nel and Marjolein Righarts, 'Natural disasters and the Risk of Violent Civil Conflict', *International Studies Quarterly* 52, 1 (2008), pp. 159–85.

23. Applying multivariate methods to a large panel of countries over more than fifty years, Slettebak finds that countries affected by climate-related disasters actually face a lower risk of civil war. See: Rune Slettebak, 'Don't Blame the Weather: Climate-Related Natural Disasters and Civil Conflict', *Journal of Peace Research* 49, 1 (2012), pp. 163–176.

24. The United Nations Office for Disaster Risk Reduction (UNISDR) defines DRR as, 'the concept and practice of reducing disaster risks through systematic efforts to analyse and manage the causal factors of disasters, including through reduced exposure to hazards, lessened vulnerability of people and property, wise management of land and the environment, and improved preparedness for adverse events'; DRM is defined as, 'the systematic process of using administrative directives, organizations, and operational skills and capacities to implement strategies, policies and improved coping capacities in order to lessen the adverse impacts of hazards and the possibility of disaster': See UNISDR website, section 'Terminology': http://www.unisdr.org/we/inform/terminology, last accessed 6 October 2014.

25. Lilianne Fan, 'Disaster as Opportunity? Building Back Better in Aceh, Myanmar and Haiti', HPG Working Paper, London: ODI, 2013, p. 2.

26. Ibid, p. 8; Government of Indonesia *et al.*, 'The Multi-Stakeholder Review of Post-Conflict Programming in Aceh: Identifying the Foundations for Sustainable Peace in Aceh', 2009.

27. Bill Guerin, 'After the tsunami, waves of corruption', *Asia Times*, 20 September 2006, http://www.atimes.com/atimes/Southeast_Asia/HI20Ae01.html, last accessed on 30 September 2014.

28. Lilianne Fan (2013), op. cit.

29. Edward Aspinall, 'Combatants to Contractors: The Political Economy of Peace in Aceh', *Indonesia* 87, 1 (2009), pp. 1–34.

30. Mohammed Hassan Ansori, 'From Insurgency to Bureaucracy: Free Aceh Moment, Aceh Party and the New Face of Conflict', *Stability* 1, 1 (2012), pp. 31–44.

31. For a refined analysis of the web of reciprocal influences between relief and religion in the case of Aceh, see Michael Feener, *Sharia as Social Engineering: The Implementation of Islamic Law in Contemporary Aceh, Indonesia*, London: Oxford University Press, 2013.

32. On 27 September 2014 the Aceh provincial parliament passed two Islamic bylaws imposing Sharia law on non-Muslims, which 'violate rights and carry cruel punishments'. See: 'Indonesia: Aceh's New Islamic Laws Violate Rights', *Human Rights Watch*, http://www.hrw.org/news/2014/10/02/indonesia-aceh-s-new-islamic-laws-violate-rights, last accessed 6 October 2014.

33. Jakarta reacted by announcing that it might overrule the mining law, which was deemed inconsistent with national legislation. See Fitri Bintang Timur, 'Scenarios for Aceh's Turning Point', *Jakarta Post*, 17 February 2014, http://m.thejakartapost.com/news/2014/02/17/scenarios-aceh-s-turning-point.html, last accessed 30 September 2014.

34. For a discussion of the alleged failure of the aid system in Haiti, see: 'Failure of the Aid System in Haiti', International Development Policy Debate, Graduate Institute of International and Development Studies, http://poldev.revues.org/1606, last accessed 30 September 2014.

35. Gilles Carbonnier, 'Official Development Assistance Once More Under Fire From Critics', *International Development Policy—Africa: 50 Years of Independence* 1 (2010), pp. 137–42.

36. David Chandler, *Resilience: The Governance of Complexity*, London: Routledge, 2014, p. 54.

37. For a literature review, see: Christopher Bene *et al.*, 'Resilience: New Utopia or New Tyranny?', Institute of Development Studies, Working Paper 405 (2012).

38. At the individual level, resilience was thought to be an inherent trait for a long time, but is increasingly understood as a state that can also be nurtured.

39. Amartya Sen, *Development as Freedom*, Oxford: Oxford University Press, 1999, p. 62.

40. Gilles Carbonnier and Achim Wennmann, 'Natural Resource Governance and Hybrid Political Orders', in David Chandler and Timothy Sisk (eds), *Routledge Handbook of International Statebuilding*, New York: Routledge, 2013, pp. 208–18.

41. Alex De Waal, 'Mission Without an End? Peacekeeping in the African Political Marketplace', *International Affairs* 85, 1 (2009), pp. 99–113.

42. David K. Leonard, 'Where are "Pockets" of Effective Agencies Likely in Weak Governance States and Why? A Propositional Inventory', Brighton Institute of Development Studies, Working Paper 306 (2008), p. 8; Wil Hout, 'Neopatrimonialism and Development: Pockets of Effectiveness as Drivers of Change', *Revue internationale de politique comparée* 20, 3 (2013), pp. 79–96.

43. Most of this section is extracted from Gilles Carbonnier and Piedra Lightfoot, 'Business in Humanitarian Crises—For Better or for Worse?', in Dennis Dijkzeul and Zeynep Sezgin (eds), *The New Humanitarians*, London: Routledge (forthcoming, 2015) and Liliana Andonova and Gilles Carbonnier, 'Business-Humanitarian Partnerships: Processes of Normative Legitimation', *Globalizations* 11, 3 (2014), pp. 349–67.

44. GHA Report 2014, Global Humanitarian Assistance, Bristol (UK): Development Initiatives, 2014, p. 7

45. Personal communication from oil firm staff.

46. Andonova and Carbonnier (2014), op. cit., p. 357.

47. Ibid.

48. This is consistent with Buchanan and Keohane's framework on the legitimacy of global governance institutions. See Allen Buchanan and Robert O. Keohane, 'The Legitimacy of Global Governance Institutions', *Ethics and International Affairs* 20, 4 (2006), pp. 405–37.

CONCLUSION

1. The quotation can be found in *The Poet at the Breakfast Table* (1872) by the American physician and poet Oliver Wendell Holmes Sr., who wrote: 'It is the province of knowledge to speak, and it is the privilege of wisdom to listen.'

2. Dennis Dijkzeul, Dorothea Hilhorst and Peter Walker, 'Introduction: Evidence-Based Action in Humanitarian Crises', *Disasters* 37, S(1), (2013), pp. 1–19. The impetus for more evidence-based policymaking arose in the early 1990s, with methodological advances in clinical trials being increasingly used in social sciences, and in applied microeconomics in particular.

3. Jyotsna Puri, Anastasia Aladysheva, Vegard Iversen, Yashodhan Ghorpade and Tilman Brück, 'What Methods May be Used in Impact Evaluations of Humanitarian Assistance?', IZA Discussion Paper No. 8755, Bonn: Institute for the Study of Labour (2015).

4. Michael Barnett, 'Humanitarianism as a Scholarly Vision', in Michael Barnett and Tom Weiss (eds), *Humanitarianism in Question: Politics, Power, Ethics* Ithaca: Cornell University Press, 2008, pp. 235–65.

5. As a side anecdote, e-mails with the file containing Chapter 4 of this book (on Terrorism Economics) have repeatedly been 'eaten up' by the Internet without the sender being ever informed that the addressees had not received the e-mail. This happened not only while I was in Lebanon, but also back in Geneva. The only way to share the draft chapter 4 was via USB key or Dropbox.

6. Marion Fourcade, Etienne Ollion and Yann Algan, 'The Superiority of Economists', *Journal of Economic Perspectives*, forthcoming (2015).

7. In the same vein, the literature on disaster impact typically considers economic

growth and other flow indicators as dependent variables, whereas greater attention should be given to stock levels, including natural capital (Chapter 5).

8. Often, this distinction between political and criminal groups does not make much difference in terms of humanitarian consequences and the resulting needs for protection and assistance.

9. Cited in Chapter 1: Jack Hirshleifer, 'The Dark Side of the Force: Western Economic Association International 1993 Presidential Address', *Economic Inquiry* 32, 1 (1994), p. 3.

10. Alfred Marshall, *Principles of Economics* (8th Edition), London: Macmillan, 1920, p. 6.

11. 'Remarks at Town Hall Meeting on the Release of the First Quadrennial Diplomacy and Development Review, "Leading Through Civilian Power"', US State Department,   http://www.state.gov/secretary/20092013clinton/rm/2010/12/152934.htm, last accessed 2 January 2015.

APPENDIX TO CHAPTER 3: PEA: THE EXAMPLE OF FOOD AID IN ANGOLA

1. The Relief Access Mapping used here is adapted from the RAM framework suggested by Philippe Le Billon in: 'The Political Economy of War: What Relief Workers Need to Know', Humanitarian Practice Network Paper 33, London: ODI, July 2000, p. 20. On the political economy of food aid, see also: David Keen, *The Benefits of Famine: A Political Economy of Famine and Relief in Southwestern Sudan, 1983–1989*, Princeton: Princeton University Press, 1994.

2. We followed an approach that has actually been advanced by Frances Stewart and Emma Samman, 'Food Aid during Civil War: Conflicting Conclusions Derived from Alternative Approaches' in F. Stewart and V. FitzGerald (eds), *War and Underdevelopment*, Vol. 1, Oxford: Oxford University Press, 2000, pp. 168–203. The authors tested the approach in a comparative case study looking at the three types of impact of food aid in Afghanistan, Mozambique and Sudan to get an overall sense of the positive or negative balance.

REFERENCES

Acemoglu, Daron and James Robinson, *Why Nations Fail: The Origins of Power, Prosperity and Poverty*, New York: Crown Business, 2012.

Acevedo, Sebastian, 'Debt, Growth and Natural Disasters: A Caribbean Trilogy', IMF Working Paper 14, 125 (2014).

Adaman, Fikret, 'Power Inequalities in Explaining the Link Between Natural Hazards and Unnatural Disasters', *Development and Change* 43, 1 (2012), pp. 395–407.

Aker, Jenny, 'Cash or Coupons? Testing the Impact of Cash Versus Vouchers in the Democratic Republic of Congo', Working Paper 320, Center for Global Development (2013).

Akerlof, George, 'The Market for "Lemons": Quality Uncertainty and the Market Mechanism', *The Quarterly Journal of Economics* 84, 3 (1970), pp. 488–500.

Albala-Bertrand, Jose-Miguel, *The Political Economy of Large Natural Disasters*, Oxford: Clarendon Press, 1993.

Ali, Hamid, 'Estimate of the Economic Cost of Armed Conflict: A Case Study from Darfur', *Defence and Peace Economics* 24, 6 (2013), pp. 503–519.

Amnesty International, 'Agonizing Choices: Syrian Refugees in Need of Health Care in Lebanon', London: Amnesty International, 2014.

Anderton, Charles and John Carter, *Principles of Conflict Economics: A Primer for Social Scientists*, New York: Cambridge University Press, 2009.

Anderton, Charles, 'Killing Civilians as an Inferior Input in a Rational Choice Model of Genocide and Mass Killing', *Peace Economics, Peace Science and Public Policy* 20, 2 (2014), pp. 327–346.

Andonova, Liliana and Gilles Carbonnier, 'Business-Humanitarian Partnerships: Processes of Normative Legitimation', *Globalizations* 11, 3 (2014), pp. 349–367.

Andreas, Peter, 'Criminalizing Consequences of Sanctions: Embargo Busting and its Legacy', *International Studies Quarterly* 49, 2, (2005), pp. 353–360.

Aning, Kwesi and John Pokoo, 'Understanding the Nature and Threats of Drug Trafficking to National and Regional Security in West Africa', *Stability* 3, 1 (2014), pp. 1–13.

REFERENCES

Ansori, Mohammed Hassan, 'From Insurgency to Bureaucracy: Free Aceh Moment, Aceh Party and the New Face of Conflict' *Stability* 1, 1 (2012), pp. 31–44.

Arbia, Ali and Gilles Carbonnier, 'Human Nature and Development Aid: IR and the Biology of Altruism', *Journal of International Relations and Development*, Forthcoming.

Arrow, Kenneth, *The Limits of Organization*, New York: Norton, 1974.

Asian Development Bank, 'From Aceh to Tacloban: Lessons from a Decade of Disaster', Development Asia, 2014.

Aspinall, Edward, 'Combatants to Contractors: The Political Economy of Peace in Aceh', *Indonesia* 87, 1 (2009), pp. 1–34.

Atran, Scott, *Talking to the Enemy: Faith, Brotherhood, and the (Un)Making of Terrorists*, New York: HarperCollins, 2010.

Axelrod, Robert, and William Hamilton, 'The Evolution of Cooperation', *Science* 211, 4489 (1981), pp. 1390–1396.

Axelrod, Robert, *The Evolution of Cooperation* (Revised ed.), New York: Perseus Books Group, 2006.

Azam, Jean-Paul and Veronique Thelen, 'Foreign Aid Versus Military Intervention in the War on Terror', *Journal of Conflict Resolution* 54 (2010), pp. 237–261.

Badiuzzaman, Mohammad, John Cameron and Syed Mansoob Murshed, 'Household Decision-making Under Threat of Violence: A Micro Level Study in the Chittagong Hill Tracts of Bangladesh', MICROCON Research Working Paper 39 (15 January 2011).

Bandyopadhyay, Subhayu and Katarina Vermann, 'Donor Motives for Foreign Aid', *Federal Reserve Bank of St. Louis Review* 95, 4 (2013), pp. 327–336.

Bardhan, Pranab and Christopher Udry, *Development Microeconomics*, Oxford: Oxford University Press, 1999

Barnett, Michael, *Empire of Humanity: A History of Humanitarianism*, Ithaca: Cornell University Press, 2011.

Baron-Cohen, Simon, *Zero Degrees of Empathy: A New Theory of Human Cruelty*, London: Penguin/Allen Lane, 2011.

Barrett, Christopher and Daniel Maxwell, *Food Aid After Fifty Years: Recasting its Role*, New York: Routledge, 2005.

Barrett, Christopher, 'Measuring Food Insecurity', *Science* 327, 5967 (2010), pp. 825–828.

Barro, Robert and José Ursúa, 'Rare Macroeconomic Disasters', *Annual Review of Economics* 4, 1 (2012), pp. 83–109.

Bastiat, Frédéric, *Ce qu'on voit et ce qu'on ne voit pas. Choix de sophismes et de pamphlets économiques*, Paris: Romillat 1850/2005.

Bates, Robert, *When Things Fell Apart: State Failure in Late Century Africa*, Cambridge: Cambridge University Press, 2008.

Batson, Daniel, *The Altruism Question: Toward a Social-psychological Answer*, Hillsdale: Lawrence Erlbaum Associates, 1991.

Beath, Andrew, Christia Fotini and Ruben Enikolopov, 'Winning Hearts and Minds through Development: Evidence from a Field Experiment in Afghanistan', Working Paper No. 2011, MIT Political Science Department (2012).

Becerra, Oscar, Eduardo Cavallo and Ilan Noy, 'Foreign Aid in the Aftermath of Large Natural Disasters', *Review of Development Economics* 18, 3 (2014), pp. 445–460.

Beirut Research and Innovation Center (BRIC), 'Survey on the Livelihoods of Syrian Refugees in Lebanon, Research Report', (November 2013).

Bene, Christopher, Rachel Godfrey Wood, Andrew Newsham and Mark Davies, 'Resilience: New Utopia or New Tyranny?' IDS Working Paper 405, Institute of Development Studies (2012).

Benson, Charlotte, and Edward Clay, 'Understanding the Economic and Financial Impacts of Natural Disasters', World Bank Disaster Risk Management Series 4 (2004).

Berman, Eli, Jacob Shapiro and Joseph Felter, 'Can Hearts and Minds Be Bought? The Economics of Counterinsurgency in Iraq', *Journal of Political Economy* 199, 4 (2011), pp. 766–819.

Biersteker, Thomas, Sue Eckert and Marcos Tourinho (eds), *Targeting Sanctions: The Impacts and Effectiveness of UN Action*, Cambridge: Cambridge University Press, forthcoming (2015).

Biestecker, Thomas, 'Trends in Terrorist Financing—A Review of the Literature', Report Prepared for Booz, Allen, & Hamilton Consultants, Washington DC, August 2011.

Bilmes, Linda, 'The Financial Legacy of Iraq and Afghanistan Schumer', Harvard Kennedy School Working Paper, RWP13–006, March 2013.

Blackorby, Charles and David Donaldson, 'Cash versus kind, self-selection, and efficient transfers', *American Economic Review* 78, 4, (1998), pp. 691–700.

Blattman, Christopher and Edward Miguel, 'Civil War', *Journal of Economic Literature* 48, 1 (2010), pp. 3–57.

Bocco, Riccardo, Pierre Harrison and Lucas Oesch, 'Recovery', in Chetail, Vincent (ed.) *Post-conflict Peacebuilding—A Lexicon*, Oxford: Oxford University Press, 2009, pp. 268–278.

Böhnke, Jan-Rasmus and Christoph Zürcher, 'Aid, Minds and Hearts: The Impact of Aid in Conflict Zones', *Conflict Management and Peace Science* 30, 5(2010), pp. 411–432.

Boyer, Pascal and Brian Bergstrom, 'Evolutionary Perspectives on Religion', *Annual Review of Anthropology* 37 (2008), pp. 111–130.

Bozzoli, Carlos and Tilman Brück, 'Agriculture, Poverty, and Postwar Reconstruction: Micro-Level Evidence from Northern Mozambique', *Journal of Peace Research* 46, 3 (2009), pp. 377–397.

Brainerd, Elizabeth and Mark V. Siegler, 'The Economic Effects of the 1918 Influenza Epidemic', CEPR Discussion Paper 3791 (2003).

Brassard, Caroline, Margaret Sherraden and Benjamin Lough, 'Emerging Perspectives on International Volunteerism in Asia', Singapore, IVCO (2010).

Brauer, Jurgen and J. Paul Dunne, *Peace Economics: A Macroeconomic Primer for Violence-Afflicted States*, Washington: US Institute of Peace, 2012.

Brück, Tilman, Olaf De Groot, and Friedrich Schneider, 'The Economic Costs of the German Participation in the Afghanistan War', *Journal of Peace Research* 48, 6 (2011), pp. 793–805.

Bryer, David, and Edmund Cairns, 'For Better? For Worse? Humanitarian Aid in Conflict', *Development in Practice* 7, 4 (1997), pp. 363–374.

Buchanan, Allen and Robert O. Keohane, 'The Legitimacy of Global Governance Institutions', *Ethics and International Affairs* 20, 4 (2006), pp. 405–437.

Burnham, Terry and Dominic Johnson, 'The Biological and Evolutionary Logic of Human Cooperation', *Analyse & Kritik* 27 (2005), pp. 113–135.

Cammett, Melani, *Compassionate Communalism: Welfare and Sectarianism in Lebanon*, Ithaca: Cornell University Press, 2014.

Cannon, Terry, 'Reducing People's Vulnerability to Natural Hazards: Communities and Resilience' Wider Research Paper 2008/34, UNU-Wider (2008).

Carbonnier, Gilles and Piedra Lightfoot, 'Business in Humanitarian Crises—For Better or for Worse?' in Dijkzeul, Dennis and Zeynep Sezgin, *The New Humanitarians*, London: Routledge (forthcoming, 2015).

Carbonnier, Gilles, 'Reason, Emotion, Compassion: Can Altruism Survive Professionalisation in the Humanitarian Sector?' *Disasters* 39, 2 (2015), pp. 189–207.

Carbonnier, Gilles, 'Humanitarian and Development Aid in the Context of Stabilization: Blurring the Lines and Broadening the Gap' in Muggah, Robert (ed.), *Stabilization Operations, Security and Development*, New York: Routledge, 2014, pp. 35–55.

Carbonnier, Gilles and Achim Wennmann, 'Natural Resource Governance and Hybrid Political Orders', in Chandler, David & Timothy Sisk (eds) *Routledge Handbook of International Statebuilding*, New York: Routledge, 2013, pp. 208–218.

Carbonnier, Gilles and Natascha Wagner, 'Resource Dependence and Armed Violence: Impact on Sustainability in Developing Countries', *Defence and Peace Economics* 25, 6 (2013), pp. 1–18.

Carbonnier, Gilles, 'Reconsidering the Secular as the Norm', *International Development Policy—Religion & Development* 4 (2013), pp. 7–12.

Carbonnier, Gilles, Alain Schoenenberger, Milad Zarin, Moez Ouni, and Lorenzo La Spada, 'Effets Economiques de l'aide Publique au Développement en Suisse', Geneva: IHEID, 2012.

Carbonnier, Gilles, 'Official Development Assistance Once More Under Fire From Critics', *International Development Policy—Africa, 50 Years of Independence* 1 (2010), pp. 137–142.

Carbonnier, Gilles, 'Security Management and the Political Economy of War', *Humanitarian Exchange* 47 (2010), pp. 18–21.

Carbonnier, Gilles, 'Privatisation and Outsourcing in Wartime: the Humanitarian Challenges', *Disasters* 30, 4, (2006), pp. 402–16.

Carbonnier, Gilles, 'Conflict, Postwar Rebuilding and the Economy: A Critical Review of the Literature', War-torn Societies Project's Occasional Paper 2, Geneva: UNRISD, 1997.

Carpenter, Jeffrey and Caitlin M. Meyers, 'Why Volunteer? Evidence on the Role of Altruism, Image and Incentives', *Journal of Public Economics* 94, 11–12 (2010), pp. 911–920.

Carr, Stuart, Lori Foster Thompson, Walter Reichman, Ishbel McWha, Leo Marai, Malcolm MacLachlan and Peter Baguma, 'Humanitarian Work Psychology: Concepts to Contributions' White Paper Series, International Affairs Committee of the Society for Industrial and Organizational Psychology (2013).

Carter, Joseph, 'Aiding Afghanistan: How Corruption and Western Aid Hinder Afghanistan Development', *Foreign Policy Journal* (18 June 2013), pp. 107–124.

Casey-Stuart, Maslen (ed.), *The War Report 2012*, Oxford: Oxford University Press, 2013.

Catusse, Myriam, 'La question sociale aux marges des soulèvements arabes: Leçons libanaises et marocaines', *Critique internationale* 61 (2013/14), pp. 19–34.

Chandler, David, *Resilience: The Governance of Complexity*, London: Routledge, 2014

Chen, Shaohua and Ravallion, Martin, 'Absolute Poverty Measures for the Developing World, 1981–2004,' Policy Research Working Paper 4211, The World Bank, (2007).

Chhibber, Ajaz and Rachid Laajaj, 'The Interlinkages Between Natural Disasters and Economic Development', in Guha-Sapir, Debarati and Indhira Santos (eds), *The Economic Impacts of Natural Disasters*, Oxford: Oxford University Press, 2013.

Chick, Paul, Daniel Slomka and Seo Young So, 'Negotiating a Change of Behavior with Non-State Armed Groups', Applied Research Project for Geneva Call, Mimeo, The Graduate Institute, Geneva, 2012.

Child, Travers, 'Hearts and Minds Cannot be Bought: Ineffective Reconstruction in Afghanistan', *The Economics of Peace and Security Journal* 9, 2 (2014), pp. 43–49.

Chou, Tiffany, 'Does Development Assistance Reduce Violence? Evidence from Afghanistan', *The Economics of Peace and Security Journal* 7, 2 (2012), pp. 5–13.

Chowdhury, Abdur and Syed Mansoob Murshed, 'Conflict and Fiscal Capacity,' *Defence and Peace Economics* (2014), published online (DOI:10.1080/10242694. 2014.948700).

Churchill, Craig and Michal Matul (eds), 'Protecting the Poor: A Microinsurance Compendium', Vol. II, Geneva: ILO, 2012.

Churchill, Craig, 'Protecting the Poor: A Microinsurance Compendium', Geneva: ILO, 2006.

REFERENCES

Coase, Ronald, 'The Nature of the Firm', *Economica* 4, 16 (1937), pp. 386–405.

Coghlan, Benjamin, Richard Brennan, Pascal Ngoy, David Dofara, Brad Otto, Mark Clements, and Tony Stewart, 'Mortality in the Democratic Republic of Congo', *Lancet* 367, 9504 (2006), pp. 44–51.

Cohen, Charles and Eric Werker, 'The Political Economy of 'Natural' Disasters', Working Paper 08–040, Harvard Business School (21 November 2008).

Cohn, Alain, Ernst Fehr and Michel Maréchal, 'Business Culture and Dishonesty in the Banking Industry' *Nature* (2014 advanced online publication).

Colgan, Jeff, *Petro-Aggression: When Oil Causes War*, Cambridge: Cambridge University Press, 2013.

Collier, Paul and Anke Hoeffler, 'Aid, Policy, and Peace: Reducing the Risks of Civil Conflict' *Defense and Peace Economics* 13, 6 (2002), pp. 435–450.

Collier, Paul, Lani Elliott, Havard Hegre, Anke Hoeffler, Marta Reynal-Querol, and Nicholas Sambanis, *Breaking the Conflict Trap: Civil War and Development Policy*, Washington/Oxford: The World Bank and Oxford University Press, 2003.

Collier, Paul. 'Economic Causes of Civil Conflict and Their Implications for Policy' in Crocket, Chester, Fen Hampson and Pamela Aall (eds), *Leashing the Dogs of War: Conflict Management in a Divided World*, Washington: USIP, 2007, pp. 197–218.

Collier, Peter and David Horowitz, *The Rockefellers: An American Dynasty*, New York: Holt, Rindhart and Winston, 1976.

Collinson, Sarah, Samir Elhawary, and Robert Muggah, 'States of Fragility: Stabilisation and its Implications for Humanitarian Action,' *Disasters* 34, 3 (2010), pp. 275–96.

Comte, Auguste, *Catéchisme positiviste*, Editions du Sandre, Paris: 1852/2009.

Connable, Ben, and Martin Libicki, *How Insurgencies End*, Santa Monica: Rand, 2010.

Cooley, Alexander and James Ron, 'The NGO Scramble: Organizational Insecurity and the Political Economy of Transnational Action', *International Security* 27, 1 (2002), pp. 5–39.

Corley, Christopher, 'The Liberation Tigers of Tamil Eelam,' in Freeman, Michael (ed.), *Financing Terrorism: Case studies*, Surrey: Ashgate, 2012.

Cramer, Christopher, *Civil War is Not a Stupid Thing: Accounting for Violence in Developing Countries*, London: Hurst, 2006.

Crost, Benjamin, Joseph Felter, and Patrick Johnston, 'Aid Under Fire: Development Projects and Civil Conflict', *American Economic Review* 104, 6 (2014), pp. 1833–1856.

Cummins, J. David, 'CAT Bonds and Other Risk-Linked Securities: State of the Market and Recent Developments,' *Risk Management and Insurance Review* 11, 1 (2008) pp. 23–47.

Daly, Patrick and Caroline Brassard, 'Aid Accountability and Participatory

REFERENCES

Approaches in Post-Disaster Housing Reconstruction', *Asian Journal of Social Science* 39, 4 (2011), pp. 508—533.

Danish Refugee Council, 'Unconditional Cash Assistance via E-Transfer: Implementation Lessons Learned: Winterization Support via CSC Bank ATM Card', DRC Lebanon, February 2014.

Das, Saudamini, 'Storm Protection by the Mangroves in Orissa: An Analysis of the 1999 Super Cyclone', SANDEE Working Paper 25–07, South Asian Network of Development and Environmental Economics (2007).

Davies, Thomas Richard, 'The Transformation of International NGOs and Their Impact on Development Aid', *International Development Policy—Aid, Emerging Economies and Global Policies*, 3 (2012).

Dawkins, Richard, *The Selfish Gene*, Oxford: Oxford University Press, 1976.

De Long, Bradford J. and Barry Eichengreen, 'The Marshall Plan: History's Most Successful Structural Adjustment Program', NBER Working Paper No. 3899, Cambridge, MA: National Bureau of Economic Research (1991).

De Ree, Jopper and Elenonora Nillesen, 'Aiding Violence or Peace? The Impact of Foreign Aid on the risk of Civil Conflict in sub-Saharan Africa', *Journal of Development Economics* 88, 2 (2009), pp. 301–313.

De Waal, Alex, 'Mission Without an End? Peacekeeping in the African Political Marketplace' *International Affairs* 85, 1 (2009), pp. 99–113.

De Waal, Frans, 'Putting the Altruism Back into Altruism: The Evolution of Empathy', *Annual Review of Psychology* 59 (2008), pp. 279–300.

Devarajan, Shantayanan, Andrew Sunil Rajkumar, and Vinaya Swaroop, 'What does Aid to Africa Finance?' Development Research Group, Washington: The World Bank, 1999.

Devereux, Michael, 'Cash Transfers and Social Protection', paper presented at the Regional Workshop on Cash Transfer Activities in Southern Africa (Johannesburg), SARPN, 9–10 October 2006.

Devereux, Stephen, 'Sen's Entitlement Approach: Critiques and Counter-critiques', *Oxford Development Studies* 29, 3 (2001), pp. 245–263.

Dietrich, Christian, 'UNITA's Diamond Mining and Exporting Capacity', in Cilliers, Jakkie and Christian Dietrich (eds), *Angola's War Economy: The Role of Oil and Diamonds*, Pretoria: Institute for Security Studies, 2000, pp. 275–294.

Dijkzeul, Dennis and Zeynep Sezgin (eds), *The New Humanitarians: Principles and Practice*, London: Routledge (forthcoming, 2005).

Dijkzeul, Dennis, Dorothea Hilhorst and Peter Walker, 'Introduction: Evidence-Based Action in Humanitarian Crises', *Disasters* 37, 1 (2013), pp. 1–19.

Djankov, Simeon, José Montalvo and Marta Reynal-Querol, 'The Curse of Aid', *Journal of Economic Growth* 13, 3 (2008), pp. 169–194.

Dube, Oeindrila and Juan Vargas, 'Commodity Price Shocks and Civil Conflict: Evidence from Colombia', *Review of Economic Studies* 80 (2013), pp. 1384–1421.

Duffield, Mark, *Development, Security and Unending War: Governing the World of Peoples*, Cambridge: Polity, 2007.

Dunant, Henry, *A Memory of Solferino*, Reprinted in Geneva: ICRC, 1862/1959.

Dunn, Sophia, Mike Brewin and Aues Scek, 'Cash and Voucher Monitoring Group: Final Monitoring Report of the Somalia Cash and Voucher Transfer Programme', ODI (2013).

Enders, Walter and Todd Sandler, 'Causality Between Transnational Terrorism and Tourism: The Case of Spain', *Terrorism* 14, 1 (1991), pp. 49–58.

Esman, Milton and Ronald Herring, *Carrots, Sticks, and Ethnic Conflict: Rethinking Development Assistance*, Ann Arbour: University of Michigan Press, 2003.

Fan, Lilianne, 'Disaster as Opportunity? Building Back Better in Aceh, Myanmar and Haiti', HPG Working Paper, November 2013, ODI, London.

Fassin, Didier, *Humanitarian Reason: A Moral History of the Present*, Berkeley: University of California Press, 2012, p. 249.

Fearon, James, 'Rationalist Explanations for War', *International Organizations* 49, 39 (1995), pp. 379–414.

Fearon, James, Humphreys Macartan and Jeremy Weinstein, 'Can Development Aid Contribute to Social Cohesion after Civil War? Evidence from a Field Experiment in Post-conflict Liberia', *American Economic Review: Papers & Proceedings* 99, 2 (2009), pp. 287–291.

Feener, Michael, *Sharia as Social Engineering: The Implementation of Islamic Law in Contemporary Aceh, Indonesia*, London: Oxford University Press, 2013.

Fehr, Ernst and Bettina Rockenbach, 'Human Altruism: Economic, Neural, and Evolutionary Perspectives', *Current Opinion in Neurobiology* 14 (2004), pp. 784–790.

Feyzioglu, Tarhan, Vinaya Swaroop and Min Zhu, 'A Panel Data Analysis of the Fungibility of Foreign Aid', *World Bank Economic Review* 12, 1 (1998), pp. 29–58.

Findley, Michael, Josh Powell, Daniel Strandow, and Jeff Tanner, 'The Localized Geography of Foreign Aid: A New Dataset and Application to Violent Armed Conflict', *World Development* 39, 11 (2011) pp. 1995–2009.

Fishtein, Paul and Andrew Wilder, 'Winning Hearts and Minds? Examining the Relationship between Aid and Security in Afghanistan', Feinstein International Center, Tufts University, 2012.

Fiszbein, Ariel, Norbert Shady, Francisco H.G. Ferreira, Margaret Grosh, Niall Keleher, Pedro Olinto, and Emmanuel Skoufias, 'Conditional Cash Transfers: Reducing Present and Future Poverty', World Bank Policy Research Report 47603, Washington DC: The World Bank, 2009.

Fourcade, Marion, Etienne Ollion, and Yann Algan, 'The Superiority of Economists', *Journal of Economic Perspectives*, forthcoming (2015).

Fountain, Philipp, 'Religion and Disaster Relief: Rethinking their Relationship in Asia'. Paper presented at a seminar on Religious Studies, Victoria University of Wellington, March 2014.

REFERENCES

Frank, Robert, Thomas Gilovich and Dennis Regan, 'Does Studying Economics Inhibit Cooperation?' *Journal of Economic Perspectives* 7, 2 (1993), pp. 159–171.

Freeman, Michael (ed.), *Financing Terrorism: Case studies*, Surrey: Ashgate, 2012.

Frey, Bruno and Heinz Buhofer, 'Prisoners and Property Rights,' *Journal of Law and Economics* 31, 1 (1988), pp. 19–46.

Frey, Bruno and Simon Lüchinger, 'Countering Terrorism: Beyond Deterrence', in: Morgan, Matthew (ed.), *The Impact of 9/11 on Politics and War: The Day that Changed Everything?*, London: Palgrave Macmillan, 2009, pp. 131–139.

Frey, Bruno, *Dealing with Terrorism—Stick or Carrots?*, Cheltenham: Edward Elgar, 2004.

Frey, Bruno, *Modern Political Economy*, New York: Halsted Press, 1978.

Friedman, Milton, *Capitalism and Freedom*, 2nd Edition, Chicago: University of Chicago Press, 1982.

Gaibulloev, Khusrav and Todd Sandler, 'The Adverse Effect of Transnational and Domestic Terrorism on Growth in Africa,' *Journal of Peace Research* 48, 3 (2011), pp. 355–371.

Gardeazabal, Javier, 'Methods for Measuring Aggregate Cost of Conflict' in Garfinkel, Michelle and Stergios Skaperdas (eds), *Handbook of the Economics of Peace and Conflict*, New York: Oxford University Press, 2012, pp. 227–251.

Garfinkel, Michelle and Stergios Skaperdas, 'Economic Perspectives on Peace and Conflict' in Garfinkel, Michelle and Stergios Skaperdas (eds), *The Oxford Handbook of the Economics of Peace and Conflict*, New York: Oxford University Press, 2012.

Garfinkel, Michelle, 'Arming as a Strategic Investment in a Cooperative Equilibrium,' *American Economic Review* 21, 1 (1980), pp. 43–68.

Gates, Carolyne, *The Merchant Republic of Lebanon: Rise of an Open Economy*, Oxford and London: Center for Lebanese Studies and I. B. Tauris & Co. Ltd, 1998.

Geneva Declaration on Armed Violence and Development, The Global Burden of Armed Violence, Geneva, 2008.

Global Humanitarian Assistance, 'GHA Report 2014', Bristol (UK): Development Initiatives, 2014.

Global Humanitarian Assistance, 'GHA Report 2015', Bristol (UK): Development Initiatives, 2015.

Global Witness, 'A Crude Awakening: The Role of the Oil and Banking Industries in Angola's Civil War and the Plunder of State Assets', Global Witness, London (1999).

Graeber, David, *Debt: the First 5000 Years*, Brooklyn: Melville House, 2011.

Greenhill, Romilly, 'Real Aid: Making Technical Assistance Work', *Action Aid*, 2006.

Grislain-Letrémy, Céline, 'Natural Disasters: Exposure and Underinsurance', INSEE, Série des documents de travail de la Direction des Études et Synthèses Économiques, G2013/12, 2013.

Grossman, Herschel, 'Foreign Aid and Insurrection,' *Defense Economics* 3, 4 (1992), pp. 275–288.

REFERENCES

Guha-Sapir, Debarati and Indhira Santos, 'The Increasing Costs and Frequency of Natural Disasters' in Guha-Sapir, Debarati and Indhira Santos (eds), *The Economic Impacts of Natural Disasters*, Oxford: Oxford University Press, 2013.

Guha-Sapir, Debarati and Philippe Hoyois, 'Measuring the Human and Economic Impact of Disasters', Report produced for the UK Government Office of Science (Foresight Project). 'Reducing Risks of Future Disasters: Priorities for Decision Makers', 27 November 2012, pp. 6–13.

Guidolin, Massimo and Eliana La Ferrara, 'The Economic Effects of Violent Conflict: Evidence from Asset Market Reactions' *Journal of Peace Research* 47, 6 (2010), pp. 671–684.

Gurenko, Eugene, Rodney Lester, Olivier Mahul, and Serap Oguz Gonulal, 'Earthquake Insurance in Turkey', Washington: The World Bank, 2006.

Gurr, Ted, *Why Men Rebel*, Princeton: Princeton University Press, 1970.

Haavelmo, Trygve, *A Study of the Theory of Economic Evolution*, Amsterdam: North Holland, 1954.

Haggard, Stephan, Jean-Dominique Lafay, and Christian Morrisson, *The Political Feasibility of Adjustment in Developing Countries*, Paris: OECD Development Centre, 1995.

Halperin, Eran, Ruthie Pliskin, Tamar Saguy, Varda Liberman and James J. Gross, 'Emotion Regulation and the Cultivation of Political Tolerance', *Journal of Conflict Resolution* 58, 6 (2014), pp. 1110–1138.

Hamilton, Kirk, 'Accounting for Sustainability: Measuring Sustainable Development: Integrated Economic, Environmental and Social Frameworks', Paris: OECD, 2014.

Hann, Chris and Keith Hart, *Economic Anthropology: History, Ethnography, Critique*, Cambridge: Polity, 2011.

Harb, Charles and Rim Saab, 'Social Cohesion and Intergroup Relations: Syrian Refugees and Lebanese National in the Bekaa and Akkar', American University of Beirut and Save the Children, Beirut (2014).

Harrison, Mark, 'An Economist Looks at Suicide Terrorism', *World Economics* 7, 3 (2006), pp. 1–15.

Healy, Sean and Sandrine Tiller, 'Where is Everyone? Responding to Emergencies in the Most Difficult Places: A Review of the Humanitarian Aid System's Response to Displacement Emergencies in Conflict Contexts in South Sudan, Eastern Democratic Republic of Congo and Jordan, 2012–13', London: MSF, 2014.

Henrich, Joseph, Jean Ensminger, Richard McElreath, Abigail Barr, Clark Barrett, Alexander Bolyanatz, Juan Camilo Cardenas, Michael Gurven, Edwins Gwako, Natalie Henrich, Carolyn Lesorogol, Frank Marlowe, David Tracer, and John Ziker 'Markets, Religion, Community Size, and the Evolution of Fairness and Punishment', *Science* 327, 5972 (2010), pp. 1480–1484.

Hewitt, Kenneth (ed.), *Interpretations of Calamity*, Boston: Allen and Unwin, 1983.

Blaikie, Piers, Terry Cannon, Ian Davis, and Ben Wisner, *At Risk: Natural Hazards, People's Vulnerability, and Disasters*, London: Routledge, 1994.

REFERENCES

Hidrobo, Melissa, John Hoddinott, Amber Peterman, Amy Margolies, and Vanessa Moreira, 'Cash, Food, or Vouchers? Evidence from a Randomized Experiment in Northern Ecuador', *Journal of Development Economics* 107, C (2014), pp. 144–156.

Hippen, Benjamin 'Organ Sales and Moral Travails: Lessons from the Living Kidney Vendor Program in Iran', *Policy Analysis*, 614, Washington: Cato Institute, 2008.

Hirsch, John, *Sierra Leone: Diamonds and the Struggle for Democracy*, Boulder: Lynne Rienner, 2001.

Hirshleifer, Jack, *The Dark Side of the Force: Economic Foundations of Conflict Theory*, Cambridge: Cambridge University Press, 2001.

Hirshleifer, Jack, 'The Dark Side of the Force', Western Economic Association International 1993 Presidential Address, *Economic Inquiry* 32, 1 (1994), pp. 1–10.

Hirshleifer, Jack, 'Conflict and Rent Seeking Success Functions: Ratio vs. Difference Models of Relative Success', *Public Choice* 63, 2 (1989), pp. 101–112.

Hirshleifer, Jack, 'The Analytics of Continuing Conflict', *Synthese* 76, 2 (1988), pp. 201–233.

Hirshleifer, Jack, *Economic Behavior in Adversity*, Chicago: University of Chicago Press, 1987.

Homer-Dixon, Thomas, *Environment, Scarcity, and Violence*. Princeton: Princeton University Press, 1999.

Hopkins, Raymond, 'The Political Economy of Foreign Aid' in Tarp, Finn (ed.), *Foreign Aid and Development: Lessons Learnt and Directions for the Future*, London: Routledge, 2000.

Hout, Wil, 'Neopatrimonialism and Development: Pockets of Effectiveness as Drivers of Change', *Revue internationale de politique comparée* 20, 3 (2013), pp. 79–96.

Hudson, David and Andrian Leftwich, 'From Political Economy to Political Analysis', *Development Leadership Program*, Research Paper 25, June 2014. pp. 8–9.

Huebner, Bryce and Marc Hauser, 'Moral Judgments About Altruistic Self-Sacrifice: When Philosophical and Folk Intuitions Clash', *Philosophical Psychology* 24, 1 (2011), pp. 73–94.

Hufbauer, Gary, Jeffrey Schott, Kimberly Elliott and Barbara Oegg, *Economic Sanctions Reconsidered*, 3rd Edition, Washington: The Peterson Institute of International Economics, 2007.

Hughs, Kathleen, and Steve Zyck, 'The Relationship Between Aid, Insurgency, and Security. Part One and Two', Civil-Military Fusion Center Monthly Report on Afghanistan, 2011.

ICJ, *Military and Paramilitary Activities in and against Nicaragua (Nicaragua v. United States of America)*, ICJ, Judgment, 27 June 1986.

ICTY, *The Prosecutor v. Dusko Tadic, Decision on the Defence Motion for Interlocutory Appeal on Jurisdiction*, IT-94-1-A, 2 October 1995.

ICTY, *The Prosecutor v. Ramush Haradinaj, Idriz Balaj and Lahi Brahimaj (Haradinaj et al.)*, Trial Chamber Judgment, IT-04-84-T, 3 April 2008.

REFERENCES

IFRC, 'The Code of Conduct for the International Red Cross and Red Crescent Movement and NGOs in Disaster Relief', Geneva: IFRC.

Inter-Agency Standing Committee (IASC), 'Multi-Cluster/Sector Initial Rapid Assessment (MIRA)', 2012.

Inter-Agency Standing Committee, 'IASC Guidelines on Mental Health and Psychosocial Support in Emergency Settings', 2007.

Internal Displacement Monitoring Center/Norwegian Refugee Council, 'Global Overview 2014: People Internally Displaced by Conflict and Violence', Geneva: Internal Displacement Monitoring Center/Norwegian Refugee Council, May 2014.

International Rescue Committee, 'Emergency Economies: The Impact of Cash Assistance in Lebanon', August 2014.

Jabbi, Mbemba, Marte Swart, and Christian Keysers, 'Empathy for Positive and Negative Emotions in the Gustatory Cortex', *NeuroImage* 34, 4 (2007), pp. 1744–1753.

Jackson, Ashley and Abdi Aynte, 'Talking to the Other Side: Humanitarian Negotiations with Al-Shabaab in Somali', HPG Working Paper, December 2013, ODI, London.

Jackson, Stephen, 'Fortunes of War: The Coltan Trade in the Kivus', Background research for HPG Report 13, 2003, ODI, London.

Jean, François and Jean-Christophe Rufin, *Economie des Guerres Civiles*, Paris: Hachette, 1996.

Jerven, Morton, *Poor Numbers: How We are Misled by African Development Statistics and What to do About it*, Ithaca: Cornell University Press, 2013.

Justino, Patricia, Tilman Bruck and Philip Verwimp (eds), *A Micro-level Perspective on the Dynamics of Conflict, Violence, and Development*, Oxford: Oxford University Press, 2013.

Kahneman, Daniel and Amos Tversky, 'Prospect Theory: An Analysis of Decisions and Risk', *Econometrica* 47, 2 (1979), pp. 263–291.

Kahneman, Daniel, *Thinking, Fast and Slow*, London: Allen Lane, 2011.

Kalyvas, Stathis, *The Logic of Violence in Civil War*, Cambridge: Cambridge University Press, 2006.

Keen, David, *Useful Enemies. When Waging Wars is More Important than Winning Them*, New Haven: Yale University Press, 2012.

Keen, David, *The Benefits of Famine: A Political Economy of Famine and Relief in Southwestern Sudan, 1983–1989*, Princeton: Princeton University Press, 1994.

Kellet, Jan and Dan Sparks, 'Disaster Risk Reduction: Spending Where it Should Count', Global Humanitarian Assistance Briefing Paper, 2012.

Kenny, Chares, 'Disaster Risk Reduction in Developing Countries: Costs, Benefits and Institutions', *Disasters* 36, 4, (2012), pp. 559–588.

Kenny, Chares, 'Why do People Die in Earthquakes? The Costs, Benefits and Institutions of Disaster Risk Reduction in Development Countries', Policy Research Working Paper 4823, The World Bank, Washington DC, 2009.

Keucheyan, Razmig, *La nature est un champ de bataille: Essai d'écologie politique*, Paris: Zones, 2014.

Keynes, John M., *How to Pay for the War*, New York: Harcourt, Brace, and Howe, Inc., 1940.

Keynes, John M., *The Economic Consequences of Peace*, New York: Harcourt, Brace, and Howe, Inc., 1919.

Kim, Namsuk, 'How Much More Exposed are the Poor to Natural Disasters? Global and Regional Measurement', *Disasters* 26, 2 (2012), pp. 195–211.

Klare, Michael, *Resource Wars*, New York: Holt, Henry & Co, Inc., 2002.

Klein, Naomi, *The Shock Doctrine: The Rise of Disaster Capitalism*, New York: Picardor, 2007.

Koenigs, Michael, Liane Young, Ralph Adolphs, Daniel Tranel, Fiery Cushman, Marc Hauser, and Antonio Damasio, 'Damage to the Prefrontal Cortex Increases Utilitarian Moral Judgements', *Nature* 446, 7138 (2007), pp. 908–911.

Kolm, Serge-Christophe, 'Introduction to the Economics of Altruism, Giving, and Reciprocity', in Kolm, Serge-Christophe and Jean Mercier Ythier, *Handbook of Economics of Giving, Altruism and Reciprocity*, Amsterdam: North-Holland, 2006, pp. 1–122.

Koubi, Vally, Tobias Bohmelt, and Thomas Bernauer, 'Do Natural Resources Matter for Interstate and Intrastate Armed Conflict?' *Journal of Peace Research* 51, 2, (2014), pp. 227–243.

Krueger, Alan, 'What Makes a Homegrown Terrorist? Human Capital and Participation in Domestic Islamic Terrorist Groups in the U.S.A.' *Economics Letters* 101, 3 (2008), pp. 293–296.

Krueger, Alan, *What Makes a Terrorist? Economics and the Roots of Terrorism*, Princeton: Princeton University Press, 2007.

Kunreuther, Howard and Erwann Michel-Kerjan, 'Natural Disasters', Copenhagen Consensus Center, 2012.

Le Billon, Philippe, 'The Political Economy of War: What Relief Workers Need to Know', Humanitarian Practice Network Paper 33, London: ODI, July 2000.

Le Billon, Phillipe, *Wars of Plunder: Conflicts, Profits and the Politics of Resources*. London, New York: Hurst and Columbia University Press, 2012.

Leiderer, Stephan, 'Fungibility and the Choice of Aid Modalities—The Red Herring Revisited', Working Paper 68, UNU-WIDER (2012).

Leonard, David, 'Where are 'Pockets' of Effective Agencies Likely in Weak Governance States and Why? A Propositional Inventory', IDS Working Paper 306, Institute of Development Studies, Brighton (2008).

Loayza, Norman, Eduardo Olaberria, Jamele Rigolini, and Luc Christiaensen, 'Natural Disasters and Growth—Going Beyond the Averages.' World Bank Policy Research Working Paper 4980, The World Bank, 2009.

REFERENCES

Lujala, Päivi, 'Deadly Combat over Natural Resources', *Journal of Conflict Resolution* 53, 1 (2009), pp. 50–71.

Luterbacher, Urs and Carmen Sandi, 'Breaking the Dynamics of Emotions and Fear in Conflict and Reconstruction', *Peace Economics, Peace Science and Public Policy* 20, 3 (2014), p. 489.

Mack, Andrew 'Armed Conflicts', in Lomborg, Bjorn (ed.) *Global Problems, Smart Solutions. Costs and Benefits*, Cambridge: Cambridge University Press, 2013, pp. 62–71.

Marshall, Alfred, *Principles of Economics*, 8th Edition, London: Macmillan, 1920.

Marshall, Monty and Ted Robert Gurr, 'Peace and Conflict', Center for International Development and Conflict Management University of Maryland, 2005.

Marwell, Gerald and Ruth Ames, 'Economists Free Ride, Does Anyone Else?', *Journal of Public Economics* 15, 3 (1981), pp. 295–310.

Maslach, Christina and Michael Leiter 'Early Predictors of Job Burnout and Engagement', *Journal of Applied Psychology* 93, 3 (2008), pp. 498–512.

Maslow, Abraham, 'A Theory of Human Motivation', *Psychological Review* 50, 4 (1943), pp. 370–96.

Maxwell, Daniel and Nisar Majid, 'Another Humanitarian Crisis in Somalia? Learning from the 2011 Famine', Feinstein International Center, Tufts University, August 2014.

Mehmood, Sultan, 'Terrorism and the Macroeconomy: Evidence from Pakistan', *Defence and Peace Economics*, 25, 5 (2014), pp. 509–534.

Meierhans, Alexandra, Victor Bresch and Sabina Voicu, 'Expatriate Taxation and the Evolution of the Humanitarian Sector', Applied Research Project for MSF-Switzerland, Mimeo, The Graduate Institute, Geneva, 2012.

Merari, Ariel, 'The Readiness to Kill and Die: Suicidal Terrorism in the Middle East' in Reich, Walter (ed.), *Origins of Terrorism: Psychologies, Ideologies, Theologies, States of Mind*, 2nd Edition, Washington, DC: Woodrow Wilson Center and Johns Hopkins University Press, 1998, pp. 192–207.

Meron, Theodor, 'International Humanitarian Law from Agincourt to Rome', *International Law Studies* 75 (1999), pp. 301–311.

Michel-Kerjan, Erwann, Ivan Zelenko, Victor Cardenas and Daniel Turgel, 'Catastrophe Financing for Governments: Learning from the 2009–2012 MultiCat Program in Mexico', OECD Working Papers on Finance, Insurance and Private Pensions No 9, Paris: OECD, 2011.

Mitri, Dalya, 'Challenges of Aid Coordination in a Complex Crisis: An Overview of Funding Policies and Conditions Regarding Aid Provision to Syrian Refugees in Lebanon', Civil Society Knowledge Center, 2014.

Moret, Erica, 'Humanitarian Impacts of Economic Sanctions on Iran and Syria', *European Security* (26 February 2014), pp. 1–21.

Morisson, Kevin, 'Oil, Nontax Revenue, and the Redistributional Foundations of Regime Stability', *International Organization* 63, 1 (2009), pp. 107–138.

REFERENCES

Mourey, Alain, *Nutrition Manual for Humanitarian Action*, Geneva: ICRC, 2008.

Muggah, Robert (ed.), *Stabilization Operations, Security and Development—States of Fragility*, New York: Routledge, 2014.

Nel, Philip and Marjolein Righarts, 'Natural disasters and the Risk of Violent Civil Conflict' *International Studies Quarterly* 52, 1 (2008), pp. 159–185.

Neumayer, Eric, Thomas Plümper and Fabian Barthel, 'The Political Economy of Natural Disaster Damage', *Global Environmental Change* 24, 1 (2013), pp. 8–19.

Neusner, Jacob, and Bruce Chilton (eds), *Altruism in World Religions*, Washington: Georgetown University Press, 2005.

Nielson, Richard, Michael Findley, Zachary Davis, Tara Candland, and Daniel Nielson, 'Foreign Aid Shocks as a Cause of Violent Armed Conflict', *American Journal of Political Science* 55, 1 (2011), pp. 219–232.

Nunn, Nathan and Nancy Qian, 'US Food Aid and Civil Conflict', *American Economic Review* 104, 6 (2014), pp. 1630–66.

O'Keefe, Phil, Ken Westgate, and Ben Wisner, 'Taking the Naturalness Out of Natural Disasters', *Nature* 260 (1976), pp. 566–567.

OCHA, 'Saving Lives Today and Tomorrow. Managing the Risk of Humanitarian Crises', Office for the Coordination of Humanitarian Affairs, 2014.

Olson, Mancur. 'Dictatorship, Democracy, and Development', *American Political Science Review* 87, 3 (1993), pp. 567–576.

Olssen, Ola and Eyerusalem Siba, 'Ethnic Cleansing or Resource Struggle in Darfur? An empirical analysis', *Journal of Development Economics* 103, C (2013), pp. 299–312.

Oxfam and WFP, 'Executive Brief: Engaging with Markets in Humanitarian Response', 10 July 2013.

Pape, Robert, *Dying to Win: The Strategic Logic of Suicide Terrorism*, New York: Random House, 2005.

Parker, Ben, 'Humanitarian Besieged', *Humanitarian Exchange* 59, November 2013.

Pictet, Jean, *The Fundamental Principles of the Red Cross: Commentary*, Geneva: ICRC, 1979.

Piliavin, Jane, 'Altruism and Helping: The Evolution of a Field: The 2008 Cooley-Mead Presentation', *Social Psychology Quarterly* 72, 3 (2009), pp. 209–225.

Pinker, Steven, *The Better Angels of Our Nature: The Decline of Violence in History and Its Causes*, New York: Viking Books, 2011.

Platteau, Jean-Philippe and Darwin Ontiveros, 'Understanding and Information Failure in Insurance: Evidence from India', Working Paper 1301, Department of Economics, University of Namur, 2014.

Polman, Linda, *The Crisis Caravan: What's Wrong with Humanitarian Aid?* New York: Metropolitan Books, 2010.

Power, Samantha, *A Problem from Hell: America and the Age of Genocide*, New York: Basic Books, 2013.

REFERENCES

Pugh, Michael, Neil Cooper and Jonathan Goodhand, *War Economies in a Regional Context: Challenges of Transformation*, Boulder (CO): Lynne Rienner, 2004.

Puri, Jyotsna, Anastasia Aladysheva, Vegard Iversen, Yashodhan Ghorpade and Tilman Brück, 'What Methods May be Used in Impact Evaluations of Humanitarian Assistance?' IZA Discussion Paper No. 8755, Bonn: Institute for the Study of Labour (2015).

Raddatz, Claudio, 'Are External Shocks Responsible for the Instability of Output in Low Income Countries?' *Journal of Development Economics* 84, 1 (2007), pp. 155–187.

Redfield, Peter, *Life in Crisis: The Ethical Journey of Doctors without Borders*, Los Angeles: University of California Press, 2013.

Rettberg, Angelika, Ralf Leiteritz, and Carlo Nasi, 'Entrepreneurial Activity and Civil War in Columbia', WIDER Working Paper 06, UNU-WIDER (2010).

Richards, Paul, 'The Political Economy of Internal Conflict in Sierra Leone', Working Paper 21, The Netherlands Institute of International Relations (2003).

Riddell, Roger, *Does Foreign Aid Really Work?*, Oxford: Oxford University Press, 2007.

Riesebrodt, Martin, *The Promise of Salvation: A Theory of Religion*, Chicago: University of Chicago Press, 2010.

Rizzolatti, Giacomo, Corrado Sinigaglia, and Frances Anderson, *Mirrors in the Brain: How Our Minds Share Actions, Emotions, and Experience*, Oxford: Oxford University Press, 2008.

Romer, Paul, 'The Origins of Endogenous Growth', *The Journal of Economic Perspectives* 8, 1 (1994), pp. 3–22.

Ryfman, Philippe, *La question humanitaire*, Paris: Ellipses, 1999.

Ryfman, Philippe, *Une histoire de l'humanitaire*, Paris: La Découverte, 2008.

Sabates-Wheeler, Rachel and Philip Verwimp, 'Extortion with Protection. Understanding the Effect of Rebel Taxation on Civilian Welfare in Burundi', *Journal of Conflict Resolution* 58, 8 (2014), pp. 1474–1499.

Salti, Nisreen and Jad Chaaban, 'The Role of Sectarianism in the Allocation of Public Expenditure in Postwar Lebanon', *International Journal of Middle East Studies* 42, 4 (2010), pp 637–655.

Sandler, Todd, 'New Frontiers of Terrorism Research: An Introduction', *Journal of Peace Research* 48, 3 (2011), pp. 279–286.

Sassoli, Marco, Antoine Bouvier, and Anne Quintin, *How Does Law Protect in War?*, Geneva: ICRC, 2011.

SCF, 'Household Economy Approach. A Resource Manual for Practitioners', Development Manual 6, Save the Children (2000).

Schneider, Friedrich, Tilman Brück and Daniel Meierrieks, 'The Economics of Terrorism and Counter-Terrorism: A Survey (Part I and II)', Working Paper 44 and 45, European Security Economics (EUSECON), 2011.

Schumer, Charles and Carolyn Maloney, 'War at any Price: Total Economic Costs of

REFERENCES

the War Beyond the Federal Budget', a Report by the US Joint Economic Committee of Majority Staff Chairman, November 2007.

Schumpeter, Joseph, *Capitalism, Socialism and Democracy*, New York: Harper, 1947.

Sen, Amartya, *Development as Freedom*, Oxford: Oxford University Press, 1999.

Sen, Amartya, *Poverty and Famines: An Essay on Entitlement and Deprivation*, Oxford: Clarendon Press, 1981.

Sen, Amartya, *Resources, Values and Development*, Oxford: Basil Blackwell, 1984.

Serneels, Pieter and Marijke Verpoorten, 'The Impact of Armed Conflict on Economic Performance: Evidence from Rwanda', *Journal of Conflict Resolution* (first published on December 30, 2013 as doi:10.1177/0022002713515409).

Sharma, Manohar, 'An Assessment of the Effects of the Cash Transfer Pilot Project on Household Consumption Patents in Tsunami-Affected Areas of Sri Lanka', IFPRI, 2006.

Shibli, Rabih, 'Reconfiguring Relief Mechanisms: The Syrian Refugee Crisis in Lebanon', Research Report of the Issam Fares Institute, The American University of Beirut, February 2014.

Shortland, Anja, Katerina Christopoulou and Charalampos Makatsoris, 'War and Famine, Peace and Light? The Economic Dynamics of Conflict in Somalia 1993–2009', *Journal of Peace Research* 50, 5 (2014), pp. 545–561.

Skees, Jerry, Barry Barnett and Anne Murphy, 'Creating Insurance Markets for Natural Disaster Risk in Lower Income Countries: the Potential Role for Securitization', *Agricultural Finance Review* 68, 1 (2008), pp. 151–167.

Skidmore, Mark and Hideki Toya, 'Do Economic Disasters Create Long-Run Growth?' *Economic Inquiry* 40, 4 (2002), pp. 664–687.

Sletteback, Rune, 'Don't Blame the Weather: Climate-Related Natural Disasters and Civil Conflict' *Journal of Peace Research* 49, 1 (2012), pp. 163–176.

Smith, Adam, *The Theory of Moral Sentiments*, London: A. Millar, 1759.

Smith, Ron, 'The Economic Cost of Military Conflict' *Journal of Peace Research* 51, 2 (2014), pp. 245–256.

Smith, Ron, *Military Economics*, London: Palgrave, 2009.

Snyder, Richard and Ravi Bhavnani, 'Diamonds, Blood and Taxes: A Revenue-Centered Framework for Explaining Political Order', *Journal of Conflict Resolution* 49, 4 (2005), pp. 563–597.

Stewart, Frances ane Emma Samman, 'Food Aid during Civil War: Conflicting Conclusions Derived from Alternative Approaches' in Stewart, F. & V. FitzGerald (eds). *War and Underdevelopment*, Vol. 1, Oxford: Oxford University Press, 2000, pp. 168–203.

Stiglitz, Joseph and Linada Bilmes, *The Three Trillion Dollar War: The True Cost of the Iraq Conflict*, London: Allen Lane, Penguin Books, 2008.

Stirk, Chloe, 'Humanitarian Assistance from Non-State Donors: What is it Worth?' Global Humanitarian Assistance Briefing Paper, Development Initiative, 2014.

REFERENCES

Taylor, Glyn, Abby Stoddard, Adele Harmer, Katherine Haver, and Paul Harvey, 'The State of the Humanitarian System', ALNAP & ODI, London, 2012.

Terry, Fiona, 'The Impact of MSF's Withdrawal from Somalia in 2013', MSF's Medical Care under Fire Project, MSF, Geneva, April 2014.

Thow, Andrew, Fernando Espada, Marybeth Redheffer, Daniela Ruegenberg, Andrea Noyes, Rodolpho Valente, Nathalie Guillaume, Mark Turner, and Nina Doyle, 'Saving Lives Today and Tomorrow: Managing the Risk of Humanitarian Crises', OCHA & DARA, 2014.

Tilly, Charles, *Coercion, Capital and European States, AD 990–1992*, Cambridge: Blackwell, 1992.

Titmuss, Richard, *The Gift Relationship: From Human Blood to Social Policy*, London: George Allen and Unwin, 1970.

Trivers, Robert, 'The Evolution of Reciprocal Altruism', *The Quarterly Review of Biology*, 46, 1 (1971), pp. 35–57.

Turner, Ginger, Farah Said and Uzma Afzal, 'Microinsurance Demand After a Rare Flood Event: Evidence from a Field Experiment in Pakistan', *The Geneva Papers on Risk and Insurance* 39 (2014), pp. 201–223.

UN/OCHA, 'Overview of Global Humanitarian Response 2014', Geneva: OCHA, 2013.

UN, 'Strengthening of the Coordination of Humanitarian Emergency Assistance of the United Nations', UNGA, UN Doc. A/RES/46/182, 78th plenary meeting, 19 December 1991.

UNISDR, 'Global Assessment Report on Disaster Risk Reduction', UNISDR, Geneva, 2013.

United States Army, *Counterinsurgency FM 3–24 (2006)*, Boulder: Paladin Press, 2007, Section 2–5.

UNODC, 'Not Just in Transit: Drugs, the State and Society in West Africa', Independent Report of the West Africa Commission on Drugs, UNODC, Vienna, 2014.

UNODC, 'Afghanistan Opium Survey 2012', UNODC, Vienna, 2013.

UNODC, *United Nations Convention against Transnational Organized Crime*, 2000.

UNODC, 'World Drug Report 2012', UNODC, Vienna, 2012.

UNSC, 'Security Council Committee: Imposes Limited Air Embargo and Financial Embargo on the Taliban', UNSC Resolution S/RES/1267 (1999), 15 October 1999.

UNSC, 'Letter dated 26 June 2014 from Panel of Experts on the Central African Republic established pursuant to the Security Council resolution 2127 (2013) addressed to the President of the Security Council', UNSC, S/2014/452, 1 July 2014.

UNSC, 'Letter Dated 22 January 2014 from the Chair of the Security Council Committee Pursuant to Resolutions 1267 (1999) and 1989 (2011) Concerning Al-

Qaida and Associated Individuals and Entities Addressed to the President of the Security Council', S/2014/41, 23 January 2014.

UNSC, 'Report of the Panel of Experts on the Illegal Exploitation of Natural Resources and Other Forms of Wealth of the Democratic Republic of the Congo', *UNSC*, S/2001/357, 12 April 2001.

Venton, Courtenay, Catherine Fitzgibbon, Tenna Shitarek, Lorraine Coulter, and Olivia Dooley, 'The Economics of Early Response and Disaster Resilience: Lessons from Kenya and Ethiopia', DFID, London, 2012.

Vines, Alex, 'Angola: Forty Years of War', in Batchelor, Peter and Kingma Kees (eds), *Demilitarisation and Peace-Building in Southern Africa—Volume II: National and Regional Experiences*, Aldershott: Ashgate, 2004.

Viscusi, Kip and Joseph Aldy, 'The Value of a Statistical Life: A Critical Review of Market Estimates Throughout the World' *Journal of Risk and Uncertainty* 27, 1 (2003), pp. 5–76.

Voltes-Dorta, Augusto, Juan Luis Jiménez and Ancor Suárez-Alemán, 'The Impact of ETA's Dissolution on Domestic Tourism in Spain', *Defence and Peace Economics* (2015), DOI: 10.1080/10242694.2015.1025485.

Voors, Maarten, Eleonora Nillesen, Philip Verwimp, Erwin Bulte, Robert Lensink, and Daan van Soest, 'Does Conflict affect Preferences? Results from Field Experiments in Burundi', HiCN Research Working Papers 71, Households in Conflict Network, Brighton, 2010.

Walker, Peter and Catherine Russ, 'Professionalising the Humanitarian Sector: A Scoping Study', Report commissioned by Enhancing Learning & Research for Humanitarian Assistance, 2010.

Walker, Peter and Daniel Maxwell, *Shaping the Humanitarian World*, London: Routledge, 2009.

Weber, Max, *From Max Weber: Essays in Sociology*, New York: Oxford University Press, 1946.

Weinstein, Jeremy, *Inside Rebellion: The Politics of Insurgent Violence*, Cambridge: Cambridge University Press, 2006.

Weiss, Thomas, *Humanitarian Business*, Malden: Polity Press, 2013.

Welsch, Heinz, 'The Social Cost of Civil Conflict: Evidence from Surveys of Happiness', *Kyklos* 61, 2 (2008), pp. 320–340.

Wennmann, Achim, 'Economic Dimensions of Armed Groups: Profiling the Financing, Costs, and Agendas and their Implications for Mediated Engagements', *International Review of the Red Cross* 93, 882 (2011), p. 333–352.

Wennmann, Achim, 'Grasping the Financing and Mobilization Cost of Armed Groups: A New Perspective on Conflict Dynamics', *Contemporary Security Policy* 30, 2 (2009), pp. 265–280.

Wennmann, Achim, 'Negotiated Exits from Organized Crime? Building Peace in Conflict and Crime-affected Contexts', *Negotiation Journal* (2014), pp. 255–273.

REFERENCES

Wieviorka, Michel, *La Violence*, Paris: Balland, 2004.

Williams, Gareth, 'Study on Disaster Risk Reduction, Decentralization and Political Economy', The Political Economy of Disaster Risk Reduction, Analysis Prepared as UNDP's Contribution to the GAR 2011, March 2011.

Wirtz, Angelika, 'Natural Disasters and the Insurance Industry', in Guha-Sapir, Debarati and Indhira Santos (eds), *The Economic Impacts of Natural Disasters*, Oxford: Oxford University Press, 2013.

Wolfers, Justin and Eric Zitzewitz, 'Using Markets to Inform Policy. The Case of the Iraq War', *Econometrica* 76, 302 (2009), pp. 225–250.

World Bank, 'Lebanon: Economic and Social Impact Assessment of the Syrian Conflict', Washington: The World Bank, 2013.

World Bank, 'Lebanon Roadmap of Priority Interventions for Stabilization: Strategy for Mitigating the Impact of the Syrian Conflict', Washington: The World Bank, 15 November 2013.

World Bank, *World Development Report 2011: Conflict, Security, and Development*, Washington: The World Bank, 2012.

World Bank and the United Nations, 'Natural Hazards, Unnatural disasters: the Economics of Effective Prevention', Washington: The World Bank, 2010.

World Food Programme, 'Comparative Review of Market Assessments Methods, Tools, Approaches and Findings', Rome: WFP, September 2013.

The Worldwatch Institute, 'State of the World 2005—Redefining Global Security', New York: W. W. Norton & Company, 2005.

WFP, UNHCR, and UNICEF, 'Vulnerability Assessment of Syrian Refugees in Lebanon (VASyR 2013)', 2013.

WFP, UNHCR, and UNICEF, 'Vulnerability Assessment of Syrian Refugees in Lebanon (VASyR 2014)', 2014.

Xiao, Yu and Uttara Nilawar, 'Winners and Losers: Analysing Post-Disaster Spatial Economic Demand Shift', *Disasters* 77, 4 (2013), pp. 646–668.

Young, Joseph and Michael Findley, 'Can Peace be Purchased? A Sectoral-Level Analysis of Aid's Influence on Transnational Terrorism', *Public Choice* 149, 3/4 (2011), pp. 365–381.

INDEX

Afghan National Solidarity Program
(NSP)(2002): 120–1
Afghanistan: 4, 13, 45, 47–8, 89, 100,
109, 114, 119–21, 178, 181–2, 187,
198; Badghis Province, 38; Faryab
Province, 38; GNI of, 45; K&R
activity in, 109; Kabul, 121; Operation Enduring Freedom (2001–14),
106–7; poppy production in, 79, 97,
125; presidential election campaign
(2014), 82; war profiteering in, 79
African Union (AU): African Risk
Capacity, 140
Agora: censoring of (1999), 93
Aid Worker Security Database: 108
altruism: 24–6, 196, 202; as biological
trait, 27–8; as cultural construct,
28–30; definitions of, 25; kin, 24;
non-kin, 25, 27; religiously-motivated, 25
American University of Beirut: 162
Angola: Civil War (1975–2002), 11,
80, 200; WFP food aid provided
to, 93
anthropology: 6, 202; economic, 13;
social, 124
armed conflict: 4–6, 8, 11, 13–15, 18,
33, 37, 39, 46, 52–3, 72, 99, 197–8;

active, 49; conflict magnitude, 50;
definitions of, 48–9; explanatory
frameworks for, 13; in non-conflict
settings, 52–3; political economy of,
13; presence in economic modelling,
17; victims of, 23, 32
al-Assad, Bashar: regime of, 18
Association of Southeast Asian Nations
(ASEAN): ASEAN Agreement on
Disaster Management and Emergency Response (AADMER), 136;
member states of, 141–2
Australia: 76–7, 118; Darwin, 77;
ODA as percentage of military
expenditure, 182
Aznar, José María: electoral defeat of,
106

al-Baghdadi, Abu Bakr: family of, 1
Bangladesh: 128; cyclone shelter con-
struction in, 58
Al Barakaat: closure of overseas offices
of, 114
Barre, Siad: regime of, 91
Beirut Research and Innovation Center
(BRIC): studies conducted by, 161,
164
Belgium: 54, 70

Bemba, Jean-Pierre: leader of MLC, 69–70

Bill and Melinda Gates Foundation: funding of, 43

Black Plague: transformative impact of, 179

Bosnia-Herzegovina: 42

Bosnian War (1992–5): 42

Bozizé, François: removed from power (2013), 83

Brazil: 54

building back better (BBB): 131, 177–9, 192; concept of, 184; criticisms of, 185–6

business-humanitarian partnerships (BHPs): institutional integrity of, 191; legitimacy of, 190–1; potential benefits of, 190; use for humanitarian organizations, 190

bureaucrats: 5, 34, 62, 121; humanitarian, 26; organizational theory view of, 25

Burkina Faso: 140

Burundi: rebel taxation in, 79

Bush, George W.: electoral victory of (2004), 76

Cambodia: 41, 142

Canada: 118, 143; ODA as percentage of military expenditure, 182; use of 3D stabilization approach, 181

capital: accumulation of, 15; formation of, 74; human, 152; human stocks, 134; investment, 85

capitalism: 15

CARE (Cooperative for Assistance and Relief Everywhere): 63

Caribbean Catastrophe Risk Insurance Facility (CCRIF): launch of (2007), 143

cash/voucher assistance: 167–9,

171–2; benefits of, 169–70; examples of, 168–9; phasing out, 172–3; shortcomings of, 170–1; use in LICs, 171; use in needs assessment, 167, 174–5

Catholic Relief Services (CRS): 60

Catholic University of Louvain: Centre for Research on the Epidemiology of Disasters (CRED), 54, 57; Emergency Events Database (EM-DAT), 54–5

Cato Institute: 31

Central African Republic (CAR): 3–4, 13, 83; Bangui, 159; Civil War (2012–15), 42; vulnerability surveys in, 158–9

Centre for Humanitarian Dialogue (HD): 'Handbook for Securing Access, Assistance and Protection for Civilians in Armed Conflict' (2004), 21

Chad: 182

China, People's Republic of: 28, 41, 87; Great Sichuan Earthquake (2008), 134

Chomsky, Noam: 34

Christianity: 38, 64, 162, 202; moral values of, 65

civil-society organizations (CSOs): 60

climate change: 138; adaptation, 186

Clinton, Bill: UN Special Envoy for Tsunami Recovery in Southeast Asia, 185; UN Special Envoy to Haiti, 129

Clinton, Hillary: 203

cocoa: impact of First Ivorian Civil War on, 73; production, 97

coffee: cultivation, 86; price shocks, 86

Cold War: 11, 13, 181; end of, 2, 39, 45, 49, 65, 82, 95, 183

Colombia: 86, 100, 181; K&R activity in, 109

coltan: commercialization of 69–70; pricing of, 68–9

Colombia: 51; cocoa production in, 97

community-based organizations (CBOs): 60

community-driven development (CDD) programmes: 122–4; eligibility for, 123

conflict theory: 20, 199; contest model, 17; development of theory, 17

Congo, Republic of the: Brazzaville, 156

Cornell University: International Terrorism: Attributes of Terrorism Events (ITERATE), 104

cost-benefit analysis: 2, 17–18, 21, 25–6, 123–4, 130, 145, 175; informed, 202; use of VSL in, 106

costs of war: 71–3; accounting approaches, 72; contingent valuation methods, 72–3; economic modelling, 72; event studies, 73

counterinsurgency: 119, 123

counterterrorism: 6, 114, 123; legislation, 100, 105–6, 118–19; targeted sanctions, 114–16

Democratic Republic of the Congo (DRC): 5, 51, 67, 73, 78, 83, 151; Bukavu, 75; coltan mining in, 68–70; impact of Dot-Com Bubble in, 96; informal miners in, 68–70; Kinshasa, 151–2; Kisangani, 67, 69–70; North Kivu, 69, 187; rejection rape victims in, 75; South Kivu, 75, 187

Denmark: ODA as percentage of military expenditure, 182; use of 3D stabilization approach, 181

disaster risk management (DRM): 139, 142, 148, 177–8, 183, 188–9;

disaster risk reduction (DRR), 183–4, 186

disasters: 5–6, 9, 19, 23, 37, 39, 42, 45–6, 49, 57–8, 127–8, 130–1, 145–8; allocation of ODA to prevention and preparedness, 145–6; cat bonds, 138–9, 148; economies, 4–5, 7–8; events, 54, 56; insuring against, 134–8, 201; long-term impact of, 132–3; natural, 54, 129–30, 140; natural hazards, 129–31; ODA fluctuation following, 132; prevention, 40; relief, 24, 41; risk-linked securities (RLS), 136–7; victims, 15, 32

Dominican Republic: 128

Dot-Com/Internet Bubble (1997–2000): 67; connection to coltan pricing, 69; impact on DRC, 96

Drilon, Franklin: Philippine Senate President, 142

Dunant, Henry: 3; *Memory of Solferino*, 34; role in founding of Red Cross, 63

Ebola: outbreak (2014), 12

Economist, The: 139

Ecuador: WFP budget in, 171

Egypt: 105; Syrian refugee population in, 168

Eisenhower, Dwight D.: 76

El Salvador: Civil War (1979–92), 11, 101

Emergency Market Mapping and Assessment (EMMA): concept of, 157–8

Ethiopia: 41–2, 47, 91, 204

European Union (EU): 43, 100, 115–16, 143

Euskadi Ta Askatasuna (ETA): 108; terrorist attacks conducted by, 105

Farabundo Martí de Liberación nacional (FMLN): 101

Financial Action Task Force (FATF): Special Recommendations against Terrorist Financing, 114

First Geneva Convention (1864): 3, 22

First World War (1914–18): 14, 180

Folha 8: censoring of (1999), 93

Food and Agricultural Organization (FAO), 155; foreign direct investment (FDI): 43–5, 163

France: 110; ODA as percentage of military expenditure, 182; Paris, 39; Revolution (1789–99), 12

Free Aceh Movement (GAM): 185

French Overseas Departments: 143

Fuerzas Armadas Revolucionarias de Colombia (FARC): funding efforts of, 79; narcotics activity of, 79

Gage, Phineas: 28

Gandhi, Rajiv: assassination of (1991), 80

Geneva Call: Deeds of Commitment, 77

Geneva Declaration on Armed Violence and Development: 52–3; concept of, 52

Germany: Hamburg, 135; Mecklenburg, 135; military of, 106–7; use of 3D stabilization approach, 181

Gibson, Mel: 91

Giuliani, Rudolph: 105

Global Counterterrorism Forum (GCTF): Algiers Memorandum on Good Practices on Preventing and Denying the Benefits of Kidnapping for Ransom by Terrorists, 111

Global Facility for Disaster Reduction and Recovery (GFDRR): 'Advancing Disaster Risk Financing and Insurance in ASEAN Member States' (2012), 141–2

Global Humanitarian Assistance (GHA) Programme: 41; Report (2014), 42, 45, 163

Global War on Terror (GWOT): 99; estimated cost of, 105

Global Witness: 'A Crude Awakening' (1999), 93

globalization: 52, 60; expansion of, 65, 81

GlobeMed Lebanon: 166

gold: 15, 161; mining of, 68; pricing of, 156

Guatemalan Historical Clarification Commission: 20

Guatemalan National Revolutionary Unity (Unidad Revolucionaria Nacional Guatemalteca)(URNG): human rights abuses committed by, 20

Guinea Bissau: 83

Guinea-Conakry: 12

Gulf Cooperation Council (GCC): humanitarian aid channelled via Lebanese sectarian groups (2011–13), 166

Haiti: 5, 128; Earthquake (2010), 42, 58, 129–30, 185

Hariri, Saad: leader of Sunni Muslim Future Movement, 163

Havel, Vaclav: support for Operation Allied Force (1999), 38

Hearst, Patty: kidnapping of (1974), 110–11

Henry V: 3

Hezbollah: 162; declared as terrorist organization by US State Department (1997), 167; services provided by, 163

HIV/AIDS: 66

homo economicus: 29, 31; concept of, 24

Households in Conflict Network (HiCN): definition of armed conflict, 48–9

human development indices (HDI): 76

humanitarian aid: 8–9, 41, 47, 59, 84, 88, 97, 132–3, 154, 163, 165; aid diversion, 90–2; as share of ODA, 43, 45; as war resource, 88–91; definitions of, 39–40; design and delivery of, 58; funding provided for, 4, 41–4, 46–7, 50, 53, 59; international, 12, 42, 166; official (OHA), 43; political economy of, 94–5; politicization of, 23, 33; private, 42, 188; programs, 32

humanitarian crisis: 2, 6–8, 11, 42, 95, 175, 177, 195–7, 202–3; chronic crises, 178; influence of business sector in, 200; political economy of, 6; study of, 15, 19, 22; transformative impact of, 177–9

humanitarian economics: 9, 195–7, 201–3; concept of, 4; potential benefits of, 4–5, 199; potential development of, 199–200

humanitarian interventions: 15–16

humanitarian labour market: 37; growth of, 60; local, 61; segmentation of, 60–1; supply, 164

humanitarian market: 38, 52, 193, 201; international, 45–6; supply side of, 40–1

humanitarian organizations: 8, 11, 20–1, 40–3, 58–9, 77–8, 81, 92–4, 96, 100, 158–9, 192, 200; bilateral aid agencies, 168; Dunantist/principle-centred, 63–4; faith-based, 64; funding of, 42; independence of, 33, 124; multilateral aid agencies, 168; needs assessment practices of, 156–7; risk of transferring to terrorist actors, 118; taxing of, 61–2; use of BHPs, 190; use of Red Cross principles by, 23

humanitarianism: 14, 19, 22, 24, 32, 34–5, 38–9, 64–5, 195, 202–3; concept of, 23; emergence of, 12; humanity principle, 32; impartiality principle, 32; independence principle, 33; neutrality principle, 33; professionalization of, 26, 34

Hundred Years' War (1337–1453): 3; Battle of Agincourt (1415), 3–4

Hussein, Saddam: regime of, 116

Hyogo Framework of Action (HFA): 136

imperialism: economic, 19, 195

India: 134; domestic disaster relief and risk reduction funding in, 41; GNI of, 45; Odisha, 134

Indian Ocean Tsunami (2004): 42, 147, 184; humanitarian aid following, 80, 184–5

Indonesia: Aceh, 59, 147, 184–5; Agency for the Rehabilitation and Reconstruction of Aceh and Nias (BRR), 184–5; government of, 184; Indonesian Disaster Management Law (2006), 147; insurance penetration in, 136; Merapi Volcano, 145; presidential elections (2006), 185; Yogyakarta, 145

industrialization: 179

informal money transfer systems (IMTS): surveillance of, 114

information and communications technology (ICT): sector: 191; innovations, 191–2; investments in, 67

Inter-Agency Standing Committee (IASC): 61

Internal Displacement Monitoring Centre (IDMC): 51

internally-displaced persons (IDPs):
50–2, 65; qualification as, 46
International Committee of the Red
Cross (ICRC): 21, 23, 46, 59, 63,
66, 155–6; founding of (1863), 22,
24; funding of, 43; Kisangani water
treatment plant operations, 70;
personnel of, 100–1, 155
International Court of Justice (ICJ):
Nicaragua v. United States (1986),
39
International Federation of Red Cross
and Red Crescent Societies (IFRC):
25
International Food Policy Research
Institute (IFPRI): 171
International Movement of the Red
Cross and Red Crescent: 25, 58,
189, 191; Code of Conduct for
(1994), 64
Market Analysis Guidance (MAG),
158; Rapid Analysis of Markets
(RAM), 158
international humanitarian law (IHL):
3–4, 20–1, 39, 77, 81, 97, 100, 190;
case law, 48; threshold of applicability for armed violence, 52; violations
of, 96, 125, 189
International Rescue Committee
(URC): 73
International Save the Children alliance: 60
Iran: 31; sanctions targeting, 115–16
Iraq: 5, 42–3, 45, 52, 86, 89, 100,
116–17, 119–20, 178, 182, 187,
198, 204; Erbil, 84; Kirkuk, 84; oil
fields of, 84; Operation Iraqi Freedom (Iraq War)(2003–11), 73–4,
76, 105–6; Shia population of, 117;
Sunni population of, 117; Syrian
refugee population in, 168

Islam: 141; Ramadan, 91; Sharia, 141,
200; Shia, 117, 162–3; Sunni, 117,
162–3, 165; Zakat, 43
Islamic Relief: 63
Islamic State of Iraq and Syria (ISIS):
18, 43, 86; financing of, 110, 124;
K&R activity of, 110; members of,
1; seizure of oil fields (2014), 84,
116–17
Islamism: 18
Israel: territory occupied by, 162
Italy: Sicily, 179
Ivory Coast: First Civil War (2002–7),
73

Japan: 56–7, 138, 143; Fudai, 145, 147;
Fukushima Disaster (2012), 128;
Kobe Earthquake (1995), 57, 132;
Tohoku Tsunami (2012), 57, 128,
145, 147
Jordan: Syrian refugee population in,
168

Kabila, Laurent Désiré: 78
Kant, Immanuel: concept of 'categori-
cal imperative', 29
Kenya: 140, 181; Lamu, 87
Kiir, Salva: 88
Kosovo War (1998–9): Operation Al-
lied Force (1999), 38
Krugman, Paul: 83
Kurdistan: Iraqi, 84
Kuwait: 31, 41, 166

Laos: 142
League of Nations: 63
Lebanon: 2, 8, 100, 166; Akkar, 162;
Arsal, 1, 162; Baalbek, 162; Bank
Libano-Française, 168; Beirut, 1;
Bekaa Valley, 1; borders of, 162;
Christian population of, 163; CSC

bank, 168; economy of, 163; government of, 1, 150; July War (2006), 162; labour supply in, 164; military of, 1; sectarianism in, 162–3; Shia population of, 162–3; Syrian refugee population of, 150, 157, 159–63, 165, 167–8, 171, 175, 196

'Lebanon Roadmap of Priority Interventions for Stabilization from the Syrian Conflict' (2013): provisions of, 173

Liberation Tigers of Tamil Eelam (LTTE): funding efforts of, 80

Liberia: 5, 12, 123; GNI of, 45

Lindberg, Charles: kidnapping and murder of son of (1932), 110

Lord's Resistance Army (LRA): predatory practices of, 82–3, 97

low-income countries (LICs): 47, 151; living standards in, 156; mortality rate in, 57; use of cash/voucher assistance in, 171

lower middle-income countries (LMICs): 47

Machar, Riek: 88

Machiavelli, Niccòlo: view of war, 15

macroeconomics: 73–4, 97, 133; analysis, 104

Malawi: 139

Mali: 83, 100

Mandela, Nelson: 66

Mangkusubroto, Kuntoro: 184

Marie-Antoinette, Queen: 12

Market Information and Food Insecurity Response Analysis (MIFIRA): 157

Marshall Plan (1948): 180–1

Maryland University: Center for International Development and Conflict Management, 50

Maslow, Abraham: hierarchy of needs, 30

Mastercard: 168

Mauritania: 140

Médecins Sans Frontières (MSF): 22, 60–1; funding of, 43; *Humanitarian Negotiations Revealed*, 21; personnel of, 12; 'Where is Everyone?', 5; withdrawal from Somalia (2013), 62, 92

Mexico: 48; debt crisis (1982), 180; Federal Government of, 138; Fund for National Disasters, 138; K&R activity in, 109

micro-insurance: 140–1; development of, 139–40; flood, 144; weather-indexed, 140

middle-income countries (MICs): 151, 155, 173; living standards in, 156

Miller, George: *Mad Max* (film series), 91

Mongolia: agricultural sector of, 143

Mouvement pour la Liberation du Congo (MLC): 69–70

Mozambique: 140

Munich Re: 54, 135, 142; findings on annual disaster losses, 135–6

Myanmar: 5, 142; Cyclone Nargis (2008), 57–8, 117, 134; sanctions targeting, 117

NASDAQ Composite Index: 67, 69

needs assessment: 7, 46, 96, 151, 153–4, 173–4, 187; cultural standards issues, 155–6; focus on household economic security, 156; market analysis, 156–8; use of cash/voucher assistance, 167, 174–5; vulnerability surveys, 158–60

neoclassical economics: 13–14, 17, 195

Netherlands: 128; Holland, 136; insurance penetration in, 136; use of 3D stabilization approach, 181

neutrality: concept of, 23
New York Times, The: 113
Nicaragua: Contra War (1981–90), 39
Niger: 140, 171
Nigeria: 51, 93, 140
non-governmental organizations (NGOs): 58–60, 165–6, 168; advocacy, 190; humanitarian, 46, 189; international (INGOs), 60, 62, 168; multi-mandated, 63; targeting in K&R, 109
North Atlantic Treaty Organization (NATO): airstrike campaigns of, 38
Norway: ODA as percentage of military expenditure, 182
Norwegian Refugee Council: 118
al-Nusra Front: members of, 1

Office for the Coordination of Humanitarian Affairs (OCHA), 5, 21, 41, 118
official development assistance (ODA): 44, 89–90, 97, 119, 147, 180–2, 186; allocation to disaster prevention and preparedness, 145–6; as percentage of gross national income (GNI), 45; definitions of, 39; fluctuation following disasters, 132; humanitarian aid as percentage of, 39, 45; use as foreign policy instrument, 181; Western, 117
oil: 20, 87–8, 94, 124, 177, 185, 189; embargoes, 116; extraction, 130; impact of Iraq War on price, 73; offshore exploitation, 86; price shocks, 86
Organization for Economic Co-operation and Development (OECD): Development Assistance Committee (DAC), 39–43, 45, 181
organizational culture: 26

organizational theory: view of bureaucrats, 25
organized criminal groups (OCGs): 82; trading activity of, 83
Overseas Development Institute (ODI): studies of, 90–1
Oxfam International: 60, 63, 161

Pacific Catastrophe Risk Insurance: 143
Pakistan: 104, 119, 181–2; Floods (2010), 144
Palestine: 100, 102
Palestinian Territories: 5, 118; Gaza Strip, 47; Second Intifada (2000–5), 156; West Bank, 47
Paul, Ron: 144
Pharmaciens sans frontières: 63
Philippine Institute of Volcanology and Seismology: 130
Philippines: 89; CDD programme in, 122–3; insurance penetration in, 136; Manila, 142; Mount Pinatubo volcanic eruption (1991), 130; Senate, 142; Typhoon Hayan (2013), 142
Philippines Risk and Insurance Scheme for Municipalities (PRISM): concept of, 142
political economy analysis (PEA): 68, 94–6, 158, 199; benefits of, 96, 200
Portugal: 15, 179
property rights: 2–3, 14; enforcement of, 17
proxy means testing (PMT): concept of, 152; shortcomings of, 152–3
public-private partnerships (PPPs): 135, 148; potential use in disaster risk governance, 141

al-Qaeda: affiliates of, 90, 108; financing of, 113; sanctions targeting, 115 randomized control trials (RCTs): 120, 197

Rassemblement Congolais pour la Démocratie (RCD): funding of, 70; RCD-Goma (RCD-G), 70; RCD-Kisangani (RCD-K), 70; Société Minière des Grands Lacs (SOMIGL), 70

rational choice theory: 20, 76, 96; application to study of terrorism, 101–2; concept of, 14

rationality: 11–12, 18, 26; bounded, 29, 31, 94, 202; teleological, 32

Rawls, John: 23

refugees: 8, 41, 43, 50–1, 65; income sources, 160–1; Palestinian, 50–1, 159–60; qualification as, 46; Syrian, 150, 155–7, 159–62, 165, 167–8, 171, 175, 189–90, 196

resilience: 186–8; concept of, 186–7

Ricardo, David: 15

Rockefeller, John D: 177

Rockefeller Foundation: 140

Rosenstein-Rodan, Paul: World Bank Chief Economist, 92

Russian Empire: 179

Rwanda: 69–70; Civil War (1990–3/1994), 72; Genocide, 72

Sandler, Todd: definition of terrorism, 101

Saudi Arabia: 166

Save the Children Fund (SCF): Household Economy Approach (HEA), 155

Schumpeter, Joseph: notion of 'creative destruction', 131

Schweizer, Albert: 38

Second Congo War (1998–2003): belligerents of, 69

Second Sudanese Civil War (1983–2005): Comprehensive Peace Agreement (CPA), 87

Second World War (1939–45): 14, 68, 71, 76–7

Sen, Amartya: 128, 154; conceptualization of famine, 155; definition of entitlement, 154–5

Sendai Framework for Disaster Risk Reduction: approval of (2015), 144

Senegal: 140

Al-Shabaab: funding activity of, 90–1; K&R activity of, 110; territory held by, 90

Sharkas, Anas: family of, 1

Sierra Leone: 5, 12

Smith, Adam: 33; thoughts on sympathy, 27–8

Society for Worldwide Interbank Financial Telecommunication (SWIFT): 113

Somalia: 5, 47, 73, 90–1, 100, 114, 118, 181–2; Civil War (1986–), 73; food aid provided to, 90; Mogadishu, 90, 92; MSF withdrawal from (2013), 62, 92

South Africa: Apartheid, 80

South Sudan: 13, 47, 87–8, 151, 156, 187; Civil War (2013–), 42, 159; government of, 87–8; Independence of (2011), 86–7; Juba, 87; Unity State, 87

Spain: 105; Basque Country, 105; Madrid Train Bombing (2004), 101, 106

Spanish Flu: transformative impact of, 180

Sri Lanka: 5, 114, 181, 204

stabilization: 9, 75, 89, 122, 177–81, 184, 186, 192; '3D' approach, 181; packages, 181; use as foreign policy instrument, 181–2 statebuilding: 7, 15, 63, 89, 116, 177, 182; bottom-up 188, 192, 203; contribution of war to, 83; funding of, 89; top-down, 188

Sudan: 47, 51, 82, 182; Darfur Conflict (2003–), 71, 85, 158; GDP per capita, 71; Khartoum, 87; Port Sudan, 87; sanctions targeting, 115

Sudanese People's Liberation Movement/Army (SPLM/A): 87

Sunni Muslim Future Movement: members of, 163

Sustainable Development Goals: 9

Sweden: 140

Swiss Re: 54, 135, 138; Sharia compliant variant of reinsurance, 141

Switzerland: Geneva, 37, 51; Glarus, 135

Syria: 1, 5, 43, 48, 51, 84, 86, 100, 116, 155; Aleppo, 110; borders of, 162; Civil War (2011–), 5, 8, 30, 42, 49, 52, 149, 163, 167, 169, 196; Damascus, 5

Taliban: removed from power (2002), 89; war profiteering activity of, 79

Tamils: diaspora of, 80

Targeting Working Group: 159

terrorism: 6, 99–100, 103–4, 123–4; countering the financing of (CFT), 107, 113–14, 116–18; definitions of, 100–1; economic impact of, 104–5; financing of, 107–8; kidnap and ransom (K&R), 108–13, 124; rational choice analysis view of, 101–2; suicide, 102–3; transnational, 104

terrorism economics: 5, 8, 99–100, 196

Third Geneva Convention (1949): provisions of, 3

transnational criminal organizations

(TCOs): 18, 68, 77; definitions of, 82

Tsarnaev, Dzhokhar: role in Boston Marathon Bombings (2013), 101

Tsarnaev, Tamerlan: role in Boston Marathon Bombings (2013), 101

Tufts University: Feinstein International Center, 158

Turkey: 41, 43; Ceyhan, 84; government of, 137; Syrian refugee population in, 168; Turkish Catastrophe Insurance Pool (TCIP): 137

Typhoon Hayan (2013): 131

Uganda: 61, 69–70, 171

Ukraine: 5

Uniao Nacional para a Independência Total de Angola (UNITA): 93; loss of funding, 80

United Arab Emirates (UAE): 166

United Kingdom (UK): 15, 43, 110, 118, 140; Department for International Development (DFID), 91; London, 128; use of 3D stabilization approach, 181

United Nations (UN): 33, 46–7, 58, 34, 84, 115, 165, 173, 189; Analytical Support and Monitoring Team of the Al-Qaida Sanctions Committee, 108; Charter of, 63; Convention against Transnational Organized Crime, 82; Financial Tracking Service (FTS), 31; General Assembly (UNGA), 63; *Natural Hazard— Unnatural Disasters* (2010), 131; oil-for-food programme, 116; Overview of Global Humanitarian Response (2014), 46; 'Panel of Experts on the Illegal Exploitation of Natural Resources and Other Forms of Wealth of the Democratic Republic of the

Congo', 70; personnel of, 21, 185; Regional Refugee and Resilience Plan, 175; Resolution 2133, (2014), 111–12; Resolution on Strengthening of the coordination of Humanitarian Emergency Assistance (1991), 63; sanctioned peacekeeping operations, 45; Security Council, 70, 108, 111–12, 116, 124; targeted sanctions used by, 115–17; Universal Declaration of Human Rights (1948), 107; use of 3D stabilization approach, 181

United Nations Children's Fund (UNICEF), 160, 191

United Nations Development Programme (UNDP), 164

United Nations High Commissioner for Refugees (UNHCR), 50–1, 149, 160–1, 165–8, 171, 175

United Nations International Strategy for Disaster Reduction (UNISDR), 142

United Nations Office on Drugs and Crime (UNODC), 83, 89

United Nations Relief and Works Agency for Palestine Refugees in the Near East (UNRWA), 51, 149

United States of America (USA): 19, 28–9, 56–7, 100, 118; 9/11 Attacks, 62, 99, 101, 105, 111, 113–14, 178; Boston Marathon Bombings (2013), 101; Central Intelligence Agency (CIA), 89; charitable giving habits in, 29; Commander's Emergency Response Programs (CERP), 119–21; Congress, 116, 144; Department of Defense, 122; Flood Insurance Reform Act, 144; Homeowner Flood Insurance Affordability Act (2014), 144; Huntsville, AL, 180; Hurricane Katrina (2005), 57, 128,

180; Hurricane Sandy (2012), 131, 144; National Flood Insurance Program (NFIP), 144; New Orleans, LA, 128; New York, 37, 67, 124, 180; State Department, 167, 203; Treasury Department, 114; US Army Counterinsurgency (COIN) Field Manual, 119–20

University of Maryland: Global Terrorism Database (GTD), 104

upper middle-income countries (UMICs): 47, 150

Uppsala Conflict Data Program (UCDP): 49; definition of armed conflict, 48

urbanization: 27, 127, 129, 136, 138; rapid, 55

US Geological Survey: 130

utilitarianism: 23, 28, 31

value of a statistical life (VSL): 56, 75, 105–7; concept of, 106; in high-income countries, 106; income elasticity of, 107; use in cost-benefit analysis, 106

value/quality of life: 75; data collection, 75; empirical studies, 76

Venezuela: K&R activity in, 109

Vietnam War (1955–75): 11

voluntourism: 24

Vulnerability Assessment of Syrian Refugees (VASyR): findings of, 160, 162, 166

Wamba dia Wamba, Ernest: 70

Wamura, Kotaku: Mayor of Fudai, 145

war economies: 4, 8, 68, 71, 80–1, 100; analysis, 67; concept of, 68; conflict finance, 68, 77; criminal/informal activities, 68, 77, 79–81; international trade/financial relations, 68–9; survival activities, 68 war profiteering: 76–7, 80; aid diversion, 90–2; in civil conflicts, 85–6; mobilizing/maintenance costs 78; territorial control, 78–80

War Report 2012: findings of, 48

Weber, Max: 65; view of bureaucrats, 26

Willis Re: 142

Wilson, Woodrow: 63

World Bank: 138–9, 143, 147, 163, 173; 'Advancing Disaster Risk Financing and Insurance in ASEAN Member States' (2012), 141–2; Livestock Insurance, 143; Living Standard Measurement Study (LSMS), 153–4; *Mind, Society and Behavior* (World Development Report)(2015), 31; *Natural Hazard— Unnatural Disasters* (2010), 131; personnel of, 92–3, 164

World Food Programme (WFP), 93, 157, 160–1, 164, 166–9, 171

World Health Organization (WHO): disability adjusted life years (DALYs), 75

World Vision International: 60, 63

Worldwide Atrocities Dataset: 18

Yemen: 171

Zaire: 80